Fodor's 2001

CW00324240

Hong Kong

The complete guide, thoroughly up-to-date

Packed with details that will make your trip

The must-see sights, off and on the beaten path

What to see, what to skip

Mix-and-match vacation itineraries

City strolls, countryside adventures

Smart lodging and dining options

Essential local do's and taboos

Transportation tips, distances, and directions

Key contacts, savvy travel tips

When to go, what to pack

Clear, accurate, easy-to-use maps

Background essays on food and culture

Fodor's Travel Publications • New York, Toronto, London, Sydney, Auckland
www.fodors.com

Fodor's Hong Kong 2001

EDITORS: Amy Karafin, Laura M. Kidder, William Travis

Editorial Contributors: Denise Cheung, Tobias Parker, Sean Rocha, Lara Wozniak

Editorial Production: Ira-Neil Dittersdorf

Maps: David Lindroth, *cartographer*; Rebecca Baer, Robert Blake, *map editors*

Design: Fabrizio La Rocca, *creative director*; Guido Caroti, *art director*; Jolie Novak, *photo editor*; Melanie Marin, *photo researcher*

Cover Design: Pentagram

Production/Manufacturing: Yexenia Markland, Robert Shields

Cover Photograph: Jeffrey Aaronson/Network Aspen

Copyright

Special Sales

Fodor's Travel Publications are available at special discounts for bulk purchases for sales promotions or premiums. Special editions, including personalized covers, excerpts of existing guides, and corporate imprints, can be created in large quantities for special needs. For more information contact your local bookseller or write to Special Markets, Fodor's Travel Publications, 280 Park Ave., New York, NY 10017. Inquiries from Canada should be directed to your local Canadian bookseller or sent to Random House of Canada, Ltd., Marketing Department, 2775 Matheson Blvd. E, Mississauga, Ontario L4W 4P7. Inquiries from the United Kingdom should be sent to Fodor's Travel Publications, 20 Vauxhall Bridge Road, London, England SW1V 2SA.

PRINTED IN THE UNITED STATES OF AMERICA

10 9 8 7 6 5 4 3 2 1

Important Tip

Although all prices, opening times, and other details in this book are based on information supplied to us at press time, changes occur all the time in the travel world, and Fodor's cannot accept responsibility for facts that become outdated or for inadvertent errors or omissions. So **always confirm information when it matters,** especially if you're making a detour to visit a specific place.

CONTENTS

ON THE ROAD WITH FODOR'S

VERY VACATION is important. So here at Fodor's we've pulled out all stops in preparing *Fodor's Hong Kong*. To help you zero in on what to see in Hong Kong, we've created great neighborhood walks. And to direct you to the places that are truly worth your time and money, we've rallied the team of endearingly picky know-it-alls we're pleased to call our writers. Having seen all corners of Hong Kong, Macau, and South China, they're real experts. If you knew them, you'd poll them for tips yourself.

Hong Kong native **Denise Cheung** has combined a career in journalism with a taste for travel that has taken her far and wide. Particularly enamored of Hong Kong's booming restaurant scene, she has written for a number of publications, including the *South China Morning Post* and *HK* magazine about food and lifestyle. She has also worked in the hospitality industry and is familiar with the travel business.

Tobias Parker, who updated the Lodging chapter for this edition, arrived in Hong Kong in 1996 shortly before his government's departure. After renouncing the world of print publishing, where he was an editor and journalist for a number of books and magazines, he joined the on-line industry. As content manager for the Hong Kong Tourist Association's Web site, he built up their on-line presence and developed the successful weekly *Hong Kong This Week*.

Sean Rocha lived in Hong Kong for three years in the early 1990s, working first as a political strategist for a legislative councillor during the territory's first democratic elections and then as a stock market analyst. He still managed to retreat to Macau so often that many Macanese assumed he lived there. He left Asia in 1994 and spent three years in Cairo writing a novel (and part of *Fodor's Egypt*) before returning to New York. After a stint at the *Paris Review*, he is now the director of literary programs at PEN American Center, the international writers organization.

Lara Wozniak, is a U.S. lawyer and senior features writer for *Hong Kong iMail*, a daily English-language newspaper in Hong Kong. She also regularly contributes to American, Canadian, and British newspapers and magazines. She wrote the Nepal chapter for the *Fodor's Nepal, Tibet, and Bhutan, 1st edition,* and updated the Smart Travel Tips, Nightlife and the Arts, Outdoor Activities and Sports, Shopping, and Side Trip to South China chapters for this edition.

We'd also like to thank Ajay and Shveta Kapur, Ronald and the Acconci family, Dan Hickey, Connie Hong, the Hong Kong Tourist Association, Chantal Hooper, Anna Yee and Ana Vong, and Gus Whitcomb for their kind assistance in preparing this edition.

Don't Forget to Write

We love your feedback—positive and negative—and follow up on all suggestions. Contact the Hong Kong editors at editors@fodors.com or c/o Fodor's, 280 Park Ave., New York, New York 10017. And have a wonderful trip!

Karen Cure
Editorial Director

Hong Kong

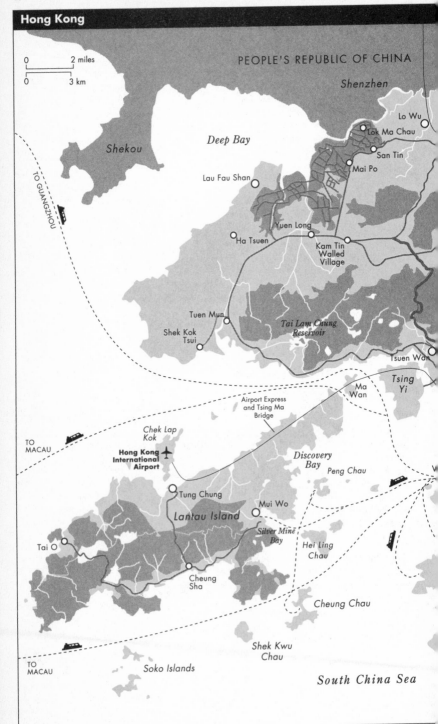

0 — 2 miles
0 — 3 km

PEOPLE'S REPUBLIC OF CHINA

Shenzhen

Lo Wu

Lok Ma Chau

San Tin

Shekou

Deep Bay

Mai Po

Lau Fau Shan

TO GUANGZHOU

Yuen Long

Ha Tsuen

Kam Tin Walled Village

Tuen Mun

Shek Kok Tsui

Tai Lam Chung Reservoir

Tsuen Wan

Tsing Yi

Ma Wan

Airport Express and Tsing Ma Bridge

TO MACAU

Chek Lap Kok

Hong Kong International Airport

Discovery Bay

Peng Chau

Tung Chung

Mui Wo

Lantau Island

Silver Mine Bay

Tai O

Hei Ling Chau

Cheung Sha

Cheung Chau

TO MACAU

Shek Kwu Chau

Soko Islands

South China Sea

Crooked Island

N

Sheung
Shui

Fanling

Wu Kau
Tang

Plover Cove
Reservoir

Tolo Channel

Grass
Island

Taipo

Kam Shan

Pan
Chung

Tolo Harbour

NEW TERRITORIES

Chek
Keng

Shatin

Sai Kung

Ho Chung

High Island

Sung Dynasty Village

Port Shelter

KOWLOON

Basalt
Island

Victoria

Victoria
Harbour

Kowloon
Bay

Yau Tong

Tai Wan
Tau

Junk Bay

HONG KONG

Tei Tong
Tsui

Tung Lung
Chau

Shek O

Stanley

Lamma
Island

Stanley
Peninsula

Po Toi
Islands

KEY

Ferry Lines
Rail Lines

World Time Zones

Numbers below vertical bands relate each zone to Greenwich Mean Time (0 hrs.).
Local times frequently differ from these general indications,
as indicated by light-face numbers on map.

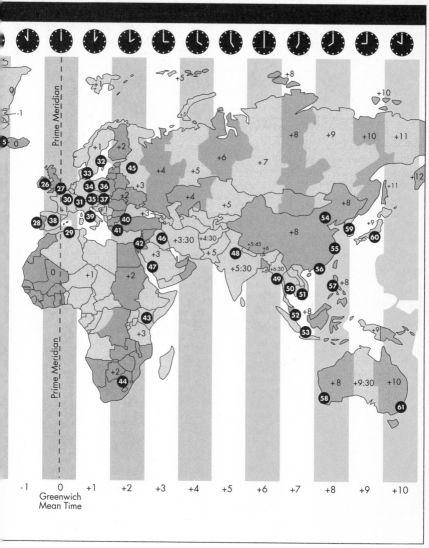

SMART TRAVEL TIPS A TO Z

Basic Information on Traveling in Hong Kong, Savvy Tips to Make Your Trip a Breeze, and Companies and Organizations to Contact

AIR TRAVEL

BOOKING YOUR FLIGHT

Most people choose a flight based on price, but because of the time and distance involved in traveling to Hong Kong, there are other issues to consider. These include connections, departure times, and a carrier's frequent-flyer partners, which allow you to credit mileage earned on one airline to your account with another.

When you book **look for nonstop flights** and **remember that "direct" flights stop at least once.** Try to avoid connecting flights, which require a change of plane.

Nonstop flights from the United States to Hong Kong are rare; if you're coming from the United States, you'll probably take a direct flight, which requires at least one stop, or a connecting flight, which requires a change of aircraft (and sometimes airline). Some flights, especially nonstops, may depart only on certain days of the week.

CARRIERS

➤ To Hong Kong: **Asiana** (☎ 800/227–4262). **Canadian** (☎ 800/426–7000). **Cathay Pacific Airways** (☎ 800/233–2742 in the U.S.; 800/268–6868 in Canada). **China Airlines** (☎ 800/227–5118). **Continental** (☎ 800/231–0856). **Korean Air** (☎ 800/438–5000).**Northwest** (☎ 800/447–4747).**Qantas** (☎ 800/227–4500). **Singapore Airlines** (☎ 800/742–3333). **UnitedAirlines** (☎ 800/241–6522). **Virgin Atlantic** (☎ 800/862–8621).

➤ To Macau: **Asiana** (☎ 800/227–4262). **Korean Air**(☎ 800/438–5000). **Northwest**(☎ 800/447–4747).

➤ From the U.K.: **Cathay Pacific Airways** (☎ 020/7/747–8888). **Virgin Atlantic**(☎ 01293/747747). **British Airways** (☎ 0345/222111).

CHECK-IN & BOARDING

Check in at least two hours before departing from Hong Kong International Airport at Check Lap Kok. If you plan on taking the train to the airport, check in your luggage at the Airport Express Railway station on Hong Kong Island. You must check in at least three hours in advance for this service.

Assuming that not everyone with a ticket will show up, airlines routinely overbook planes. When everyone does, the airlines ask for volunteers to give up their seats. In return, these volunteers usually get a certificate for a free flight and are rebooked on the next flight out. If there are not enough volunteers, the airline must choose who will be denied boarding. The first to get bumped are passengers who checked in late and those flying on discounted tickets, so **get to the gate and check in as early as possible,** especially during peak periods.

Always **bring a government-issued photo I.D. to the airport.** You may be asked to show it before you are allowed to check in.

CUTTING COSTS

The least expensive airfares to Hong Kong must usually be purchased in advance and are nonrefundable. It's smart to **call a number of airlines, and when you are quoted a good price, book it on the spot**—the same fare may not be available the next day. Always **check different routings** and look into using different airports. Travel agents, especially low-fare specialists (☞ Discounts & Deals, *below*), are helpful.

Consolidators are another good source. They buy tickets for scheduled international flights at reduced rates from the airlines, then sell them at prices that beat the best fare available directly from the airlines, usually without restrictions. Sometimes you can even get your money back if you need to return the ticket. Carefully read the fine print detailing penalties for changes and cancellations, and **confirm your consolidator reservation with the airline.**

When you **fly as a courier,** you trade your checked-luggage space for a ticket deeply subsidized by a courier service. There are restrictions on when you can book and how long you can stay.

➤ CONSOLIDATORS: **Cheap Tickets** (☎ 800/377–1000). **Discount Airline Ticket Service** (☎ 800/576–1600). **Unitravel** (☎ 800/325–2222). **Up & Away Travel** (☎ 212/889–2345). **World Travel Network** (☎ 800/409–6753).

ENJOYING THE FLIGHT

For more legroom, **request an emergency-aisle seat.** Don't sit in the row in front of the emergency aisle or in front of a bulkhead, where seats may not recline. If you have dietary concerns, **ask for special meals when booking.** These can be vegetarian, low-cholesterol, or kosher, for example. On long flights, try to maintain a normal routine, to help fight jet lag. At night, **get some sleep.** By day, **eat light meals, drink water** (not alcohol), and **move around the cabin** to stretch your legs.

Airlines flying into Hong Kong usually no longer permit in-flight smoking. Check with your carrier before booking the flight. Smoking is also not permitted within the airport (the fine is HK $1,000) or on the Airport Express Railway.

FLYING TIMES

Flying time to Hong Kong is between 17 and 20 hours from New York or Chicago (via Vancouver or Honolulu), 13 hours direct from Los Angeles or 12¼ from San Francisco. Macau is a 20-minute flight from Hong Kong.

HOW TO COMPLAIN

If your baggage goes astray or your flight goes awry, complain right away. Most carriers require that you **file a claim immediately.**

➤ AIRLINE COMPLAINTS: U.S. Department of Transportation **Aviation Consumer Protection Division** (✉ C-75, Room 4107, Washington, DC 20590, ☎ 202/366–2220, airconsumer@ost.dot.gov, www.dot.gov/airconsumer). **Federal Aviation Administration Consumer Hotline** (☎ 800/322–7873).

RECONFIRMING

If you are flying on a mainland Chinese airline, reconfirm your ticket at least 24 hours in advance before leaving Hong Kong. You can also call your travel agent to do this for you. Other airlines might not be as strict as the Chinese airlines operating out of Hong Kong. Check with your travel agent or contact your carrier when booking your flight.

AIRPORTS & TRANSFERS

The gateway to Hong Kong is the new Hong Kong International Airport at Chek Lap Kok. Like its predecessor, however (which was known universally as Kai Tak), HKIA is never called by its official name; it's universally referred to as **Chek Lap Kok.** The new airport is mammoth, five times the size of the old one; the passenger terminal is a mile long and could encompass those at Heathrow and JFK combined. It is also well marked and employs a helpful staff. Note that because the Arrival Hall is so vast passengers often have trouble finding those who come to meet them. (An unofficial meeting place is the McDonald's between the two arrival gates.) Remember to hold on to HK$50 for the airport tax, payable on departure from the country. It is only levied on those 12 years and older and is waived for all transit and transfer passengers who arrive and leave on the same day.

The nearby **Macau International Airport** gives you more flight options; from here you can simply connect with sea transport for the one-hour journey to Hong Kong.

➤ AIRPORT INFORMATION: **Hong Kong International Airport** (☎ 852/2181–0000). **Macau International Airport** (☎ 853/785–448).

SMART TRAVEL TIPS A TO Z

TRANSFERS TO AND FROM HONG KONG INTERNATIONAL AIRPORT

The high-speed, high-frequency **Airport Express Railway** whisks passengers between the airport and Kowloon in 19 minutes via the spectacular Tsing Ma Bridge, and to and from Hong Kong Island (Central) in 23 minutes. This is the most convenient and economical way to get to and from the airport. There is plenty of luggage space, leg room, and comfortable seating with television screens on the backs of the passenger seats showing tourist information and the latest news. **Hot Line:** ☎ 2881–8888.

A newsworthy feature of this new train is in-town check-in, whereby you **check your luggage, get your boarding pass, and pay departure tax while still on Hong Kong Island.** To do this, you must purchase an Airport Express ticket and get to the train station three hours before your flight. Some people check in early in the day—the office is open 6 AM–1 AM— and board the train of their choice later on. The Airport Express station is connected to the MTR's Central station (albeit via a long, underground walkway with no luggage carts). One-way fare to or from Central is HK$70; from Kowloon, HK$60. Round-trip tickets valid for one month cost HK$120 for both destinations.

The Airport Express also runs a **free shuttle bus** between major hotels and its Hong Kong or Kowloon Stations. To board, you must show your ticket, boarding pass, or Airport Express ticket.

Airbus has eight routes covering just about every hotel and hostel in Hong Kong, Kowloon, and the New Territories. Prices range from HK$20 to HK$45 for the one-hour trip. Information: ☎ 2745–4466.

A 24-hour **Airport Shuttle** bus departs major hotels every 30 minutes and costs HK$120. Reservations: ☎ 2377–0733.

A number of regular public buses serve the airport; though cheaper (HK$23 and under), these take longer than express options. For more information: **Cityflyer** (☎ 2873–0818). **Kowloon Motor Bus** (☎ 2745–4466). **Long Wing Bus Company** (☎ 2786–6036).

Taxis from the airport cost up to HK$400 for Hong Kong Island destinations and up to HK$320 for Kowloon destinations, plus HK$5 per piece of luggage.

DCH Limo Service (☎ 2262–1888, FAX 2753–6768) is located at Kiosk 4 in the Arrival Hall. Depending on the zone and the type of car, limo rides from the airport range from HK$450 to HK$600. A pick-up service is available at the same rates, as is a car service at HK$300–HK$360 per hour, minimum two hours.

DUTY-FREE SHOPPING

In Hong Kong, the only place you can buy duty-free liquor and tobacco is at the Hong Kong International Airport. Ten duty-free liquor and tobacco shops are located at the restricted boarding level, with two pre-order shops on the nonrestricted departures check-in level. The shops are open from 7 AM to 11:30 PM. Airport tax is not levied on transit and transfer passengers.

BOAT & FERRY TRAVEL

The century-old **Star Ferry** is a Hong Kong landmark. Double-bowed, green-and-white vessels connect Hong Kong Island with Kowloon in just eight minutes; the ride costs HK$2.20 upper deck, HK$1.70 lower deck. Ferries also run to and between Wanchai and Tsim Sha Tsui; both rides cost HK$5.

Two companies, **Hong Kong & Yau Ma Tei Ferry Company** and **Discovery Bay Transportation Services**, run various ferries from Central to the outlying islands of Lantau, Cheung Chau, Lamma, and Ping Chau. For schedules, call **HYF** (☎ 2525–1108), **Discovery Bay** (☎ 2987–7351), or the **HKTA Visitor Hot Line** (☎ 2508–1234). (Note: The high-speed ferries to Discovery Bay, which run 24 hours a day, are located on the Star Ferry Concourse.) Printed schedules are obtainable at the HKTA Information and Gift Centres at two locations: the Star Ferry Concourse, Kowloon, and The Center, 99 Queen's Road Central, Central. Return fares vary from HK$15 to HK$50.

FARES & SCHEDULES

Call the **Hong Kong Tourist Association (HKTA) Visitor Hot Line** (☎ 2508–1234), or stop in at the **HKTA Visitor Information and Gift Centres** (✉ The Center, 99 Queen's Road Central, Central; ✉ Star Ferry Concourse, Kowloon).

For individual company schedules call **Star Ferry** (☎ 2366–2576 or 2845–2324), the **Hong Kong & Yau Ma Tei Ferry Company** (☎ 2525–1108), or **Discovery Bay** (☎ 2987–7351).

For information about ferry service to Macau and locations in China, *see* Macau A to Z *in* Chapter 8 *and* South China A to Z *in* Chapter 9.

BUS TRAVEL

Double-decker buses run from 6 AM to midnight, and cover most parts of Hong Kong. Bus drivers usually don't speak English, so you may have to ask other passengers for help or you must know exactly where you want to disembark.

When determining bus direction, buses ending with the letter L will eventually connect to the Kowloon-Canton Railway; buses ending with the letter M connect to an MTR station; and buses ending with the letter X are express buses.

As with other big cities, buses can be quite busy during rush hours, public holidays, and at weekends, so it's best to use them during nonpeak times.

Maxicabs and minicabs both seat 16 people. Maxicabs are cream-colored, with green roofs, a route number and fixed price prominently displayed. Minibuses are also cream but have red roofs. Minibuses display both fares and destinations (albeit in very small English letters), though these can change based on demand. Maxicabs and minibuses are both quick, though they cost slightly more than buses. Both can be waved down at any point.

Smoking is not permitted on public transportation.

FARES & SCHEDULES

Call the **HKTA Visitor Hot Line** (☎ 2508–1234) or, for double-decker-bus route maps, stop in at the **HKTA Information and Gift Centres** (✉ The Center, 99 Queen's Road Central, Central; ✉ Star Ferry Concourse, Kowloon).

PAYING

Double-decker bus fares range from HK$1.20 to HK$45; the fare is paid entering the bus. Maxicab fares range from HK$1.50 to HK$18. Similarly, you pay as you board. Minibus fares range from HK$2 to HK$20, but you pay as you exit. For all three types of transportation you must pay exact change.

Long-staying visitors should consider purchasing an "Octopus" stored-value card, which you can use on the city bus as well as the Mass Transit Railway, Kowloon-Canton Railway, Light Rail, and Airport Express.

BUSINESS & TRADE SERVICES & CONTACTS

BUSINESS CENTERS

Hong Kong supports many business centers outside hotels, and some are considerably cheaper than hotel facilities. Others cost about the same but offer private desks (from HK$250 per hour for desk space to upward of HK$8,000 a month for a private office). Amenities include a private address and phone-answering and forwarding services. Many centers are affiliated with accountants and lawyers who can expedite company registration. Some will even process visas and wrap gifts for you.

Harbour International Business Centre (✉ 2802 Admiralty Centre Tower I, 18 Harcourt Rd., ☎ 2529–0356, 𝔽𝔸𝕏 2861–3420) provides typing, secretarial support, and office rentals. Reservations are not required.

The **American Chamber of Commerce** (✉ Bank of America Tower, Room 1904, 12 Harcourt Rd., Central, Hong Kong Island, ☎ 2526–0165, 𝔽𝔸𝕏 2810–1289) can arrange a Breakfast Briefing Program at your hotel for a fee based on group size. The chamber hosts luncheons and seminars, and

SMART TRAVEL TIPS A TO Z

the Young Professionals Committee holds cocktail parties at least once a month. Facilities include a library and China trade services.

Other business organizations of note are **AMS Management Service Ltd.** (✉ Wilson House, 19–27 Wyndham St., 18th floor, Central, ☎ 2846–3100, FAX 2810–7002), **Brauner's Business Centre** (✉ Kowloon Centre, 29–43 Ashley Rd., Room 903–5, 9th floor, Tsim Sha Tsui, ☎ 2376–2855, FAX 2376–3360), **Business Executive Centre** (✉ Kinwick Centre, 32 Hollywood Rd., 23rd floor, Central, ☎ 2827–7322, FAX 2827–4227), **Business Station** (✉ East Wing Duke Wellington House, 14–24 Wellington St., 5th floor, Central, ☎ 2521–0630, FAX 2521–7601; ✉ Cosmos Bldg., 8–11 Lan Kwai Fong, 6th floor, Central, ☎ 2523–6810, FAX 2530–5071), and **Central Executive Business Centre** (✉ Central Bldg., 1 Pedder St., 11th floor, Central, ☎ 2841–7888, FAX 2810–1868).

CELLULAR PHONES

Hong Kong Telecom International (HKTI) rents cellular phones from offices throughout Hong Kong. The 24-hour office is at Hermes House, 10 Middle Road, in Tsim Sha Tsui (☎ 2888–7184 or 2888–7185), though phones can only be rented between 9 and 6; another **main office** is at 1 D'Aguilar St., Central (☎ 2810–0660).

CHAMBERS OF COMMERCE

American Chamber of Commerce in Hong Kong (✉ Bank of America Tower, 12 Harcourt Rd., Room 1904, Central, Hong Kong Island, ☎ 2526–0165, FAX 2810–1289).

Australian Chamber of Commerce (✉ Lucky Building, 39 Wellington St., 4th Floor, Central, Hong Kong Island, ☎ 2522–5054, FAX 2877–0860.

British Chamber of Commerce (✉ Tung Wai Commercial Building, 109–111 Gloucester Rd., Room 1401–2, Wanchai, Hong Kong Island, ☎ 2824–2211, FAX 2824–1333).

Chinese Manufacturers' Association (✉ CMA Bldg., 64–66 Connaught Rd., 5th floor, Central, Hong Kong Island, ☎ 2542–8600, FAX 2541–4541).

Federation of H.K. Industries (✉ 407 Hankow Centre, 5–15 Hankow Rd., Kowloon, ☎ 2732–3188, FAX 2721–3494.

Hong Kong General Chamber of Commerce (✉ United Centre, 95 Queensway, 5th floor, Hong Kong Island, ☎ 2529–9229, FAX 2527–9843).

Hong Kong Japanese Chamber of Commerce and Industry (✉ Hennessy Centre, 500 Hennessy Rd., 38th floor, Causeway Bay, Hong Kong Island, ☎ 2577–6129, FAX 2577–0525).

Hong Kong Productivity Council (✉ HKPC Bldg., 78 Tat Chee Ave., Kowloon Tong, ☎ 2788–5678, FAX 2788–5900).

Indian Chamber of Commerce Hong Kong (✉ Hoseinee House, 69 Wyndham St., 38th floor, Central, Hong Kong Island, ☎ 2523–3877, FAX 2845–0300).

Swedish Chamber of Commerce (✉ Allied Capital Resource Bldg., 32–38 Ice House St., 10th floor, Central, Hong Kong Island, ☎ 2525–0349, FAX 2537–1843).

CONVENTION CENTER

The **Hong Kong Convention and Exhibition Centre** (✉ 1 Expo Dr., Wanchai, Hong Kong Island, ☎ 2582–8888, FAX 2802–0000) is a state-of-the-art, 693,000-square-ft complex on the Wanchai waterfront, capable of handling 140,000 visitors a day. There are five exhibition halls and two main convention halls; the section jutting into the harbor hosted the 1997 handover ceremony. The largest complex in Asia, the center houses two hotels, the 600-room Grand Hyatt, and the 900-room New World; an apartment block; and a 54-story trade center/office building.

COPY SERVICES

All hotels and business centers have photocopy machines, as do many stores scattered throughout Hong Kong. For heavy-duty, oversize, and color copying, try **Xerox** (✉ Central: New Henry House, 10 Ice House St., 2nd floor, ☎ 2524–9799, FAX 2845–9271; Admiralty: United Centre, Unit 34, 95 Queensway, 2nd floor,

☎ 2527–6162, FAX 2529–5416; Wanchai: Shanghai Ind. Investment Bldg., 58 Hennessy Rd., ☎ 2528–0761, FAX 2865–0799; Tsim Sha Tsui: China Hong Kong City, 33 Canton Rd., Shop 3, 2nd floor, ☎ 2736–6011, FAX 2736–6278).

FAX SERVICES

The Post Office and Hong Kong Telecom International (HKTI) offer a joint service called "Postfax." Inquire at the **General Post Office** (✉ 2 Connaught Rd., next to Star Ferry Terminal, Central, Hong Kong, ☎ 2921–2222) to see which post offices have the service. Postfax is available at **Hong Kong Telecom**'s 24-hour office (✉ Hermes House, 10 Middle Rd., Tsim Sha Tsui, Kowloon, ☎ 2843–9466).

MESSENGERS

Most business centers offer delivery service, and you can sometimes arrange a delivery through your hotel concierge. There's a good chance that both, however, will contact DHL's local courier service. Major buildings and various MTR stations have numerous **DHL Express Centres** (☎ 2765–8111); the company will also pick up from your hotel. Price is based on weight and distance.

OVERNIGHT MAIL

The post office has an overnight express service called Speedpost. Large international couriers in Hong Kong include **DHL** (☎ 2765–8111, FAX 2334–1228), **Federal Express** (☎ 2730–3333, FAX 2730–6588), and **UPS** (☎ 2735–3535, FAX 2738–5070).

TELEX

If your business center is closed and you want to avoid a hotel surcharge, **Hong Kong Telecom International** has one 24-hour office to handle public telephone, fax, and telex: ✉ Hermes House, 10 Middle Road (across the street from the Sheraton) in Tsim Sha Tsui, Kowloon (☎ 2724–8322).

TRADE INFORMATION

Hong Kong Trade Development Council (✉ Office Tower Convention Plaza, 1 Harbour Rd., 38th floor, Hong Kong Island, ☎ 2584–4333, FAX 2824–0249). The TDC has 51 overseas offices, including 12 in the U.S. and one in the U.K.

Trade Department (✉ Trade Department Tower, 700 Nathan Rd., Kowloon, ☎ 2392–2922, FAX 2789–2435).

Industry Department (✉ Ocean Centre, 5 Canton Rd., 14th floor, Kowloon, ☎ 2737–2573, FAX 2730–4633).

BUSINESS HOURS

Nearly all businesses, even tourist-related ones, will shut down for major holidays such as Chinese Lunar New Year, Christmas, and New Year's.

BANKS & OFFICES

Banks are open weekdays 9–4:30 and Saturday 9–12:30. Cash machines are plentiful. Office hours are more or less the same as in the West—9 to 5 or 6. Some offices are open 9–noon on Saturday. Lunch hour is from 1 to 2 pm; don't be surprised if the office closes during lunch.

MUSEUMS & SIGHTS

Museums and sights are usually open six days a week from 9 to 5. Each site picks a different day, usually a Monday or Tuesday, for its day off. Call the destination before visiting.

PHARMACIES

Pharmacies are generally open from about 10 AM until about 9 PM. There are no 24-hour pharmacies.

SHOPS

Stores usually open around 10 AM and stay open until 9 or 9:30 PM, especially in tourist and residential areas. Here's an estimate of store hours by neighborhood: Central, 10–6; Causeway Bay and Wanchai, 10–9:30; Tsim Sha Tsui East, 10–7:30; Tsim Sha Tsui, Yau Ma Tei, and Mong Kok, 10–9.

CAMERAS & PHOTOGRAPHY

You are neither permitted to photograph customs and immigration procedures at border crossings nor allowed to photograph the police or military. At sites where photography is barred there are usually clearly marked NO PHOTOGRAPHY signs.

Although Hong Kong is picturesque, it can be quite cloudy, smoggy, or foggy, so be prepared for poor lighting at times.

Victoria Peak and Repulse Bay both offer visually stunning backdrops for photographs, but don't miss the unforgettable urban scenery of neon-lit streets at night or crowded market scenes by day.

➤ PHOTO HELP: **Kodak Information Center** (☎ 800/242–2424). *Kodak Guide to Shooting Great Travel Pictures,* available in bookstores or from Fodor's Travel Publications (☎ 800/533–6478; $16.50 plus $5.50 shipping).

EQUIPMENT PRECAUTIONS

Always **keep your film and tape out of the sun.** Carry an extra supply of batteries, and **be prepared to turn on your camera or camcorder** to prove to security personnel that the device is real. Always **ask for hand inspection of film,** which becomes clouded after repeated exposure to airport X-ray machines, and **keep videotapes away from metal detectors.**

FILM & DEVELOPING

Kodak and Fuji color film are easy to find in hotel shops, corner grocery stores, and camera shops throughout Hong Kong. Expect to pay about $28HK (around US$3.50) for a 36-exposure roll of 200 film. For insta-matic cameras, you will pay about $100HK (around US$12.50) for a 10-picture pack of Polaroid Spectra Instant Film. One-hour developing is available at Kodak express stalls in malls, hotels, and street corners in Hong Kong. Expect to pay $6 (around $48HK) to $10 (around $80HK) for the speedy service.

CAR RENTAL

Avoid renting a car in Hong Kong. Driving conditions, traffic jams, and parking are bound to make life more difficult. Public transportation is excellent here, and taxis are inexpensive. If you do decide to rent a car, you may want to hire a driver as well; this can be arranged through your hotel. The fee is HK$800–HK$1,200 for the first four hours (depending on

car model) and HK$200–HK$300 for each subsequent hour.

➤ MAJOR AGENCIES: **Alamo** (☎ 800/522–9696; 020/8759–6200 in the U.K.). **Avis** (☎ 800/331–1084; 800/331–1084 in Canada; 02/9353–9000 in Australia; 09/525–1982 in New Zealand). **Budget** (☎ 800/527–0700; 0870/607–5000 in the U.K., through affiliate Europcar). **Dollar** (☎ 800/800–6000; 0124/622–0111 in the U.K., through affiliate Sixt Kenning; 02/9223–1444 in Australia). **Hertz** (☎ 800/654–3001; 800/263–0600 in Canada; 020/8897–2072 in the U.K.; 02/9669–2444 in Australia; 09/256–8690 in New Zealand). **National Car Rental** (☎ 800/227–7368; 020/8680–4800 in the U.K., where it is known as National Europe).

Rates begin at $90 per day and $372 per week for an economy car with air-conditioning, automatic transmission, and unlimited mileage.

➤ LOCAL AGENCIES: **Ace Hire Car** (✉ 16 Min Fat St., Happy Valley, ☎ 2893–0541; turn left at Hong Kong Bank). **Fung Hing Hire Co.** (✉ 58 German St., ground floor, Happy Valley, ☎ 2572–0333) rents chauffeured cars only.

CUTTING COSTS

To get the best deal, **book through a travel agent who will shop around.** Payment must be made before you leave home.

INSURANCE

When driving a rented car you are generally responsible for any damage to or loss of the vehicle as well as for any property damage or personal injury that you may cause. Before you rent see what coverage your personal auto-insurance policy and credit cards already provide.

REQUIREMENTS & RESTRICTIONS

Your own driver's license is valid in Hong Kong, but an International Driver's Permit is always a good idea; it's available from the American and Canadian automobile associations and, in the U.K., from the Automobile Association or Royal Automobile Club. These permits are universally recognized, so having one in your wallet may save you a problem with the local authorities.

SURCHARGES

Before you pick up a car in one city and leave it in another, **ask about drop-off charges or one-way service fees,** which can be substantial. Note, too, that some rental agencies charge extra if you return the car before the time specified in your contract. To avoid a hefty refueling fee, **fill the tank just before you turn in the car,** but be aware that gas stations near the rental outlet may overcharge.

CHILDREN IN HONG KONG

If you are renting a car, don't forget to **arrange for a car seat** when you reserve.

FLYING

If your children are two or older, **ask about children's airfares.** As a general rule, infants under two not occupying a seat fly at greatly reduced fares or even for free. When booking, **confirm carry-on allowances** if you're traveling with infants. In general, for babies charged 10% of the adult fare you are allowed one carry-on bag and a collapsible stroller; if the flight is full, the stroller may have to be checked or you may be limited to less.

Experts agree that it's a good idea to use safety seats aloft for children weighing less than 40 pounds. Airlines set their own policies: U.S. carriers usually require that the child be ticketed, even if he or she is young enough to ride free, since the seats must be strapped into regular seats. Do **check your airline's policy about using safety seats during takeoff and landing.** And since safety seats are not allowed just everywhere in the plane, get your seat assignments early.

When reserving, **request children's meals or a freestanding bassinet** if you need them. But note that bulkhead seats, where you must sit to use the bassinet, may lack an overhead bin or storage space on the floor.

LODGING

Most hotels in Hong Kong allow children under a certain age to stay in their parents' room at no extra charge, but others charge for them as extra adults; be sure to **find out the cutoff age for children's discounts.**

PRECAUTIONS

The traffic flows by quickly, so be especially careful to warn children to look both ways. Otherwise Hong Kong is as safe as any major city in the world. Simply use common sense.

SIGHTS & ATTRACTIONS

Places that are especially appealing to children are indicated by a rubber duckie icon in the margin.

SUPPLIES & EQUIPMENT

Baby supplies such as diapers range in price from $64HK (around US$8) for a box of 30 medium-sized Huggies to $76HK (around US$12) for a box of 28 extra-large Pampers, and are widely available throughout the city. Similarly, a variety of brands of baby-powder milk, sold in 1 kilogram–sized tin containers, are available for about $136HK (around US$17) Heinz baby foods, Johnson & Johnson lotions and powders, and Gerber plastic nursers and silicone nipples are all readily found. You can shop in supermarkets, or at pharmaceutical/cosmetics chain stores such as **Watson's** (☎ 2915–9055) or **Fanda Perfume Co., Ltd.** (☎ 2526–6623), which are scattered throughout Hong Kong. Call for the nearest location.

TRANSPORTATION

Most public transportation services charge half price for children under 12.

COMPUTERS ON THE ROAD

Hong Kong is computer-friendly. If your spare battery or adapter fails you, no worries; you can buy a new one in Hong Kong. In general, for computer purchases make sure the product's voltage compatibility is that of your home country and verify that all parts, pieces, and an international warranty are packed with your purchase. Shop around, as prices may vary within a few months. Consider purchasing your product with a credit card, which might increase the price by 3 to 5 percent, but will make it easier if you need to return or claim a refund for your purchase from the manufacturer or store once you return home.

SMART TRAVEL TIPS A TO Z

While using surge protection is a good computer habit, you'll have no worries plugging your computer directly into the socket at a Hong Kong hotel or business building. The electricity is stable.

CONCIERGES

Concierges, found in many hotels, can help you with theater tickets and dinner reservations: a good one with connections may be able to get you seats for a hot show or prime-time dinner reservations at the restaurant of the moment. You can also turn to your hotel's concierge for help with travel arrangements, sightseeing plans, services ranging from aromatherapy to zipper repair, and emergencies. Always, **always tip** a concierge who has been of assistance (☞ Tipping, *below*).

CONSUMER PROTECTION

Whenever shopping or buying travel services in Hong Kong, **pay with a major credit card** so you can cancel payment or get reimbursed if a problem occurs. Note, however, that this will increase the price of your purchase by 3 to 5 percent. If you're doing business with a particular company for the first time, **contact your local Better Business Bureau and the attorney general's offices** in your own state and the company's home state, as well. Have any complaints been filed? Finally, if you're buying a package or tour, always **consider travel insurance** that includes default coverage (☞ Insurance, *below*).

➤ BBBs: **Council of Better Business Bureaus** (✉ 4200 Wilson Blvd., Suite 800, Arlington, VA 22203, ☎ 703/276–0100, FAX 703/525–8277 www.bbb.org).

CRUISE TRAVEL

Cruise ships in Hong Kong tend to cater to a mix of passengers from Hong Kong, Singapore, Thailand, and Malaysia alongside Westerners. The large cruise lines are beginning to expand their range of itineraries; in the meantime, you can **book a cruise with a local operator** that specializes in a specific part of Southeast Asia.

➤ CRUISE LINES: **Star Cruise** (✉ Ocean Centre, 5 Canton Rd., No. 1,

15th floor, Tsim Sha Tsui, ☎ 2317–7711) runs cruises out of Hong Kong.

CUSTOMS & DUTIES

When shopping, **keep receipts** for all purchases. Upon reentering the country, **be ready to show customs officials what you've bought.** If you feel a duty is incorrect or object to the way your clearance was handled, note the inspector's badge number and ask to see a supervisor. If the problem isn't resolved, write to the appropriate authorities, beginning with the port director at your point of entry.

IN HONG KONG

Except for the usual prohibitions against narcotics, explosives, firearms, and ammunition (all but narcotics must be declared upon arrival and handed over for safekeeping until departure), and modest limits on alcohol, tobacco products, and perfume, you can bring anything you want into Hong Kong, including an unlimited amount of money.

Nonresident visitors may bring in, duty-free, 200 cigarettes or 50 cigars or 250 grams of tobacco, and 1 liter of alcohol.

IN AUSTRALIA

Australian residents who are 18 or older may bring home $A400 worth of souvenirs and gifts (including jewelry), 250 cigarettes or 250 grams of tobacco, and 1,125 ml of alcohol (including wine, beer, and spirits). Residents under 18 may bring back $A200 worth of goods. Prohibited items include meat products. Seeds, plants, and fruits need to be declared upon arrival.

➤ INFORMATION: **Australian Customs Service** (Regional Director, ✉ Box 8, Sydney, NSW 2001, ☎ 02/9213–2000, FAX 02/9213–4000).

IN CANADA

Canadian residents who have been out of Canada for at least 7 days may bring home C$500 worth of goods duty-free. If you've been away less than 7 days but more than 48 hours, the duty-free allowance drops to C$200; if your trip lasts 24–48 hours, the allowance is C$50. You may not pool allowances with family members. Goods claimed under the C$500 exemption may follow you by mail; those claimed under the lesser exemptions must accompany you. Alcohol and tobacco products may be included in the 7-day and 48-hour exemptions but not in the 24-hour exemption. If you meet the age requirements of the province or territory through which you reenter Canada, you may bring in, duty-free, 1.14 liters (40 imperial ounces) of wine or liquor *or* 24 12-ounce cans or bottles of beer or ale. If you are 16 or older you may bring in, duty-free, 200 cigarettes and 50 cigars. Check ahead of time with Revenue Canada or the Department of Agriculture for policies regarding meat products, seeds, plants, and fruits.

You may send an unlimited number of gifts worth up to C$60 each duty-free to Canada. Label the package UNSOLICITED GIFT—VALUE UNDER $60. Alcohol and tobacco are excluded.

➤ INFORMATION: **Revenue Canada** (✉ 2265 St. Laurent Blvd. S, Ottawa, Ontario K1G 4K3, ☎ 613/993–0534; 800/461–9999 in Canada, FAX 613/957–8911, www.ccra-adrc.gc.ca).

IN NEW ZEALAND

Homeward-bound residents 17 or older may bring back $700NZ worth of souvenirs and gifts. Your duty-free allowance also includes 4.5 liters of wine or beer; one 1,125-ml bottle of spirits; and either 200 cigarettes, 250 grams of tobacco, 50 cigars, or a combination of the three up to 250 grams. Prohibited items include meat products, seeds, plants, and fruits.

➤ INFORMATION: **New Zealand Customs** (Custom House, ✉ 50 Anzac Ave., Box 29, Auckland, New Zealand, ☎ 09/359–6655, FAX 09/359–6732).

IN THE U.K.

From countries outside the EU, including Hong Kong, you may bring home, duty-free, 200 cigarettes or 50 cigars; 1 liter of spirits or 2 liters of fortified or sparkling wine or liqueurs; 2 liters of still table wine; 60 ml of perfume; 250 ml of toilet water; plus £136 worth of other goods, including gifts and souvenirs. If returning from outside the EU, prohibited items include meat products, seeds, plants, and fruits.

➤ INFORMATION: **HM Customs and Excise** (✉ Dorset House, Stamford St., Bromley, Kent BR1 1XX, ☎ 020/7/202–4227).

IN THE U.S.

U.S. residents who have been out of the country for at least 48 hours (and who have not used the $400 allowance or any part of it in the past 30 days) may bring home $400 worth of foreign goods duty-free.

U.S. residents 21 and older may bring back 1 liter of alcohol duty-free. In addition, regardless of your age, you are allowed 200 cigarettes and 100 non-Cuban cigars. Antiques, which the U.S. Customs Service defines as objects more than 100 years old, enter duty-free, as do original works of art done entirely by hand, including paintings, drawings, and sculptures.

You may also send packages home duty-free: up to $200 worth of goods for personal use, with a limit of one parcel per addressee per day (except alcohol or tobacco products or perfume worth more than $5); label the package PERSONAL USE and attach a list of its contents and their retail value. Do not label the package UNSOLICITED GIFT or your duty-free exemption will drop to $100. Mailed items do not affect your duty-free allowance on your return.

➤ INFORMATION: **U.S. Customs Service** (✉ 1300 Pennsylvania Ave. NW, Washington, DC 20229, www.customs.gov; inquiries ☎ 202/354–1000; complaints c/o ✉ Office of Regulations and Rulings; registration of equipment c/o ✉ Resource Management, ☎ 202/927–0540).

DINING

The restaurants we review are the cream of the crop in each price category. Prices are indicated as follows:

CATEGORY	COST*
$$$$	over $64
$$$	$38–$64
$$	$13–$38
$	under $13

per person, not including 10% service charge

SMART TRAVEL TIPS A TO Z

MEALS & SPECIALTIES

With more than 9,000 restaurants, Hong Kong has food to please every palate.

Hong Kong is famous for its Cantonese restaurants, since most residents trace their roots to Guangdong (Canton) Province. The Cantonese are noted for cooking foods you might not think edible. As the saying goes, if it has four legs and isn't a table, the Cantonese will steam, stir-fry, or boil it. Specialties include pigeon, shark's-fin soup, and abalone.

You shouldn't leave Hong Kong without trying the Cantonese specialty dim sum. These light snacks, served for lunch or breakfast in local tea-houses as well as fine restaurants, are usually served in steaming bamboo baskets. Dim sum includes a variety of dumplings, buns, and pastries containing meat and vegetables.

Of course, you can also find restaurants serving specialties from throughout China. Peking foods use noodles and dumplings and are strongly spiced with coriander, peppers, and garlic. Shanghainese cuisine is typically seasoned with sugar, soy sauce, and wine. Late autumn is the best time to try a Shanghainese specialty, freshwater hairy crabs. Szechuan food includes some of the spiciest dishes in China (check the chili codes on the menus) but not all dishes are spicy.

Seafood is a year-round favorite in Hong Kong. Plentiful and delicious, live fish and shellfish are kept in tanks at many restaurants, so you can hand pick your dinner and be assured of freshness. Steamed garoupa (grouper) and poached shrimp with chili and soy sauce are two specialties.

MEALTIMES

Dim sum restaurants normally open about 7:30 AM and close about 2:30 PM. Some are shut between 10 and 11:30 AM. Dim sum restaurants often teem with people on the weekends, so expect to wait at the more popular places.

Western-style restaurants, such as Irish pubs and steak houses, are open from about 11 am to 11 pm daily; dinner is busiest, around 7 PM.

Unless otherwise noted, the restaurants listed in this guide are open daily for lunch and dinner.

PAYING

Try not to be shocked when you get your bill. You'll be charged for everything, including tea, rice, and even those side dishes placed automatically on every table, which are often mistaken for complimentary snacks. Tips are expected (10% average gratuity) at most restaurants, even if the bill includes a service charge.

RESERVATIONS & DRESS

Reservations are always a good idea; we note only when they're essential, which is often the case at lunchtime (between 1 and 2) or at dinnertime (between 7 and 10) on weekends. Book as far ahead as you can, and reconfirm as soon as you arrive. We mention dress only when men are required to wear a jacket or a jacket and tie.

WINE, BEER & SPIRITS

The drinking age in bars is 18, and is fairly strictly enforced. You can find most brands of imported alcohol and an excellent array of imported beers as well as the locally brewed San Miguel. Most nightlife spots offer happy-hour specials, sometimes starting as early as 3 PM and continuing until 10 PM.

DISABILITIES & ACCESSIBILITY

Hong Kong is not the easiest of cities for people in wheelchairs, and few ramps or other provisions for access are provided. Progress is being made, however; the airport, City Hall, the Academy for Performing Arts, and the Hong Kong Arts Centre have made efforts to assist people in wheelchairs. For more information, consult the *Hong Kong Access Guide for Disabled Visitors,* available from the Hong Kong Tourist Association (HKTA). The guide lists those rare places that have special facilities for people with disabilities, in addition to the best access to hotels, shopping centers, government offices, consulates, restaurants, and churches.

LODGING

When discussing accessibility with an operator or reservations agent, **ask hard questions.** Are there any stairs, inside *or* out? Are there grab bars next to the toilet *and* in the shower/tub? How wide is the doorway to the room? To the bathroom? For the most extensive facilities meeting the latest legal specifications, **opt for newer accommodations.**

TRANSPORTATION

The vast airport has moving walkways that transport arriving or departing passengers from the most remote gates in about 70 seconds. Ramps, lifts, and escalators are provided for unavoidable changes of level.

While taxis in Hong Kong do not adapt to special needs of passengers with physical disabilities, walking aids such as wheelchairs and crutches are carried free of charge.

The Kowloon Canton Railway (KCR), which operates along North East New Territories, has lifts at all stations except the Racecourse Station. The KCR Light Rail, which operates in the North West New Territories, has ramps from the street to the platform at all stations. The Mass Transit Railway (MTR), which services Hong Kong and Kowloon and also connects to Tung Chungk and the Chek Lap Kok airport, has ramps or lifts at 19 stations. For **MTR** enquiries, call ☎ 2881–8888.

Ancillary facilities such as tactile guide paths, escalator audible devices, and light emitting diode (LED) display boards are available at most stations.

The lower deck on the ferries is more accessible than the upper deck for passengers using wheelchairs.

➤ COMPLAINTS: **Disability Rights Section** (✉ U.S. Department of Justice, Civil Rights Division, Box 66738, Washington, DC 20035-6738, ☎ 202/514–0301 or 800/514–0301; TTY 202/514–0301 or 800/514–0301, FAX 202/307–1198) for general complaints. **Aviation Consumer Protection Division** (☞ Air Travel, *above*) for airline-related problems. **Civil Rights Office** (✉ U.S. Department of Transportation, Departmental Office of Civil Rights, S-30, 400 7th St. SW, Room 10215, Washington, DC 20590, ☎ 202/366–4648, FAX 202/366–9371) for problems with surface transportation.

TRAVEL AGENCIES

In the United States, the Americans with Disabilities Act requires that travel firms serve the needs of all travelers. Some agencies specialize in working with people with disabilities.

➤ TRAVELERS WITH MOBILITY PROBLEMS: **Access Adventures** (✉ 206 Chestnut Ridge Rd., Rochester, NY 14624, ☎ 716/889–9096, dltravel@prodigy.net), run by a former physical-rehabilitation counselor. **CareVacations** (✉ 5-5110 50th Ave., Leduc, Alberta T9E 6V4, ☎ 780/986–6404 or 877/478–7827, FAX 780/986–8332, www.carevacations.com) for group tours and cruise vacations. **Flying Wheels Travel** (✉ 143 W. Bridge St., Box 382, Owatonna, MN 55060, ☎ 507/451–5005 or 800/535–6790, FAX 507/451–1685, thq@ll.net, www.flyingwheels.com).

➤ TRAVELERS WITH DEVELOPMENTAL DISABILITIES: **New Directions** (✉ 5276 Hollister Ave., Suite 207, Santa Barbara, CA 93111, ☎ 805/967–2841 or 888/967–2841, FAX 805/964–7344, newdirec@silcom.com, www.silcom.com/ânewdirec/).

DISCOUNTS & DEALS

Be a smart shopper and **compare all your options** before making decisions. A plane ticket bought with a promotional coupon from travel clubs, coupon books, and direct-mail offers may not be cheaper than the least expensive fare from a discount ticket agency. And always keep in mind that what you get is just as important as what you save.

DISCOUNT RESERVATIONS

To save money, **look into discount reservations services** with toll-free numbers, which use their buying power to get a better price on hotels, airline tickets, even car rentals. When booking a room, always **call the hotel's local toll-free number** (if one is

SMART TRAVEL TIPS A TO Z

available) rather than the central reservations number—you'll often get a better price. Always ask about special packages or corporate rates.

When shopping for the best deal on hotels and car rentals, **look for guaranteed exchange rates,** which protect you against a falling dollar. With your rate locked in, you won't pay more, even if the price goes up in the local currency.

➤ AIRLINE TICKETS: ☎ 800/FLY–4–LESS.

➤ HOTEL ROOMS: **Steigenberger Reservation Service** (☎ 800/223–5652, www.srs-worldhotels.com). **Travel Interlink** (☎ 800/888–5898, www.travelinterlink.com). **VacationLand** (☎ 800/245–0050, sales@vacationasia.com, www.vacation-land.com).

PACKAGE DEALS

Don't confuse packages and guided tours. When you buy a package, you travel on your own, just as though you had planned the trip yourself. Fly/drive packages, which combine airfare and car rental, are often a good deal. In cities, ask the local visitors' bureau about hotel packages that include tickets to major museum exhibits or other special events.

ELECTRICITY

To use your U.S.-purchased electric-powered equipment, **bring a converter and adapter.** The electrical current in Hong Kong is 220 volts, 50 cycles alternating current (AC); in Macau it's also 220 volts, 50 cycles. Some outlets in Hong Kong take plugs with three round prongs, while others use plugs with two square prongs. There is no standard plug size in Macau; check with your hotel regarding its setup.

If your appliances are dual-voltage, you'll need only an adapter. Don't use 110-volt outlets marked FOR SHAVERS ONLY for high-wattage appliances such as blow-dryers. Most laptops operate equally well on 110 and 220 volts and so require only an adapter.

EMBASSIES

➤ AUSTRALIA: **Australian Consulate** (✉ Harbour Centre, 25 Harbour Rd., 24th floor, Wanchai, ☎ 2827–8881, FAX 2585–4459).

➤ CANADA: **Canadian Consulate** (✉ Tower 1, Exchange Sq., 8 Connaught Pl., 11th–14th floors, Hong Kong Island, ☎ 2810–4321, FAX 2810–8736).

➤ NEW ZEALAND: **Consulate General** (✉ Central Plaza, Central, Hong Kong, ☎ 2525–5044).

➤ UNITED KINGDOM: **British Trade Commission** (✉ Visa Section, 1 Supreme Court Rd., 3rd floor, Hong Kong Island, ☎ 2901–3111).

➤ UNITED STATES: **U.S.Consulate** (✉ 26 Garden Rd., Hong Kong Island, ☎ 2523–9011, FAX 2845–1598).

EMERGENCIES

Locals and police are usually quite helpful in an emergency situation. Most police officers speak some English or will contact someone who does.

➤ EMERGENCY SERVICES: **Police, fire, and ambulance** (☎ 999). **Hong Kong Police and Taxi Complaint Hotline** (☎ 2527–7177).

➤ HOSPITALS: **Prince of Wales Hospital** (✉ 30–32 Ngan Shing St., Shatin, New Territories, ☎ 2632–2211), **Princess Margaret Hospital** (✉ 2–10 Princess Margaret Hospital Rd., Laichikok, Kowloon, ☎ 2990–1111), **Queen Elizabeth Hospital** (✉ 30 Gascoigne Rd., Kowloon, ☎ 2958–8888), **Queen Mary Hospital** (✉ 102 Pok Fu Lam Rd., Hong Kong, ☎ 2855–3111), and **Tang Shiu Kin Hospital** (✉ 282 Queen's Rd. East, Hong Kong, ☎ 2291–2000).

➤ 24-HOUR PHARMACIES: There are no 24-hour pharmacies, however **Watson's** (☎ 2915–9065) and **Fanda Perfume Co., Ltd.** (☎ 2526–6623) both have pharmacy departments and numerous shops throughout the city; they are usually open until 9 PM.

ENGLISH-LANGUAGE MEDIA

English-language newspapers are available in Hong Kong. Two English television channels broadcast local English programs weekday mornings and evenings and all day on weekends and holidays. Satellite and Cable TV are also available.

BOOKS

Most bookstores throughout the city have English-language selections.

➤ BOOKSTORES: **Bookazines Ltd.** (✉ Pacific House, 20 Queen's Rd., Central, ☎ 2521-1649) has a wide selection of books and magazines.

NEWSPAPERS & MAGAZINES

English newspapers printed in Hong Kong include the *South China Morning Post, Hong Kong iMail,* the *Asian Wall Street Journal,* the *International Herald Tribune,* and *USA Today International.* The *HK* and the *BC Magazine* are free. The former is an alternative weekly tabloid, the latter a monthly magazine; both provide comprehensive weekly listings.

RADIO & TELEVISION

There are 13 radio channels, with everything from Cantonese pop music to English news. Stations with English-speaking disc jockeys include: RTHK Radio 3 (AM 567 or 1584, FM 97.9 or 106.8), which airs news, finance, and current affairs; RTHK Radio 4 (FM 97.6 to 98.9), which plays Western and Chinese classical music; and RTHK Radio 6 (AM 675), which airs the BBC World Service relay. Metro Plus (AM 1044) has regional news, finance programs, and international music.

English-language television channels include ATV World and TVB Pearl. Satellite selections include Star and AUSTV; on cable you can get BBC, CNN, ESPN, and HBO.

ETIQUETTE & BEHAVIOR

It won't hurt to **brush up on your use of chopsticks.** Silverware is common in Hong Kong, but it might be seen as a respectful gesture if you try your hand at chopsticks. Dining is a communal event. Everyone orders at least one dish, which are then placed in the center of the table and shared. Your meal will usually include rice or soup. It is considered proper to hold the bowl close to your lips and shovel the rice or soup into your mouth.

Smoking is common in Hong Kong, yet you should know that in July 1998 smoking was officially banned in all indoor public areas, including malls, banks, department stores, and supermarkets.

Hong Kong is extremely crowded; pushing, shoving, and gentle nudges are commonplace. As difficult as this may be to accept, it's not considered rude, it's unavoidable. Becoming angry or taking offense to an inadvertant push is considered rude.

However, while a gentle shove on the streets may be common, it is not typical of strangers to be excessively touchy-feely with one another. A gregarious hug and boisterous hello will be off-putting to Hong Kongers who don't know you. When you are first meeting local people, try to be low-key and subdued, even if its not in your nature.

BUSINESS ETIQUETTE

Hong Kongers have a keen sense of hierarchy in the office. Egalitarianism may be admired in the United States, but it's often insulting in Hong Kong. **Let the tea lady get the tea** and coffee—that's what she's there for. Your assistant or Chinese colleague is thought to have better things to do than make copies or deliver messages. Hong Kongers are very attached to business cards, presumably because they're tangible evidence of one's place in the hierarchy. **Have plenty of cards available** (printed, if possible, in English on one side and Chinese on the other). Exchange cards by proffering yours with both hands and a slight bow, and receiving one in the same way.

GAY & LESBIAN TRAVEL

Criminal sanctions on homosexual relations between consenting adults in Hong Kong were lifted in 1991.

➤ LOCAL RESOURCES: *Contacts,* a magazine covering the local gay scene, is available for HK$35 at the **Fetish Fashion** boutique (✉ 32 Cochrane St., mezzanine floor, Central, ☎ 2544–1155). Among popular nightspots are **Flex** (✉ 7 Glenealy Rd., Central, ☎ 2967–1832, **Petticoat Lane** (✉ 2 Tun Wo La., Midlevels, ☎ 2973–0642), and **Propaganda** (✉ 1 Hollywood Rd., Central, ☎ 2868–1316), the largest gay and lesbian bar in Hong Kong.

Hong Kong's **AIDS Hot Line** can be reached at ☎ 2780–2211.

➤ GAY- & LESBIAN-FRIENDLY TRAVEL AGENCIES: **Different Roads Travel** (⊠ 8383 Wilshire Blvd., Suite 902, Beverly Hills, CA 90211, ☎ 323/651–5557 or 800/429–8747, FAX 323/651–3678, leigh@west.tzell.com). **Kennedy Travel** (⊠ 314 Jericho Turnpike, Floral Park, NY 11001, ☎ 516/352–4888 or 800/237–7433, FAX 516/354–8849, main@kennedytravel.com, www.kennedytravel.com). **Now Voyager** (⊠ 4406 18th St., San Francisco, CA 94114, ☎ 415/626–1169 or 800/255–6951, FAX 415/626–8626, www.nowvoyager.com). **Skylink Travel and Tour** (⊠ 1006 Mendocino Ave., Santa Rosa, CA 95401, ☎ 707/546–9888 or 800/225–5759, FAX 707/546–9891, skylinktvl@aol.com, www.skylinktravel.com), serving lesbian travelers.

HEALTH

FOOD & DRINK

The major health risk for travelers overseas is traveler's diarrhea, caused by eating contaminated fruit or vegetables or drinking contaminated water. **Watch what you eat:** stay away from ice, uncooked food, and unpasteurized milk and milk products. Note, too, that eating raw shellfish has been associated with recent hepatitis outbreaks in Hong Kong. **Drink only bottled water** or water that has been boiled for at least 20 minutes, even when you're brushing your teeth. Expect to pay HK$7 to HK$20 for a liter bottle of distilled water.

OVER-THE-COUNTER REMEDIES

Familiar over-the-counter medications such as aspirin, Tylenol, etc., are available in supermarkets such as Wellcome or even 7-Eleven shops, which are scattered throughout the city. The drugstore chains **Watson's** (☎ 2915–9065) and **Fanda Perfume Co., Ltd** (☎ 2526–6623) both have pharmacy departments and numerous shops throughout the city.

HOLIDAYS

Major holidays in Hong Kong include New Year's (the first weekday in January), Chinese New Year, Easter, Labour Day (May 1), National Day (Oct. 1), and Christmas and Boxing Day (Dec. 25 and 26). There are also numerous Chinese holidays throughout the year.

INSURANCE

The most useful travel insurance plan is a comprehensive policy that includes coverage for trip cancellation and interruption, default, trip delay, and medical expenses (with a waiver for preexisting conditions).

Without insurance you will lose all or most of your money if you cancel your trip, regardless of the reason. Default insurance covers you if your tour operator, airline, or cruise line goes out of business. Trip-delay covers expenses that arise because of bad weather or mechanical delays. Study the fine print when comparing policies.

If you're traveling internationally, a key component of travel insurance is coverage for medical bills incurred if you get sick on the road. Such expenses are not generally covered by Medicare or private policies. U.K. residents can buy a travel insurance policy valid for most vacations taken during the year in which it's purchased (but check preexisting-condition coverage). British and Australian citizens need extra medical coverage when traveling overseas.

Always **buy travel policies directly from the insurance company**; if you buy them from a cruise line, airline, or tour operator that goes out of business you probably will not be covered for the agency or operator's default, a major risk. Before making any purchase, **review your existing health and home-owner's policies** to find what they cover away from home.

➤ TRAVEL INSURERS: In the U.S.: **Access America** (⊠ 6600 W. Broad St., Richmond, VA 23230, ☎ 804/285–3300 or 800/284–8300, FAX 804/673–1583, www.previewtravel.com); **Travel Guard International** (⊠ 1145 Clark St., Stevens Point, WI 54481, ☎ 715/345–0505 or 800/826–1300, FAX 800/955–8785, www.noelgroup.com). In Canada: **Voyager Insurance** (⊠ 44 Peel Center Dr., Brampton,

Ontario L6T 4M8, ☎ 905/791–8700; 800/668–4342 in Canada).

➤ INSURANCE INFORMATION: In the U.K.: **Association of British Insurers** (✉ 51–55 Gresham St., London EC2V 7HQ, ☎ 020/7/600–3333, FAX 020/7/696–8999, info@abi.org.uk, www.abi.org.uk). In Australia: **Insurance Council of Australia** (☎ 03/9614–1077, FAX 03/9614–7924).

LANGUAGE

Hong Kong's official languages are English and Chinese. The most commonly spoken Chinese dialect is Cantonese, but Mandarin—the official language of China, known in Hong Kong as Putonghua—is gaining in popularity. Macau's official languages are Portuguese and Chinese, but many people speak some English. Here, too, Mandarin is growing in popularity.

In hotels, major restaurants, stores, and tourist centers, almost everyone speaks English. This is not the case, however, with taxi drivers, bus drivers, and workers in small shops, cafés, and market stalls.

Language study courses are available, but most last at least one month. Contact the Chinese Language Centre at the Chinese University of Hong Kong (www.cuhk.edu.hk/lac) for more information.

LODGING

Hong Kong hotels operate on the European Plan, i.e., with no meals included. Rooms have private baths unless otherwise noted.

The lodgings we review are the cream of the crop in each price category. We always list the facilities available, but we don't specify whether they cost extra; so when pricing accommodations, always ask what's included and what's not.

CATEGORY	COST*
$$$$	over $310
$$$	$225–$310
$$	$150–$225
$	under $150

All prices are for a double room, not including 10% service charge and 3% tax.

Bargain lodging has become increasingly rare in Hong Kong. If none of our moderately priced suggestions pan out, try the **STB Hostel** (✉ HK Ltd., Great Eastern Mansion, 255–261 Reclamation St., 2nd floor, Mong Kok, Kowloon, ☎ 2710–9199, FAX 2385–0153), which has dorm-style sleeping quarters, or the **YMCA International House** (✉ 23 Waterloo Rd., Yau Ma Tei, Kowloon, ☎ 2771–9111, FAX 2771–5238).

APARTMENT RENTALS

If you want a home base that's roomy enough for a family and comes with cooking facilities, **consider a furnished rental.** These can save you money, especially if you're traveling with a group. Home-exchange directories sometimes list rentals as well as exchanges.

Hong Kong landlords usually require a minimum one-month stay for apartment rentals. Contact real-estate agencies to find out what is currently available.

Hong Kong & Shanghai Hotels Ltd. (✉ 8/F St. Georges House, 2 Ice House St., Central, ☎ 2840–7788, FAX 2845–5526) and **Eaton House** (✉ 380 Nathan Rd., Kowloon, ☎ 2710–1800, FAX 2388–6971) both handle rentals area wide.

HOSTELS

No matter what your age, you can **save on lodging costs by staying at hostels.** The Hong Kong Youth Hostels Association is a full member of the International Youth Hostel Federation (Hostelling International). The main hostels, **Ma Wui Hall** (✉ Top of Mt. Davis Path, Mt. Davis, Western District, Hong Kong, ☎ 2817–5715) and **Bradbury Lodge** (✉ 66 Ting Kok Road, Tai Mei Tuk Tai Po, New Territories, ☎ 2662–5123) are easily accessible by public transport. Both are less than $HK 50 per night.

➤ ORGANIZATIONS: **Hostelling International—American Youth Hostels** (✉ 733 15th St. NW, Suite 840, Washington, DC 20005, ☎ 202/783–6161, FAX 202/783–6171, www.hiayh.org). **Hostelling International–Canada** (✉ 400–205 Catherine St., Ottawa, Ontario K2P 1C3, ☎ 613/237–7884,

FAX 613/237–7868, www.hostellingintl. ca). **Youth Hostel Association of England and Wales** (✉ Trevelyan House, 8 St. Stephen's Hill, St. Albans, Hertfordshire AL1 2DY, ☎ 01727/855215 or 01727/845047, FAX 01727/844126, www.yha.uk). **Australian Youth Hostel Association** (✉ 10 Mallett St., Camperdown, NSW 2050, ☎ 02/ 9565–1699, FAX 02/9565–1325, www. yha.com.au). **Youth Hostels Association of New Zealand** (✉ Box 436, Christchurch, New Zealand, ☎ 03/ 379–9970, FAX 03/365–4476, www. yha.org.nz).

HOTELS

All hotels listed have private baths unless otherwise noted.

➤ TOLL-FREE NUMBERS: **Best Western** (☎ 800/528–1234, www.bestwestern. com). **Choice** (☎ 800/221–2222, www. hotelchoice.com). **Four Seasons** (☎ 800/332–3442, www.fourseasons. com). **Hilton** (☎ 800/445–8667, www. hiltons.com). **Holiday Inn** (☎ 800/ 465–4329, www.holiday-inn.com). **Inter-Continental** (☎ 800/327–0200, www.interconti.com). **La Quinta** (☎ 800/531–5900, www.laquinta. com). **Marriott** (☎ 800/228–9290, www.marriott.com). **Nikko Hotels International** (☎ 800/645–5687, www. nikko.com). **Omni** (☎ 800/843–6664, www.omnihotels.com). **Ramada** (☎ 800/228–2828. www.ramada.com). **Renaissance Hotels & Resorts** (☎ 800/ 468–3571, www.hotels.com). **Sheraton** (☎ 800/325–3535, www.sheraton. com).

MAIL & SHIPPING

Hong Kong has an excellent reputation for its postal system. Airmail letters to any place in the world should take 3 to 8 days.

➤ POST OFFICES: The Kowloon Central Post Office (✉ 10 Middle Rd., Tsim Tsa Shui) and the General Post Office (✉ 2 Connaught Rd., Central) are open 8 AM to 6 PM Monday through Saturday.

OVERNIGHT SERVICES

Overnight delivery services are available throughout the city. You will find drop-off boxes or offices in most subway stations, malls, and hotels. For the office nearest you, call the company. **DHL** (☎ 2765–8111), **Federal Express** (☎ 2730–3333), **United Parcel Service** (☎ 2735–3535).

POSTAL RATES

Letters sent from Hong Kong are thought of as going to one of two zones. Zone 1 includes China, Japan, Taiwan, South Korea, South-East Asia, Indonesia, and Asia. Zone 2 is everywhere else. International airmail costs HK$2.10 for a letter or postcard weighing under 10 grams mailed to a Zone 1 address, and HK$2.60 for a letter sent to a Zone 2 address. For each additional 10 grams, you will be charged HK$1.10 for Zone 1 and HK$1.20 for Zone 2.

RECEIVING MAIL

The **General Post Office** and **Kowloon Central Post Office** have poste restante counters.

Travelers with American Express cards or traveler's checks can receive mail at the **American Express** office (✉ 5 Queen's Rd., Central, ☎ 2811–6888). Have mail addressed c/o Client Mail Service at this address.

MONEY MATTERS

Prices throughout this guide are given for adults. Substantially reduced fees are almost always available for children, students, and senior citizens. For information on taxes, *see* Taxes, *below.*

ATMS

Reliable and safe, ATMs are widely available throughout Hong Kong. If your card was issued from a bank in an English-speaking country, the instructions on the ATM machine will appear in English.

CREDIT CARDS

Throughout this guide, the following abbreviations are used: **AE**, American Express; **DC**, Diner's Club; **MC**, Master Card; and **V**, Visa.

CURRENCY

Units of currency are the Hong Kong dollar ($) and the cent. Bills come in denominations of 1,000, 500, 100, 50, 20, and 10 dollars. Coins are 10, 5, 2, and 1 dollar and 50, 20, and 10 cents. At press time the Hong Kong dollar was fixed at approximately 7.8

dollars to the U.S. dollar, 6.52 to the Canadian dollar, and 12.5 to the pound sterling. The image of Queen Elizabeth II will not appear on new coins, but the old ones are still valid.

The official currency unit in Macau is the pataca, which is divided into 100 avos. Bank notes come in five denominations: 500, 100, 50, 10, and 5 patacas. Coins are 5 and 1 patacas and 50, 20, and 10 avos. The pataca is pegged to the Hong Kong dollar (within a few cents); at press time there were 8 patacas to the U.S. dollar. **Hong Kong currency circulates freely in Macau but not vice versa,** so remember to change your patacas before you return to Hong Kong.

CURRENCY EXCHANGE

There are no currency restrictions in Hong Kong. You can exchange currency at the airport, in hotels, in banks, and through private money changers scattered through the tourist areas. For the most favorable rates, **change money at banks.** You'll get better rates from a bank or money changer than from a hotel; just **beware of money changers who advertise "no selling commission"** without mentioning the "buying commission" you must pay when you exchange foreign currency or traveler's checks for Hong Kong dollars.

➤ EXCHANGE SERVICES: **International Currency Express** (☎ 888/278–6628 for orders, www.foreignmoney.com). **Thomas Cook Currency Services** (☎ 800/287–7362 for telephone orders and retail locations, www. us.thomascook.com).

TRAVELER'S CHECKS

Do you need traveler's checks? It depends on where you're headed. If you're going to rural areas and small towns, go with cash; traveler's checks are best used in cities. Lost or stolen checks can usually be replaced within 24 hours. To ensure a speedy refund, buy your own traveler's checks—don't let someone else pay for them: irregularities like this can cause delays. The person who bought the checks should make the call to request a refund.

Dress in Hong Kong is generally informal. From May through September, Hong Kong's high humidity warrants light clothing; but air-conditioning in hotels and restaurants can be arctic, so bring a sweater or shawl for evening use indoors. Don't forget your swimsuit and sunscreen; several hotels have pools, and you may want to spend some time on one of Hong Kong's many beaches. In October, November, March, and April, a jacket or sweater should suffice, but from December through February bring a raincoat or a light overcoat. At any time of year it's wise to **pack a folding umbrella.**

In your carry-on luggage, **pack an extra pair of eyeglasses or contact lenses** and **enough of any medication you take** to last the entire trip. You may also ask your doctor to write a spare prescription using the drug's generic name, since brand names may vary from country to country. In luggage to be checked, **never pack prescription drugs or valuables.** To avoid customs delays, carry medications in their original packaging. And don't forget to carry with you the addresses of offices that handle refunds of lost traveler's checks.

CHECKING LUGGAGE

Airlines flying *out* of Hong Kong are strictly enforcing carry-on rules, particularly among holders of economy tickets. Coach-class passengers are allowed only one bag, measuring not more than 9 x 14 x 22 inches and weighing not more than 20 kilograms, in addition to a handbag or briefcase. Business-class passengers get two bags, first-class passengers three.

How many carry-on bags you can bring with you is up to the airline. Most allow two, but not always, so make sure that everything you carry aboard will fit under your seat or in the overhead bin, and get to the gate early. Note that if you have a seat at the back of the plane, you'll probably board first, while the overhead bins are still empty.

If you are flying internationally, note that baggage allowances may be determined not by piece but by weight—generally 88 pounds (40 kilograms) in first class, 66 pounds (30 kilograms) in business class, and 44 pounds (20 kilograms) in economy.

Airline liability for baggage is limited to $1,250 per person on flights within the United States. On international flights it amounts to $9.07 per pound or $20 per kilogram for checked baggage (roughly $640 per 70-pound bag) and $400 per passenger for unchecked baggage. You can buy additional coverage at check-in for about $10 per $1,000 of coverage, but it excludes a rather extensive list of items, shown on your airline ticket.

Before departure, **itemize your bags' contents** and their worth, and label the bags with your name, address, and phone number. (If you use your home address, cover it so potential thieves can't see it readily.) Inside each bag, **pack a copy of your itinerary.** At check-in, **make sure that each bag is correctly tagged** with the destination airport's three-letter code. If your bags arrive damaged or fail to arrive at all, file a written report with the airline before leaving the airport.

PASSPORTS & VISAS

When traveling internationally, **carry your passport even if you don't need one** (it's always the best form of I.D.) and **make two photocopies of the data page** (one for someone at home and another for you, carried separately from your passport). If you lose your passport, promptly call the nearest embassy or consulate and the local police.

ENTERING HONG KONG

Citizens of the U.K. need only a valid passport to enter Hong Kong for stays of up to 6 months. Australian, Canadian, New Zealand, and U.S. citizens need only a valid passport to enter Hong Kong for stays up to 3 months. It is best to have at least six months' validity on your passport before traveling to Asia.

PASSPORT OFFICES

The best time to apply for a passport or to renew is in fall and winter. Before any trip, check your passport's expiration date, and, if necessary, renew it as soon as possible.

➤ AUSTRALIAN CITIZENS: **Australian Passport Office** (☎ 131–232, www.dfat.gov.au/passports).

➤ CANADIAN CITIZENS: **Passport Office** (☎ 819/994–3500 or 800/567–6868, www.dfait-maeci.gc.ca/passport).

➤ NEW ZEALAND CITIZENS: **New Zealand Passport Office** (☎ 04/494–0700, www.passports.govt.nz).

➤ U.K. CITIZENS: **London Passport Office** (☎ 0990/210–410) for fees and documentation requirements and to request an emergency passport.

➤ U.S. CITIZENS: **National Passport Information Center** (☎ 900/225–5674; calls are 35¢ per minute for automated service, $1.05 per minute for operator service).

REST ROOMS

Public rest rooms are difficult to find in Hong Kong. Clean, western-style rest rooms (as opposed to squatters, which are merely holes in the ground) are even more difficult to find. Although the situation is gradually improving, bring tissues or a toilet-paper roll. Using hotel and restaurant bathrooms is the best bet for a clean environment.

RICKSHAWS

Because rickshaws are a tourist attraction rather than a common mode of transportation, prices run high. Rates are supposed to be around HK$50 for a five-minute ride, but rickshaw operators are merciless. A posed snapshot can cost almost as much as a ride. When you hire a rickshaw or take an operator's picture, **bargain aggressively and agree on the price in advance.**

SAFETY

Hong Kong is a relatively safe city day or night. The Hong Kong Police who served under the British government continue to maintain law and order. Avoid carrying large amounts of cash or valuables. Pickpockets are an increasing problem in Hong Kong.

SENIOR-CITIZEN TRAVEL

To qualify for age-related discounts, **mention your senior-citizen status up front** when booking hotel reservations (not when checking out) and before you're seated in restaurants (not when paying the bill). When renting a car, ask about promotional car-rental discounts, which can be cheaper than senior-citizen rates.

➤ EDUCATIONAL PROGRAMS: **Elderhostel** (✉ 75 Federal St., 3rd floor, Boston, MA 02110, ☎ 877/426–8056, FAX 877/426–2166, www.elderhostel.org). **Interhostel** (✉ University of New Hampshire, 6 Garrison Ave., Durham, NH 03824, ☎ 603/862–1147 or 800/733–9753, FAX 603/862–1113, www.learn.unh.edu).

SHOPPING

If you buy and ship home Chinese lacquer or other breakable keepsakes, **buy an all-risk insurance policy.** Ivory has long been a prized souvenir of trips to the Orient, but in 1990 the Hong Kong government imposed a stringent policy on the import and export of this bone derivative. As a result, you must **get an import license from your country of residence, as well as an export license to take ivory out of Hong Kong.** Failure to comply may result in a fine and forfeiture of the purchase. If you're considering buying ivory, check with the **Hong Kong Department of Agriculture and Fisheries** (☎ 2733–2235), as well as your home consulate or trade commission, for the latest regulations. Remember that all goods—with the exceptions of alcohol, tobacco, petroleum, perfume, cosmetics, and soft drinks—are duty-free everywhere in Hong Kong, not just in "duty-free" stores. Bargaining, even at street markets, has become increasingly rare.

Beware of merchants who claim to be giving you a "special" price; you may not get what you actually pay for.

STUDENTS IN HONG KONG

To save money, **look into deals available through student-oriented travel agencies.** You need only a valid student ID card to qualify. Members of international student groups are also eligible.

➤ I.D.s & SERVICES: **Council Travel** (CIEE; ✉ 205 E. 42nd St., 14th floor, New York, NY 10017, ☎ 212/822–2700 or 888/268–6245, FAX 212/822–2699, info@councilexchanges.org,

www.councilexchanges.org), for mail orders only, in the U.S. **Travel Cuts** (✉ 187 College St., Toronto, Ontario M5T 1P7, ☎ 416/979–2406 or 800/667–2887, www.travelcuts.com) in Canada.

SUBWAY TRAVEL

The four-line Mass Transit Railway (MTR) links Hong Kong Island to Kowloon (the shopping area Tsim Sha Tsui) and parts of the New Territories. Trains run frequently and are safe and easy to use. Station entrances are marked with a simple line symbol resembling a man with arms and legs outstretched. You buy tickets from ticket machines; change is available at the stations' Hang Seng Bank counters. Fares range from HK$4 to HK$26.

DISCOUNT PASSES

The special Tourist Ticket (HK$25) can save you money. Another bulk-value possibility is the Stored Value Ticket, which also provides access to the above-ground Kowloon Canton Railway (KCR). Tickets are HK$70, HK$100, and HK$200.

➤ SUBWAY INFORMATION: **Mass Transit Railway** (MTR; ☎ 2881–1888). HKTA Visitor Hot Line (☎ 2508–1234).

TAXES

Hong Kong levies a 10% service charge and a 3% government tax on hotel rooms.

TAXIS

Taxis in Hong Kong and Kowloon are usually red. A taxi's roof sign lights up when the car is available. Fares in urban areas are HK$15 for the first 2 km (1 mi) and HK$1.20 for each additional ⅕ km (⅒ mi). There is luggage surcharge of HK$5 per large piece, and surcharges of HK$20 for the Cross-Harbour Tunnel, HK$30 for the Eastern Harbour Tunnel, and HK$45 for the Western Harbour Tunnel. The Tsing Ma Bridge surcharge is HK$30. The Aberdeen, Lion Rock, and Junk Bay tunnels also carry small surcharges (HK$3–HK$8). Taxis cannot pick up passengers where there are double yellow lines. Note that it's hard to find a taxi around 4 PM.

SMART TRAVEL TIPS A TO Z

Many taxi drivers do not speak English, so you may want to **ask someone at your hotel to write out your destination in Chinese.**

Outside the urban areas, taxis are green (blue on Lantau Island). Cabs in the New Territories cost less than urban taxis: HK$11.80 for the first 2 km (1 mi) and HK$1.10 for each additional ⅕ km (⅒ mi). Urban taxis may travel into rural zones, but rural taxis must not cross into urban zones. There are no interchange facilities for the two, so **do not try to reach an urban area using a green taxi.**

COMPLAINTS

Taxis are usually reliable, but if you have a problem **note the taxi's license number,** which is usually on the dashboard. The police hot line for complaints is ☎ 2527–7177.

TELEPHONES

Hong Kong phone numbers are comprised of eight digits. The local telephone system is efficient and telephone owners pay a flat monthly fee, not a per-call tariff; international calls are inexpensive relative to those in the United States. You can expect a clear-sounding connection. Directory assistance is helpful.

AREA & COUNTRY CODES

The country code for Hong Kong is 852. When dialing a Hong Kong number from abroad, drop the initial 0 from the local area code. The country code is 1 for the United States and Canada, 61 for Australia, 64 for New Zealand, and 44 for the U.K.

The country code for Macau is 853; for China, 086.

DIRECTORY & OPERATOR ASSISTANCE

Dial 1081 for directory assistance from English-speaking operators. If a number is constantly busy and you think it might be out of order, call 109 and the operator will check the line.

LOCAL CALLS

Given that your hotel will likely charge you for a local call, you might consider simply walking out of your hotel, stopping at the nearest shop and asking the shopkeeper if you can use the phone. Most locals will not charge you to you use their phone for a local call.

LONG-DISTANCE CALLS

You can dial direct from many hotel and business centers, but always with a hefty surcharge. Dial 013 for international inquiries and for assistance with direct dialing. Dial 10010 for operator-assisted calls to most countries, including the United States, Canada, and the U.K. Dial 10011 for credit-card, collect, and international conference calls.

You can also make long-distance calls from **Hong Kong Telecom International** (✉ Shop 116, Prince's Building, Des Voeux Rd., Central, ☎ 2810–0660, and ✉ TST Hermes House, Kowloon, ☎ 2888–7184 or 2888–7185). Here you dial direct from specially marked silver-colored phone booths that take phone cards (available from Hong Kong Telephone Company's retail shops and 7-Eleven convenience stores throughout the island). The cards have values of HK$25, HK$50, and HK$100, and multilingual instructions for their use are posted in the phone booths.

LONG-DISTANCE SERVICES

AT&T, MCI, and Sprint access codes make calling long distance relatively convenient, but you may find the local access number blocked in many hotel rooms. First ask the hotel operator to connect you. If the hotel operator balks, ask for an international operator, or dial the international operator yourself. One way to improve your odds of getting connected to your long-distance carrier is to travel with more than one company's calling card (a hotel may block Sprint, for example, but not MCI). If all else fails, call from a pay phone.

➤ ACCESS CODES: **AT&T Direct** (☎ 800/435–0812). **MCI WorldPhone** (☎ 800/444–4141). **Sprint International Access** (☎ 800/877–4646).

PUBLIC PHONES

To make a local call from a pay phone, use a HK$1 coin or, at some phones, a credit card. Pay phones are not hard to find, but locals generally pop into a store and ask to use the phone there, as local calls are free on residence and business lines. Many small stores keep their telephone on the counter facing the street.

Watch for multimedia Powerphones, whose touch screens allow you to check E-mail and send faxes as well as phone home.

TIME

Hong Kong is 12 hours ahead of Eastern Standard Time and 7 hours ahead of Greenwich Mean Time.

TIPPING

Hotels and major restaurants add a 10% service charge. In the more traditional Chinese restaurants, a waiter will bring small snacks at the beginning of the meal and charge them to you even if you did not order them; this money takes the place of a service charge. It is customary to leave an additional 10% tip in all restaurants, and in taxis and beauty salons.

TOURS & PACKAGES

Because everything is prearranged on a prepackaged tour or independent vacation, you'll spend less time planning—and often get it all at a good price.

BOOKING WITH AN AGENT

Travel agents are excellent resources. But it's a good idea to collect brochures from several agencies as some agents' suggestions may be influenced by relationships with tour and package firms that reward them for volume sales. If you have a special interest, **find an agent with expertise in that area**; ASTA (☞ Travel Agencies, *below*) has a database of specialists worldwide.

Make sure your travel agent knows the accommodations and other services of the place they're recommending. Ask about the hotel's location, room size, beds, and whether it has a pool, room service, or programs for children, if you care about these. Has your agent been there in person or sent others whom you can contact?

Do some homework on your own, too: local tourism boards can provide information about lesser-known and small-niche operators, some of which may sell only direct.

BUYER BEWARE

Each year consumers are stranded or lose their money when tour operators—even large ones with excellent reputations—go out of business. So **check out the operator.** Ask several travel agents about its reputation, and try to **book with a company that has a consumer-protection program.** (Look for information in the company's brochure.) In the United States, members of the National Tour Association and the United States Tour Operators Association are required to set aside funds to cover your payments and travel arrangements in the event that the company defaults. It's also a good idea to choose a company that participates in the American Society of Travel Agents' Tour Operator Program (TOP); ASTA will act as mediator in any disputes between you and your tour operator.

Remember that the more your package or tour includes the better you can predict the ultimate cost of your vacation. Make sure you know exactly what is covered, and **beware of hidden costs.** Are taxes, tips, and transfers included? Entertainment and excursions? These can add up.

➤ TOUR-OPERATOR RECOMMENDATIONS: **American Society of Travel Agents** (☞ Travel Agencies, *below*). **National Tour Association** (NTA; ⊠ 546 E. Main St., Lexington, KY 40508, ☎ 606/226–4444 or 800/682–8886, www.ntaonline.com). **United States Tour Operators Association** (USTOA; ⊠ 342 Madison Ave., Suite 1522, New York, NY 10173, ☎ 212/599–6599 or 800/468–7862, FAX 212/599–6744, ustoa@aol.com, www.ustoa.com).

TRAIN TRAVEL

The **Kowloon–Canton Railway** (KCR) has 13 commuter stops on its 34-km (22-mi) journey through urban Kowloon (from Kowloon to Lo Wu) and the new cities of Shatin and Taipo on its way to the Chinese border. The main station is at Hung Hom, Kowloon, where you can catch express trains to China. Fares range from HK\$7.50 to HK\$40. The KCR meets the MTR at the **Kowloon Tong** station (☎ 2602–7799). In the New Territories, the **Light Rail Transit**

SMART TRAVEL TIPS A TO Z

connects Tuen Mun and Yuen Long
(☎ 2468–7788).

TRAVEL CARD

The electronic Octopus Card
(HK$100) is accepted on the MTR,
Kowloon Canton Railway (KCR),
Kowloon Motor Bus (KMB), and
Citybus. You can buy the card at
ticket offices and HKTA outlets; you
place a refundable deposit of HK$50
on it, then reload it with HK$50 or
HK$100 increments at Add Value
machines. For more information call,
HKTA (⊠ The Center, 99 Queen's Rd.
Central, Central; ⊠ Star Ferry Con-
course, Kowloon, ☎ 2508–1234).

TRAMS

STREET TRAMS

Trams run along the north shore of
Hong Kong Island from Kennedy
Town (in the west) all the way through
Central, Wanchai, Causeway Bay,
North Point, and Quarry Bay, ending
in the former fishing village of
Shaukiwan. A branch line turns off in
Wanchai toward Happy Valley, where
horse races are held in season. Destinations are marked on the front of
each tram; the fare is HK$2. Avoid
trams at rush hours, which are generally 7:30–9 AM and 5–7 PM each
weekday.

PEAK TRAM

Dating from 1888, this railway rises
from ground level to Victoria Peak
(1,305 ft), offering a panoramic view
of Hong Kong. Both residents and
tourists use it; most passengers board
at the lower terminus between Garden Road and Cotton Tree Drive.
(The tram has five stations.) The fare
is HK$18 one-way, HK$28 round-
trip, and the tram runs every 10–15
minutes daily from 7 AM to midnight.
A free shuttle bus runs between the
lower terminus and the Star Ferry.

TRANSLATION SERVICES

CIAP Hong Kong (⊠ 2A, Tower 10,
Pak Pat Shan, Red Hill, Hong Kong,
☎ 2697–5114). **Translation Business**
(⊠ 13D, Chinaweal Centre, 414–424
Jaffe Rd., Wanchai, ☎ 2893–5000).
Polyglot Translations (⊠ 14B Time
Centre, 53 Hollywood Rd., Central,
☎ 2851–7232).

TRANSPORTATION

Comprised of a collection of islands
in the South China Sea and a chunk
of the Chinese mainland, Hong Kong
may have more varieties of transportation than any other city in the
world.

Ferries (☞ Boat & Ferry Travel, *above*)
and a **subway system** (☞ Subway
Travel, *above*) connect Hong Kong
Island with the Kowloon peninsula
and the Outer Islands.

Buses (☞ Bus Travel, *above*) run
throughout Hong Kong Island,
Kowloon, and the New Territories,
and along a number of routes linking
the two sides of the harbor.

Hong Kong Island has two kinds of
trams (☞ Trams, *above*): a street-
level tram that runs across the north
shore, and the Peak Tram, a funicular
railway that climbs Victoria Peak.

Trains (☞ Train Travel, *above*) travel
north from Kowloon serving cities all
the way to the Chinese border. You
can also opt for a limousine (the
Mandarin and the Peninsula hotels
rent chauffeur-driven Rolls-Royces), a
car with driver (☞ Car Rental, *above*),
or a touristy rickshaw (☞ Rickshaws,
above).

TRAVEL AGENCIES

A good travel agent puts your needs
first. Look for an agency that has been
in business at least five years, emphasizes customer service, and has someone on staff who specializes in your
destination. In addition, **make sure
the agency belongs to a professional
trade organization.** The American
Society of Travel Agents (ASTA), with
27,000 agents in some 170 countries,
is the largest and most influential in
the field. Operating under the motto
"Integrity in Travel," it maintains and
enforces a strict code of ethics and
will step in to help mediate any agent-
client disputes if necessary. ASTA also
maintains a Web site that includes a
directory of agents. (If a travel agency
is also acting as your tour operator,
see Buyer Beware *in* Tours & Packages, *above*.)

➤ LOCAL AGENT REFERRALS: **American Society of Travel Agents** (ASTA;
☎ 800/965–2782 24-hr hot line,

FAX 703/684–8319, www.astanet.com).
Association of British Travel Agents
(✉ 68–71 Newman St., London W1P
4AH, ☎ 020/7/637–2444, FAX 020/7/
637–0713, abta.co.uk, www.abtanet.
com). **Association of Canadian Travel
Agents** (✉ 1729 Bank St., Suite 201,
Ottawa, Ontario K1V 7Z5, ☎ 613/
521–0474, FAX 613/521–0805, acta.
ntl@sympatico.ca). **Australian Federation of Travel Agents** (✉ Level 3, 309
Pitt St., Sydney 2000, ☎ 02/9264–
3299, FAX 02/9264–1085, www.afta.
com.au). **Travel Agents' Association
of New Zealand** (✉ Box 1888,
Wellington 10033, ☎ 04/499–0104,
FAX 04/499–0827, taanz@tiasnet.co.nz).

VISITOR INFORMATION

For general Hong Kong and Macau
information before you go, contact
the **Hong Kong Tourist Association
(HKTA)** and **Macau Government
Tourist Office** locations below. When
you arrive, stop by an HKTA information center in Hong Kong.

➤ IN THE U.S.: **HKTA** (✉ 590 5th
Ave., Suite 590, New York, NY 10036,
☎ 212/869–5008, FAX 212/730–2605;
✉ 610 Enterprise Dr., Suite 200, Oak
Brook, IL 60521, ☎ 630/575–2828,
FAX 630/575–2829; ✉ 10940 Wilshire
Blvd., Suite 1220, Los Angeles, CA
90024, ☎ 310/208–4582, FAX 310/
208–1869). **Macau Government Tourist Office** (✉ Box 350, Kenilworth, IL
60043, ☎ 847/251–6421 or 800/331–
7150, FAX 847/256–5601).

➤ IN CANADA: **HKTA** (✉ 9 Temper-
ance St., 3rd floor, Toronto, Ontario
M5H 1Y6, ☎ 416/366–2389, FAX 416/
366–1098).

➤ IN THE U.K.: **HKTA** (✉ 6 Grafton
St., London W1X 3LB, ☎ 0711/530–
7100, FAX 020/7/533–7111). **Macau
Government Tourist Office** (✉ 1
Battersea Church Rd., London SW11
3LY, ☎ 020/7/771–7006, FAX 020/7/
771–7059).

➤ IN AUSTRALIA: **HKTA**(✉ Level 4,
Hong Kong House, 80 Druitt St.,
Sydney NSW200, ☎ 612/928–3083,
FAX 612/929–3383).

➤ IN HONG KONG: **HKTA** (✉ Star
Ferry Concourse, Kowloon; ✉ The
Center, 99 Queen's Rd. Central,
Central, Hong Kong Island; ✉ Hong

Kong International Airport). For
round-the-clock phone assistance,
call the multilingual **Visitor Hot Line**
(☎ 2508–1234). For a printout of
specific details, contact the 24-hour
fax information service (FAX 900/
6077–1128).

➤ U.S. GOVERNMENT ADVISORIES: **U.S.
Department of State** (✉ Overseas
Citizens Services Office, Room 4811
N.S., 2201 C St. NW, Washington,
DC 20520, ☎ 202/647–5225 for
interactive hot line, 301/946–4400
for computer bulletin board, FAX 202/
647–3000 for interactive hot line);
enclose a self-addressed, stamped,
business-size envelope.

WALKING

If you're not defeated by heat, Hong
Kong is a pleasant place to stroll. On
Hong Kong Island you might enjoy a
walk through the very traditional
Western district, where life has changed
little over the years. If you really like
to roam, **take a long hike in the New
Territories or on Lantau Island.** The
HKTA has self-guided tours of these
distinct areas; each includes a map
and detailed instructions for connecting the dots.

WEB SITES

Do check out the World Wide Web
when you're planning. You'll find
everything from current weather
forecasts to virtual tours of famous
cities. Fodor's Web site, www.fodors.
com, is a great place to start your on-
line travels. When you see a ✪ in this
book, go to www.fodors.com/urls for
an up-to-date link to that destination's
site.

WHEN TO GO

Hong Kong's high season, October
through late December, is popular for
a reason: the weather is pleasant, with
sunny days and cool, comfortable
nights. January, February, and sometimes early March are cold and dank,
with long periods of overcast skies
and rain. March and April can be
either cold and miserable or sunny
and beautiful. By May the temperature
is consistently warm and comfortable.

June through September is typhoon
season, when the weather is hot,
sticky, and very rainy. Typhoons

(called hurricanes in the Atlantic) must be treated with respect, and Hong Kong is prepared for these blustery assaults; if a storm is approaching, the airwaves will crackle with information, and your hotel and various public institutions will post the appropriate signals. When a No. 8 signal is posted, Hong Kong and Macau close down completely. Head immediately for your hotel and stay put. This is serious business—bamboo scaffolding can come hurtling through the streets like spears, ships can be sunk in the harbor, and large areas of the territory are often flooded.

Macau's summers are slightly cooler and wetter than Hong Kong's.

Climate in Hong Kong

The following are average daily maximum and minimum temperatures for Hong Kong.

Jan.	64F	18C	May	82F	28C	Sept.	85F	29C
	56	13		74	23		77	25
Feb.	63F	17C	June	85F	29C	Oct.	81F	27C
	55	13		78	26		73	23
Mar.	67F	19C	July	87F	31C	Nov.	74F	23C
	60	16		78	26		65	18
Apr.	75F	24C	Aug.	87F	31C	Dec.	68F	20C
	67	19		78	26		59	15

➤ FORECASTS: **Weather Channel Connection** (☎ 900/932–8437), 95¢ per minute from a Touch-Tone phone.

1 DESTINATION: HONG KONG

FROM CHINA TO CHINA

WHEN YOU FLY to Hong Kong, try to get a window seat. As you approach the coast of China you'll see a few small, rocky islands, tiny fishing boats, and sailboats in the channels leading into Hong Kong Harbour—the most spectacular harbor in the world.

Hong Kong is Cantonese for "fragrant harbor," a name inspired either by the incense factories that once dotted Hong Kong Island or by the profusion of scented pink *Bauhinias,* the national flower (whose representation has recently replaced colonial insignias).

Hong Kong is on the southeast coast of China, at the mouth of the Pearl River, on the same latitude as Hawaii and Cuba. By air, it's 2¾ hours from Beijing, 20 hours from New York, 12¼ hours from San Francisco, and 13 hours from London. It consists of three parts: Hong Kong Island, roughly 82 square km (32 square mi); Kowloon, 9 square km (3½ square mi); and the New Territories, about 945 square km (365 square mi). Its land mass grows, however, through land-reclamation projects, causing Hong Kong Harbour to narrow.

The name Hong Kong refers to the overall territory as well as to the main island, which is across the harbor from Kowloon. The island's principal business district is officially named Victoria, but everyone calls it Central. The island also contains the districts of Wanchai, Causeway Bay, Repulse Bay, Stanley, and Aberdeen. Kowloon includes Tsim Sha Tsui, Tsim Sha Tsui East, Hung Hom, Mong Kok/Yau Ma Tei, and the area north to Boundary Street. The New Territories begin at Boundary Street and extend north to the border with mainland China, encompassing the container port, the former Kai Tak airport, most of the major factories, and the outlying islands.

Hong Kong is 98% Chinese. Although the territory's official languages are English and Cantonese, the use of Mandarin (or *Putonghua*), China's official language, is on the rise. Many other languages and dialects are spoken here, including Hakka (the language of a group of early settlers from China), Tanka (the language of the original boat people who came here some 5,000 years ago), and Shanghainese. Among the nationalities living in Hong Kong, some 150,000 Filipinos make up the largest foreign community; most are women working as maids and nannies (*amahs* in local parlance), and can be seen socializing in Statue Square on their day off, usually Sunday.

The three great strands of Chinese thought—Buddhism, Taoism, and Confucianism—together with Christianity make up Hong Kong's major religions, and you'll see signs of them everywhere. Chinese people tend toward eclecticism in their beliefs, so the distinctions between faiths are often blurred. It's not uncommon for the same person to put out food and incense for his departed ancestors at Spring Festival time, invite a Taoist priest to his home to exorcise unhappy ghosts, pray in a Buddhist temple for fertility, and take communion in a Christian church.

Hong Kong's earliest visitors are believed to have been people of Malaysian-Oceanic origin who came here by boat about 5,000 years ago. Their geometric-style drawings are still visible on rocks in Big Wave Bay (on Hong Kong Island) and on Po Toi Island. The earliest structure found so far is the 1,600-year old Han Dynasty tomb at Lei Cheng Uk Museum. More than 600 years later, the Tang Dynasty left lime kilns full of seashells—an archaeological mystery, as there are no clues indicating how or why the lime was used.

Records from the 13th century tell us Sung Dynasty loyalists fled China with their child emperor to escape the invading Mongols. The last of the Sung Dynasty emperors, a 10-year-old boy, is said to have spent a night in the late 1270s near the site of Hong Kong's former airport. One of his men is credited with naming Kowloon, which means "nine dragons" (he counted eight mountain peaks that resembled dragons and added one for the emperor, who was also considered a dragon). The boy was the only Chinese emperor believed to have set foot in what is now Hong Kong. Today, anyone visiting Po Lin Monastery, high in the mountains of Lantau Island, will pass Shek Pik Reservoir, where innumerable Sung Dynasty coins were found during the reservoir's excavation.

Western traders first appeared in the Hong Kong area in 1513. The first were Portuguese, but they were soon followed by the Spanish, Dutch, English, and French. All were bent on making fortunes trading porcelain, tea, and silk. Until 1757 the Chinese restricted all foreigners to neighboring Macau, the Portuguese territory 64 km (40 mi) across the Pearl River estuary. After 1757, traders (but not their families) were allowed to live just outside Canton for about eight months each year. Canton—also known by its Chinese name, Guangzhou—is only 30 minutes from Hong Kong by plane or three hours by train or Hovercraft.

Trading in Canton was frustrating for the foreigners. It took at least 20 days for messages to be relayed to the emperor; local officials had to be bribed; and Chinese justice seemed unfair. For Western traders, life in Canton consisted of a lot of buying and little selling. At that time China was the world's premier source of silk, tea, porcelain, and textiles—they wanted nothing from the West except silver, until the British started offering opium.

THE SPREAD OF the opium habit and the growing outflow of silver alarmed high Chinese officials as early as 1729. They issued edicts forbidding importation of the drug, but these rules were regularly circumvented. Then, in 1839, a heroic and somewhat fanatical imperial commissioner, Lin Ze-xu (Lin Tse-hsu), laid siege to the foreign factories in Canton and detained the traders until they surrendered more than 20,000 chests of the drug, almost a year's worth of trade. The Westerners also signed bonds promising to desist from dealing opium forever, upon threat of death. The opium was destroyed. The British continued to press the issue, however, and the resulting tension between the government and foreign traders led to the Opium Wars and a succession of unequal treaties enforced by superior British firepower. The most important of these treaties required China to cede the island of Hong Kong to Britain; later, another treaty added Kowloon. Finally, in 1898, China leased the New Territories to

Britain for 99 years—it was the expiration of this lease that led to the handover in 1997.

British-ruled Hong Kong flourished from the start of trade, especially the trade in opium, which was not outlawed in Hong Kong until after World War II. The population grew quickly, from 4,000 in 1841 to more than 23,000 in 1847, as Hong Kong attracted anyone anxious to make money or to escape the fetters of feudalism and family.

Each convulsion on the Chinese mainland—the Taiping Rebellion in the mid-1800s, the 1911 republican revolution, the rule of warlords of the 1920s, the 1937 Japanese invasion—pushed another group of refugees into Hong Kong. Then Japan invaded Hong Kong itself. The population, 1.4 million just before the Japanese arrived, dropped to a low of 600,000 by 1945. Many Hong Kong residents were forced to flee to Macau and the rural areas of China. Older locals still remember the Japanese period with bitterness.

The largest group of Chinese refugees came in the wake of the Chinese civil war between the Nationalists and the Communists, which ended with a Communist victory in 1949. Many refugees, especially the Shanghainese (including the shipping family of Hong Kong's new chief executive, Tung Chee-hwa), brought capital and business skills. Hong Kong's population was 1.8 million in 1947; by 1961 it stood at 3.7 million. And for 25 days in 1962, when food was in short supply in China, Chinese border guards allowed 70,000 Chinese to walk into Hong Kong.

DURING CHINA'S antilandlord, anticapitalist, and antirightist campaigns, and especially during the Cultural Revolution (1967–76), more and more refugees risked both imprisonment and the sharks in Mirs Bay to reach Hong Kong. In 1967, inspired by the leftist fanaticism of the Red Guards in China, local sympathizers and activists in Hong Kong set off bombs, organized labor strikes, and demonstrated against the British rulers and Hong Kong's Chinese policemen. They taunted the latter by asking, "Will the British take you when they go?" But the revolutionaries did not have popular support, and the disruptions in Hong Kong lasted less than a year.

In the 30 years after the establishment of the People's Republic of China in 1949–50, about a half million mainlanders came to Hong Kong, disillusioned with communism and eager for a better standard of living for themselves and their families.

Until October 1980 the Hong Kong government had a curious "touch-base" policy—a critical game of hide-and-seek, or survival of the fittest. Any Chinese who managed to get past the barbed wire, attack dogs, and tough border patrols to the urban areas was allowed to stay and work. Local industries needed labor then. At first, a similarly lenient policy was applied to Vietnamese refugees who arrived between 1975 and 1982: more than 100,000 were allowed to work in Hong Kong pending transfer to permanent homes abroad, and 14,000 were given permanent-resident status. As the number of countries willing to take the Vietnamese dwindled, however, Hong Kong detained the 20,000 most recent arrivals in closed camps resembling prisons, in the hope that no more boat people would choose to make the trip. Amid much controversy and the dismay of human rights groups, all of the detained Vietnamese were returned to Vietnam before the handover.

In the early 1980s a worldwide recession made jobs harder to find. As the population continued to increase, the standard of services in Hong Kong began to deteriorate. After consulting China, the government decreed that everyone had to carry a Hong Kong identification card. Now, after the handover, mainlanders can apply to the Chinese government to request settlement in Hong Kong, but entries are restricted.

The fate of Hong Kong after the expiration of the New Territories lease on June 30, 1997, was the question hanging over the colony from the moment British Prime Minister Margaret Thatcher set foot in Beijing in September 1982 to start talks with China's paramount leader Deng Xiaoping. Stating from the outset that he intended to take back all of Hong Kong, Deng set the tone for a series of acrimonious talks at which no negotiations were possible. Though only the New Territories (NT) lease was due to expire, Hong Kong was not a viable entity without it: the NT consists of 97% of the land. Since Deng would not countenance a partial solution, a full return was inevitable. Discussions between China and Britain

lasted for nearly two years, with China applying pressure by announcing in early 1984 that if no solution were found by September 1984 it would declare one unilaterally. With that, British resistance buckled; so the final agreement was broadly in line with China's wishes: Hong Kong would become a Special Administrative Region (SAR) under the Chinese flag, with a Chinese leader (called a chief executive) and a 50-year guarantee of autonomy, effective July 1, 1997. The deal was labeled "One Country, Two Systems."

Hong Kong's economy did not react well to this political uncertainty. Land prices fell. The stock market plunged by as much as 50% from late 1981 to late 1983. The Hong Kong dollar plummeted in value, careening from HK$5.7 to the U.S. dollar at the end of 1981 to almost HK$10 in September 1983. This forced the government to intervene, albeit reluctantly. For stabilization's sake, the currency was pegged at HK$7.80 to the U.S. dollar with a unique Exchange Rate Mechanism, and this peg still stands, though it does make Hong Kong vulnerable to overseas inflationary pressures.

One of the greatest concerns for Hong Kongers was the issue of post-handover citizenship, since the British, fearful of a wave of Chinese moving to the U.K., offered them only a second-class passport that allowed Hong Kongers to travel as British citizens but did not give them the right of abode in the U.K. As a result, emigration—mainly to Canada, Australia, Britain, the United States, New Zealand, and Singapore—reached record levels, topping out at some 60,000 skilled Hong Kongers (and their families) annually, from doctors and architects to computer technicians and teachers, as they sought to acquire a foreign passport that would give them a sanctuary in the event that post-handover Hong Kong became intolerable. Many of them continued to do business in the territory, however, so as soon as they acquired their passports the flow reversed and they returned—along with their newfound prowess in English and experience abroad, making them one of the most sought-after groups for headhunters seeking to fill executive positions.

When the handover finally came, it was beamed live around the world and watched by hundreds of millions. At the stroke of midnight ushering in July 1, 1997, Prince Charles, representing his mother, Queen Elizabeth II, officially handed over this British Crown Colony 156 years, 5 months, and 10 days after Royal Navy captain Charles Elliot claimed Hong Kong Island for Queen Victoria. The recipient was China's President Jiang Zemin, the late Deng Xiaoping's chosen heir, who claimed the prize for the motherland in the vast Hong Kong Convention and Exhibition Centre in front of 5,000 specially invited guests (among them British Prime Minister Tony Blair and U.S. Secretary of State Madeleine Albright). Those watching also saw the heavens open—more rain fell that week than Hong Kong normally gets in a year—and a rain-soaked Prince Charles, accompanied by an equally drenched Chris Patten, the last British governor, sailed away in the the the Royal Yacht *Britannia* in the wee hours of July 1. Royal standards flying high, the royal yacht sailed slowly through the harbor, trailed by a Royal Navy destroyer, to join the waiting British fleet and lead it away from what had often been called the last jewel in Britain's colonial crown. Back in the Convention Centre, celebrations continued.

The rain itself inspired local commentary: were the gods washing the Brits away or weeping for them? In any case, the downpour ruined the grand entrance of the People's Liberation Army, which had timed the arrival of its main body of troops for 6:30 AM July 1—just in time for live, prime-time coverage in the United States. The soldiers duly arrived, standing at rigid attention in the backs of open trucks in a watery deluge, but the rain put a damper on the intended visual effect.

The new Special Administrative Region (SAR) government convened the Provisional Legislative Council (LegCo; Hong Kong's parliament) in the first few hours of its rule to swear in its members. The first step taken by the LegCo, at the behest of the Central Government, was to repeal the Bill of Rights that the last British governor, Chris Patten, had managed to get passed in order to calm those apprehensive of the future. As draconian as the repeal sounds, what was implemented instead was the original, long-standing British law concerning assembly. Under political pressure, the SAR Government eased the restrictions on police notification, so Hong Kong still has its annual Tiananmen memorial demonstrations and other anti-Chinese events. Demonstrations, sit-ins, marches, signature campaigns, and petitions are frequent events, as one group or another tries to influence or complain about an SAR law or proposed legislation. The protest events are always covered live and uncensored by the media, and the only police in evidence are traffic police. The traditional Sunday outdoor forum, in which issues are debated openly—and often with the participation of top government officials and legislators—is still avidly covered and reported by the local media. Not anticipated before the handover was mainland China's acceptance of some of its own dissidents' living freely in Hong Kong. Labor leader Han Dongfang, for example, was expelled in 1993 after being imprisoned for his part in the June 4, 1989, Tiananmen Square demonstrations. Though marooned here, he is nonetheless free to give speeches, comment openly on events here and on the mainland, edit his own labor bulletin, and host his own radio show. (The SAR government did bar dissident exiles such as Wang Dan from coming to Hong Kong in spring 1999 for a 10th-anniversary Tiananmen memorial gathering.)

W ITH THE BENEFIT of a few years' hindsight, the handover looks anticlimactic. The rest of the world was always more apprehensive about Chinese rule than were most Hong Kongers. For most Hong Kongers, business takes precedence over all other issues and it was the Asian crisis, which hit within a month of the handover, that became the real news of 1997 and the years that followed. The very month Hong Kong came into being, Thailand experienced a run on its currency, the baht, the defense of which eventually cost the country most of its foreign exchange. Malaysia was next, then Indonesia, exacerbated by the fall of Suharto. Hong Kong's banks were heavily exposed in all of these markets. By autumn 1997, with a prestigious World Bank–IMF Conference in town, Hong Kong was busy defending its currency and its 15-year-old peg against the U.S. dollar, which now had become not just a financial mechanism but a political symbol of stability. China, despite economic problems of its own, helped Hong Kong's defense by promising not to devalue the yuan. Unlike some of its neighbors, the SAR had ample foreign reserves and, most important, virtually no debt; still, Hong Kong's stock and futures markets reeled with each currency attack from the big hedge funds. The side effects were high interest rates and high inflation, making Hong Kong one of the most expensive places in the world to live and do business. On August 24, 1998, the SAR Government purchased HK$15 billion (US$1.92 billion) worth of stock to drive prices up; the hedge funds retreated, cutting their losses. In June 1998, the government put forth an economic rescue package, its third, that froze land sales, the major source of government income, until March 31, 1999.

But for all the uncertain moments, the SAR pulled through it (as, now, has much of Asia) and with the stock market soaring it is easy to forget the economy was ever imperiled. Indeed, except for a few other small differences—the increasing use of Mandarin on television and in the streets, the Hong Kong Jockey Club's decision to drop the 'Royal' that once preceded its name—the changes wrought by the handover are mostly ones of increasing integration between the local and mainland economies, a process that has been under way for at least two decades. Culturally, Hong Kong Chinese have long been akin to the southern Chinese, but these ties have been strengthened since Hong Kong's terrestrial TV stations have been received in south China, displaying Hong Kong's lifestyle for all to see. The rest of China may have been protected from the outside world, but southern China was not. Hong Kong went to bat for China time and time again with the U.S. government to obtain and keep China's Most Favored Nation status, arguing that if it were denied, Hong Kong's economy would be more adversely affected than China's.

Ironically, the biggest post-handover controversy surrounded the issue of Right of Abode—not, this time, about who from Hong Kong gets to live in the U.K. but who from the mainland can move to Hong Kong. The Basic Law guarantees this right to certain groups of people who have connections here, mainly children of Hong Kong residents who were not eligible for residency under the British. Most of these children—numbering between 200,000 and 1.6 million, depending on the estimate—live in China. Their waiting time for a one-way permit (i.e., authorized emigration) is 10 years, and corruption among those waiting is rampant. The Hong Kong courts ruled that these children had the right to move to the territory but amid much controversy the SAR executive, Tung Chee-hwa, appealed to the mainland to overrule, which it did. While most Hong Kongers were relieved not to face inundation by a million mainland children, many were concerned that this establishes a bad precedent that would erode local judicial autonomy.

Another challenge that put Hong Kong on the front pages of the world press was the bird flu that struck in January 1998. The U.S. Centers for Disease Control had a virologist in Hong Kong just 24 hours after hearing the news. With the memory of previous flu pandemics this century still fresh—Hong Kong's 1968 flu claimed 700,000 lives—microbiologists and virologists sought to isolate the new strain when it jumped species (from chickens to humans). This one claimed nine lives out of 18 victims; to control the disease, 1.5 million chickens were slaughtered on the Hong Kong side of the border alone, and every market, street stall, and farm was scoured. Eight weeks later, the return of this staple food to the markets and to the restaurant and dining-room tables was cause for Hong Kong–wide celebration.

The issue of Hong Kong's deteriorating natural environment has managed to unite all sides of the political spectrum. Water quality has long been a problem, with beaches being periodically closed due to pollution. But what has drawn renewed and unwelcome attention is the severe deterioration in air quality. (Foreigners' main complaints about Hong Kong are high prices and pollution.) When the SAR was finally forced by public opinion to place pollution meters at street level for more accurate readings, the results were shocking. Pollution levels are now reported like the weather, with warnings issued on bad days. The main culprits are diesel taxis, minibuses, buses, and trucks, whose industries have lobbied against environmental legislation. When the SAR's chief executive convened an International Advisory Board (with stars such as Rupert Murdoch and retired Federal Reserve Board chairman Paul Volker) to collect advice on keeping Hong Kong competitive in the new millennium, they spoke not of economics but of the outdoors.

Indeed, perhaps the greatest sign that Hong Kong is operating quite comfortably under Chinese rule is the very fact that political debate has, for the most part, centered on such quotidien issues as chickens and pollution rather than the much-feared crackdown on individual liberty. Graves are still swept on the Ching Ming and Chung Yeung holidays. The Buddha's birthday has been added to the official holiday list but the four-day Easter weekend and the two-day Christmas–Boxing Day respite remain on the calendar as well. The local press, though subject to some self-censorship, still thrives; international reporting, publishing, and broadcasting continue unabated. Great debates rage in the local print and electronic media, both pro and con the SAR's, or China's, latest action or pronouncement. And everyone has time to check up on the stock market.

— By Jan Alexander and Saul Lockhart;
updated by Sean Rocha

WHAT'S WHERE

Hong Kong Island

Hong Kong is a dazzling melee of human life and enterprise. From the harbor, the city's latest architectural wonders stand against a green-mountain backdrop, while on the other side of the island beaches and quieter villages slow the pace considerably. Moving clockwise, beginning with the harbor districts, Western and Central are two of the liveliest areas, full of markets, other shopping, restaurants, businesses— you name it. South of these, Midlevels, with its agglomeration of apartment towers, and Victoria Peak rise above the din of downtown. Wanchai, the next district east, was once of ill repute but now the preferred locale for an upscale night on the town. After that is Causeway Bay, another shopping haven. North Point is on the northeast corner; its principal tourist offerings are a market and a ferry pier. Shek O lies at a distant remove on the southeastern peninsula, a pleasant village with a beach for an afternoon's escape.

At the bottom of Hong Kong Island, Stanley was a fishing village in the 19th century. Now mostly residential, it, too, has a pleasant beach, an interesting market, and restaurants that make a trip here worthwhile. Working your way back to the western part of the island you'll find the amusements of Ocean Park (with its Middle Kingdom section) and the large town of Aberdeen, followed by Repulse Bay, named for the HM *Repulse,* which the British used to break the ring of pirates that occupied this area.

Kowloon

Bustling Kowloon occupies the tip of the peninsula across from Hong Kong Island. Tsim Sha Tsui, at the bottom of the peninsula, is crammed full of shops, restaurants, and businesses. Yau Ma Tei, on the western side of Kowloon, is noted for two temples, more practical shops, and great markets, such as the Jade Market and the Temple Street night market.

New Territories

Because of its distance (which in fact is not great) from the commercial hubs of Hong Kong Island and Kowloon, travelers often overlook the attractions of the New Territories. Parts of the area retain their isolated, rural character, even if to find them you must make your way past massive housing developments called new towns, built to house the burgeoning population. Shatin is one of these towns, with its ultramodern racecourse belonging to the Hong Kong Jockey Club and the very old Temple of Ten Thousand Buddhas. To the east, the village of Sai Kung has wonderful restaurants, and its Country Park is one of the most spectacular in the SAR.

Outer Islands

As popular getaways for locals and tourists alike, the islands around Hong Kong in the South China Sea have unique charms of their own, from beaches and old fishing villages to hiking trails and remote, ancient Buddhist monasteries. There are three main islands. Lantau is the largest, larger actually than Hong Kong Island, and has the Polin Monastery, with the largest reclining Buddha in the world. Lamma Island is famous for its restaurants, Cheung Chau for its shops.

Macau

A tiny geographical remnant of the 16th-century Portuguese spice trade, Macau provides a pleasant respite from the nonstop bustle of Hong Kong, 65 km (40 mi) to the east. Construction has taken away some of the island's quieter charms, but

Portuguese influence—especially in the food—is yet another fascinating Eurasian variation played out in the South China Sea. Macau is a peninsula, connected by bridge to Taipa Island, which is in turn connected to Coloane Island by a causeway. Both islands are easy to reach and have many attractions of their own.

PLEASURES AND PASTIMES

Beaches

Surprising as it may seem, splendid beaches are all over the area, some of which are well maintained by the government and served by lifeguards. **Repulse Bay** is a sort of Chinese Coney Island. Around the corner is the smaller and less crowded **Deep Water Bay; Turtle Cove** is isolated and beautiful; Shek O's **Big Wave Bay** has a Mediterranean feel; and among New Territory and Outer Island beaches, **Pak Sha Chau** has lovely golden sands, while **Lo Sho Ching** is popular with local families.

Chinese Culture

There are so many ways of taking in day-to-day Chinese phenomena—at restaurants, in street markets where the very sense of an individual's personal space is so dramatically different than in the West, in ancient Chinese temples, in a karaoke bar, at the hands of a fortune teller, or in parks watching the morning tai-chi-chuan ritual. Embrace as much of Hong Kong as you can. You'll never forget it.

Restaurants

Aside from New York, no other city in the world can match the distinct variety and integrity of cuisines consumed in Hong Kong. One of the most exciting aspects of being on Chinese soil is the opportunity to eat authentic Chinese food. At the same time, at a cultural crossroads like Hong Kong, the steamy, aromatic tastes of pan-Asian cuisine are another unique culinary opportunity. Approach menus with a spirit of adventure, and you might enjoy some foods you otherwise might shy away from.

Shopping

Hong Kong has the best shopping in the world, if you work at it. Although the thought of crowded streets, mind-boggling choices, and endless haggling can be daunting, no place makes big spending easier than this center of international commerce. Even self-declared nonshoppers are tempted to part with their money, and some have admitted to enjoying the experience.

The variety of goods is astonishing: international designer products, expensive treasures, handcrafted folk items from all over Asia. Just as remarkable is the physical array of places to shop, from sophisticated boutique-lined malls to open-air markets and shadowy alleyways.

NEW AND NOTEWORTHY

Nineteen ninety-nine was Hong Kong's second full year under Chinese rule. For the next 50 years Hong Kong will be a Special Administrative Region (SAR) before fully rejoining China. Under the Basic Law, Hong Kong's constitution, Hong Kong will remain highly independent of China under the "One Country, Two Systems" concept. Laws in place before the handover have remained basically unchanged.

Hong Kongers, while never experiencing a true democracy, live in one of the freest and most transparent of all Asian countries (even though it was for so long a colony, with all the political domination that term implies). Hong Kongers are known more for their industriousness than for their political convictions, and have accepted the handover without incident. Many have emotionally embraced the idea of returning to the motherland. On the other hand, they are all too aware that Hong Kong's way of life, its freedom and rule of law, are not mirrored in the PRC, and they are guarding these rights jealously. Political scientists are waiting to see how Hong Kong will change China as well as vice versa. With **Macau** having reverted to China on December 20, 1999, also under the "One Country, Two Systems" banner, the outcome of these historic events will shape the future of China's quest to regain Taiwan.

The Feng Shui Tour is a four-hour jaunt that lets you explore Hong Kong's architecture while learning about the Chinese art of feng shui. Many of the city's most famous buildings were designed to adhere to this system of beliefs, which translates as "wind water" and concerns man's relationship to nature. Adherence to the principles of feng shui is supposed to ensure good luck, health, prosperity, wealth, love, and general happiness. Contact the Hong Kong Tourist Association (HKTA) for more information.

South China continues to grow as a side-trip destination for visitors to Hong Kong. The great city of Guangzhou (still better known as Canton), a major port for more than 2,000 years, is at last being discovered by travelers from the West. Among the newest attractions is the Guangdong Museum of Art, a world-class facility that displays the best in contemporary Chinese art, including fine sculpture and ceramics. Border town Shenzhen is still the country's fastest-growing city economically, with amusement parks a particular focus vis-à-vis tourism. In addition to the Lilliputian kitsch-filled parks Splendid China and Window of the World, two more parks have opened up in the last year—Happy Valley and Future Times. The former is a Western-style amusement park packed with heart-pounding rides; the latter is a loud, indoor kiddie affair that's transformed by night into a bizarre rave party hosted by DJs from neighboring Hong Kong.

FODOR'S CHOICE

Dining

★ **Petrus.** A superb view, a fine selection of wine, and sumptuous dishes with artistic flair have earned this French restaurant's prestigious reputation. $$$$

★ **Yü.** A creative East-and-West menu and posh decor make this the best seafood restaurant in town and arguably the best restaurant in Hong Kong. $$$$

★ **Cafe Deco Bar and Grill.** Combining Hong Kong chic and pan-Asian cuisine with panoramic views from atop Victoria Peak, this has become an island favorite. $$$

★ **The Verandah.** Classical colonial elegance with contemporary European cuisine await you at this restaurant overlooking Repulse Bay. $$$

★ **Yung Kee.** What you expect from Cantonese dining—lightning-fast preparation, high-energy service, and reasonable prices—is what you get at Yung Kee, which is why so many people keep coming back. $$–$$$

★ **Afonso III, Macau.** Try this simple café for a unique experience of Portuguese cuisine, where the chef prepares food the way his grandmother did. $$

★ **Wu Kong.** Friendly service with authentic cooking in this traditional Shanghainese restaurant ensures you a delightful northern Chinese meal. $$

★ **Great Shanghai Restaurant.** This restaurant wins no awards for its decor, but it's excellent for culinary adventurers and those who prefer the bold flavors of Shanghai food to the more delicate flavors of local Cantonese fare. $–$$

Lodging

★ **Island Shangri-La, Hong Kong Island.** This hotel, which towers above the Pacific Place complex, has spacious rooms and spectacular views of the Peak and Victoria Harbour. $$$$

★ **Mandarin Oriental, Hong Kong Island.** The Mandarin matches convenience with luxury, making it one of the world's great hotels. Celebrities and VIPs agree. $$$$

★ **Peninsula, Kowloon.** The Pen is the ultimate in colonial elegance, with its mix of European ambience and Chinese details. $$$$

★ **Pousada de São Tiago, Macau.** This traditional Portuguese inn is built into the ruins of a 17th-century fortress and incorporates ancient trees and natural springs into its design. The furnishings were custom-made in Portugal and Hong Kong. $$$

★ **Garden View International House, Hong Kong Island.** This small, attractive hotel overlooks the botanical gardens and the harbor. $

Parks, Gardens, and Walks

★ **Dragon's Back in Shek O Country Park.** Bring your hiking boots and canteen and escape the urban madness on a moderately hilly trail where banana leaves grow to lengths of 3 ft and the view of the sea is nothing short of spectacular.

★ **Lantau Island, Shek Pik to Tai O.** If you're a seasoned hiker, try this wondrous all-day stretch of the Lantau Trail, which passes the Shek Pik Reservoir and a half dozen tucked-away monasteries on its way down to the pristine seaside village of Tai O.

★ **Lou Lim Ioc Garden, Macau.** For a lovely respite in Macau, stroll through this Soochow-style enclosed garden, a miniature bamboo forest, a lake, and a traditional nine-turn bridge.

★ **Coloane Park, Macau.** On the southernmost of Macau's three islands, Coloane Park has a remarkable walk-in aviary with more than 200 bird species (some quite rare), a nature trail, and a fascinating collection of exotic trees and shrubs.

Excursions

★ The view of the coastline from the **Ocean Park cable car.** From here you'll think you're riding over the Mediterranean as you gaze down at a panorama of mountains, pastel villas, and the vast blue sea.

★ Crossing the harbor on the **Star Ferry,** first class. Breathing the air of the South China Sea is vital to any experience of Hong Kong, whose very existence owes itself to the crossing of seas—not to mention today's stunning views.

★ A 30-minute **junk trip** through Macau's Inner Harbour, organized by the Maritime Museum, brings up close the life of the fishing population and the booming Chinese suburb on the opposite shore.

Street Markets

★ **Bird Garden, Kowloon.** The bird garden consists of various courtyards filled with trees and 70 stalls selling birds, cages, and such accoutrements as tiny porcelain feeders and fresh grasshoppers.

★ **Rua de Cinco de Outubro, Macau.** Here in traditional Chinese Macau, street markets offer incredible bargains in name-brand clothing, made under license in local factories.

Temples and Shrines

★ **The Temple of 10,000 Buddhas, Shatin.** You have to climb nearly 500 steps to reach this wonder, but with its 13,000 statues and gilded, mummified holy man, in addition to views of Amah Rock, it's worth the effort.

★ **Po Lin Buddhist Monastery, Lantau Island.** Built on a grander scale than most temple complexes in Hong Kong, Po Lin Monastery is home to Southeast Asia's tallest bronze Buddha, more than 100 ft high.

★ **A-Ma Temple, Macau.** Named for a sea goddess who, according to custom, saved a humble junk from a storm, A-Ma is the oldest and perhaps the most beautiful temple in Macau.

Museums

★ **Hong Kong Museum of Art.** This is the place in town to see ancient Chinese scrolls and sculpture along with the work of the Territory's own contemporary masters.

★ **Hong Kong Museum of History.** See what Hong Kong looked like more than 6,000 years ago, when tigers and other animals ranged over the islands. Scenes of Neolithic life, life-size dioramas, military displays, and artifacts trace the territory's development up to the present.

★ **The Maritime Museum, Macau.** From its dragon boats to pirate-chasing *lorchas,* Portuguese voyage charts, and navigation equipment, the ship-shape Maritime Museum provides a fascinating view of seagoing Macau.

Nightlife

★ The tiny streets of Central's **Lan Kwai Fong** area hide more than 100 restaurants and bars of every description and ethnic orientation, with celebrants often spilling out onto the streets with their drinks. It's a superb way to start, spend, or end an evening.

★ **Crazy Paris Show at Hotel Lisboa, Macau.** Girls, girls, girls (wait, was that a boy in there?)—if that's what you're after, this Paris- and Vegas-style show is the best around.

Taste Treats

★ **Dim sum** for lunch anywhere. Since you've come to the source, this is one tradition you can't pass up.

★ A market-stall Chinese breakfast of **congee** (rice porridge) at Kowloon Park Road and Haiphong Road, Kowloon. Some of these foods are so exotic that we can't recommend them to everyone, but this is a quintessential Hong Kong experience.

★ **Afternoon tea** in the grand lobby of the Peninsula Hotel. Dignified and utterly civilized, this legacy of the British presence in Hong Kong can lift you beyond the Peninsula's own elegance to another era entirely.

Special Events

★ **Candlelight parades.** Two parades, one in honor of the mid-autumn moon and another at the Dragon Boat Festival in June, are both resplendent with traditional costumes, music, and general merrymaking.

★ **Bun Festival (May) on Cheung Chau.** To placate vengeful spirits of the dead, villagers offer fresh-baked buns in the form of three 50-ft-high bun towers outside the Pak Tai Temple. Bring a camera to capture the parade of elaborate floats and an altar of papier-mâché gods.

★ **Horse racing.** All of Hong Kong loves to gamble, and there's no better way to see a cross section of the population, from the boxes to the bleachers, than taking your chances. Whether you win or not, you'll find the mood contagious. The HKTA runs tours to both racecourses.

★ **Fringe Festival.** Experience the best of Hong Kong's avant-garde theater, music, and art at the unique Fringe Club, housed in a historic building that used to be a dairy depot. The festival is held on various dates in January and February.

★ **The Good Friday Passion Parade, Macau.** A statue of Christ is carried through the streets in procession on the first weekend of Lent, with the stations of the cross erected along the way.

FESTIVALS AND SEASONAL EVENTS

Top seasonal events in Hong Kong include the Chinese New Year, the Hong Kong Arts Festival, the Hong Kong Food Festival, and the Dragon Boat Festival. The most colorful shindigs of all are the many lunar festivals celebrated throughout the year. Contact the HKTA for exact dates and more information.

JAN.➤ The Fringe Club's **City Festival** showcases an assortment of international and local drama, dance, music, and light entertainment.

LATE JAN.–EARLY FEB.➤ The **Hong Kong Marathon** consists of three hot races—a full marathon, a half-marathon, and a 10K race. The event attracted nearly 7,000 athletes last year, including many well-known foreign distance runners.

FEB.➤ The **Chinese New Year** has the city at a virtual standstill as shops shut down for three days and people don their best to visit friends and relatives.

FEB.➤ For the **Spring Lantern Festival,** streets and homes are decorated with brightly colored lanterns for the last day of Chinese New Year celebrations.

LATE FEB.–EARLY MAR.➤ The **Hong Kong Arts Festival** showcases four weeks of world-class music, dance, and drama from around the globe.

HKTA offices worldwide have schedules and information.

EARLY MAR.➤ The **Hong Kong Open Golf Championship** is held at the Hong Kong Golf Club.

SPRING

MID-MAR.➤ The annual **Hong Kong Food Festival** is a two-week smorgasbord of events, including cooking classes with world-renowned chefs, tours of famous restaurants and teahouses, and an amusing waiters' race and cheerleading competition.

LATE MAR.–EARLY APR.➤ The **Rugby Sevens** is the world's premier seven-a-side rugby tournament usually held over Easter weekend in a sold-out 40,000-seat stadium.

EARLY APR.➤ The **Ching Ming Festival,** literally "bright and clear" is when families visit the burial plots of ancestors and departed relatives.

APR.➤ The **Hong Kong International Film Festival** focuses on hot spots in global cinema as well as special sections on restored Mandarin classics, commendable locally made films, and many other Asian productions.

APR.➤ The **Hong Kong Open** tennis tournament attracts some of the biggest names in the sport.

LATE APR.➤ For the **Birthday of Tin Hau,** goddess of the sea, fisher-

men decorate their boats and converge on seaside temples to honor her, especially around the Tin Hau Temple in Junk Bay.

MAY➤ The **Birthday of Lord Buddha** is celebrated on the eighth day of the fourth moon. The devout flock to major Buddhist shrines like the Temple of 10,000 Buddhas at Shatin or Po Lin Monastery on Lantau.

MAY➤ The **Bun Festival** on Cheung Chau Island attracts thousands for a three-day rite dedicated to placating the spirits of the dead. It culminates in a grand procession.

JUNE➤ The **Dragon Boat Festival** pits long, multi-oared dragon-head boats against one another in races to commemorate the hero Chu Yuen, a fourth-century scholar who supposedly threw himself into a river to protest the corruption of government officials, causing local fishermen to race to save him.

SUMMER

JULY 1➤ **Return to Motherland Day** marks the day that Hong Kong reverted to Chinese sovereignty in 1997.

MID-AUG.➤ The **Seven Sisters (Maiden) Festival** is a celebration for lovers, and a time when young girls pray for a good husband.

AUG.➤ The **Hungry Ghosts Festival** is a time when food is set out and elaborate ceremonies are performed to placate the angry roaming spirits of those buried without proper funeral rites, forgotten by their families, or deceased with no descendents to care for their grave sites.

AUTUMN

SEPT.➤ The **Chinese Opera Fortnight** presents traditional Cantonese, Peking, Soochow, Chekiang, and Chiu Chow operas in the City Hall Theatre, Concert Hall, and Ko Shan Theatre.

SEPT.➤ The **Mid Autumn Festival,** also known as the Lantern or Moon Festival, sees crowds with candle lanterns gather in parks and other open spaces sharing *yue bing* or "moon cakes," which are stuffed with red-bean or lotus-seed paste. Such hearty foods are said to symbolize happiness and completion.

LATE SEPT. OR EARLY OCT.➤ The **Birthday of Confucius** honors the revered philosopher.

MID-OCT.➤ The **Chung Yeung Festival** commemorates a Han Dynasty tale about a man taking his family to high ground to avoid disaster. Like the Ching Ming festival, this is a time to clean family graves and make offerings.

LATE OCT. OR EARLY NOV.➤ The **Festival of Asian Arts** showcases more than 150 artistic events (dance, music, and theater) from as far afield as Australia, Bhutan, Hawaii, and Mongolia. It is held biennially, in even-numbered years.

LATE NOV.➤ The **Macau Grand Prix** takes over the city streets for a weekend.

MID-DEC.➤ The **Hong Kong Judo Championship** takes place at Queen Elizabeth Stadium.

2 EXPLORING

Hong Kong is back: the buzz, energy, and reckless optimism of fortunes being made (and occasionally lost) have returned after a brief lull sparked by the Asian crisis. Yet the audacity of this city, which was crafted out of barren rock and political turmoil, still inspires—and its streets once again surge and swirl with enterprise, hitting the visitor like a shot of adrenaline.

Updated by
Sean Rocha

T O STAND ON THE TIP OF KOWLOON PENINSULA and look out across the harbor to the full expanse of the Hong Kong island skyline—as awesome in height as Manhattan's, but only a few blocks deep and strung along the entire north coast—is to see the triumph of ambition over fate. Whereas it took Paris and London 10 or 20 generations to build the spectacular cities we know today, and New York six, Hong Kong built almost everything you see before you in the time since today's young investment bankers were born. It is easy to perceive this tremendous creation of wealth as an inevitable result of Hong Kong's strategic position, but at any point in the Territory's history things might have happened slightly differently, and the island would have found itself on the margins of world trade rather than at the center.

When the 30-square-mi island of Hong Kong was ceded to the British after the Opium War of 1841, it consisted, in the infamous words of the British minister at the time, of "barren rock" whose only redeeming feature was the adjacent deep-water harbor. For the British, though, it served another purpose: Hong Kong guards the eastern edge of the Pearl River Delta, and with it access to Guangzhou (Canton), which in the mid-19th century was China's main trading port. By controlling Hong Kong, Britain came to control the export of Chinese products such as silk and tea, and to corner the Chinese market for Western manufactured goods and opium. The scheme proved highly profitable.

If British trade were all Hong Kong had going for it, however, its prosperity would have faded with said empire. No, the real story of Hong Kong begins in the 1920s, when the first wave of Chinese refugees settled here to avoid civil unrest at home. They were followed in the '30s and '40s by refugees fleeing in advance of invading Japanese soldiers. But the biggest throngs of all came after the 1949 Communist revolution in China—mostly from the neighboring province of Guangdong, but also from Fujian, Shanghai, and elsewhere. Many of these new arrivals came from humble farming backgrounds, but many others had been rich, and had seen their wealth and businesses stripped away by the revolutionaries. They came to Hong Kong poorer than their families had been in generations, yet by virtue of their labor their descendants are the wealthiest generation yet.

Hong Kong has always lived and breathed commerce, and it is the territory's shrines to Mammon that will make the strongest impression when you first arrive. The Central district has long been thick with skyscrapers bearing the names of banks and conglomerates, yet it continues to build more, squeezing them into irregular plots of land that would seem insufficient for buildings half the size. When that doesn't work, the city simply reclaims more land from the harbor and builds on it almost before it dries. For a few years it will be obvious which land is new and which is old as the ground is turned and foundations laid, but soon enough the two will meld into one, just as they have before: you now have to walk four blocks from the Star Ferry terminal, through streets shaded by office towers, to reach Queen's Road, the former waterfront. A visitor may well ask what one can know for sure in this world if not where the earth ends and the oceans begin, but Hong Kongers have gotten used to such vagaries.

Watching young investment bankers out on a Friday night in Hong Kong's nightspot haven of Lan Kwai Fong, reveling in their outrageous good fortune at being in this place at this time in history, one can't help but wonder whether this can possibly last. A heady, end-of-an-era ex-

Hong Kong Island

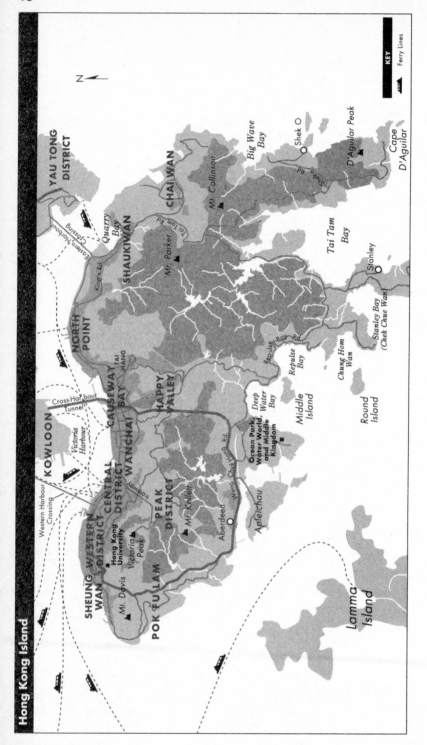

N

KEY

Ferry Lines

YAU TONG DISTRICT

Eastern Crossing

Quarry Bay

Big Wave Bay

Shek O

CHAI WAN

D'Aguilar Peak

Cape D'Aguilar

Mt. Collinson

Tai Tam Rd.

SHAUKIWAN

King's Rd.

Mt. Parker

Tai Tam Bay

NORTH POINT

Stanley

TAI HANG

Repulse Bay Rd.

Stanley Bay (Chek Chue Wan)

Cross-Harbour Tunnel

CAUSEWAY BAY

HAPPY VALLEY

Chung Hom Wan

KOWLOON

WANCHAI

Repulse Bay

Victoria Harbour

CENTRAL DISTRICT

Deep Water Bay

Middle Island

Round Island

Western Harbour Crossing

Tai Hom Rd.

Ocean Park, Water World and Middle Kingdom

SHEUNG WAN

WESTERN DISTRICT

PEAK DISTRICT

Mt. Kellett

Wong Chuk Hang Rd.

Aberdeen

Apleichau

Hong Kong University

Victoria Peak

Mt. Davis

POK FU LAM

Lamma Island

Hong Kong Mass Transit Railway

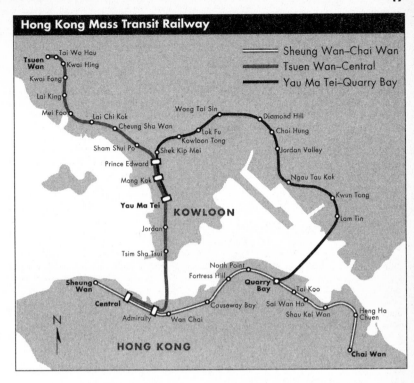

uberance to it all—a decadence that portends doom ahead. Yet visitors to Hong Kong have felt this same sentiment for almost a century and a half and, save for the rare economic downturn, the day of reckoning has not come. Indeed, that it is so palpable on its streets today is a sign that the good old days are back, because one of those rare exceptions came in 1997—not with the handover to China, which many expected to create problems, but with the Asian crisis, which took almost everyone by surprise. For a moment in 1997 and '98, it seemed Hong Kongers would have to permanently scale back their ambitions. But then the moment passed and the usual breakneck growth returned.

Rapid change has not been limited to Hong Kong Island or the crowded Kowloon Peninsula, but extends up through the "new towns" of the New Territories. Some of these, like Shatin, were rice paddies 20 years ago and now form thriving cities of a half million people. The most ambitious project of all is the one you see on arrival: the leveling of Chek Lap Kok, an uninhabited island of rock and scrub, to make way for Hong Kong's stylish, ultra-efficient new international airport. Arriving in Hong Kong may now lack the rooftop-grazing shock of flying into the old Kai Tak, but you're whisked through the airport in no time and can then zip into Central in just 23 minutes on the Airport Express train.

Amid all the change it can be easy (even for residents) to forget that most of Hong Kong has nothing to do with business or skyscrapers: three-quarters of it is actually rural land and wilderness. A bird's-eye view reveals the 236 islands that make up the lesser-known part of Hong Kong; most are nothing but jagged peaks and tropical scrub, just as Hong Kong Island itself once was. Others are time capsules of ancestral China, with tiny temples, fishing villages, and small vegetable farms. Even Hong Kong Island, so relentlessly urban on its north coast, consists mostly of rolling green hills and sheltered bays on its south side. So whether you're looking for the hectic Hong Kong or the relaxed one, both are easy enough to find—indeed, sometimes only a few minutes apart.

HONG KONG ISLAND

Comprising just 77 square km (30 square mi), Hong Kong Island is where the action is, from high finance to nightlife to luxury shopping. As a result—even though Kowloon is just a short ride away—many residents feel little reason to ever leave the island. One of Hong Kong's unexpected pleasures is that, despite what sometimes feels like unrelenting urbanity, property development has actually been restricted to a few small areas. As a result, a 20-minute taxi ride from downtown Central can have you breathing fresh air and seeing only lush green vegetation.

Hong Kong has few historical landmarks (largely because soaring property values have long since caused most older buildings to be torn down and replaced) and no more than a handful of cultural sights, but it pulses with an extraordinarily dynamic contemporary life. In general, the commercial and shopping districts are on the island's north coast, interspersed with the ubiquitous apartment blocks, while the towns on the rest of the island tend to be more residential. Each district has a name (and the name of its MTR stop usually corresponds) and a slightly distinct character, but the borders tend to blur together.

Central Hong Kong, in the middle of the island's north side, is a gleaming modern business enclave containing the stock exchange, dozens of banks, deluxe hotels, and upmarket shops.

The **Western** district lies, sure enough, to the west of the Central district and consists primarily of small shops, markets, ladder streets, and rows of traditional shop houses.

The **Midlevels** area runs halfway up the Peak behind Central and consists of high-rise luxury apartment blocks soaring straight out of the tropical bush.

Victoria Peak, an exclusive residential area, is the highest (1,805 ft) of a small range of hills in the middle of the island, high above Midlevels. Reached via the Peak Tram or zigzagging roads, it offers spectacular views and a selection of restaurants.

Wanchai, east of Central, was once famed for its nightlife, as immortalized in Richard Mason's novel *The World of Suzie Wong* and the ensuing movie. It still has plenty of bars, but it's now better known for its convention center, smart offices, and wide range of restaurants.

Causeway Bay, just east of Wanchai, was once a middle-class Chinese community but is now primarily a business and tourist area filled with offices, hotels, restaurants, and department stores.

Deep Water Bay, Repulse Bay, and Stanley, are prestigious residential areas on the south side of the island with a few beaches and the famous souvenir-hunter's paradise, Stanley Market.

Shek O, a pleasant seaside village on the southeast coast, has a mixture of modest village houses and baronial mansions.

Central and Western Districts

The office towers and opulent shopping centers of Hong Kong's core business district occupy one of the most expensive stretches of land on earth. It may be fitting, then, that Central also houses nearly every major investment and commercial bank, fashion designer, and luxury-goods boutique the world has yet produced. The streets are often so crowded with bankers and shoppers that the pedestrian can feel like a salmon trying to swim upstream to spawn. Fortunately, most of the buildings are connected by elevated walkways, which can also be handy in the rain. Bear in mind that on Sunday, many Central shops close and the district teems with thousands of maids, mostly Filipinas, who spend their day off in the public gardens.

The Western district is gradually becoming more like Central, but it still retains a traditional feel that many other areas have lost. Most of the buildings are high-rises (and older and more run-down than those in Central), but it's in some of the small alleys off Western's main streets that the old China Coast comes alive. Traditional shops sell dried sea horses, curled snakes, salted fish, aromatic mushrooms, herbal medicines, steaming noodles, and, of course, tea, by the glass or by the bushel.

Numbers in the text correspond to numbers in the margin and on the Central and Western Districts map.

A Good Walk

Walking is by far the best way to get around Central and Western, and orientation is easy since the harbor is always north. Start at the **Star Ferry Terminal** ①, where sturdy green-and-white boats deposit passengers arriving from Kowloon. With your back to the harbor (and stepping out from the awning to get a better view), you can see many of Hong Kong's most significant buildings, as well as a number of practical landmarks. Just in front of you is a parking garage, to the east (left) of which is the shuttle to the Peak Tram and the unattractive City Hall complex. To your right is the General Post Office, a squat white building, and behind it is the towering **Jardine House** ②, with its many round windows, and the marble-and-mirrored-glass stripes of Exchange Square, which houses the stock exchange and the American Club and has a bus terminal underneath. Just north of Exchange Square are the new Airport Express terminal and, along the water, the piers for ferries to the outlying islands.

Follow the awnings to the right and go through the underground walkway to **Statue Square** ③. The intriguing Victorian/Chinese hybrid building on the east side of the square is the **Legislative Council Building** ④. Along the southern end of the square are the buildings of Hong Kong's three note-issuing banks: the Art Deco former headquarters of the **Bank of China** ⑤, the spectacular strut-and-ladder facade of the **Hongkong & Shanghai Bank (HSBC)** ⑥, and, pressing up against it, the rose-colored wedge of Standard Chartered Bank. The HSBC building is one of the most important buildings in 20th-century architecture; walk under it and look up into the atrium through the curved glass floor, or go inside for a view of its details. Exiting HSBC on the south side, cross the street (Queen's Road Central) and turn left past the giant Cheung Kong building (on your right) and Chater Garden (on your left) until you come to the triangle-scheme Bank of China building, with its adjacent Chinese waterfall garden. This is the new headquarters of the largest mainland-Chinese bank and was built a few years before the handover in an effort to architecturally one-up its local rival, HSBC.

Head back on Queen's Road Central toward HSBC and walk until you get to the intersection with Pedder Street, where you'll find **The Landmark** ⑦, the mother of all luxury shopping centers. Having paid your respects, exit and turn left (south) on Pedder Street and walk straight up the hill until you pass the colonial red-and-white-striped building on the left that hosts the Fringe Club, an avant-garde arts center. At the five-street intersection, a sharp right takes you into Lan Kwai

Fong, a prime entertainment district, but veering right gets you to **Wyndham Street** ⑧ and the start of a breathtaking series of antiques and Oriental-rug galleries. At the old Central Police Station, Wyndham Street turns into Hollywood Road, and you'll see an overpass that forms a link in the open-air **Midlevels Escalator** ⑨. Join up with it by turning left up an incline; once aboard, take it all the way up the hill until you see an elaborate metalwork gate on the left. The gate hides a small garden and the tranquil **Jamia Mosque** ⑩, built in 1915.

Follow the escalator back downhill to **Hollywood Road** ⑪, perhaps stopping for a meal in the hip Staunton Street area en route. Turn left on Hollywood Road and follow the antiques shops to the colorful **Man Mo Temple** ⑫. To reach the curio and trinket shops of **Upper Lascar Row** ⑬ (also known as **Cat Street**), walk down the steps of Ladder Street, just across from Man Mo Temple. Continue down to **Queen's Road** ⑭ and turn left (west) to see a bit of the old Hong Kong that may otherwise seem to have disappeared. Turn right on Cleverly Street, then left. Both **Bonham Strand East and West** ⑮ have plenty of little shops to explore, as does the adjacent **Wing Lok Street** ⑯. Follow Bonham Strand West to **Des Voeux Road West** ⑰ to see the food and medicine shops. When you're just about ready to turn back, head toward the harbor and follow Connaught Road east until you come to the cream-and-brown **Western Market** ⑱, built in 1906 and lovingly restored. From here it's an easy tram ride back to Central.

TIMING

Allow a full day, perhaps two if you want to spend any appreciable time shopping for antiques. It's physically possible to walk from the Star Ferry Terminal to Cat Street in three hours, but you won't be able to see anything in depth. The Man Mo Temple will add 20 minutes. The second half of the walk, from Cat Street to Western Market, will take an hour or two.

Sights to See

⑤ Bank of China. In the politics of Hong Kong architecture, the stylish Art Deco building that served as the old Bank of China headquarters was the first trump: built after World War II, it was 20 ft higher than the adjacent Hongkong & Shanghai Bank (HSBC). It is now one of the smallest buildings in Central, utterly dwarfed by the imposing new structure HSBC built in the mid-1980s. The Bank of China refused to take this challenge lying down, however, and commissioned the Chinese-American architect I. M. Pei to build a new headquarters nearby. The result, the **Bank of China Tower,** completed in 1990, is a masterful twisting spire of replicating triangles, and was the first building to break the ridgeline of Victoria Peak. It may not be as innovative as the new HSBC building, but it dominates Hong Kong's urban landscape and embodies the post-handover balance of power. The old building now houses Sin Hua Bank and, on the top floor, David Tang's exclusive China Club, which manages to be both postmodern and nostalgic for pre-Communist Shanghai.

★ **⑮ Bonham Strand East and West.** A major thoroughfare in one of Hong Kong's most charmingly traditional areas, Bonham Strand is lined with shops selling goods that evoke the old China Coast trade merchants. A few shops sell live snakes, whose meat is used in winter soups to ward off colds and whose gall bladders reputedly improve vigor and virility. Bonham Strand West, in particular, is known for its Chinese medicines and herbal remedies. Many of its old shops have their original facades, and inside, the walls are lined with drawers and shelves of jars filled with hundreds of pungent ingredients such as wood barks and insects. These are consumed dried and ground up, infused in hot water or tea, or taken as powders or pills.

⑰ Des Voeux Road West. You'll recognize the tram tracks when you get to the west end of ☞ **Bonham Strand West.** On the left (south) side of the street are a cluster of shops selling preserved foods—everything from dried and salted fish to black mushrooms to vegetables—and herbal medicines. This is a good area for lunchtime dim sum.

⑪ Hollywood Road. Many of Hong Kong's best antiques, furniture, and classical-art galleries are concentrated on ☞ **Wyndham Street**, at the road's eastern end. As the road heads west, the shops gradually move downmarket, selling mostly porcelain, curios, and not-very-old trinkets masquerading as ancient artifacts. Look to the left for a sign saying POSSESSION STREET, where Captain Charles Elliott of the British Royal Navy stepped ashore in 1841 and claimed Hong Kong for the British empire. It's interesting to note how far today's harbor is from this earlier shoreline—the result of a century of aggressive land reclamation.

OFF THE BEATEN PATH **HONG KONG MUSEUM OF MEDICAL SCIENCES** – This new museum, tucked away in an Edwardian-style building behind a small park in Midlevels, is worth the climb through tiny back streets for anyone interested in the history of Chinese medicine in Hong Kong. Exhibits compare the uses of Chinese and Western medicines and show Chinese medicines of both animal and herbal origin as well as a traditional Chinese medical practitioner's equipment. Several other rooms are devoted to Western medical subjects. To get here from Hollywood Road, follow Ladder Street behind Man Mo Temple, going south and uphill to Square Street, which veers right, then left to Caine Lane. Follow a circular path up about 300 ft around Caine Lane Garden, a park with colorful stucco structures, until you reach Number 2. ✉ *2 Caine La., Midlevels, Hong Kong,* ☏ *2549–5123,* ⅏ *2559–9458.* ⌸ *HK$10.* ☉ *Tues.–Sat. 9–5:30, Sun. 1–5.*

★ **⑥ Hongkong & Shanghai Bank.** With its distinctive ladder facade, this striking building is a landmark of modern architecture. Designed by Sir Norman Foster as the headquarters of Hong Kong's premier bank (you'll see it depicted on most of the paper money) and completed in 1985, the building sits on four props, which allow you to walk under it and look up through its glass belly into the soaring atrium within. Imposing as that may be, the building is most interesting for its sensitive use of high-tech details: the mechanics of everything from the elevators' gears and pulleys to the electric signs' circuit boards are visible through smoked glass. In addition to its architectural triumph, the building served a symbolic function as well: built at a time of insecurity vis-à-vis China at a cost of almost US$1 billion, it was a powerful statement that the bank had no intention of taking its money out of the Territory. ✉ *Queen's Rd. Central, across from Statue Sq.*

⑩ Jamia Mosque. This attractive gray-and-white mosque was built by HMH Essack Elias of Bombay in 1915, and it shows its Indian heritage in the perforated arches and decorative work on the facade. The mosque itself is not open to non-Muslims, but it occupies a small, verdant enclosure that offers a welcome retreat from the city. It once had a nice view down toward the water, but that was recently disrupted by a new apartment tower—one of many now ringing this site. ✉ *Shelley St., just off Midlevels Escalator.*

② Jardine House. To the west of the Star Ferry Terminal, recognizable by its signature round windows, this 1973 building was once the tallest in Central. It houses Jardine, Matheson & Co., the greatest of the old British hongs (trading companies) that dominated trade with imperial China.

Central and Western Districts

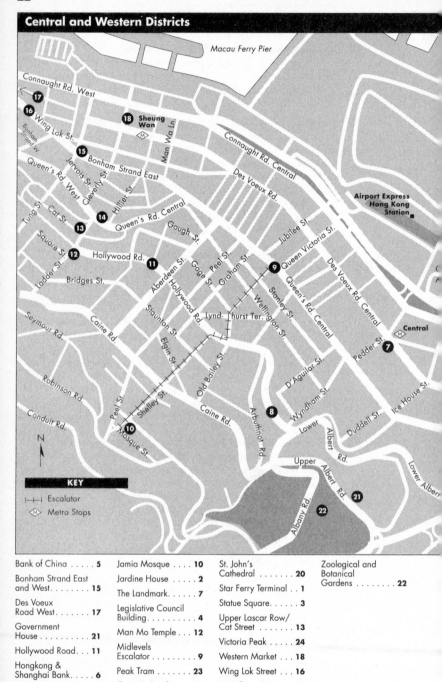

Macau Ferry Pier

Connaught Rd. West

Wing Lok St.

Sheung Wan

Man Wa Ln.

Connaught Rd. Central

Des Voeux Rd.

Airport Express Hong Kong Station

Bonham Strand W

Bonham Strand East

Queen's Rd. West

Jervois St.

Cleverly St.

Hillier St.

Queen's Rd. Central

Gough St.

Jubilee St.

Queen Victoria St.

Des Voeux Rd. Central

Tung St.

Cat St.

Square St.

Ladder St.

Hollywood Rd.

Bridges St.

Aberdeen St.

Gage St.

Peel St.

Graham St.

Queen's Rd. Central

Hollywood Rd.

Stanley St.

Wellington St.

Central

Seymour Rd.

Caine Rd.

Staunton St.

Elgin St.

Lynd-hurst Ter.

Pedder St.

Ice House St.

Robinson Rd.

Peel St.

Shelley St.

Old Bailey St.

Caine Rd.

Arbuthnot Rd.

D'Aguilar St.

Wyndham St.

Duddell St.

Lower Albert

Conduit Rd.

Mosque St.

Lower Albert Rd.

N

Upper Albert Rd.

Albany Rd.

KEY

⊢─⊣ Escalator

Ⓜ Metro Stops

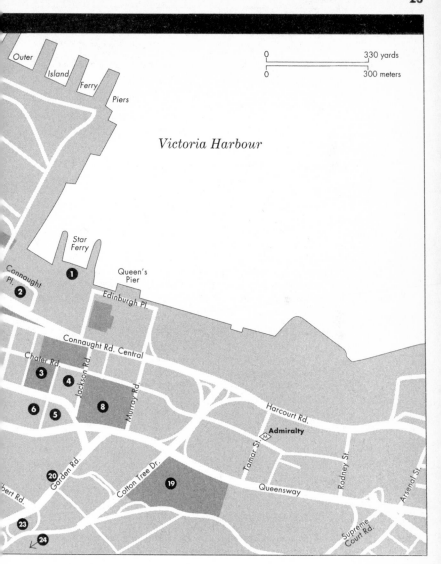

Victoria Harbour

Jardines has come a long way from the days when it trafficked opium, and its investment-banking arm, Jardine Fleming, is one of the most respected in Asia. ⊠ *Connaught Pl., across from the Central Post Office.*

❼ The Landmark. Few fashion designers, watch craftsmen, or other makers of luxury goods do not have—or do not crave—a boutique in the Landmark. The building is no longer the city's poshest, but its Pedder Street location is still priceless, and it has its own MTR entrance. Live concerts are occasionally performed near the fountain in the high-ceiling atrium. ⊠ *Des Voeux Rd. between Ice House and Pedder Sts.* ⊙ *Building, daily 9 AM–midnight; most shops, 10–6.*

❹ Legislative Council Building. Built for the Supreme Court in 1912 and now home to the Legislative Council (known as LegCo), this building is one of the few grand Victorian structures left in this area. Note the Chinese-style eaved roof, a modest British concession to local culture. The council had no real power in the British days, but starting in 1991 it did have a majority of elected members who challenged the administration every Wednesday. Since the handover in 1997, mainland attempts to muzzle LegCo's pro-democracy members have been only moderately successful, so it continues to serve as a forum for debate, if not as an organ of political power. In front of the Council Building is the **Cenotaph,** a monument to all who lost their lives in the two world wars. ⊠ *Statue Sq. at Jackson Rd.*

⓬ Man Mo Temple. Built in 1847 and dedicated to the gods of literature and of war—Man and Mo, respectively—this is Hong Kong Island's oldest temple. It now serves primarily as a smoke-filled haven for elderly women paying respects; ashes flutter down onto your clothes from the spirals of incense hanging from the beams. The statue of Man is dressed in green and holds a writing brush, while Mo is dressed in red and holds a sword. To their left is a shrine to Pao Kung, god of justice, whose face is painted black; to the right is Shing Wong, god of the city. The temple bell, cast in Canton in 1847, and the drum next to it are sounded to attract the gods' attention when a prayer is being offered. To check your fortune, stand in front of the altar, take one of the small bamboo cylinders available there, and shake it until one of the sticks falls out. The number on the stick corresponds to a written fortune. The English translation of said fortune is in a book that the temple will happily sell you. ⊠ *Hollywood Rd. at Ladder St.* ⊙ *Daily 8–6.*

❾ Midlevels Escalator. Completed in 1993, this is actually a ½-mi-long combination of escalators and walkways that provide free, glass-covered transport up or down the steep incline between Central and Midlevels. The painless uphill climb provides a view of small Chinese shops and gleaming residential high-rises, as well as the ☞ **Jamia Mosque** (built in 1915), at Shelley Street. **Staunton Street,** one level above Hollywood Road, is now known as Hong Kong's SoHo (South of Hollywood), with an eclectic collection of cafés and bars, including the Sherpa Himalayan Coffee Shop.

Plan to ride the escalators up between 10:20 AM and 11:30 PM. From 6 to 10 AM the escalators move downhill, so commuters living in Midlevels can get to work in Central; and after 11:30 they shut down. You can get off at any point and explore the side streets, whose vendors sell porcelain, clothes, and antiques (not necessarily authenticated). Almost every building has a tiny makeshift altar to the ancestors, usually made of red paper with gold Chinese characters, with offerings of fruit and incense. ⊠ *Enter across from Central Market, at Queen's Rd. Central and Jubilee St.* ⊙ *Daily 6 AM–11:30 PM.*

⑭ Queen's Road. This street once ran along the waterfront. It is, at various points, one of Hong Kong's most prestigious shopping addresses and among its quaintest and most traditional streets.

Of the countless shops and market stalls selling dried herbs, live snakes, and everything else imaginable to treat the body's vital energies, the **Eu Yan Sang Medical Hall** (⊠ 152 Queen's Rd. Central) is the one to visit for an education in traditional Chinese medicines. Glass cases display reindeer antlers, dried fungi, ginseng, and other standard medicinal items; English-language cards explain some of the items' uses, and men behind the counters will happily sell you purported cures for anything from the common cold to impotence (the cure for the latter is usually slices of reindeer antler boiled into tea). A note of caution: look all you want, but remember that Chinese medicines are not regulated by the Hong Kong government, and anything that sounds dubious or dangerous might be just that.

★ **❶ Star Ferry Terminal.** Since 1898 the ferry terminal has been the gateway to the island for commuters and travelers coming from Kowloon. First-time visitors are all but required to cross the harbor on the Star Ferry at least once and ride around Hong Kong Island on a double-deck tram. In front of the terminal you will usually see a few red rickshaws; once numbering in the thousands, these two-wheel man-powered taxis are all but gone. ⊠ *Enter terminal through tunnel next to Mandarin Hotel, Connaught Rd. and Connaught Pl.* ☒ *1st class HK$2.20, 2nd class HK$1.70.* ☉ *6 AM–midnight.*

OFF THE
BEATEN PATH

HONG KONG DOLPHIN WATCH – The Chinese white dolphin (actually from pink to dark gray, and found in waters from South Africa to Australia) is on its way to extinction in the South China Sea, mainly because of dredging for the new airport. Hong Kong Dolphin Watch sponsors a Dolphin Discovery Cruise three or four times a week—there's no guarantee, but on most trips you'll catch one or two dolphins playing in the water. The trip, which departs from Queen's Pier (next to City Hall), makes for an enjoyable day at sea, and tickets help raise money to build a sanctuary that would ensure the dolphins' survival. The cost includes a buffet lunch. Try to reserve at least two weeks in advance. ⊠ Box 4102, Central, Hong Kong, ☎ 2984–1414, ℻ 2984–7799. ☒ Weekdays HK$280, weekends HK$350.

❸ Statue Square. This piece of land was gifted to the public by the ☞ **Hongkong & Shanghai Bank** (whose headquarters dominate the southern end), with the proviso that nothing built on it could block the bank's view of the water. The square is named for the statue of Sir Thomas Jackson, Bart. (1841–1915), who was the bank's chief manager for more than 30 years in the late 19th century. The square is surrounded by some of the most important buildings in Hong Kong, including those housing the **Hong Kong Club,** the ☞ **Legislative Council,** and the ☞ **Bank of China,** and has an entrance to the Central MTR station. On Sunday it hosts thousands of Filipina maids enjoying their day off.

NEED A
BREAK?

On the west side of Statue Square is the **Mandarin Oriental Hotel** (⊠ 5 Connaught Rd., ☎ 2522–0111), one of the finest hotels in the world. The mezzanine coffee lounge is a pleasant place to have a drink, or you can people-watch at the **Captain's Bar,** where billion-dollar deals are consummated over cognac.

⑬ Upper Lascar Row. Cat Street, as Upper Lascar Row is often called, is a vast flea market. You won't find Ming vases here—or anything else of significant value—but you may come across an old Mao badge or an antique pot or teakettle.

More worthwhile for the art or antiques collector is the section of shops and stalls known as **Cat Street Galleries** (✉ 38 Lok Ku Rd.), adjacent to the flea market, open 10–6 every day but Sunday. This is a new and growing complex, with galleries selling every kind of craft, sometimes old but more often new. You can rest your feet and have coffee in the convenient little European café Somethin' Brewin'.

18 **Western Market.** Erected in 1906, this is the only surviving segment of a larger market building built in 1858. It functioned as a produce market for 83 years and included living quarters for coolies and inspectors in the four corner towers. Threatened with demolition, it was exquisitely restored and turned into a unique shopping outlet. Alas, they've never gotten the retail mix quite right, filling the place with souvenir and trinket shops on the ground floor, fabrics on the middle floor, and a Chinese restaurant on the top floor. The building, however, gorgeously decorated with Chinese bunting, is worth a trip. ✉ *323 Connaught Rd. W.* ⊙ *Daily 10 AM–11:45 PM.*

16 **Wing Lok Street.** You can still find fascinating traditional items on this street (off Queen's Road Central), as it's lined with Chinese shops selling dried fish and seafood, rattan goods, medicines, and the engraved seals called chops. You can have your initials engraved in Roman letters or Chinese characters on a chop made of plastic, bone, or jade. (Ivory is also available all over Hong Kong, but it's illegal to bring it into the United States.) It takes about an hour to engrave a chop, which you can pick up later or the following day.

★ 8 **Wyndham Street.** The galleries that pack the curving block of Wyndham Street from the Fringe Club to where Wyndham becomes Hollywood Road can be approached more as a collection of miniature museums than as mere shops. Their showrooms hold some spectacular antique furniture, art, and artifacts (albeit perhaps smuggled out of their countries of origin) at prices that, while not cheap by any means, are a fraction of what they would be outside the region. Most stores are open daily from 10 to 7, though some have shorter hours or close altogether on Sunday. Here is a rough guide, starting from the western end: the **Oriental Rug Gallery, Oriental Carpets Gallery,** and **Mir Oriental Carpets** specialize in rugs from the Middle East and Central Asia. **Artemis** has gorgeous but expensive furniture, along with statuary and stone work. **MinGei Antiques** has Chinese furniture and an interesting collection of birdcages. **Zitan** has chests and old doors, many in a more authentic state than the restored pieces sold elsewhere. **Zee Stone Gallery** specializes in Tibetan arts, including silverwork, silk hangings, and robes. **Ad Lib** has kilnwork, statues, and the ubiquitous Ming and Qing Dynasty reproduction furniture. **Teresa Coleman Fine Arts,** opposite the police station at the corner of Pottinger Street, is among the premier galleries in Asia, with an ability to find little treasures others miss, like embroidered dragon robes and collars or vibrant-blue "kingfisher" jewelry. **Chu's** focuses on artifacts from Tibet, including carpets and chests. **Schoeni** has an antiques gallery here but is better known as a promoter of contemporary mainland Chinese art. For more on shopping, ☞ Chapter 7.

From Central to the Peak

The Midlevels is the wide band of land south of Central that runs halfway up Victoria Peak. Long one of Hong Kong's most desirable residential districts, it is now lined with towering apartment blocks that cling precariously to the hillside. Bisecting it is the **Midlevels Escalator** (☞ above), which connects Central Market with some of the area's main residential roads. Free of charge and protected from the elements, the escalator has proved a great way to move commuters and tourists through the congested city without destroying the landscape. The Midlevels is also worth a visit to see Hong Kong University, the Botanical Gardens, and some of Hong Kong's few remaining examples of Victorian apartment architecture, though the latter are disappearing rapidly.

Victoria Peak, high above Midlevels, is known simply as the Peak, and soars 1,805 ft above sea level. Residents here take special pride in the positions to which they have, quite literally, risen; theirs is the most exclusive residential area on the island—perhaps in all of Asia.

Numbers in the text correspond to numbers in the margin and on the Central and Western Districts map.

A Good Tour

Start your walk at 2 Queen's Road Central, diagonally across the street from Chater Garden. Head uphill on Garden Road and cross the street at the pedestrian overpass to Cotton Tree Drive. You should be facing **Hong Kong Park** ⑲, where you'll find the **Museum of Tea Ware** and a large aviary and conservatory.

Leave the garden and return to Garden Road. On the right heading up Garden Road is **St. John's Cathedral** ⑳. Continue up the road and turn right on Upper Albert Road, passing the former **Government House** ㉑. Farther up Garden Road are the United States Consulate General and the **Zoological and Botanical Gardens** ㉒.

Stroll through the gardens, zoo, and aviary. Swing back down Garden Road, cross it, and go to the **Peak Tram** ㉓, just behind St. John's Building (not to be confused with the cathedral). Take the tram to **Victoria Peak** ㉔.

For a scenic alternative to the Peak Tram, you can catch Bus 15 or a cab from Central. Both go through the steep roads of the residential areas of Midlevels, a route just as beautiful as the tram's. You can also get to the Peak on the Number 1 minibus from the terminal behind the former HMS *Tamar* site (now occupied by the People's Liberation Army), next to the City Hall complex.

TIMING
This walk is largely uphill and is complicated somewhat by the elaborate road system that crisscrosses the area. The entire route takes about four hours. Allow about 40 minutes for the Museum of Tea Ware and at least 45 minutes to stroll through Hong Kong Park's greenhouses and aviary, both of which can get crowded. Add another half hour or more for the zoo at the Zoological and Botanical Gardens. The tram ride up the mountain will take about 20 minutes. Allow about an hour for the Peak.

Sights to See

㉑ **Government House.** Constructed in 1855, this handsome white Victorian building was the official residence of the British governor. During the Japanese Occupation it was significantly rebuilt, so it now exhibits a subtle Japanese influence, particularly the eaved roof. The SAR's chief executive, Tung Chee Hwa, had no wish to reside here, so Government House is used periodically for state occasions. It is not open to the public. ✉ *Upper Albert Rd., just west of Garden Rd.*

★ ☙ ⑲ **Hong Kong Park.** Hoarding 25 acres of prime real estate, this park has to be one of the world's most valuable. Built by the Hong Kong Jockey Club with the abundant revenues from its racetracks, it comprises lakes, gardens, sports areas, a café, a rain-forest aviary with 500 species of birds, and a greenhouse with 200 species of tropical and arid-region plants. Although some of the artificial rocks and waterfalls in the lower gardens can feel a little unnatural, the park is a blessedly quiet and lush oasis within the urban melee.

The park also contains Flagstaff House, the former official residence of the commander of the British forces and the city's oldest colonial building (built in 1846). The house is now the **Museum of Tea Ware**, which has a fascinating exhibit chronicling the history of tea and its various accessories (including the famous Yixing tea ware) from the 7th century on. Who knew, for example, that Tibetan cream tea could be made with cheese by-products, or that the method of steeping leaves in water came relatively late, following a preference for whipped tea? ⊠ *Cotton Tree Dr. at park entrance,* ☎ *2869–0690.* ☒ *Free.* ⊙ *Thurs.–Tues. 10–5.*

㉓ Peak Tram. Housed in the Lower Peak Tram Terminus is the world's steepest funicular railway. It passes five intermediate stations on its way to the upper terminal, 1,805 ft above sea level. The tram was opened in 1880 to transport people to the top of ☞ **Victoria Peak**, the highest hill overlooking Hong Kong Harbour. Before the tram, the only way to get to the top was to walk or take a bumpy ride up the steep steps in a sedan chair. The tram has two 72-seat cars, which are hauled up the hill by cables attached to electric motors. A shuttle bus to and from the Peak Tram leaves from Edinburgh Place, next to City Hall. ⊠ *Between Garden Rd. and Cotton Tree Dr.* ☒ *HK$15 one way, HK$28 round-trip.* ⊙ *Daily every 10–15 mins 7 AM–midnight.*

㉑ St. John's Cathedral. Completed in 1849, this Anglican cathedral was built with Canton bricks in the shape of a cross. It serves as a good example of both Victorian-Gothic and Norman architecture. ⊠ *4–8 Garden Rd. up from Queen's Rd. Central, on west side of the street just past the large parking lot.* ⊙ *Daily 9–5, Sun. services.*

★ ㉔ Victoria Peak. Known in Chinese as Tai Ping Shan, or Mountain of Great Peace, the Peak is Hong Kong's one truly essential sight. On a clear day, nothing rivals the view of the dense, glittering string of skyscrapers that line Hong Kong's north coast and the carpet of buildings that extend to the eight mountains of Kowloon. It's well worth timing your visit to see the view both by day and at night, perhaps by taking in a meal at one of the restaurants near the upper terminus. The Peak is more than just a view, however; it also contains extensive parkland, perfect for a picnic or a long walk.

With the opening of the **Peak Tower**, the commercial complex of shops, restaurants, and diversions up top, the site's developers have tried to rebrand a visit to the Peak, spectacular enough in the old days, as "the Peak Experience," complete with shopping, amusement parks, and restaurants. This has been a mixed success, but children might enjoy some of the activities; The Peak Explorer is a virtual-reality ride through outer space, while the Rise of the Dragon takes you on a rail car through a series of animated scenes from Hong Kong's history, including a frighteningly accurate rendition of the 1907 typhoon that devastated the territory. There's also a Ripley's Believe It or Not Museum.

NEED A BREAK?

You won't find a more atmospheric place to eat or have a coffee than the venerable **Peak Café** (⊠ 121 Peak Rd., ☎ 2849–7868). It was saved from redevelopment by conservationists' heated protests, and the elaborate carved bar is alone enough to justify their effort (☞ Chapter 3).

㉒ **Zoological and Botanical Gardens.** A visit here is a delightful way to escape the city's traffic and crowds. In the early morning the spectacle of people practicing tai chi chuan (the ancient art of meditative shadow boxing) is an interesting sight. The quiet pathways are lined with semitropical trees, shrubs, and flowers. The zoo has jaguars and gorillas, which for years were a source of friction between the government and animal-rights groups, but the cages have been expanded to better simulate the animals' natural habitats; as a result, you can usually see the jaguars swimming in their pool or sunbathing. There is also an aviary with more than 300 species of birds, including a spectacular flock of pink flamingos. ⊠ *Upper Albert Rd., opposite Government House; enter on Garden Rd.,* ☎ *2530–0155.* 🖾 *Free.* ☉ *Daily 6:30 AM–7 PM.*

OFF THE BEATEN PATH

YAN YUEN SHEK – Also known as Lovers' Rock, Yan Yuen Shek is a shrine that some Chinese women visit daily, burning joss sticks and making offerings in hopes of finding a husband. The 6th, 16th, and 26th days of each lunar month are the most popular times, and during the Maidens' Festival, in August, fortune-tellers set up shop for the lovelorn. A visit here is best combined with a visit to the ☞ Zoological and Botanical Gardens. Leave the gardens by the upper exit, east of the aviaries; cross Garden Road and take the left fork (Magazine Gap Road) at the traffic circle. Take a sharp left onto Bowen Road, a pleasant, tree-lined street that becomes a traffic-free path all the way to Happy Valley. From there Lovers' Rock is a 20- to 30-minute stroll. To get back to town, walk to the Wong Nai Chung Gap Road traffic circle at the end of Bowen Road, where you can catch Bus 15 or 15B to the Peak or Bus 6 or 61 back to Exchange Square, or you can take a taxi.

Wanchai

Wanchai was once one of the five *wan*—areas the British set aside for Chinese residences—but it developed a reputation for vice and became a magnet for sailors on shore leave, as during the Vietnam War. How times have changed: Wanchai is still as risqué an area as Hong Kong has to offer, but that says more about the city's overall respectability than it does about its available indulgences. For all its bars and massage parlors, Wanchai is now so safe that it seems a pale version of the "Wanch" of Richard Mason's novel *The World of Suzie Wong*.

The city's high real-estate prices have inevitably turned parts of Wanchai into an area of office towers, but it comes as a pleasant surprise to see how many crowded little alleys remain. A chance wrong turn can lead you into an outdoor wet market, a tiny furniture maker's shop, or an age-old temple. At night, the area comes alive (☞ Chapter 5) with bars, restaurants, and discos, as well as establishments offering some of Wanchai's more traditional services.

Numbers in the text correspond to numbers in the margin and on the Wanchai, Causeway Bay, Happy Valley, and North Point map.

A Good Walk

Walking is the best way to get around Wanchai, as the district's charms are more in its atmosphere than in specific sights. Take a circular walking tour starting from the junction of Queensway and **Queen's Road East** ① (a 10-minute ride from Central by tram or Bus 5, or a few blocks from the Admiralty MTR stop). Continue on Queen's Road East and turn left onto Wanchai Road, a busy market area selling a variety of foods, clothing, and household goods. This is a good place for browsing, especially in the narrow side alleys. To the left, several small lanes lead to Johnston Road and more tram lines; this area contains many shops that make rattan furniture, picture frames, and curtains to order. Turn left on Johnston Road and follow the edge of Southorn Playground, a popular meeting place, especially for those looking for a game of cards or Chinese chess.

Luard Road—along with cross streets Hennessy, Lockhart, and Jaffe roads—is the heart of Old Wanchai. At night the area is alive with multicolor neon signs and a lively trade in bars, pubs, massage parlors, and restaurants. Hennessy Road, which roughly follows the line of the original harborfront, is another good place to browse. Walk east on Hennessy Road to Fleming Road and turn north. Continue to Harbour Road, then head west to the **Academy for Performing Arts and Hong Kong Arts Centre** ②, in two adjacent buildings that function as the core of Hong Kong Island's cultural activity.

Continue on Harbour Road to Seafront Road and the **Hong Kong Convention and Exhibition Centre** ③. Circle back to Harbour Road and head east for a look at the **Central Plaza** ④, one of the world's tallest buildings. From here you can taxi back to your hotel, catch the MTR at the Wanchai station, or continue walking along the harborfront to the Wanchai Ferry pier for a ferry to Kowloon.

TIMING

If you stop to take in views and exhibits, this walk takes about two hours.

Sights to See

② **Academy for Performing Arts and Hong Kong Arts Centre.** Hong Kong is often maligned, not least by its foreign residents, as a cultural desert, but these two adjacent buildings help defuse this charge, with excellent facilities for both exhibits and the performing arts. Find out about the busy schedule of activities—dance, classical music, and theater by local and visiting artists—in local newspapers or at the ticket reservations office. While you're at the Arts Centre, visit the **Pao Gallery** (fourth and fifth floors), which hosts both local and international exhibits. The Academy for Performing Arts was financed with horse-racing profits donated by the Hong Kong Jockey Club. ⊠ *2 Harbour Rd., Wanchai,* ☎ *2582–0256.* ▢ *Free.* ☉ *Daily 10–8.*

NEED A BREAK?	The restaurant at the **Hong Kong Arts Centre** has a soup and salad buffet daily for HK\$65. ⊠ 2 Harbour Rd., Wanchai. ☉ Daily 10–9.

④ **Central Plaza.** In Asia's ongoing race to build ever-taller skyscrapers, this office complex (completed in 1992) briefly held the title as the region's tallest. It has long since been surpassed, but at 78 stories it's still quite striking. ⊠ *Harbour Rd. and Fleming Rd.*

③ **Hong Kong Convention and Exhibition Centre.** The original center opened in 1988 as one of the largest and best-equipped meeting facilities in the world, but—in typical Hong Kong fashion—it was quickly deemed insufficient. Needing a suitable venue for the 1997 handover ceremonies, the city decided to build, in a mad, furious dash, the extension that now sits so prominently on a spit of reclaimed land jutting into the harbor. With its glass walls and swooping curved roof, it's an outstanding venue for annual international trade fairs, regional conferences, and hundreds of local events. An exceptionally long walk through the centre yields a few celebratory sculptures commemorating the handover and a waterfront promenade with views of a not-very-distant Kowloon. It forms the core of the complex that includes the Convention Plaza office tower, a block of service apartments, and two hotels, the Grand Hyatt and the Renaissance Harbour View. ⊠ *Enter on Harbour Rd. between Fenwick Rd. and Fleming Rd.*

Next to the Convention and Exhibition Centre is the **Grand Hyatt Hotel.** From its polished marble and enormous Chinese vases to the jungle-size flower displays and grand staircases, this hotel just manages to stay on the tasteful side of opulence. The second-floor lounge is an exceptionally relaxing place to sit and chat over a drink or two.

❶ **Queen's Road East.** It's choked with traffic day and night, but this busy shopping street is packed with diversions. You'll pass rice and food shops and stores selling rattan and traditional furniture, curtains, picture frames, paper lanterns, and Chinese calligraphic materials. Shortly before reaching the Hopewell Centre, you may notice the altar of the **Tai Wong Temple** and smell its smoldering joss sticks.

Causeway Bay, Happy Valley, and North Point

Causeway Bay, one of Hong Kong's best shopping areas, also has a wide range of restaurants and a few sights. Much of the district is easily reached from Central by the tram that runs along Hennessy Road, or by the MTR to the Causeway Bay station.

The areas east of Victoria Park offer little for first-time visitors. North Point and Quarry Bay are both undeniable parts of the "real" Hong Kong, which means they're full of offices, apartment blocks, and factories. From Causeway Bay you can ride the tram for a few miles through these areas, perhaps the best way to get a feel for the environment.

Numbers in the text correspond to numbers in the margin and on the Wanchai, Causeway Bay, Happy Valley, and North Point map.

A Good Tour

If you come by taxi, a good starting point is the **Hong Kong Yacht Club** ⑤, which overlooks the **Cargo Handling Basin** ⑥. Stroll around the harbor and have a look at the **Noonday Gun** ⑦ and the boats in the **Causeway Bay Typhoon Shelter** ⑧. From Gloucester Road, which runs by the Noonday Gun, you can walk to **Victoria Park** ⑨, where you can roam at leisure and, on a nice day, have lunch or beverages in the outdoor restaurant. Exit from there onto Causeway Road, and walk or take a taxi to **Tin Hau Temple** ⑩. Take another taxi to **Kwun Yum Temple** ⑪. Continue uphill on Tai Hang Road (a 15-minute walk or a brief ride by taxi or Bus 11) to **Aw Boon Haw (Tiger Balm) Gardens** ⑫, then taxi to the **Happy Valley Racetrack** ⑬.

From here go to Chai Wan, site of the **Law Uk Folk Museum.** You can take a taxi from the racetrack all the way to Chai Wan, or ask to be dropped off at the Tin Hau MTR station. From here take the Island Line (the only line that stops here, designated in blue on the maps) in the direction of Chai Wan. Get off at Chai Wan, the end of the line, eight stops from Tin Hau. Follow signs to the museum, hidden on a small side street a five-minute walk from the MTR station.

TIMING

Allow four to five hours so you'll have plenty of time to stroll around the park, catch taxis, and find the museum. Try to set out late in the morning, just after rush hour, as the traffic in Causeway Bay—both pedestrian and vehicular—can be extremely daunting. The busiest intersection is right in front of the Sogo department store, which, with its skyscraper-size advertisements, looks a bit like an Asian Times Square.

0   330 yards

0   300 meters

KEY

⬧ M   Metro Stops

Victoria Harbour

Wanchai
Ferry Pier

Hung Hing Rd.

❸

❻

Seafront Rd.

❷

Harbour Rd.

❹

Harbour Dr.

Gloucester Rd.

Stewart Rd.

Tonnochy Rd.

Marsh Rd.

Canal Rd. West

Bowrington Rd.

Fenwick St.

Luard Rd.

Jaffe Rd.

O'Brien Rd.

Lockhart Rd.

Fleming Rd.

Wanchai Rd.

Admiralty

Hennessey Rd.

M **Wanchai**

❶

*Southorn
Playground*

Thomson Rd.

Johnston Rd.

*Morrison
Hill*

Queen's Rd. East

Spring Garden Ln.

Cross St.

Wanchai Rd.

Queen's Rd. East

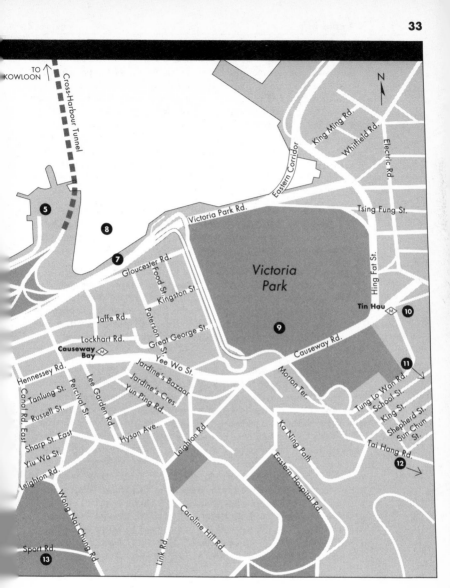

Sights to See

★ ⓒ ⑫ **Aw Boon Haw (Tiger Balm) Gardens.** Built in 1935 with profits from sales of a popular menthol balm, the gardens were the pet project of two Chinese brothers, who also built a mansion here. Eight acres of hillside are pocked and covered with grottoes and pavilions filled with garishly painted statues and models of Chinese gods, mythical animals, and scenes from fables and parables. An ornate seven-story pagoda contains Buddhist relics and the ashes of monks and nuns. It's great fun to explore, especially for children. Be forewarned: some Taoist and Buddhist scenes are decidedly gruesome. At press time, the financial troubles of the gardens' owners had its future in some doubt. ⊠ *Tai Hang Rd., Happy Valley.* 🎫 *Free.* ☉ *Daily 9:30–4.*

⑥ **Cargo Handling Basin.** West of the Yacht Club and east of the Wanchai Ferry pier (which sends ferries to Kowloon), you can watch the unloading of boats bringing cargo ashore from ships anchored in the harbor. ⊠ *Hung Hing Rd.*

⑧ **Causeway Bay Typhoon Shelter.** This boat basin was originally built as a bad-weather haven for sampan dwellers. In the 1960s and '70s, tourists could have dinner on a sampan, but this is no longer possible, as the number of fishing families who live in those small open-air boats has dwindled and the basin has filled with pleasure craft. A few traditional sampans, crewed primarily by elderly toothless women, still putter around ferrying owners to their sailboats.

⑬ **Happy Valley Racetrack.** Hong Kong punters are the world's most avid horse-racing fans, and the track in Happy Valley—opened soon after the British first arrived in the territory—is one of their headquarters (the other being the newer, larger track in Shatin, in the New Territories). Races alternate between the tracks but are generally held in Happy Valley on Wednesday night or weekends from September through June. The joy of the Happy Valley track, even for those who aren't into horses, is that it's smack in the middle of the city and surrounded by towering apartment blocks—indeed, people whose balconies hang over the backstretch often have parties on racing days. Only members are admitted to the track, but you can obtain a special visitor's pass if you've been in Hong Kong for less than three weeks and are over 18. You'll need to present your passport and its tourist-visa stamp as proof. ⊠ *Hong Kong Jockey Club, 2 Sports Rd., Happy Valley,* ☎ *2966–8111 or 2966–8364.* 🎫 *HK$50 for entrance badge.*

⑤ **Hong Kong Yacht Club.** The yacht club is worth a visit, but it's not open to the public, so try to find a local who is a member (or knows one) to give you guest privileges. If you belong to a yacht club at home, you may have reciprocal guest privileges. Once inside, you're surrounded by display cabinets full of silver prize trophies and welcomed by a delightfully old-fashioned bar with magnificent views of the harbor. On weekends the place hums with activity, especially when there are races, common from spring through fall. The South China Sea Race to Manila is held every two years at Easter time; call the race office (☎ 2891–0013) for details. ⊠ *Off Hung Hing Rd.,* ☎ *2832–2817.*

⑪ **Kwun Yum Temple.** A shrine to the goddess of mercy has stood on this site for 200 years, but the current structure is mostly new, dating from 1986. Constructed on top of a huge boulder, it has a high ceiling and gallery and is very popular with local worshipers. ⊠ *Lin Fa Kung St. W.* ☉ *Daily 9–nightfall.*

⑦ **Noonday Gun.** "In Hong Kong they strike a gong and fire off a noonday gun," wrote Noël Coward in his song "Mad Dogs and Englishmen." They still fire that gun at noon each day from a small enclosure overlooking the Yacht Club Basin and Typhoon Shelter, which is reached via a long walk (follow the signs) through the parking garage next to the Excelsior Hotel. The tradition was started by Jardine Matheson and Co., the great hong that inspired James Clavell's novels *Taipan* and *Noble House*: Jardine would fire a salute each time their *taipan*, who ruled over the company like a lord, would enter or leave the harbor. This angered the local governor, who ordered the company to use a gun instead of a cannon, and to fire it only as a noontime signal. The gun itself, with brass work polished bright, is a 3-pound Hotchkiss that dates back to 1901. ⊠ *Across from Excelsior Hotel, 281 Gloucester Rd.*

NEED A BREAK?	Have coffee or lunch in the first-floor coffee shop of the **Excelsior Hotel** (⊠ 281 Gloucester Rd., ☎ 2894–8888), overlooking the Yacht Club, and gaze at the yachts docked in the harbor.

⑩ Tin Hau Temple. Located on a street of the same name off Causeway Road (behind Park Cinema on the southeast side of Victoria Park), this temple is one of several in Hong Kong similarly named and dedicated to the goddess of the sea. Its decorative roof and old stone walls are worth a peek; the date of construction is unknown, but the temple bell was made in 1747. ⊠ *Tin Hau St. off Causeway Rd.*

⑨ Victoria Park. Beautifully landscaped with trees, shrubs, flowers, and lawns, the park has an aviary and recreational facilities for swimming, lawn bowling, tennis, roller-skating, and even go-cart racing. The Lantern Carnival is held here in mid-autumn, with the trees a mass of colored lights. Just before Chinese New Year (late January–early February), the park hosts a huge flower market. Early every morning the park fills with hundreds of tai chi chuan practitioners. ⊠ *Gloucester Rd.*

OFF THE BEATEN PATH	**LAW UK FOLK MUSEUM** – It's worth a trip to the end of the MTR line to see this 200-year-old house, which belonged to a family of Hakkas, the farmers who originally inhabited Hong Kong Island and the peninsula all the way into what is now southern Guangdong. Decorated in period style, the museum displays rural furniture and farm implements. Photos show you what bustling, industrial Chai Wan looked like in the 1930s, when it was a peaceful bay inhabited only by fishermen and squatters. ⊠ *14 Kut Shing St.,* ☎ *2896–7006. 1 block from Chai Wan station; outside station turn left and follow Kut Shing St. as it turns to the right.* ⊡ *Free.* ☉ *Tues.–Sat. 10–1 and 2–6, Sun. 1–6.*

South Side

One of Hong Kong's unexpected pleasures is that, for all the unrelenting urbanity of the north coast of the island, the south side consists largely of rolling green hills and a few residential areas that have sprung up around picturesque bays. A few points of interest nestle within the rolling hills. You can't cover this area on foot, but you can take a city bus or taxi from Central to either Stanley or Shek O (a 20- to 30-minute ride) and walk around.

Numbers in the text correspond to numbers in the margin and on the South Side map.

A Good Tour

Start the tour at **Hong Kong University** ①, which you can easily reach by taxi from Central; visit the **Fung Ping Shan Museum** on campus. From here take a taxi around the western end of the island to **Aberdeen** ②, with its teeming harbor full of sampans. Take a bus or a sampan to **Apleichau Island** ③.

If you have children in tow, you might want to take a taxi east of Aberdeen to **Ocean Park** and **Middle Kingdom** ④ and spend the day here; or you can skip the theme parks and taxi from Aberdeen along the scenic coastal road to **Deep Water Bay** ⑤ and **Repulse Bay** ⑥. Taxi from there to **Stanley** ⑦, where the main attraction is shopping at Stanley Market. Finally, stop at **Shek O** ⑧, the easternmost village on the island's south side.

From Shek O the round-island route continues back to the north, to the housing and industrial estate of Chai Wan, where you can choose between a fast journey back to Central on the MTR or a slow ride to Central on the double-deck tram that crosses the entire north side of the island via Quarry Bay, North Point, and Causeway Bay.

TIMING

If your time in Hong Kong is short, you can see all of these sights in a day, though it might make sense to limit yourself to, say, Stanley and Shek O. If you want to squeeze everything in, set out early in the morning and plan to make Shek O your dinner stop. Alternatively, you could easily spend an entire day shopping in Stanley and another day on the beach at Shek O or hiking through Shek O Country Park.

Shek O is worth visiting only in good weather. You can hike there year-round, while the beach is best from June through November.

Sights to See

❷ **Aberdeen.** Named after an English lord, not the Scottish city, Aberdeen got its start as a refuge for pirates some 200 years ago. After World War II Aberdeen became fairly commercial as the *tanka* (boat people) attracted tourists to their floating restaurants. You'll notice the famous Jumbo restaurant just offshore, its faux-Chinese decorations shrouded in lights. The tanka continue to live on houseboats, and although they may appear picturesque to passersby, their economic conditions are depressing.

You can still see much of traditional Aberdeen, such as the **Aberdeen Cemetery** (✉ Aberdeen Main Rd.), with its enormous gravestones, and side streets where you'll find outdoor barbers at work and any number of dim sum restaurants. In the harbor, some 3,000 junks and sampans are interspersed with floating restaurants, and you will undoubtedly be invited on board for a ride through the harbor. Use one of the licensed operators, which depart on 20-minute tours daily from 8 to 6 from the main Aberdeen seawall opposite Aberdeen Centre. Groups can bargain: A trip for 4–6 people should cost from HK$100 to HK$150. Individual tickets are HK$40.

Also in Aberdeen is a famous **Tin Hau temple,** whose ancient original bell and drum are still used at its opening and closing each day. Currently in a state of decline, this is one of several shrines to the goddess of the sea celebrated in the Tin Hau Festival in April and May, when hundreds of boats converge along the shore.

❸ **Apleichau (Duck's Tongue) Island.** To get here, take a bus across the bridge or arrive by sampan. Apleichau Island has a boat-building yard where junks, yachts, and sampans are constructed, almost all without formal plans. Look to your right when crossing the bridge for a superb view of the harbor and its countless junks. Vehicles are not allowed to stop on the bridge, so you'll have to walk back if you want to take a picture.

On your left are boats belonging to members of the Marina Club and the slightly less exclusive Aberdeen Boat Club, as well as the famous Jumbo Floating Restaurant. Quiet and unspoiled just a decade ago, Apleichau is now bursting at the seams with development—both public housing and a number of gleaming new private residential estates and shopping malls.

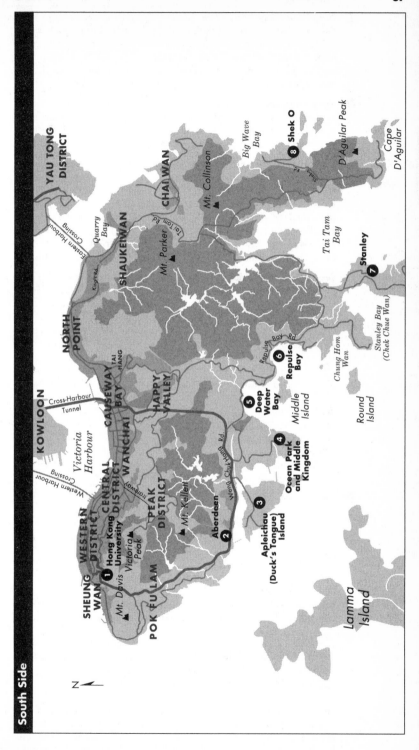

❺ Deep Water Bay. Situated on Island Road, just to the east of Ocean Park, this bay was the setting for the film *Love Is a Many Splendoured Thing,* and its deep coves are still lovely. Nearby are the manicured greens of the exclusive Hong Kong Golf Club. Not surprisingly, the area has become a multimillionaires' enclave and is home to Hong Kong's richest man, Li Ka-shing, a very private real-estate tycoon.

❶ Hong Kong University. Established in 1911, the university has almost 10,000 undergraduate and graduate students. Most of its buildings are spread along Bonham Road, the most interesting of which is the 19th-century University Hall, designed in a hybrid Tudor Gothic style.

The university's **Fung Ping Shan Museum** holds an excellent collection of Chinese antiquities (ceramics and bronzes, some dating from 3000 BC, fine paintings, lacquerware, and carvings in jade, stone, and wood). It also houses the world's largest collection of Nestorian crosses from the Yuan Dynasty (1280–1368), and some superb ancient pieces: ritual vessels, decorative mirrors, and painted pottery. The museum is a bit out of the way, but it's a must for the curious and the true Chinese art lover. ✉ *94 Bonham Rd.,* ☎ *2859–2114.* ✁ *Free.* ☉ *Mon.–Sat. 9:30–6.*

❹ Ocean Park and Middle Kingdom. The Hong Kong Jockey Club built these two attractions, just east of Aberdeen. One of the world's largest oceanariums, **Ocean Park** (☎ 2873–8888) occupies 170 acres overlooking the sea. On the lowland side are gardens, parks, and a children's zoo. A cable car with spectacular views of the entire south coast can take you to the headland side and to Ocean Theatre, the world's largest marine-mammal theater, where dolphins and a killer whale perform for crowds of up to 4,000. There are also various rides, including a mammoth roller coaster. The park is open daily 10–6 and charges HK$140 per person (which includes entrance to Middle Kingdom). **Middle Kingdom** is a theme park depicting architecture, arts, crafts, and industry through 3,000 years of Chinese history; it's open daily 10–6, and admission is included in the Ocean Park ticket. The complex has cultural shows, souvenir shops, and restaurants. Note that Water World, which used to adjoin the site, has closed and the plans for redevelopment are uncertain. ✉ *Wong Chuk Hang Rd.*

❻ Repulse Bay. Named after the British warship HMS *Repulse* (not, as some local wags say, after the pollution of its waters), the beach is a wonderful place to while away an afternoon. This was the site of the famed Repulse Bay Hotel, which gained notoriety in December 1941 when invading Japanese clambered over the hills behind it and entered its gardens, which were being used as headquarters by the British. After a brief battle, the British surrendered. The hotel was demolished in 1982 and eventually replaced with a luxury residential building, but replicas of its Repulse Bay Verandah Restaurant and Bamboo Bar were opened in 1986, run by the same people who operated the hotel.

NEED A
BREAK?

To taste the experience of colonial pampering, treat yourself to British high tea at the **Repulse Bay Verandah Restaurant and Bamboo Bar.** Tea is served daily from 3 to 5:30. ✉ *109 Repulse Bay Rd.,* ☎ *2812–9988. AE, DC, MC, V.*

❽ Shek O. The easternmost village on the south side of Hong Kong Island is a popular weekend retreat. It's filled with old houses, great mansions, a superb golf course and club, a few simple restaurants, a pretty beach, and fine views, albeit marred by some ugly new housing developments. Leave the town square, full of small shops selling inflatable toys and other beach gear, and take the curving path across a footbridge to the "island" of **Tai Tau Chau,** really a large rock with a lookout for scanning the South China Sea. Little more than a century ago, this open water was ruled by pirates.

You can hike through **Shek O Country Park** in less than two hours. Look here for birds that are hard to find in Hong Kong, such as Kentish plovers, reef egrets, and black-headed gulls, as well as the colorful rufus-backed shrike and the ubiquitous, chatty bulbul.

NEED A BREAK? | A favorite place for lunch, drinks, or just alfresco lounging is Shek O's **Black Sheep Restaurant,** a small place with an eclectic menu and the kind of relaxed ambience that makes you wonder if you're still in Hong Kong. Clusters of palm fronds give it the feel of a tropical island hideaway. ⊠ *From Shek O village, turn left at the Thai restaurant by the small traffic circle, continue down the road and around the corner on the right,* ☎ *2809–2021. AE, MC, V.*

❼ Stanley. Notorious during World War II as the home of Japan's largest POW camps in Hong Kong, Stanley is now known for its picturesque beaches and its market, where casual clothing and tourist knickknacks are sold at wholesale prices. Hong Kong has dozens of shops offering similar bargains, but it's more fun to shop for them in Stanley's countrified atmosphere. You can also buy ceramics, paintings, and books. The old police station, built in 1859, is open to the public and now houses a restaurant. Past the market, on Stanley Main Street, a strip of restaurants and pubs faces the bay. On the other side of the bay is a Tin Hau temple, wedged between giant new housing estates.

KOWLOON

Kowloon Peninsula is the extension of mainland China just across the harbor from Central, bounded in the north by the string of mountains that give Kowloon its poetic name: *gau lung,* "nine dragons." Kowloon is closer to China than Hong Kong in more ways than just geography: although the island's glittering skyscrapers are suffused with international commerce, Kowloon's urban fabric is even denser but has an older look to it. The proximity of the old Kai Tak airport kept building heights down (though landings still made you feel like you were scraping Kowloon's rooftops), but with the opening of the new airport Kowloon will no doubt rival the heights of Hong Kong at some point. The peninsula boasts many of the territory's best hotels as well as a mind-boggling range of shopping options; and no visit to Hong Kong is complete without taking on the commercial chaos of Nathan Road.

The southernmost part of Kowloon is called Tsim Sha Tsui, where such landmarks as the Star Ferry Pier and the elegant Peninsula Hotel stand proudly. A series of cultural buildings lines the waterfront, including the bold, parabolic curves of the Cultural Centre and the golf ball–shaped Space Museum. North of Tsim Sha Tsui are the market districts of Jordan and Mong Kok, where you can buy everything from pirated videos to electronics to name-brand clothes at fire-sale prices. Tsim Sha Tsui is best reached by the Star Ferry, while the rest of Kowloon is easily accessible by MTR or taxi.

Numbers in the text correspond to numbers in the margin and on the Kowloon Peninsula map.

A Good Tour
From the Kowloon tip, wend your way into the urban jungle of Tsim Sha Tsui from the **Star Ferry Pier** ①, which is a 10-minute ferry ride from the pier on the Hong Kong side—and, incidentally, the most romantic way to see the harbor, day or night.

Stroll east along the pedestrian waterfront to the **Victoria Clock Tower,** then visit the **Hong Kong Cultural Centre** ②. Note the luxurious **Peninsula Hotel** ③, across from which you'll find the **Hong Kong Space Museum** ④. The **Hong Kong Museum of Art** ⑤ is behind the Space Museum.

Continue east on Salisbury Road and turn left on Chatham Road South and continue north to the corner of Cheong Wan Road, where you'll find the **Hong Kong Science Museum** ⑥ and the newly relocated **Hong Kong Museum of History** ⑦. Backtrack a bit on Chatham Road to Granville Road or Cameron Road and turn right. The next main boulevard will be **Nathan Road** ⑧. Head south a short way on Nathan Road, then turn right onto Haiphong Road to get to **Kowloon Park** ⑨.

Return to Nathan Road and continue north to Jordan Road, then make a left and then a right onto **Temple Street** ⑩. Follow Temple Street north to the **Kansu Street Jade Market** ⑪, to the west. Continue one block north of Kansu Street to the **Tin Hau Temple** ⑫.

From here you can either walk or take the MTR to Prince Edward to see the new **Bird Garden** ⑬, which replaced the old Bird Market.

The **Wong Tai Sin Temple** ⑭ is best reached by MTR. The Wong Tai Sin station is four stops from Prince Edward on the green Kwun Tong line; the temple is directly opposite the station.

TIMING

You can take this tour in one day, but it will be a tiring day, as Kowloon is crowded, noisy, and often frustrating to walk or drive through. Plan a half day to stroll from the Star Ferry Pier to the Tin Hau Temple, stopping to see sights and shops along the way. Allow at least an hour for the Space Museum and the Museum of Art, another 45 minutes for the Science Museum, and an hour for the Museum of History. Be flexible with your shopping time; you'll want to compare prices before you make decisions. If you have two days in Kowloon, take the walk from Star Ferry to Kowloon Park the first day, then start at Temple Street and continue to Wong Tai Sin Temple the next day.

Start around 10 AM to avoid rush-hour traffic. Note that all museums offer free admission on Wednesday, though they're quite inexpensive normally.

Sights to See

🖐 ⑬ **Bird Garden.** Built in 1997 on Yuen Po Street, 10 minutes from the Prince Edward MTR station, this garden replaces the old Bird Market, whose narrow streets of bird shops have been redeveloped. What the garden lacks in spontaneous tumult it makes up for with an attractive outdoor setting in the shadow of the KCR railroad tracks—and the rumble of each passing train sends the birds into a frenzy. The garden is composed of various courtyards filled with trees and surrounded by 70 stalls selling birds, cages, and such accoutrements as tiny porcelain feeders and fresh grasshoppers. Plenty of free birds also swoop in to gorge on spilled food and commiserate with their imprisoned brethren. If you walk from the MTR, you'll enjoy an aromatic approach through a street lined with flower shops. ⊠ *Yuen Po St.* 🎟 *Free.* 😕 *Daily 7 AM–8 PM.*

② **Hong Kong Cultural Centre.** This stark, architecturally controversial building (which looks better by its flattering nighttime lighting than by day) has tile walls inside and out, sloped roofs, and no windows—an irony, since the view of the harbor would be superb. Its concert hall and two theaters host almost every major artist who performs in the territory. Exhibits are occasionally mounted in the atrium, which has its own three-story metallic mural by Van Lau called *The Meeting of Yin and*

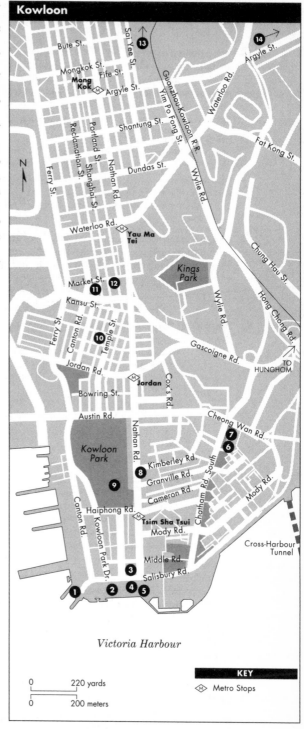

Kowloon

Yang. In front of the center is a long, two-level promenade with plenty
of seating and a view of the entire north coast of Hong Kong. ⊠ *10
Salisbury Rd.,* ☏ *2734–2010.*

★ ❺ **Hong Kong Museum of Art.** The exterior is unimaginative, but inside
are five floors of innovatively designed galleries. One is devoted to historic photographs, prints, and artifacts of Hong Kong, Macau, and other
parts of the Pearl River Delta; other galleries feature Chinese antiquities, fine art, and visiting exhibits. ⊠ *10 Salisbury Rd.,* ☏ *2734–2167.*
⊟ *HK$10.* ⊘ *Mon. and Wed.–Sat. 10–6, Sun. 1–6.*

❼ **Hong Kong Museum of History.** The museum covers a broad expanse
of Hong Kong's past with life-size dioramas. But since its move a couple of years ago to a new, ungainly building adjacent to the Science
Museum, exhibits may be limited to temporary displays. Call before
you visit. Plans to reopen the full space have been much delayed. ⊠
100 Chatham Rd. S, ☏ *2367–1124.* ⊟ *Free.* ⊘ *Mon.–Thurs. and weekends 10–6, Fri. 1–6.*

★ ⟲ ❻ **Hong Kong Science Museum.** More than 500 scientific and technological
exhibits—including an energy machine and a miniature submarine—
emphasize interactive participation. The highlight is a series of exper-
iments that test memory and cognitive ability. ⊠ *2 Science Museum
Rd., corner of Cheong Wan Rd. and Chatham Rd.,* ☏ *2732–3232.* ⊟
HK$25. ⊘ *Tues.–Fri. 1–9, weekends 10–9.*

⟲ ❹ **Hong Kong Space Museum.** Across from the Peninsula Hotel, this
dome-shape museum houses one of the most advanced planetariums
in Asia. The museum has a variety of interactive models explaining basic
aspects of space exploration (though some of these are less than lucid),
as well as flywires to let you experience weightlessness and such. It also
contains the **Hall of Solar Science,** whose solar telescope permits visitors a close look at the sun, and the **Space Theatre** (⊘ seven shows
daily from 2:30 to 8:30), with Omnimax movies on space travel,
sports, and natural wonders. Children under three are not admitted.
⊠ *10 Salisbury Rd.,* ☏ *2734–9009.* ⊟ *HK$10.* ⊘ *Mon. and Wed.–
Fri. 1–9, weekends 10–9.*

⓫ **Kansu Street Jade Market.** The old jade market was a sea of pavement
trading, but this more orderly market has 450 stalls, selling everything
from priceless ornaments to fake pendants. If you don't know much
about jade, take along someone who does or you might pay a lot more
than you should. Try to come between 10 and noon, as many traders
close shop early. ⊠ *Kansu and Battery Sts.* ⊘ *Daily 10–3:30.*

⟲ ❾ **Kowloon Park.** The former site of the Whitfield Military Barracks is now
a restful, green oasis. Signs point the way to gardens with different land-
scaping themes—the sculpture garden is particularly interesting, and the
Chinese Garden has a lotus pond, streams, a lake, and a nearby aviary
with a colorful collection of rare birds. The **Jamia Masjid and Islamic
Centre** is in the south end of the park, near the Haiphong Road entrance.
This is Hong Kong's principal mosque, albeit not its most graceful; built
in 1984, it has four minarets, decorative arches, and a marble dome.
At the northern end of the park sits an extraordinary public swimming
complex built, like so much else in the city, by the Hong Kong Jockey
Club with revenues from the races. ⊠ *Just off Nathan Rd.*

❽ **Nathan Road.** The densest shopping street in town, the so-called
Golden Mile runs for several miles both north and south and is filled
with hotels, restaurants, and shops of every description. To the left and
right are mazes of narrow streets lined with even more shops crammed
with every possible type of merchandise—jewelry, electronics, clothes,

souvenirs, and so on (☞ Chapter 7). Expect to be besieged with street hawkers trying to sell you cheap "Rolexes."

❸ Peninsula Hotel. The grande dame of Hong Kong hotels, the Peninsula is a local institution. The exterior of this sumptuous hotel commands attention with a fleet of Rolls-Royce taxis and doormen in white uniforms, while the huge colonnaded lobby has charm, grandeur, string quartets, and the sedate air of excessive wealth tastefully enjoyed. ⊠ *Salisbury Rd.,* ☎ *2366–6251.*

NEED A
BREAK?

Tsim Sha Tsui is short on quiet cafés, but the **Peninsula Hotel** serves high tea—the perfect way to rest your shopping feet in style. Nibble on a majestic array of scones and pastries in the lobby (HK$155 per person), or settle down for tea in the Verandah restaurant. ⊙ *Mon.–Sat. 2–7, Sun. 3–5.*

❶ Star Ferry Pier. The pier makes a convenient starting point for any tour of Kowloon. (It also has a bus terminal, which sends buses to all parts of Kowloon and to the New Territories.) As you face the bus station, Ocean Terminal, where luxury cruise ships berth, is on your left; inside this terminal, and in adjacent Harbour City, are miles of air-conditioned shopping arcades. To the right of the ferry pier is **Victoria Clock Tower,** which dates from 1915 and is all that remains of the old Kowloon-Canton Railway Station. (The new station, for travel within China, is a mile to the east.)

OFF THE
BEATEN PATH

Lei Cheung Uk Museum – This small museum in Sham Shui Po houses a 1,600-year-old vault and is worth a trip for its age alone. The four barrel-vaulted brick chambers form a cross around a domed vault, and the funerary objects are typical of the tombs of the Han Dynasty (AD 25–220). The vault was discovered in 1955 during excavations for the huge housing estate that now surrounds it. To get here, take Bus 2 from Kowloon's Star Ferry terminal to Tonkin Street (drops you closer), or catch the MTR to the Cheung Sha Wan station (faster trip). ⊠ *41 Tonkin St., Lei Cheng Uk Resettlement Estate.* ☎ *2386–2863.* ▭ *Free.* ⊙ *Mon.–Wed. and Fri.–Sat. 10–1 and 2–6, Sun. 1–6.*

❿ Temple Street. The heart of a busy shopping area, Temple Street is ideal for wandering and people-watching. By day you'll find market stalls with plenty of kitsch and plenty of bargains in clothing, handbags, accessories, tapes, and CDs, but the best time to come is after 8 PM, when the streets become an open-air bazaar of fortune-tellers, prostitutes, street doctors offering cures for almost any complaint, and occasionally Chinese opera.

Such nearby lanes as **Shanghai Street** and **Canton Road** are also worth a peek for their shops and stalls selling everything from herbal remedies to jade and ivory. **Ning Po Street** is known for its paper kites and for the colorful paper and bamboo models of worldly possessions (boats, cars, houses) that are burned at Chinese funerals.

⓬ Tin Hau Temple. One of Kowloon's oldest temples, this sensual site is filled with incense and crowds of worshipers. You'll probably be encouraged to have a try with the fortune sticks, known as *chim* sticks. Each stick is numbered, and you shake them in a cardboard tube until one falls out. A fortune-teller asks you your date of birth and makes predictions from the stick based on numerology. ⊠ *Market St., 1 block north of Kansu St.* ⊙ *Daily 7–5:30.*

★ **⓮ Wong Tai Sin Temple.** Have your fortune told at this large, vivid compound, whose Buddhist shrine is dedicated to a shepherd boy who was said to have magic healing powers. In addition to the main altar, the pavilions, and the arcade—where soothsayers and palm readers are happy to interpret Wong Tai Sin's predictions for a small fee—there are two lovely Chinese gardens and a Confucian Hall. ⊠ *2 Chuk Yuen Village, Won Tai Sin (in front of MTR stop)*, ☎ *2327–8141.* ⊠ *Small donation expected.* ⊙ *Daily 7–5.*

THE NEW TERRITORIES

Until a generation ago, the expansive New Territories consisted almost exclusively of farmland and traditional walled villages. Today, following a government housing program that created "new towns" such as Shatin and Tsuen Mun with up to 500,000 residents, parts of the New Territories are beginning to feel more like the rest of Hong Kong. Within its expansive 518 square km (200 square mi), however, you'll still feel far removed from the congestion and urban rigors of Hong Kong Island and Kowloon. It's here you'll find many of the area's lushest parks and therapeutic nature walks. In addition, you'll be able to sneak glimpses of traditional rural life in the restored walled villages and ancestral clan halls scattered throughout the area.

The New Territories got its name when the British acquired this area. Whereas Hong Kong Island and Kowloon were taken outright following the Opium War of 1841, the land that now constitutes the New Territories was handed over much later on a 99-year lease. It was this lease that expired in 1997 and was the catalyst for the return of the entire colony to China. Because of its size, the New Territories can be difficult to explore without a car, but between the bus, MTR, and the Kowloon–Canton Railway, you can at least get close to many sights.

Perhaps the best way to see some of the smaller villages is to go on one of the HKTA's organized tours (even if you don't think of yourself as a tour type), which loop through the region. In addition to the tours' convenience, the guides are knowledgable and helpful. The Heritage tour focuses on the territory's fast-disappearing traditional walled villages and ancestral halls. The six-hour Land Between tour takes you through the rural countryside, including Chuk Lam Shim Yuen (Bamboo Forest Monastery) and Hong Kong's tallest mountain, Tai Mo Shan. Reserve through your hotel's tour desk or at an HKTA information center (☎ 2807–6390 Mon.–Sat., 2508–1234 Sun. and holidays).

Numbers in the text correspond to numbers in the margin and on the New Territories and the Outer Islands map.

Western New Territories

A Good Tour

Start at **Sam Tung Uk Museum** ①, an 18th-century walled village in Tseun Wan. From here take a taxi to the **Yuen Yuen Institute** ②, which brings together Buddhism, Taoism and Confucianism. From there drive to **Ching Chung Koon Taoist Temple** ③, near the town of Tuen Mun, and then a little farther north to the **Miu Fat Buddhist Monastery** ④ on Castle Peak Road, which is a popular place for a vegetarian lunch. Drive from there to the **Kam Tin Walled Village** ⑤, a 17th-century enclave accessible by Bus 51.

After wandering the old village, you can drive east to go up to the peak of **Tai Mo Shan** ⑥ or drive north to visit the scenic town of **Lok Ma Chau** ⑦. End your tour at **Tai Fu Tai** ⑧, a 19th-century mansion that illustrates the conflicted political times during which it was built.

TIMING

Allow at least a full day for this tour, more depending on your pace. Plan to start in the morning and have lunch at the Miu Fat Monastery.

Sights to See

❸ Ching Chung Koon Taoist Temple. This huge temple near the town of Tuen Mun has room after room of altars, all filled with the heady scent of incense burning in bronze holders. On one side of the main entrance is a cast-iron bell with a circumference of about 5 ft—all large monasteries in ancient China rang such bells at daybreak to wake the monks and nuns for a day of work in the rice fields. On the other side of the entrance is a huge drum that was used to call the workers back in the evenings. Inside, some of the rooms are papered with small pictures; their relatives pay the temple to have these photos displayed so they can see their dearly departed as they pray. The temple also includes a retirement home, built from donations, which provides a quiet and serene atmosphere for the elderly. Colorful plants and flowers, hundreds of dwarf shrubs, ornamental fish ponds, and pagodas bedeck the grounds. ✉ *Adjacent to Ching Chung LRT station.*

❺ Kam Tin Walled Village. This village was built in the 1600s as a fortified town belonging to the Tang clan. Six walled villages surround Kam Tin, but **Kat Hing Wai** is the most popular. The original walls are intact, with guardhouses on the four corners and arrow slits for fighting off attackers; but the image of antiquity is somewhat marred by the modern homes and TV antennas looming over the ancient fortifications. Just inside the main gate is a narrow street lined with shops selling souvenirs and mass-produced oil paintings.

❹ Miu Fat Buddhist Monastery. On Castle Peak Road near Tuen Mun, Miu Fat is a popular place for a vegetarian lunch. The monastery itself is ornate, with large carved-stone animals guarding the front. Farther on is the former clan village of **Yuen Long,** now almost completely redeveloped as an industrial and residential complex. ✉ *Castle Peak Rd.* 🎟 *Free.* ⊙ *Daily 10–6.*

❶ Sam Tung Uk Museum. This walled village, built in 1786, looks more like a single large house with numerous interlocking chambers and whitewashed interior courtyards. Set in a forested area incongruously amid the residential towers and chaotic commercial life of Tsuen Wan, its construction obeys a rigid symmetry, with the ancestral hall and two common chambers forming the central axis and the more private areas flanking it. The front door is angled to face west–southwest, in keeping with feng shui principles of alignment between mountain and water. The village is easily reached by MTR; it's a five-minute walk from the Tseun Wan stop to the museum.

★ ❽ Tai Fu Tai. Built in 1865 by a scholar of the gentry class, this exquisitely preserved home reflects the European architectural influence on China, which was a result of the Western victory over China in the Opium War of 1841 and the gradual encroachment of colonialism. With loyalties divided, the scholar-gentry class decided to incorporate a few European design elements to indicate their open-mindedness. French roccoco moldings and stained glass above the doorways belie the home's traditional Qing Dynasty style. Other charming idiosyncrasies include an upper floor that allowed women to watch guests unobserved and an enclosed courtyard called a "moon playing" chamber for examining the night sky.

❻ Tai Mo Shan. Rising 3,230 ft above sea level, Tai Mo Shan—which translates as Big Hat Mountain—is Hong Kong's highest peak and the area around the peak has been cordoned off as a country park. Access is via a former military road (you can see the old British barracks, now occupied by the People's Liberation Army, en route), and a lookout about two-thirds of the way up gives you a chance to see both sides

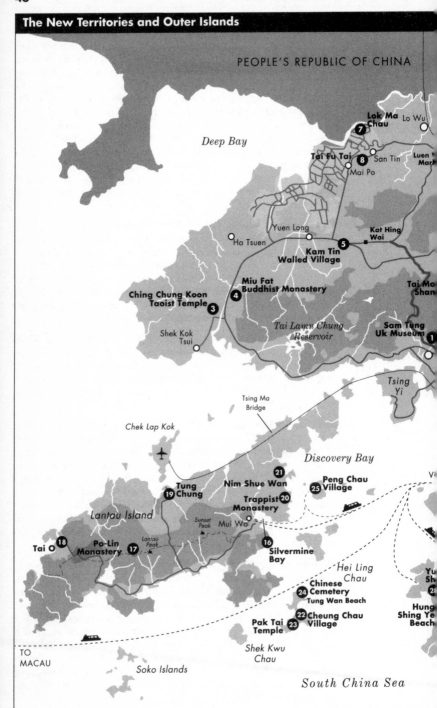

PEOPLE'S REPUBLIC OF CHINA

Deep Bay

Lok Ma Chau **7** Lo Wu

Tai Fu Tai **8** San Tin Luen Mar

Mai Po

Yuen Long Kat Hing Wai

Ha Tsuen **5**

Kam Tin Walled Village

Miu Fat Buddhist Monastery **4** Tai Mo Shan

Ching Chung Koon Taoist Temple **3**

Tai Lamu Chung Reservoir Sam Tung Uk Museum **1**

Shek Kok Tsui

Tsing Yi

Tsing Ma Bridge

Chek Lap Kok

Discovery Bay

21 Nim Shue Wan Peng Chau Village **25** Vi

19 Tung Chung

Trappist Monastery **20**

Lantau Island Sunset Peak Mui Wo

Tai O **18** Po-Lin Monastery **17** Lantau Peak

16 Silvermine Bay

Hei Ling Chau Yu Sh

Chinese Cemetery **24** Tung Wan Beach

Hung Shing Ye Beach

Pak Tai Temple **22** Cheung Chau Village

23

TO MACAU Shek Kwu Chau

Soko Islands

South China Sea

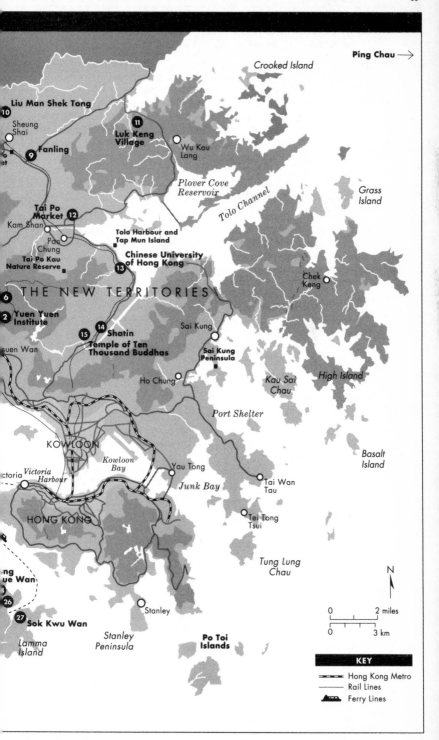

Ping Chau →

Crooked Island

Liu Man Shek Tong

⑩

Sheung
Shai

⑨ Fanling

⑪ Luk Keng
Village

Wu Kau
Lang

Plover Cove
Reservoir

Tolo Channel

Grass
Island

Tai Po
Market ⑫

Kam Shan

Pan
Chung

Tolo Harbour and
Tap Mun Island

Tai Po Kau
Nature Reserve

Chinese University
of Hong Kong

⑬

Chek
Keng

THE NEW TERRITORIES

⑥

② Yuen Yuen
Institute

⑭

⑮ Shatin

Temple of Ten
Thousand Buddhas

Sai Kung

suen Wan

Sai Kung
Peninsula

Ho Chung

Kau Sai
Chau

High Island

Port Shelter

KOWLOON

Kowloon
Bay

Yau Tong

Basalt
Island

ctoria Victoria
Harbour

Junk Bay

Tai Wan
Tau

HONG KONG

Tei Tong
Tsui

Tung Lung
Chau

N

g
ue Wan

㉖

㉗ Sok Kwu Wan

Lamma
Island

Stanley

Stanley
Peninsula

Po Toi
Islands

0   2 miles

0   3 km

KEY

▬▬▬ Hong Kong Metro
──── Rail Lines
🚢 Ferry Lines

of the territory: rolling green hills in the foreground and dense urban development in the distance. On a clear day you can even see the spire of the Bank of China building in Central.

② **Yuen Yuen Institute.** This complex of pavilions and prayer halls was built in the 1950s to bring together the three streams of Chinese thought: Buddhism (which emphasizes nirvana and physical purity), Taoism (nature and inner peace), and Confucianism (which follows the practical and philosophical beliefs of Confucius). The main three-tiered red pagoda is a copy of the Temple of Heaven in Beijing, and houses 60 statues representing the full cycle of the Chinese calendar—you can look for the one that corresponds to your birth year and make an offering of incense.

Central and Eastern New Territories

A Good Tour

Although parts of this tour are accessible by KCR train, you should consider renting a taxi and driver for the day for visiting some of the more remote sights. Otherwise, if you take a taxi to a sight you may not be able to find one to take you back.

Start from the north end of the tour and take the train to **Fanling** ⑨, then take a taxi from the KCR stop to the **Luen Wo Market.** From there, drive to the nearby village of Sheung Shui to see the ancestral hall of **Liu Man Shek Tong** ⑩, then head northeast to **Luk Keng village** ⑪, which is close to the Chinese border. It is a scenic drive past Plover Cove Reservoir to **Tai Po Market** ⑫, which runs along the streets near the Tai Po KCR stop. Wander around the market, then take the KCR south one more stop to the University station to find the **Chinese University of Hong Kong** ⑬. Take a campus bus or taxi to the **Art Gallery,** in the university's Institute of Chinese Studies Building.

Go back to the University station and take the train another stop south to the **Shatin Racecourse,** which adjoins the Racecourse station. Take a look around, then take the train one more stop south if you want to see the functional new town of **Shatin** ⑭. From here you can take a taxi to the **Temple of Ten Thousand Buddhas** ⑮, which provides a view of Amah Rock and Tai Mo Shan, Hong Kong's highest peak.

If you want to spend some time enjoying the outdoors, the Eastern New Territories has several attractive undeveloped areas: you can explore the beaches and fishing villages of **Tap Mun Island** or wander the forest and seaside trails of the **Sai Kung Peninsula.**

TIMING

Allow a couple of days for this tour. For a shorter tour, you may want to select sights that are geographically close together. If you want to visit Tap Mun Island or the Sai Kung Peninsula, set aside a separate day for each.

Sights to See

⑬ **Chinese University of Hong Kong.** The **Art Gallery** in the Institute of Chinese Studies Building is well worth a visit for its large exhibits of paintings and calligraphy from the Ming period to modern times. There are also important collections of bronze seals, carved jade flowers, and ceramics from South China. Take the KCR to University station, then a campus bus or taxi. ✉ *Tai Po Rd., Shatin,* ☎ *2609–7416.* ▨ *Free.* ☉ *Mon.–Sat. 10–4:30, Sun. 12:30–4:30. Closed holidays.*

NEED A   Across from the Chinese University campus is the popular restaurant
BREAK?   **Yucca de Lac,** which serves meals outdoors in the green hills along Tolo

Harbour, affording a pleasant view of the university. ✉ *Tai Po Rd., Ma Liu Shiu village,* ☎ *2691–1630.* ⊙ *Daily 11–11. MC, V.*

<table>
<tr><td>OFF THE
BEATEN PATH</td><td>

TOLO HARBOUR AND TAP MUN ISLAND – About a 15-minute walk from the Chinese University along Tai Po Road is the Ma Liu Shui Ferry pier, the starting point for a ferry tour of the harbor and Tap Mun Island. The ferry makes many stops, and if you take the 8:30 AM trip you'll have time to hike around Tap Mun Island and still turn back by late afternoon (☎ 2807–6177 for schedule). Tap Mun has a small village with a few Chinese restaurants, but you can also bring a picnic lunch. This trip is better by far in sunny weather. The **New Fisherman's Village**, on the southern tip of the island, is populated mainly by Hakka fisherwomen. About a half mile north, near the western shore, is the ancient village of **Tap Mun**, where you'll see old women playing mah-jongg. The huge **Tin Hau Temple**, dedicated to the goddess of the sea, is one of the oldest temples in Hong Kong and is less than ¼ mi north of the village. It sits at the top of a flight of steps that leads down into the water of the harbor; inside are old model junks and, of course, a veiled figure of the goddess herself. Go to the east side of the island to see the Tap Mun Cave and some of the best-kept beaches in the territory.

</td></tr>
</table>

⑨ Fanling. Although this town has the rather spare, functional feel of many of the new towns and may be of little interest to you, the nearby **Luen Wo Market** is one of the territory's most impressive and well worth a look. A grid of small stalls selling everything from T-shirts to pigs' lungs and the bustle and pungent aromas prove that local merchants can quickly make even a relatively newly built marketplace feel traditional.

⑩ Liu Man Shek Tong. Approached down a small, unmarked path in the village of Sheung Shui, this ancestral hall was built in 1751 and was one of few such halls that survived the antihistorical Cultural Revolution of the mid-1960s–mid-1970s. A recent restoration (completed in 1994) preserved the spectacular original roofs and ornamentation but substituted concrete walls to take the weight off the rickety pillars—at some cost to the site's aesthetic unity, unfortunately. It is interesting to note that the Liu clan, for whom this hall was built, was obsessed with education: the wood panels hung in the rear hall indicate the education levels achieved by various clan members under the old imperial civil-service-exam system of the Qing dynasty. ✉ 🆓 *Free.* ⊙ *Wed., Thurs., weekends, and public holidays 9–1 and 2–5.*

⑪ Luk Keng village. This tiny Hakka village is home to fewer than 200 residents, most of them widows. While most of the existing buildings were constructed in the 1960s (the dates are marked above the entryways), the village abuts the Luk Keng Country Park, which is an egret sanctuary, lending the place a superbly tranquil air.

<table>
<tr><td>NEED A
BREAK?</td><td>

Just outside Luk Keng village is the aptly named **Roadside Cafe,** which sells soft drinks and a few snacks. From a chair under an awning you look out over a small bridge and the nearby country park. ✉ *Bride's Pool Rd., Luk Keng village,* ☎ *2659–7274.* ⊙ *Daily until sunset.*

</td></tr>
</table>

⑭ Shatin. Whether you enter Shatin by road or rail, you'll be amazed to find this metropolis smack-dab in the middle of the New Territories. One of the so-called new towns, Shatin underwent a population explosion starting in the mid-1980s that transformed it from a town of 30,000 to a city of more than a half million in less than 15 years. It's home to the **Shatin Racecourse** (✉ Racecourse stop on KCR), Hong Kong's largest and a spectacular place to watch a race.

OFF THE
BEATEN PATH

SAI KUNG PENINSULA – To the east of Shatin, Sai Kung Peninsula is home to a few small towns and Hong Kong's most beloved nature preserve. The hikes through the hills surrounding High Island Reservoir are spectacular, and the beaches are among the Territory's cleanest, largely because they are sheltered from the effluent that flows out of the Pearl River Delta. A number of open-air seafood restaurants dot the area as well. (If you choose to eat in a seafood restaurant, note that physicians caution against eating raw shellfish here because of hepatitis outbreaks.) Take the MTR to Choi Hung and then Bus 92, Bus 96R, or Minibus 1 to Sai Kung Town. You can also take a taxi along **Clearwater Bay Road**, which will take you into forested areas and land that is only partially developed, with Spanish-style villas overlooking the sea. To cruise around the harbor, rent a *kaido* (pronounced "guy-doe"; one of the small boats run by private operators for about HK$130 round-trip), and stop at tiny **Yim Tin Tsai Island**, which has a rustic Catholic mission church built in 1890. **Sai Kung Country Park** has several hiking trails (☞ Chapter 6) that wind through majestic hills overlooking the water. This excursion will take a full day, and you should go only in sunny weather.

⑫ **Tai Po Market.** *Tai po* means "shopping place," and the town more than lives up to its name. In the heart of the region's breadbasket, Tai Po is fast becoming a utilitarian "new town," but its main open-air market is a feast for the eyes: baskets of lush green vegetables, freshly cut meat hanging from great racks overhead, fish swimming in tanks awaiting selection, and a variety of baked and steamed treats. Adjacent to the market is the 100-year-old **Man Mo Temple**; you'll smell the incense offered by worshipers. ⊠ *Take KCR to the Tai Po Market stop.* ⊙ *Daily 9–6.*

⑮ **Temple of Ten Thousand Buddhas.** You have to climb some 500 steps to reach this temple, nestled in the foothills of Shatin, but it's worth every step: inside the main temple are nearly 13,000 gilded ceramic statues of Buddha, all virtually identical. They were made by Shanghai craftsmen and donated by worshipers. From here you can also see the nearby Amah Rock. Amah means "nurse" in Cantonese, and the rock resembles a woman with a child on her back; it's popular with Chinese women. ⊠ *Shatin.* ☞ *Free.* ⊙ *Daily 9–5.*

THE OUTER ISLANDS

It's easy to forget that Hong Kong is not the only island in these parts. But for residents, the Outer Islands are a popular and important chance to escape the city and enjoy the waterfront, good seafood, and a little peace and quiet. The islands' villages are very much up to speed (and, to the regret of many, cellular phones still work here), but they run at a more humane pace. For maximum relaxation, try to come on a weekday, as the Hong Kong weekenders often come in large numbers and bring their stresses with them.

In addition to Hong Kong Island and the mainland sections of Kowloon and the New Territories, 235 islands were under the control of the British until July 1997. The largest, Lantau, is bigger than Hong Kong Island; the smallest is just a few square feet of rock. Most are uninhabited. Others are gradually being developed, but at nowhere near the pace of the main urban areas. A few of the outlying islands are off-limits, occupied by prisons or military bases. The four that are most easily accessible by ferry—Lantau, Lamma, Cheung Chau, and Peng Chau—have become popular residential areas and welcome visitors.

You can reach the islands by scheduled ferry services operated by the **Hongkong Ferry Company** (☎ 2542–3081 or 2525–1108 for recorded information). The ferries are easy to recognize by the large letters HKF on their funnels. For most destinations you'll leave from the Outlying Districts Services Pier, in Central, on the land reclamation area just west of the ☞ **Star Ferry Terminal.** Boats to Discovery Bay on Lantau leave from the Star Ferry Terminal itself. Schedules are available at the information office on the pier; round-trip fares range from HK$15 to HK$50.

Numbers in the text correspond to numbers in the margin and on the New Territories and the Outer Islands map.

Lantau

The island of Lantau lies due west of Hong Kong. At 143 square km (55 square mi), it is almost twice the size of Hong Kong Island. Hong Kong's new airport, at Chek Lap Kok, may eventually change the face of Lantau, but for the time being it's sparsely populated and makes a nice getaway from the city.

A Good Tour

Because of Lantau's size, you should plan to see either the western half (Silvermine Bay, Po Lin Monastery and Tung Chung) or the eastern half (Discovery Bay, the Trappist monastery, and perhaps Peng Chau) instead of combining both on a single visit. To do the western tour, take the ferry to the town of Mui Wo on **Silvermine Bay** ⑯, an area being developed as a commuter suburb of Hong Kong Island. Lantau is very mountainous, so for a tour of the outlying villages, plan to hike (☞ Chapter 6) or take a bus. From Mui Wo, the island's private buses head out to the **Po Lin Monastery** ⑰, home of a giant Buddha; **Tai O** ⑱, an ancient fishing village; and **Tung Chung** ⑲, which has a Sung Dynasty fort.

Although the **Trappist Monastery** ⑳ near **Nim Shue Wan** ㉑ can be reached by bus from Silvermine Bay, one alternative is to combine the monastery with other sights on the eastern end of the island by taking the ferry from Central to Discovery Bay. From there it is half-hour walk to the monastery. Ferries for Discovery Bay leave from the ☞ **Star Ferry Terminal,** and from the pier in Discovery Bay turn left and walk to Nim Shue Wan, then follow the signs to the monastery. You can also take a small passenger ferry, or kaido, between Peng Chau Island and Nim Shue Wan.

TIMING

The ferry ride from Central to Silvermine Bay takes about an hour, while the trip to Discovery Bay (via faster boats) takes about 25 minutes; after that, you can spend as long on Lantau as you like. The island is worth at least a full day's visit, even two; and you could easily spend a day on just one or two of the attractions listed below, so choose the ones that interest you most. The best overnight accommodations are at the Silvermine Beach Hotel (☞ Chapter 4); you can also stay at the Po-Lin and Trappist monasteries. The HKTA has information on these and other Lantau lodgings.

Sights to See

㉑ **Nim Shue Wan.** For quiet and solitude, take the 90-minute hike through this old fishing village—where you might see fishermen's grandchildren talking on their cellular phones—and the unspoiled woods and hills beyond to the **Trappist Monastery** (✉ Grand Master, Trappist Haven, Lantau Island, Box 5, Peng Chau, ☎ 2987–6292)(☞ below), on eastern Lantau. On the way you'll see beaches that would be beautiful except for the astounding amount of trash thrown there or washed ashore. You can spend the night in the monastery's simple accommodations, but you must make reservations well in advance.

⑰ Po Lin Monastery. Within the Precious Lotus Monastery, in Lantau's mountainous interior, is the world's tallest outdoor bronze statue of Buddha, the **Tin Tan Buddha**—measuring more than 100 ft high and weighing 275½ tons. The statue is all the more impressive for its situation at the peak of a hill, which essentially forces pilgrims to stare up at it as they ascend. The adjacent monastery, gaudy and exuberantly commercial, is known for the vegetarian meals served in the temple refectory. ⊠ *Take the bus marked* PO LIN MONASTERY *from Mui Wo and ask the driver to let you off at the monastery stop, from which you follow signs.* ☎ *Free.* ☉ *Daily dawn–dusk.*

⑯ Silvermine Bay. This area is being developed as a commuters' suburb of Hong Kong Island. You can rent bicycles in front of the **Silvermine Beach Hotel** (☞ Chapter 4) to ride around the village of Mui Wo, still surrounded by terraced fields.

⑱ Tai O. Divided into two parts connected by a modern drawbridge, the village still has many waterfront stilt houses and fishing shanties. Visit the local temple dedicated to Kuanti, the god of war, and taste the local catch at one of Tai O's seafood restaurants. ⊠ *Take the bus marked* TAI O *from Mui Wo village.*

⑳ Trappist Monastery. Despite its unexpectedly futuristic 1950s architecture, the monastery and its adjacent chapel exude a wonderfully placid air. Founded in 1951, the monastery is reached by a steep wooded path that ends at a footbridge suspended over a small stream. Like many Trappist monasteries, this one served as a working dairy for many years. The walk from Discovery Bay takes about 30 minutes, and you'll know you're on the right path if you find yourself walking through the backyards of the ramshackle huts en route. ⊠ *Follow the poorly marked concrete path from the southwest end of Discovery Bay to the forest, where the signs become more useful.* ☎ *Free.* ☉ *Daily dawn–dusk.*

⑲ Tung Chung. Here an ancient **Sung Dynasty fort** was evacuated by the Qing dynasty army in 1898, when the New Territories was leased to Britain. The fort is now an elementary school. Tung Chung's other attraction is its view of **Chek Lap Kok Airport.**

Cheung Chau

Cheung Chau, southwest of Lantau and about one hour from Central by ferry, is Hong Kong's most crowded outlying island (all things being relative), with about 22,000 people. Most of them live on the sandbar that connects the two hilly tips of this dumbbell-shape entity. Its Mediterranean flavor has attracted artists and writers from around the world, some of whom have formed an expatriate artists' colony here. Cheung Chau also draws Hong Kongers for another reason: its hotels rent by the hour (you'll see their booths in front of the ferry terminal), offering young lovers a brief escape from the congested living quarters and parental oversight of home.

There are no vehicles here—with the exception of a miniature red fire truck—so be prepared to walk around the island. As an alternative, you can take one of the small sampans that ferry year-round from Hong Kong Island to Cheung Chau's beaches, which are virtually deserted and have clear water.

TIMING
The ferry from Central takes an hour each way. You can make Cheung Chau a day trip, or you can stay in reasonable comfort at the **Cheung Chau Warwick** hotel (☞ Chapter 4), on East Bay at Tung Wan Beach, just north of Cheung Chau village.

Sights to See

㉒ Cheung Chau village. The entry into Cheung Chau's harbor, through lines of gaily bannered fishing boats, is an exhilarating experience. Cheung Chau is highly historical, with pirate caves and ancient rock carvings along the waterfront just below the Warwick hotel. Dining out here is also a joy, as there are dozens of open-air cafés on either side of the crowded sandbar township—both on the waterfront **Praya Promenade** and overlooking the main public beach at **Tung Wan.**

㉓ Pak Tai Temple. Dedicated to the protector of fishermen, this 200-year-old temple hosts the colorful, springtime Bun Festival, one of Hong Kong's most popular community galas. The festival originated in the 18th century as an appeasement for the spirits of people killed by pirates—spirits thought to wreak plagues upon the village. Beside the main altar are four whale bones from the nearby sea. ⊠ *¼ mi from ferry pier; turn left from the pier and walk along the waterfront until you see the temple, a slight uphill walk.* 🎟 *Free.* ☉ *Daily dawn–dusk.*

㉔ Chinese cemetery. These graves are generally modest and are set very close together, but each one bears a photo, etched onto a porcelain plate, of the person buried below. The ground is littered with fake money (belonging to the Bank of Hell, and denominated in the millions of dollars) that relatives burn to bring the deceased prosperity in the afterlife. ⊠ *½ mi from ferry pier; turn right from pier and walk along waterfront until you leave town, then follow paths veering left up the hill.* 🎟 *Free.* ☉ *Daily dawn–dusk.*

Lamma Island

What Lamma lacks in sights, it makes up for with an abundance of quaint, lackadaisically bustling portside village charm. The waterfront is lined with restaurants offering alfresco dining and the pleasure of exquisitely fresh seafood plucked live from tanks and cooked on the spot. Once you've feasted, you can work off the meal by taking the hour-long walk through rolling green hills that connects the two main villages.

In addition to its other attractions, Lamma is as close to a '60s bohemian scene as Hong Kong gets, full of laid-back expatriates driven out of Central by high rents. They have spawned a subculture of vegetarian restaurants and Tibetan crafts stores.

TIMING

The ferry from Central to either Sok Kwu Wan or Yung Shue Wan takes about 25 minutes and leaves from the new ferry piers in front of Exchange Square. It doesn't matter which village you go to first, since the one-hour walk between them is a Lamma highlight. Plan to visit both in a leisurely afternoon.

Sights to See

㉖ Hung Shing Ye Beach. "Beach" overstates the scale of this small, sandy oceanside strip next to the Hong Kong Electric power plant. Roughly midway between Sok Kwu Wan and Yung Shue Wan, Hung Shing Ye Beach is a pleasant place to enjoy the sun and is sometimes swimmable (don't go in if you see plastic bags or other refuse on the water). You can spend the night at the modest 12-room **Concerto Inn** (☎ 2982–1668, ℻ 2982–0022); some rooms have nice views, and the inn has a garden café.

㉗ Sok Kwu Wan. The smaller and grittier of Lamma's two villages, Sok Kwu Wan is notable mainly for the string of cavernous seafood restaurants that line the path leading from the pier. If you arrive on foot from Yung Shue Wan, however, your first glimpse of the bay from the hills will be quite stunning.

②⑧   **Yung Shue Wan.** By comparison with Sok Kwu Wan, Yung Shue Wan whirrs with activity. Formerly a farming and fishing village, it has in the past couple of decades become an enclave for expats, especially artists and journalists. Main Street is lined with small shops selling handicrafts and the occasional bohemian outpost, although the lingering smell of the fish markets is a reminder of Lamma's humbler, less cosmopolitan origins. The hub of expat community life (and a great place for vegetarian food) is the **Bookworm Café** (⌧ 79 Main St., ☎ 2982–4838), which bills itself as a "health café with net surfing and community happenings." **Lamma Fine Craft** (⌧ 61 Main St., ☎ 2982–2120) sells handmade crafts and jewelry from across the region.

Peng Chau

The tiniest of Hong Kong's four major Outer Islands, Peng Chau was once home to a few farmers, fishermen, and a fireworks factory. Although the factory has long since closed and the island has been discovered as a weekend retreat for Hong Kong's cityfolk, the portside community feeling remains.

Stand on the Peng Chau ferry quay and watch the kaido for Lantau's Trappist monastery sputter toward dark-green hills. Breathe in that stirring ambience of Hong Kong's islands—a mix of salt air, shrimp paste, and dried fish combined with a strong dose of local pride and a sense of independence, both of which have been lost in urban Hong Kong.

TIMING

The ferry from Central takes an hour each way; alternatively, you can make a short hop from Nim Shue Wan on Lantau in about 15 minutes. Go on a sunny afternoon, if possible, and plan to spend about two hours.

Sights to See

②⑤   **Peng Chau village.** The village is small and charming, and its shopping district is known for its unpretentious little stores selling locally made porcelain at remarkably low prices.

Peng Chau doesn't have Lamma's lively café scene, but the **Forest** (⌧ 38C Wing Hing St., ☎ 2983–8837) is a popular watering hole among locals, with home-style American cooking and live music several nights a week.

Other Islands

If you have extra time or a venturesome spirit, try one of Hong Kong's more out-of-the-way islands, not so easy to reach but all the more rewarding for their isolation.

Ping Chau

This minuscule island, not to be confused with Peng Chau, is 1 square mi of land in the far northeast of the New Territories, near the mainland coast. Now almost deserted, it has a checkered history. Guns and opium were smuggled out of China through Ping Chau, and during the Cultural Revolution many mainlanders swam through shark-infested waters in hope of reaching Ping Chau and the freedom of Hong Kong. The island's largest village, **Sha Tau,** is something of a ghost town, with many cottages boarded up, but here and there you'll find old farming families eager to take you in, maybe even for the night.

A large part of the island is country parkland, with footpaths overgrown with orchids, wild mint, and morning glories. Look for the strange rock formations at either end of the island. At the south end are two huge rocks known as the **Drum Rocks,** or Watchman's Tower Rocks. At the north end is a chunk of land that has broken away from the island; the Chinese say it represents the head of a dragon.

Plan your visit for a weekend and be prepared to stay the night, as the ferry to Ping Chau departs only on Saturday at 11:15 AM and returns only on Sunday at 11:15 AM. Bring camping gear, or accept lodging from villagers if they offer. Board the ferry at Ma Liu Shui, near the University KCR stop. Call the **HKTA Visitor Hot Line** (☎ 2508–1234) to confirm departure times before you go.

Po Toi Islands

This chain of three barren little fishing islands, virtually unchanged since medieval times, sits in the extreme southeast of Hong Kong's waters. Only Po Toi Island itself is inhabited (sort of), with a population of fewer than 100. It offers spectacular walks and fine seafood restaurants.

Walk uphill past primitive dwellings, many deserted, to the Tin Hau Temple, or walk east through the hamlet of Wan Tsai, past banana and papaya groves, to Po Toi's famous **rock carvings.** The geometric patterns on these rocks are believed to have been carved during the local Bronze Age, about 2,500 years ago.

Getting to the Po Toi Islands is an all-day affair and takes some planning. The most convenient way to go is by junk—to rent one call **Simpson Marine Ltd.** (☎ 2555–7349; ☞ Junking *in* Chapter 6). **Ferries** leave Aberdeen on Tuesday, Thursday, and Saturday at 9 AM and return from Po Toi at 10:30 AM the following day, so you have to stay overnight. On Sunday and holidays, however, you can get a morning ferry (10 or 11:30 from St. Stephen's Beach in Stanley) and return the same day at 3 or 4. You can make reservations by calling ☎ 2554–4059, but you'll need the help of a Cantonese speaker.

3 DINING

The surroundings may be Chinese, but cuisine in Hong Kong begins with carefully prepared Cantonese feasts and travels around the globe.

WHEREVER YOU GO IN HONG KONG, you're bound to see a restaurant sign. Establishments that sell prepared food are as old as Chinese culture itself, and because most people live in small apartments and have little space to entertain at home, restaurants are usually the chosen venues for special occasions and family gatherings. Cooking may be more varied in Hong Kong than anywhere else in the world: Cantonese cuisine (long regarded by Chinese gourmands as the most intricate and sophisticated in Asia) is joined by foods from other parts of China and nearly every other culinary region on earth. The deeply rooted Chinese love of good food extends here to French, Italian, Portuguese, British, Spanish, Australian, Japanese, Indian, Thai, Vietnamese, Korean, Mexican, and specialty American fare.

Updated by
Denise Cheung

Be advised, however, that Hong Kong's extraordinary culinary vitality is offset by some of Asia's worst restaurants. It's possible to find a hole-in-the-wall with unexpectedly exciting food, but don't expect any old neighborhood restaurant to turn out dreamy dishes.

Don't be shocked when you get your bill. You'll be charged for everything, including tea, rice, and even those side dishes placed automatically on every table, which are often mistaken for complimentary snacks. Tips are generally expected, even if the bill includes a service charge.

Restaurants in Hong Kong tend to change menus as often as people change their clothes, following the season and the clientele's tastes. Don't be surprised if your favorite dish is no longer on the list the second time you visit.

Hong Kongers regularly patronize hotel restaurants, bars, and coffee shops. Service is usually better, and the quality of the food more consistent, than in many independent restaurants.

Reservations are always a good idea; we note only when they're essential, which is often the case at lunchtime (between 1 and 2) or at dinnertime (between 7 and 10) on weekends. Unless otherwise noted, all restaurants listed are open daily for lunch and dinner. We mention dress only when men must wear a jacket or a jacket and tie.

CATEGORY	COST*
$$$$	over $64
$$$	$38–$64
$$	$13–$38
$	under $13

per person, not including 10% service charge

HONG KONG ISLAND

Central

One of the busiest sections of Hong Kong, Central is a madhouse at lunchtime, when hungry office workers crowd the streets and eateries. Most restaurants have set lunches with speedy service, making it possible for most customers to get in and out within an hour; these are generally good values. Evening dining is either formal or a quick bite followed by many drinks, especially in an area called Lan Kwai Fong. Another social area is SoHo (the area south of Hollywood Road), accessible by the long, outdoor Midlevels escalator. Almost every kind of cuisine can be found here including Spanish, Italian, Indian, Argentinian, Cuban, and Russian. Restaurants in both Lan Kwai Fong

A CHINESE SAMPLER

GASTRONOMICALLY SPEAKING, the words "Chinese cuisine" don't mean much more than the words "European cuisine." The most populous country in the world has dozens of different cooking styles, and five of these are prominent in Hong Kong:

Beijingese. Beijing cuisine, which originated in what was once called Peking, is hearty fare designed for the chilly climate of northern China—noodles, dumplings, and breads are more evident than rice. Peking duck, the perennial favorite, was originally an imperial Mongolian dish and is usually served in two (or three) courses. Mongolian or Manchurian hot pots (a sort of fondue-cum-barbecue) are northern specialties, and firm flavors—such as garlic, ginger, and leek—are popular.

Cantonese. Because 94% of Hong Kong's population comes from the Chinese province of Guangdong (Canton), Cantonese is by far the most popular culinary style. Favoring meats and fresh vegetables, the Cantonese ideal is to bring out the natural taste of each ingredient by cooking them all quickly at very high temperatures. The result is *wok chi*, a fleeting energy that requires food to be served and eaten immediately. If it's properly prepared, you will never taste fresher food.

Chiu Chow. The Chiu Chow people, from around Canton, have a gutsy, hearty cuisine that has never caught on in the West. It begins with Iron Buddha tea and moves on to thick shark's-fin soup, soya goose, whelk (snails), bird's nest, dumplings, and irresistible cold crabs served with vinegar.

Shanghainese. Shanghai is a city of immigrants, not unlike New York and Hong Kong, so it has cosmopolitan cuisine; and because it lies at the confluence of several rivers on the South China Sea, the city has especially good seafood. The rich-flavored Shanghainese hairy crabs are winter favorites. Many Shanghainese dishes are fried in sesame oil or soy sauce and can be a bit greasy. Sautéed freshwater shrimps are also a staple dish. Shanghai is also famous for its great varieties and hearty tastes of buns and dumplings.

Szechuan. Most renowned for its spicy and chili flavors, Szechuan food, also rendered *Sichuan* in English, is beloved around the world. Szechuan rice, bamboo, wheat, river fish, shellfish, chicken, and pork dishes are all prepared with plenty of salt, anise, fennel seed, chili, and coriander. The ingredients are simmered, smoked, stirred, and steamed, and the effect is an integrated flavor—the opposite of Cantonese food, in which each ingredient has its own presence. The cooking style features an eye-watering array of different chili types.

and SoHo have a somewhat contrived quality, with highly stylized theme decorating schemes and menus, along with relatively steep prices.

Asian

CANTONESE

$$$$ ✕ **Man Wah.** Even upscale Cantonese restaurants are known for their lively atmosphere, but this one is a Zen-like haven in the midst of busy Central. Silk paintings of Mandarins hang on the walls, hand-carved gold-and-ebony chopsticks polish off each place setting, and rosewood is everywhere you turn. The food is exquisite. Cantonese feasts come in many courses, and it's easy to order a half dozen dishes or more between friends. Steamed crab claws with ginger and rice wine are huge yet light, leaving plenty of room for more. The signature dish of sautéed fillet of sole with chilis in black-bean sauce is close to a work of art. A dragon's head and tail garnish the dish, which is delicately cooked to bring out the flavor of the fish. For dessert try the poached pear in tangerine tea—to be savored slowly, while you watch the ships in Victoria Harbour go by. ⊠ *Mandarin Oriental Hotel, 5 Connaught Rd.,* ☎ *2522–0111, ext. 4025. AE, DC, MC, V.*

$$–$$$ ✕ **Yung Kee.** For more than a half century, this massive eatery has served
★ Cantonese food amid riotous decor featuring writhing gold dragons. Convenient to both hotels and businesses, Yung Kee attracts a varied clientele—from office workers to visiting celebrities—all of whom receive the same cheerful, high-energy service. Roast goose is a specialty, its skin beautifully crisp. Adventurous palates must check out Yung Kee's famous thousand-year-old eggs with ginger. The preserved blackish eggs literally melt in your mouth. Seafood fanciers should try sautéed fillet of pomfret with chili and black-bean sauce, braised *garoupa* (grouper) or one of the many shark's-fin soups. ⊠ *32–40 Wellington St.,* ☎ *2522–1624. AE, DC, MC, V.*

$$ ✕ **Luk Yu Tea House.** Food takes a backseat to atmosphere in this institution. Luk is a living museum with extraordinary character—it's been in business for more than 60 years, and as such lets you catch a rare glimpse of old colonial Hong Kong from the Chinese perspective. The decor is worth a look in itself, with handsome, carved wooden doors, hardwood paneling, marble facings, and spittoons (which customers use with gusto)—and waiters dress in traditional Chinese uniform. Morning dim sum is popular with Chinese businesspeople, though the fare is no more than standard Cantonese. Reservations can be hard to get at peak hours (1 to 2) unless you're a regular. ⊠ *24–26 Stanley St.,* ☎ *2523–5464. V.*

$ ✕ **Mak's Noodles Limited.** Mak's looks just like another Hong Kong noodle shop, but it's one of the best-known noodle joints in town. The restaurant takes pride in its reputation, displaying copies of its reviews—including a write-up in *Time* magazine—at every table. The premises are clean, the attentive staff wears smart-looking uniforms, and the menu even includes some inventive dishes, such as tasty pork-chutney noodles. The real test of a good noodle shop, however, is its wontons, and here they're fresh, delicate, and filled with whole shrimp. ⊠ *77 Wellington St.,* ☎ *2854–3810. No credit cards.*

$ ✕ **Zhong Guo Song.** A hole in the wall with a difference, Zhong Guo Song serves delicious home-style Cantonese food in a hectic but clean environment with friendly service. Claiming not to use the dreaded MSG and excessive oil (which many Chinese restaurants do), the restaurant packs diners into close quarters and watches them chow down heartily on dishes such as braised garoupa (grouper) with bean curd and minced pork, scrambled eggs with little white fish, chicken in soybean sauce. Increase your carbohydrate intake with generous portions of a healthy fried rice with dried scallops and egg whites. No gimmicks here; every-

60

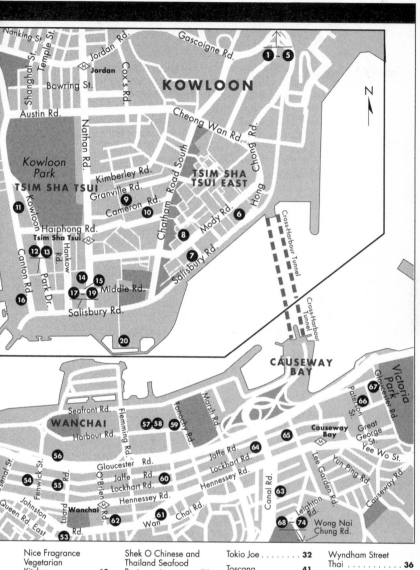

thing is just like a Chinese mother's treat, and the price is reasonable. Lunch hour gets very busy, so go early to avoid a wait. ⊠ *6 Wo On La.,* ☎ *2810–4040. No credit cards.*

HUNAN

$$$–$$$$ ✕ **Hunan Garden.** Escape the fast lane in this serene restaurant serving the cuisine of Hunan, the Chinese province where Mao Tse-tung was born. Both Hunan food and Hunan temperaments are known for being hot. Fried-fish butterflies are a highly recommended appetizer: these carp pieces, thinly sliced and deep-fried with a sweet coating, are crispy and sweet. The spicy fried chicken with chili may well set your lips and throat on fire; if you like things milder, stick with the codfish fillet with fried minced beans—the chewy and nutty bean paste goes perfectly with the fillet's soft texture. Do try the Shaoxing wine, served in tiny cups after the waiter pours it into a silver container and rests it in a bucket of hot water. Ask for lemon slices with the wine if you want a zestier aroma. Live Chinese music accompanies your meal. ⊠ *The Forum, Exchange Sq., 3rd floor,* ☎ *2868–2880. AE, DC, MC, V.*

MANCHURIAN

$$ ✕ **Bistro Manchu.** Finding cuisines of all kinds in Hong Kong is not an exaggeration. This smart little bistro serves up heart-warming, soul-soothing, and stomach-filling Manchurian cuisine. Noodles, dumplings, vegetables, meat—you won't be disappointed. Instead of the typical Chinese meat and vegetable dumplings, check out the option with tomato and egg fillings. You will be surprised how good this combination works in the light and delicate dumpling wrap. Meat lovers will not be able to resist the staple stir-fried lamb with scallions. Consume the hearty dishes with your choice from the great selection of Chinese tea. ⊠ *33 Elgin St.,* ☎ *2536–9218. Reservations recommended. AE, DC, MC, V.*

JAPANESE

$$$ ✕ **Tokio Joe.** Labeled as a place for "user-friendly Japanese food," this funky, casual Japanese joint literally serves up delicate Oriental fare with finesse yet without any intimidating formality. Creative design elements make the atmosphere fun—beautiful ceramic pots line faux-fur walls, and the food is delicately presented. Watch the chefs at work in a central bar area, preparing your favorite sushi in innovative ways. They lend a wonderfully contemporary twist to some classic dishes: the house sushi roll, for example, contains a scrumptious mixture of deep-fried soft-shell crab, avocado, and crab roe. Impressive combinations such as Super Model and Dragon's Eye promise to delight, as well as the sumptuous seafood ramen, nicely battered tempura shrimps, or the broiled sea bass. For dessert, try the homemade sesame ice cream. Service is attentive and courteous. ⊠ *16 Lan Kwai Fong,* ☎ *2525–1889. Reservations essential. AE, DC, MC, V. No lunch Sun.*

NEPALI

$$ ✕ **Nepal.** If you thirst for adventure but don't want to risk an assault on Everest, knock back a Yaktail or Yeti Foot cocktail in this tiny Nepalese restaurant. Don't be deceived by its size—it has more to offer than you might expect. Take a look at the Nepalese wood carving, the *manne* (praying tools), and the musical instruments as you enjoy the Indian/Nepalese music in the background. The *hanta tareko* (grilled eggplant) and *kaju sadeko* (fried cashew nuts) are good starters, and the special Nepalese soup, *golveda-ko-rash,* is perfect for vegetarians. The royal chicken, a light Nepalese curry, is a highly recommended entrée. End the meal with Nepalese ice cream, which is slightly firmer than Western ice cream. ⊠ *14 Staunton St.,* ☎ *2869–6212. Reservations essential. AE, DC, MC, V.*

SHANGHAINESE

$$$ ✕ **Shanghai Shanghai.** Part of the trend of retro-Chinese restaurants that try to capture the essence of Shanghai in the '30s, this newcomer is the best of the bunch. Art-deco touches, stained glass, discreet private rooms, and wooden booths achieve the nostalgic effect. The menu ranges from simple Shanghainese midnight snacks and cold appetizers, such as mock goose and smoked fish, to pricey shark's-fin soup. After 9 PM the lights dim, a chanteuse comes onstage to croon Mandarin tunes, and a song-request book is placed at every table. It's imperative you make reservations at least a week in advance, as this intimate restaurant has become a hot spot for affluent Chinese reminiscing about the good old days. ⊠ *Ritz-Carlton Hotel, 3 Connaught Rd., basement,* ☎ *2869–0328. Reservations essential. AE, DC, MC, V. Closed Sun.*

THAI

$$$ ✕ **Wyndham Street Thai.** You might mistake this place for yet another gallery on a Wyndham Street stretch of Asian art and antiques dealers. It has a rarefied atmosphere, with stark gray walls, but touches of red and turquoise and a few Thai decorations liven up the minimalist decor. The food—Thai with a Western twist—is artfully presented on large, contemporary plates. The menu, handwritten on a chalkboard that's carried to your table, changes from time to time, but certain items have been served since the restaurant opened six years ago. The crispy coconut prawns with peanut and cucumber sauce live up to all expectations. The green mango salad with char-grilled scampi is another appetizing starter. A table of four or more can try the red emperor (a delicious sea fish from Australia) in Thai sweet-and-sour sauce. For meat lovers, the roast U.S. game hen stuffed with lemongrass rice is an ace in the hole. The wine list has over 400 selections and is organized by grape. Desserts are also delicious, ranging from sorbets in flavors such as litchi to black-mango chocolate cake. Finally, refresh your palate with a Thai lemongrass tea. ⊠ *38 Wyndham St.,* ☎ *2869–6216. Reservations essential. AE, DC, MC, V. No lunch weekends.*

VIETNAMESE

$$$ ✕ **Indochine 1929.** Colonialism in Asia may be history, but many in Hong Kong retain romantic memories thereof. That may help explain the smashing success of Indochine 1929, which looks like a French plantation verandah at the height of the colonial era. The food is equally tasty and authentic; most of the ingredients used are imported twice a week from Vietnam. Highlights include the salt-and-pepper soft-shell crab, the fried beef and tomato, the stir-fried fillet of pork with shallot and lemongrass, and the fried fish Hanoi style. This is not the cheapest Vietnamese food in town, but it's arguably the best. The staff's traditional costumes—*ao dais,* straight, elegant silk gowns worn over flowing pants—and the surrounding old maps and antique fans and lamps add to the authentic atmosphere. The newly extended private area is ideal for group outings or parties. ⊠ *California Tower, Lan Kwai Fong, 2nd floor,* ☎ *2869–7399. AE, DC, MC, V. No lunch Sun.*

European

BRITISH

$$ ✕ **SoHo SoHo.** True, Britain is not considered a source of inspired cui-
★ sine, but this smart little restaurant is doing its best to change that. Calling its cuisine "Modern British," SoHo SoHo takes traditional dishes, combines them with eclectic ingredients, and transforms them into modern classics. Homemade pâté served with toasted, melt-in-your-mouth focaccia is surprisingly light—heavenly—and seared scallops served on a rocket salad with a warm, fresh pesto sauce tempt the taste buds. Sea trout, an uncommon visitor to these waters, needs very little else, but

the bed of pureed celeriac and blended almonds pushes frontiers. Rack of lamb on mashed potatoes is a meatfest, and salmon and cod-fish cakes and spinach in a mild mushroom-and-saffron sauce find their way to many a table. The restaurant's crowds are a testament to its winning formula of high-quality, delicious food, helpful service, and value for money. ⊠ *9 Old Bailey St.,* ☎ *2147–2618. AE, DC, MC, V. Closed Sun.*

CONTINENTAL

$$$$ ✕ **M at the Fringe.** Set above the Fringe Club, M sets itself apart with
★   quirky yet classy decor and a seasonal menu that mixes Continental with Middle Eastern cuisine. Both vegetarians and carnivores are well served, as in parsley salad with lemon and Parmesan or that all-time favorite, lamb chops. The combinations are as delicious as they are creative. It can be hard to choose from the long list of intriguing descriptions; highly recommended are the creamy (yet not too rich) risotto with mussels, saffron, and chili; soft-shell crabs sautéed with crispy shallots and coriander; a Turkish vegetable platter, with delicately presented veggie portions from *borek* (cheese pastry pie) to *courgette basti* (molded zucchini); and juicy yet flaky baked cod with mashed potatoes, mussels, and mussel sauce. Those with a sweet tooth should not miss the Pavlova or tart Tatin. The set lunch is a good value. ⊠ *South Block, 2 Lower Albert Rd., 1st floor,* ☎ *2877–4000. Reservations essential. AE, MC, V. Closed Sun.*

$$ ✕ **Jimmy's Kitchen.** Probably the most famous—and still one of the best—of Hong Kong's restaurants, Jimmy's first opened for business in 1928 and has been catering to a deeply devoted clientele (in one location or another) ever since. It's nicely decorated with comfortable booths, dark woodwork, lattice partitions, and brass fittings. The food is as charmingly old-fashioned as the place itself: where else in Hong Kong can you find corned beef and cabbage? Other European specialties, including borscht, Stroganoff, goulash, and bangers and mash, are accompanied by the restaurant's traditional pickled onions. The extensive and diverse menu includes a selection of Asian delights from curry to fried rice for those who fancy a bit of an Oriental flavor. The rhubarb tart is a must for dessert. ⊠ *South China Bldg., 1 Wyndham St., basement,* ☎ *2526–5293. Reservations essential for lunch. AE, DC, MC, V.*

$$ ✕ **Wyndham Street Deli.** Feast your eyes on the deli counter before sampling its goodies—fresh salads, sandwiches, quiches, breads, and cheeses that taste as good as they look, plus an array of bottled condiments from olive oil to preserves and sauces. You can't go wrong here, but the grilled vegetables and chicken pasta salads are highly recommended. Focaccia sandwiches and hot pastas also make light but satisfying meals. The deli is popular for lunch, so come before 1 or after 2 to avoid the Central office crowd, or aim for the quieter tables on the small patio in back. Leave room for one of the excellent tarts and cakes, such as lemon cheesecake. ⊠ *36 Wyndham St.,* ☎ *2522–3499. Reservations essential for lunch. AE, DC, MC, V. No dinner Sun.*

FRENCH

$$$$ ✕ **Vong.** This is designer dining. With sister establishments in London and New York, Hong Kong's Vong sits glamorously at the top of the Mandarin Oriental Hotel, overlooking Central and the harbor. Black and gold feature heavily in the visuals, creating a sophistication that's only enhanced by such details as curvaceous cutlery and chic crockery. The menu comprises the world-class innovations of celebrated chef-patron Jean-Georges Vongerichten, whose Asian-inspired French cuisine fuses flavors from both worlds. Good examples are foie gras with ginger and caramelized mango, and quail rubbed with Thai spices. Chicken marinated in lemongrass and served with sticky rice in a banana leaf is another favorite. Even the desserts are startling: the warm Valhrona chocolate cake with coconut ice cream sends a surprise torrent of molten choco-

late cascading onto your plate. Don't expect a quiet dinner, as the atmosphere is high-octane. ⌧ *Mandarin Oriental Hotel, 5 Connaught Rd., 25th floor,* ☎ *2825–4028. Reservations essential. AE, DC, MC, V.*

ITALIAN

\$\$\$–\$\$\$\$ ✕ **Toscana.** This is classical Italian dining at its finest—sumptuous, el-
★ egant, and relaxed. Huge oil paintings depicting scenes from Venice cover the walls, a high ceiling amplifies the spacious interior, elegant drapes shroud the high windows, and Italian opera softly fills the air. The opulent atmosphere is matched by the food and smooth, friendly service. The lobster and *rucola* (arugula) salad is a heavenly creation with salty bursts of caviar mixing with fresh angel hair. Tender orecchiette with shellfish ragout and baby tomatoes is a deliciously rare dish to be found in Hong Kong. The lamb comes highly recommended, especially when hiding a bed of porcini mushroom risotto and topped by foie gras and black truffle. Match these with a little-known but much sought-after wine from Chef Umberto Bombana's list, and you'll know why regulars from around the world visit whenever in town. The warm caraibe chocolate cake with homemade vanilla ice cream and almonds is a perfect finale. ⌧ *Ritz-Carlton, 3 Connaught Rd.,* ☎ *2532–2062. AE, DC, MC, V. Closed Sun.*

Vegetarian
\$–\$\$ ✕ **Eating Plus.** Healthy eating with elegant simplicity is the principle of this smart restaurant, making it a popular hangout for the health-conscious crowds. The menu does not suggest heavy meat intake, but you can easily find chicken, beef, and seafood, prepared and served to accompany your carbohydrate-rich choices. The menu includes a wide selection of noodles, ramens, pastas and rice, as well as an array of vegetables and side dishes such as eggplant medallions, crispy tofu, and chicken and vegetable skewers. A glass of freshly squeezed juice from the fruit bar completes this healthy dining experience. Located next to the Hong Kong Station, this is an excellent stop for a hearty treat before you hop on a train for the airport. ⌧ *1009, Southern International Finance Centre, 1st floor,* ☎ *2868–0599. AE, DC, MC, V.*

Western

Neighborhoods west of Central—including Sheung Wan, Saiyingpun, and Kennedy Town—are generally lumped under this unimaginative name. The farther west you wander, the fewer English signs you'll see. The part of Des Voeux Road just past Western Market is especially well known for wholesale vendors of dried seafood: shop after shop displays heaps of dried fish, shark's fins, and all manner of medicinal herbs and animal parts. Many Western shops and restaurants have not been renovated for decades. As more expatriates have moved into this area, with its cheaper rents and convenient situation, more and more restaurants have added limited English menus.

European
CONTEMPORARY

\$\$\$ ✕ **Igor's.** Here you're greeted by ghouls and vampires, led on a spooky tour, and terrorized by an assortment of mechanical monsters before being shown to the dining room. Igor's is as much a haunted house-cum-stage show as a restaurant, but eventually you'll get down to stuffing yourself with appetizers; a limited selection of entrées such as smoked salmon, steak, and chicken; and desserts—all rolled along the banquet tables on a series of trolleys. Not for the faint-hearted, this restaurant is popular with parties who want a raunchy night out. *Western Harbour Centre, 181 Connaught Rd. W,* ☎ *2108–4467. Reservations essential. DC, MC, V. Closed Mon.*

Admiralty

Since this is essentially an office area and a series of large shopping malls, much of the food is aimed at meeting the lunch needs of workers and shoppers. However, with a major cinema and several good restaurants in the Pacific Place mall, it's convenient for dinner as well.

Asian
CANTONESE

$$$ ✕ **Zen.** This upscale nouveau Cantonese eatery has the same owner as the ultrachic London restaurants of the same name. Thinly sliced pig's ears are one of the more unusual specialties, and the Peking duck is delicious (give a full day's notice if you want to try it). The more standard Cantonese dishes are quite delicately prepared and presented. Service is flawless, and the decor is contemporary, with dramatic hanging lights and a central waterfall. ✉ *The Mall, Pacific Place One, 88 Queensway,* ☎ *2845–4555. AE, DC, MC, V.*

SHANGHAINESE

$$ ✕ **Ye Shanghai** "Ye" means "night" in Chinese. And those who want to capture or recapture the spirit of old Shanghai nightlife will find this a dining experience. The setting is elegantly nostalgic, the lighting subdued, and the ceiling fans move relentlessly. Once the mood is set, start with some light appetizers such as chicken in spicy sauce or tea-leaf smoked egg. For an entrée, try the fresh and flavorful stir-fried river shrimps, accompanied by strong dark vinegar, or the sautéed minced chicken with pine nuts, served with sesame pockets. Desserts include the Shanghai staple deep-fried eggwhite stuffed with banana and mashed red-bean paste and the Japanese-inspired black-sesame ice cream. Reserve early for the comfortable booth seats or the window tables with a view of the bustling Queensway. Its shop next door, Xiao Shanghai (Small Shanghai), sells all sorts of snacks, tea, pickles, and sweets. Live music delivers golden oldies every Thursday through Saturday nights (English numbers on Thursday). ✉ *Level 3, Pacific Place, 88 Queensway,* ☎ *2918–9833. AE, DC, MC, V.*

THAI

$$ ✕ **Thai Basil.** You won't miss this relatively new kid on the block when stepping out from the Admiralty MTR Station and heading toward Pacific Place. Don't be deceived by its mall location: delicious food with reasonable prices make it a popular dining spot. An Australian chef artfully presents his myriad Oriental creations with a contemporary twist, creating deliciously innovative dishes such as scampi and banana bud with lime and mint leaves, stingray salad with green mango, and green papaya and crispy fish. Those with a sweet tooth will love the homemade ice-cream selection, from ginger to honeycomb, while the sticky banana pudding deserves two thumbs up. A dedicated exclusive dining area called The Kitchen at the back of the restaurant services well-heeled diners. ✉ *Shop 005, Pacific Place, lower ground floor,* ☎ *2537–4682. Reservations recommended for The Kitchen. AE, DC, MC, V.*

European
FRENCH

$$$$ ✕ **Petrus.** Fine modern French dining matched with glittering views
★   sums up Petrus. From the 56th floor of this five-star hotel, Petrus literally looks down on nearly all other Hong Kong restaurants in location and culinary standards. It attracts the finest and most decorated chefs from Europe to its kitchen, peppering the menu with traditional French dishes such as green asparagus with Perigord truffle, deep-fried egg and Dublin Bay prawn, and Bresse pigeon. However a closer inspection hints at tastes from many parts of the world. Black cod comes

with the Middle Eastern herb baharat and a lemon gravy. Bouillon of baby lobster with rock oysters is served with ginger, white cheese, and lime dumplings. Try the refreshing ginger ice cream for a light dessert. Naturally enough, the extensive wine list is largely French. ⊠ *Island Shangri-La, Pacific Place, Supreme Court Rd., 56th floor,* ☎ *2820–8590. Reservations essential. AE, D, MC, V.*

ITALIAN

$$$$ ✕ **Nicholini's.** Fine Italian dining at its best can be found at Conrad International hotel's signature restaurant, Nicholini's. Separated by a lounge from its French cousin, Brasserie on the Eighth, this elegant and florally decorated establishment regularly picks up awards for its fine food: it was crowned by the Italian Commissione Centrale as one of the world's finest Italian restaurants abroad in 1999. Featuring northern Italian dishes, the menu serves a wide range of pastas, fish, fowl and meat. Homemade black fettuccine with shrimp, clams, and asparagus tips is deliciously dark, while linguine with clams is a delight. The roast rack of lamb with green tomato compote is young enough to be sweet without overpowering the palate. For dessert, try a soufflé. The wine list features wines especially hand-blended for Nicholini's. ⊠ *Conrad Hotel, Pacific Place, 88 Queensway, 8th floor,* ☎ *2521–3838. AE, DC, MC, V.*

$$–$$$ ✕ **Grappa's.** Don't let the mall location mislead you. Once inside you can turn your back on the mall and let the kindly staff serve you superb Italian food. The endless selection of pastas can prolong your decision, but nothing will disappoint. With excellent coffee and a range of bottled beers, Grappa's is equally useful for a quick pick-me-up or a post-shopping rendezvous. ⊠ *132 Pacific Place, 88 Queensway,* ☎ *2868–0086. AE, DC, MC, V.*

North American

$$ ✕ **Dan Ryan's.** This popular bar is often standing room only, so call ahead
★ for a table. Apart from beer, the menu offers a smattering of international dishes—pasta and the like—but Dan Ryan is known for its great burgers and soups served in bread bowls. It's simple, rib-sticking stuff, and Dan Ryan's serves it up without fuss or formality. ⊠ *114 Pacific Place, 88 Queensway,* ☎ *2845–4600. Reservations essential. AE, DC, MC, V.*

Seafood

$$$ ✕ **Lobster Bar.** The giant tropical-fish tank at the entrance sets the scene here. As the name suggests, lobster is the feature presentation, whipped into soups, appetizers, and various entrées. The lobster bisque is creamy yet light, with great chunks of meat at the bottom. Lobster tartare, served with cucumber salad and two good-size lobster claws, fills a starter plate with fresh, succulent shredded lobster meat. For a lighter main course, the angel-hair pasta with *yabbies* (a smaller Australian cousin of the lobster) tastes as good as it sounds. The seafood selection—half a lobster thermidor, whole grilled langoustine, prawn, baked oyster, creamy scallops, crab cakes, black cod—delivers on its promise. If you must avoid the fruits of the sea, meats are also available. The space is large and elegant, decorated in blue and gold; the atmosphere is at once formal and relaxed. ⊠ *Island Shangri-La, lobby level,* ☎ *2877–3838. Reservations essential for lunch. AE, DC, MC, V.*

The Peak

On a clear day, even the views en route via tram or taxi will justify a trip to the highest dining points in Hong Kong. (Note that if there are low clouds, you won't be able to see a thing; you'll just hear the city beneath you.) Two restaurants compete for the Peak position: stick with Cafe Deco for the view, or the Peak Cafe for unbeatable atmosphere.

Asian

$$$ ✕ **Cafe Deco Bar and Grill.** If you're in Hong Kong on a clear day, take
★   the Peak tram to the top and dine at this spiffy double-decker restau-
     rant overlooking the entire city. The views are stunning, and the decor
     is Art Deco to the hilt—you can spend an age looking at original pe-
     riod fittings. The menu is international, with Chinese, Indian (the
     kitchen has a proper tandoor), Italian, Mexican, and Thai dishes.
     Some specialties make use of *ancho* chilis, or combine striped sea bass
     with fennel and pancetta. The wine list is reasonably priced, with an
     extensive selection of wines from around the world. Eat in the dining
     room, at the oyster bar, or in the ice-cream parlor. Cafe Deco is a fa-
     vorite with locals and travelers alike. ⊠ *Peak Galleria, 118 Peak Rd.,
     1st level,* ☎ *2849–5111. AE, DC, MC, V.*

$$–$$$ ✕ **Peak Cafe.** Built in 1888 as a workshop for tram engineers, this colo-
★   nial granite building was transformed into a café-restaurant in 1989.
     The outdoor dining area is a treat for alfresco enthusiasts: on a sunny
     day or a clear night, the views over Lamma Channel are incredible. When
     the clouds roll in (as they often do), the terrace is a different place, with
     mist-shrouded trees silhouetted in subtle lighting, candles glowing softly
     on the tables, and coal fires competing with condensation to keep you
     comfortable. The atmosphere is surprisingly intimate; you're far from
     the rest of the world. Inside, however, it's a different story whatever the
     weather, with big, jovial groups creating a general air of merriment. Colo-
     nial artifacts and Roaring '20s photos hang on the wall, and a high ceil-
     ing towers over the tables. Waiters are aloof and smartly casual. Favorite
     meals include a fragrant Thai duck curry, succulent satays, and a nightly
     barbecue. A tandoor turns out beautiful naan breads and various tan-
     doori dishes. The general experience is highly recommended. ⊠ *121
     Peak Rd.,* ☎ *2849–7868. Reservations essential. AE, DC, MC, V.*

Wanchai

At lunchtime Wanchai is just another jumble of people, not a partic-
ularly invigorating shopping area; but after dark it comes into its own.
This is Hong Kong's prime nightlife area, its long roads lined with flu-
orescent lights and jam-packed with taxis and wide-awake crowds. The
range of dining options is extreme—from fail-safe five-star luxury to
authentic and welcoming street-level spots with fine food.

Asian

$ ✕ **American Peking Restaurant.** Full of red and gold fixtures, this
    overdecorated restaurant has been a gastronomic Hong Kong entity for
    more than 40 years. Favorites here include hot-and-sour soup, fried and
    steamed dumplings, and, in the winter, delicious hot pots; you might
    also try the excellent beggar's chicken (so called because it's cooked in
    clay and lotus leaves), minced pigeon, and, of course, Peking duck. Each
    meal begins with complimentary peanuts and sliced cucumber in vine-
    gar—perfect for practicing chopstick skills. The name American Peking
    is fitting: the authenticity of the food is questionable, but it caters well
    to those unaccustomed to Chinese food. ⊠ *20 Lockhart Rd.,* ☎ *2527–
    7770. Reservations essential on weekends. AE, DC, MC, V.*

$ ✕ **Dumpling Shop.** If the Marco Polo story is true, you can get a taste
    of the forerunner of spaghetti *bolognese* at this clean and smart Bei-
    jingese food shop. Thick, northern-Chinese noodles arrive in a bowl ac-
    companied by a rich minced-pork sauce; it's just a matter of mixing them
    together before slurping them up. Even a small portion is enough for
    two, so be careful not to over order. Buns and dumplings, also Beijingese
    specialties, appear in abundance, such as the pan-fried spring-onion cake.

The staff is friendly and ready to assist. Leave room for the sweet bean ball—looking for all the world like a donut, it consists of sweet red-bean paste encased in a light dough made of fluffy egg whites. ⊠ *138 Wanchai Rd.,* ☎ *2836–0000. DC, MC, V (for dinner over HK$200).*

CANTONESE

$$$–$$$$ ✕ **Dynasty.** One of the two entrances to this hotel restaurant takes you past a beautiful, two-story-long chandelier to a typically subdued Cantonese environment: beige tones, mirrors, unobtrusive fixtures. The beautiful crockery—designed especially for Dynasty—combines art deco elements with a Buddhist aesthetic. Palm trees and live traditional Chinese music form a total contrast to the modernity outside the windows: neon signs pushing familiar brand names and the Wanchai Ferry traversing the harbor. The menu is extensive, comprising luxurious abalone and bird's nest along with a variety of meat, seafood, and vegetable dishes. The cold chicken marinated in yellow wine and the deep fried tofu are delectable starters. The roast pigeon marinated in champagne sauce is wonderfully prepared, with crispy skin and flavorful meat. (It's not really marinated in champagne, but in a mixture of seasonings and sauces that enhance the flavor of the meat.) Vegetarians may be intrigued by the braised bean curd with gluten puffs, straw mushrooms, and chestnuts. To finish things off, chilled sago cream with mango and grapefruit is the perfect sweet. ⊠ *Renaissance Harbour View, 1 Harbour Rd., 3rd floor,* ☎ *2802–8888. AE, DC, MC, V.*

$–$$ ✕ **Steam and Stew Inn.** You can't miss the red lanterns marking the Inn's entrance down a short alley. This hole in the wall with simple decoration dishes out healthy, home-style Cantonese cooking—it serves red rice and uses no MSG, both rare in Hong Kong. Go for the steamed fish and eggplant casserole (one of the most popular items) or one of the deep-fried dishes, of which they have a wide variety, including an irresistible deep-fried eel. Another find is the double-boiled chicken and ginseng, which helps lower the body heat. If you're concerned about cholesterol, you can request preparation with egg whites rather than whole eggs. There's also a seasonal menu, and dim sum at lunchtime. This gem was opened by a group of young professionals who craved inexpensive, healthy Chinese food, and it draws a young crowd. ⊠ *21– 23 Tai Wong St. E, Wanchai,* ☎ *2529–3913. MC, V. No lunch Sun.*

SHANGHAINESE

$$$ ✕ **Lao Ching Hing.** One of the oldest Shanghainese restaurants in Hong Kong (open since 1955), Lao Ching Hing has earned its good name over the years. From simple stuff such as the Shanghainese buns and dumplings to deluxe braised shark's fin, you're bound to find something intriguing. Chicken in wine sauce and sautéed river shrimp are popular. Also check out the famous Shanghainese dumplings and buns. For a real adventure, investigate the braised sea cucumber in brown sauce for its distinct texture and strong sauce. Try the freshwater crab if you're here in September or October. ⊠ *Century Hong Kong Hotel, 238 Jaffe Rd., basement,* ☎ *2598–6080. AE, MC, V.*

VEGETARIAN

$ ✕ **Nice Fragrance Vegetarian Kitchen.** Ingredients as simple as bean curd, mushrooms, and taro are whipped into unexpected and delicious forms here. Don't be surprised to see a whole fish on the next table: taro paste molded into a fish shape and deep-fried is one of the most popular dishes in Chinese vegetarian cooking. Crispy on the outside and succulent inside, the "fish" is served with a tangy sweet-and-sour sauce. Assorted vegetables wrapped in a sheet of bean curd form a flavorful combo that might surprise your palate, and a delicious fried rice with both tomato and white sauce will please those who can't make up their mind which way to go. Vegetarian dim sum and a snack counter at the door round out the offerings. ✉ *105–107 Thomson Rd.,* ☎ *2838–3608 or 2838–3067. AE, DC, MC, V.*

VIETNAMESE

$ ✕ **Saigon Beach.** This tiny place can seat only about 20, so avoid coming here at rush hour unless you don't mind standing in line. The decor, an amalgam of nautical paraphernalia—cheap plastic fish hung from nets, folding chairs, and Formica tables, isn't likely to impress. Rather, the authentic Vietnamese fare and the opportunity to rub convivial elbows with people who know the place well more than make up for the unprepossessing environs. Soft-shell crab and lemon chicken, washed down with French 33 beer, are always a pleasure. ✉ *66 Lockhart Rd.,* ☎ *2529–7823. No credit cards.*

European
ITALIAN

$$$$ ✕ **Grissini.** It's named after the Italian breadstick, and you won't miss the aroma of a long one baking visibly in the oven as you walk in. Grissini specializes in Milanese cuisine. The antipasto *misto* is a collection of delicately presented appetizers including tomato and fresh buffalo mozzarella—some of the best in town. The Venetian green-pea risotto with glazed goose liver is simply divine. Entrées range from seafood to veal and lamb, but it's more exciting to try the potato- and herb-filled rabbit saddle with black-truffle sauce, or the osso bucco signature dish. Not to be outdone, the Wine Gallery houses 1,000 bottles of mainly new– and old–world Italian wines. Sabayon parfait with almond praline and aged balsamic vinegar brings the meal to a climax. ✉ *Grand Hyatt, 1 Harbour Rd., 2nd floor,* ☎ *2588–1234. Reservations essential. AE, DC, MC, V.*

International
ECLECTIC

$$ ✕ **Grand Cafe.** Grander than you'd expect for a coffee shop, the Grand Cafe has an impressive menu. "Sandwich" is interpreted loosely here—marinated lamb fillet on naan bread is one option—and you can opt for quesadillas, pastas, and Asian-style noodles and rice in addition to such proteins as free-range chicken, pan-fried veal chops, and oven-glazed king prawns. Start with a salad or a creative appetizer such as steamed asparagus with cold-pressed olive oil, poached egg, and shaved Parmesan, a dish that outperforms the fare at far pricier restaurants. The Hainanese chicken rice with soup is as flavorful and ample as this traditional Chinese dish is meant to be. Desserts—sorbets, tarts, and cakes—are heavenly. The café draws both locals and tourists, not to mention a few long-term resident sparrows, who flutter around overhead and enjoy whatever crumbs diners will share with them. ✉ *Grand Hyatt Hotel, 1 Harbour Rd.,* ☎ *2588–1234, ext. 7273. AE, DC, MC, V.*

$–$$ ✕ **Open Kitchen.** This sit-down cafeteria in the Hong Kong Arts Centre has a large selection of good food and a nice view of the harbor. It's ideal for a pre- or post-performance meal or coffee. Flavors range from Malaysian *laksa*—a rich and flavorsome noodle with bean curd, shrimp, fish ball, and spices—and Indian curries to fresh Italian pasta and fish-and-chips, not to mention a nice selection of pastries for dessert or coffee. The spacious and quiet seating areas are always tidy, and you can linger and read here undisturbed. The balcony area offers an excellent view of the Victoria Harbour. ✉ *Hong Kong Arts Centre, 2 Harbour Road, 6th floor,* ☎ *2827–2923. AE, MC, V (for over HK$150).*

Causeway Bay

Home to a series of large Japanese department stores, Causeway Bay is one of Hong Kong's busiest shopping districts and becomes a real cultural phenomenon on Saturday afternoon. The density of the population can be overwhelming. Several pubs are in the vicinity, but they're not concentrated on one strip; likewise, there are several good restaurants, but they can be hard for the uninitiated to find. Times Square, a huge, modern shopping mall, has four floors of restaurants in one of its towers, serving international cuisines including Korean, French, steak, and regional Chinese.

Asian

CANTONESE

$$$$ ✗ **Forum.** The name of this prestigious restaurant connotes two things: chef Yeung Koon Yat and his special abalone. Yeung has earned an international reputation with his Ah Yat abalone. The price is steep, but if you want to experience this luxurious Oriental ingredient, you really must come here. Your beautiful abalone is boiled and braised to perfection and served with a rich brown sauce—one of the most extravagant dishes in Cantonese cooking. Shark's-fin soup and bird's nest are the next two stars, and if you want to leave with some cash in hand, you can choose from several more-affordable Cantonese dishes. ⊠ *485 Lockhart Rd.,* ☎ *2891–2516, AE, DC, MC, V.*

$$ ✗ **Dim Sum.** Most restaurants in Hong Kong serve dim sum only at
★ lunchtime, but this elegant jewel breaks with tradition and serves it from dusk till dawn. The menu goes beyond Cantonese morsels from the essential *har gau* (steamed shrimp dumpling) to northern choices such as chili prawn dumplings, Beijing onion cakes, and steamed buns. The creative lobster bisque and abalone dumplings are popular picks. Lunch reservations are not taken on weekends, so there's always a long line. Arrive early, or admire the antique telephones and posters of old Chinese advertisements while you wait. Happy Valley is near Causeway Bay, but not near the MTR; take a tram or a cab to get here. ⊠ *63 Sing Woo Rd., Happy Valley,* ☎ *2834–8893. AE, DC, MC, V.*

European

CONTEMPORARY

$$–$$$ ✗ **Talk of the Town (ToTT's).** Talk of the Town sits atop the Excelsior Hotel, looking down on Causeway Bay and the marina. The funky decor, which includes zebra-stripe chairs, a central oval bar, and designer tableware, is matched by the East-meets-West cuisine. Caesar salad with tandoori chicken is a good example of the culinary collision, and just as appetizing is the lobster-tail salad. The red-crab bisque in baby papaya is a house specialty, while soba noodle with crab spring rolls is light yet absolutely flavorsome. The grilled rare tuna steak is another longstanding favorite, and the sampler platter of desserts is a grand finale. Live music kicks in late during the evening, offering a chance to burn a few calories on the dance floor. ⊠ *Excelsior Hotel, 281 Gloucester Rd.,* ☎ *2837–6786. AE, DC, MC, V.*

FRENCH

$$$ ✗ **W's Entrecote.** W's is a dining dictatorship: you can order steak, steak, or steak. Your only choices have to do with size and cooking time. Some call this the best steak in town, and the price includes a salad and as many fries as you can eat. The wine list is French, as is the interior: red-and-white checked tablecloths and French posters. Perched at the top of bustling Times Square, it's ideal for a bout of protein and carbohydrate replenishment after battling the crowds. ⊠ *1303 Times Square, 13th floor,* ☎ *2506–0133. AE, DC, MC, V.*

ITALIAN

$$ ✗ **Fat Angelo's.** People cram into this place—partly for the lively atmosphere, but mostly for the huge piles of pasta that weigh down the tables. Fat Angelo's is an Italian-American–style diner, its green-checked tablecloths and wooden chairs watched from the walls by prints of elder Italian commonfolk. Portions come in "big" (serving five–eight) and "not so big" (serving two–four). Favorites are the mounds of steamed green-lipped mussels in tomato sauce, massive meatballs, roast chicken with rosemary, and pastas of every kind. Linguini with pesto is hearty and fulfilling. Meals come with a salad and a bread basket. Wine is served in water glasses. ⊠ *414 Jaffe Rd.,* ☎ *2574–6263. AE, DC, MC, V.*

Seafood

$$–$$$ ✗ **Island Seafood & Oyster Bar.** Tucked into a Causeway Bay shopping area that was once Hong Kong's Food Street, this laid-back spot is drawing foodies back. The deliciously fresh oysters come in several varieties from around the world. Pick them as creamy or firm as you like from the oyster bar, where the staff will happily make suggestions and serve the sexy mollusk on ice or cooked hot to your taste. (Note that eating raw shellfish can put you at risk for hepatitis.) Read the chalkboard for daily specials, which are bound to include seafood and meat. ⊠ *Shop C, Towning Mansion, 50–56 Paterson St.,* ☎ *2915–7110. AE, DC, MC, V.*

Aberdeen

Seafood

$$–$$$ ✗ **Jumbo Floating Restaurant.** This is it—the floating restaurant you see on postcards. A huge, pagoda-shape building that burns with a thousand lights at night, it floats replete with a throne for all those visiting emperors. It sounds more like a sightseeing outing than a meal, and indeed it's one of the most interesting dining experiences you may have in Hong Kong. Jumbo comprises three floating outlets—Tai Pat, Sea Palace, and Jumbo Palace, where you eat "on board." Naturally enough, seafood is the draw, and it's made the old-fashioned way: you peer into the fish tank, pick your prey, and it shows up on your table in minutes. (There's also an à la carte menu.) You get here by shuttle ferry; ferries depart every 2–3 minutes from Shum Wan Pier, every 15 minutes from Aberdeen Pier. *Shum Wan Pier Path, Wong Chuk Hang,* ☎ *2553–9111. AE, DC, MC, V.*

Repulse Bay

The south side of Hong Kong Island is a string of beaches, rocky coves, and luxury developments, and Repulse Bay, 20 minutes by bus from Central, comprises all three. Popular on weekends and in summer, its beach is one of the best on the island, and The Repulse Bay complex houses a number of quality restaurants and shops along with serviced apartments.

Asian

PAN-ASIAN

$$–$$$ ✗ **Spices.** Alfresco dining is something of a rarity in Hong Kong, but at Spices you can dine on classic Asian food surrounded by lawns and patios. (If the weather fails, there's an elegant interior.) The menu here flies from India to Japan and back again. Singaporean satay of beef, chicken, and lamb and Indonesian *kuwe udang goreng* (deep-fried prawn cakes) make good starters. Main courses include Indian tandoori plates, Vietnamese fried soft-shell crabs, Japanese beef *shogayaki* (pan-fried fillet with sake sauce), and Malaysian *char kwayt teow* (seafood fried noodles). Curry lovers can try different versions, with varying degrees of spice, from India, Vietnam, Singapore, and Indonesia; these involve mutton, duck, chicken, seafood, and even oxtail. Combine them with one of several Indian breads. ⊠ *The Repulse Bay, 109 Repulse Bay Rd.,* ☎ *2812–2711. AE, DC, MC, V.*

European
CONTEMPORARY

$$$ ✕ **The Verandah.** Step into another era here: the walls are white; the
★ doors are dark wood; fans spin silently high overhead; champagne-cock-
tail trolleys cross the cool, granite-tile floor; palm trees wave through
the arched teak windows; and tuxedoed waiters attend to your every
whim. A pianist entertains while budding Bogarts and Bergmans act
out (or watch) the romance. The Verandah is an unashamed celebra-
tion of the halcyon days of colonial rule, and creates popular appeal
by serving an excellent Sunday brunch and daily afternoon tea. It
comes into its own at night, however, when the chef designs innova-
tive and impressive combinations. Boston lobster with scrambled egg
topped with sevruga caviar, for instance, perfectly blends the essence
of each of the three ingredients. Other culinary specialties include
mustard-crumbled rack of lamb, giant sea scallops with green as-
paragus and basil, and slowly braised Atlantic salmon with Burgundy
snail ragout. For dessert, Verandah's soufflé is a classic. ✉ *109 Re-
pulse Bay Rd.,* ☎ *2812–2722. AE, DC, MC, V.*

Stanley Village

A visit to Stanley Village reveals another side of Hong Kong: a much
slower pace of life than in the city. After exploring the market, historical
sights, and beaches, take a leisurely meal at one of the top-notch but
laid-back restaurants scattered around, some of which have harbor views.

European
FRENCH

$$–$$$ ✕ **Lucy's.** There's something incredibly comforting about Lucy's. The
★ lighting is low, the decor is warm, and the waiters are friendly and ca-
sual, creating a generally laid-back atmosphere. This intimate restaurant
draws regulars back again and again. A colorful chalkboard lists the chef's
recommendations for the day as well as a list of wines from around the
globe. The food is fresh and lovingly presented with familiar tastes com-
bined in dishes that lack any pretentiousness but deliver full flavor and
satisfaction. Starters such as leek and Gruyère tart with delicious short
pastry, and roasted vegetables with soft fresh mozzarella and cheese souf-
flé deserve a thumbs-up. A good selection of vegetarian dishes includes
grilled courgette and goat cheese stack. Lamb fillet with mushroom and
rosemary is gorgeous, and duck breast on a bed of red cabbage and crunchy
snow peas, enhanced by a red wine, is amazingly tender and sweet. Warm
chocolate pudding with melting crème anglaise sends you home happy.
✉ *64 Stanley Main St.,* ☎ *2813–9055. MC, V.*

$$–$$$ ✕ **Stanley's French Restaurant.** A recent move up the road has not di-
★ minished Stanley's appeal. Both floors now have beautiful harbor
views from balconies, adding to the romantic quasi-Mediterranean atmo-
sphere. The colors are soft; wood blends nicely with eye-catching tiles,
and the curtains match the pretty cushions on the wrought-iron chairs.
Mardi Gras parade posters in French and sketches of Parisian ladies
of the night look down from the walls. The glazed quail with Roque-
fort-cheese mousse is a marriage made in heaven, and the warm lob-
ster salad with artichoke heart is a favorite. Seasonal items are featured
on a daily chalkboard and tend to be in great demand. Finish the evening
off with a light soufflé or a selection of cheeses from the Swiss Alps.
The ninth-floor suite, which seats up to 30 and has its own kitchen, is
ideal for private functions. ✉ *90B Stanley Main St., 1st–2nd floors,*
☎ *2813–8873. Reservations essential. AE, DC, MC, V.*

Shek O

Shek O is a tiny seaside village, but it has a few decent open-air restaurants. And once you've made the trek—the longest overland trip possible from Central—you'll need some sustenance.

Asian

CHINESE-THAI

$ ✕ **Shek O Chinese and Thailand Seafood Restaurant.** Nothing particularly stands out about the food or aesthetics here, but this place is a legend—it's just such *fun.* On summer weekends, people arrive en masse and sit for hours despite the relentless heat. The curious hybrid cuisine ensures plenty of rice, noodle, and fish dishes. The *tom yung kung* (spicy prawn and coconut soup) is guaranteed to bring color to your cheeks; the green curry is a safe chicken choice; and the honey-fried squid is amazing. The festive ambience is a real experience, and you'll eat heartily without breaking the bank. ✉ *303 Shek O Village (main intersection, next to the bus stop),* ☎ *2809–4426. Reservations essential on weekends. AE, DC, MC, V (for over HK$300).*

KOWLOON

Parts of Kowloon are among the most densely populated areas on the planet, and support a corresponding abundance of restaurants. Many hotels, planted here for the view of Hong Kong Island (spectacular at night), also have excellent restaurants, though they're uniformly expensive. You may have just as much luck walking into places on a whim, though of course you'll take your chances. Some of the best food in Kowloon is served in the back streets, where immigrants from Vietnam, Thailand, and all over Asia keep their native cooking skills sharp.

Kowloon City

Locals flock to Kowloon City for casual, authentic, tasty meals at affordable prices.

Asian

CANTONESE

$–$$ ✕ **Tso Choi Koon.** If you're of delicate constitution, or insist on fine food, pass on this home-style Cantonese restaurant. Tso Choi (Rough Dishes) is not everyone's cup of tea. Tripe lovers and haggis fans, however, might like to try the Chinese versions of some of their favorites: fried pig tripe, fried pig brain (served as an omelet), double-boiled pig brain . . . you get the idea. The older Hong Kong generation still likes this stuff; younger folks may demur. The wary can opt for creamy congee, fried chicken, or a fish fillet. ✉ *17–19A Nga Tsin Wai Rd.,* ☎ *2383–7170. No credit cards.*

THAI

$ ✕ **Golden Orchid Thai Restaurant.** Only a five-minute walk from the former Kai Tak Airport, Golden Orchid serves some of the best and most innovative Thai cuisine in the territory. The curried crab and the seafood curry in pumpkin are excellent. Proactive eaters should not miss *mein come,* a kind of Thai leaf served with little bowls of spices and fixings such as fried coconut, peanuts, garlic, chili, lime, and dried shrimp. Wrap your choices in the leaf and delve in. The steamed seafood cakes, served in Thai stone pots, are also delicious. Try the roasted pork-neck slices, prawn cakes, and rice with olives. Unlike most restaurants on planet Earth, the Golden Orchid neither levies a service charge nor accepts tips, making this already cheap place a major bargain. ✉ *12 Lung Kong Rd.,* ☎ *2383–3076. MC, V.*

THE DIM SUM EXPERIENCE

A **VISIT TO HONG KONG** is not complete without a visit to a dim sum restaurant. Dim sum is the staple food in Hong Kong and is always accompanied by Chinese tea. Served from before dawn to around 5 or 6 pm, these traditional Cantonese daytime tidbits are miniature works of art. More than 2,000 kinds of dim sum are in the Cantonese repertoire, and most dim sum restaurants prepare 100 varieties daily. Don't belittle these bite-size morsels, though. Many are filled with such ingredients as pork, prawns, rice, and flour, and can efficiently fill up your stomach before you even notice it.

In the old days, dim sum restaurants were always associated with noise. Trolleys filled with steaming dishes were pushed around in restaurants while dim sum ladies shouted the names of the dishes. Today, in many of Hong Kong's hundreds of dim-sum restaurants, a dim sum order form awaits you at the table and is subsequently stamped as your dishes arrive.

Generally steamed in bamboo steamers, panfried, baked, or deep-fried, the buns, crepes, and cakes are among the world's finest hors d'oeuvres. Many are minor culinary achievements—such as a soup with prawns served in a translucent rice-pastry shell, or a thousand-layer cake, or the ubiquitous spring roll. Most items come in a serving for three or four, allowing diners to share a good variety of delicacies around a table. Although every restaurant has its own dim sum menu, certain traditional items can be found in almost all dim sum outlets.

Popular dim sum items you need to know before a fun and fulfilling dim sum hunting meal include:

Cha siu bao: barbecued pork buns

Cha siu so: baked barbecued pork pastry

Cheong fun: steamed rice rolls (with various fillings such as prawns, beef, barbecued-pork buns and more)

Chun kuen: spring rolls

Dan tart: baked egg tarts

Har gau: steamed prawn dumplings with a light translucent wrap

Har kok: deep-fried prawn dumplings

Lou mei gai: glutinous rice wrapped in lotus leaf

Ngau yuk: steamed beef balls

Siu mai: steamed pork dumplings

Don't be surprised, however, if you discover some novelty items that you, or even your Hong Kong friends, have never heard of. Dim sum chefs in Hong Kong like to come up with innovative ideas and introduce creative elements to make a dim sum meal satisfying.

Sai Kung

Renowned for its seafood restaurants and neighborhood hill-walking tracks, Saikung is a town worth investigating. Many restaurants run adjoining seafood shops, so you can select fresh catch from tanks and have it cooked to order—steamed, fried, sautéed, or deep-fried with salt and pepper. You'll also find a good selection of Western restaurants serving delicious food with an easy, intimate, and laid-back ambience.

International

$$ ✕ **Jaspa's.** What could be better than heading straight to a cozy restaurant after a day out in the countryside? Here the food is always deliciously fulfilling, perfect after a day walking in the hills or fun-seeking in the water. Whether sitting out on the terrace or indoors, an enjoyable dining experience is guaranteed. Goat cheese parcel makes a delectable starter, and tasty Jaspa's chicken fajitas arrives on your table sizzling hot. Pasta with bay bugs and lamb chop never disappoint. The hearty food and friendly service makes Jaspas a key culinary attraction in Sai Kung. ⊠ *13 Sha Tsui Path,* ☎ *2792–6388. AE, MC, V.*

Seafood

$$–$$$ ✕ **Chung Thai Food Restaurant and Sea Food.** As its name suggests, this seafood corner is best known for both Chinese and Thai cooking, prepared separately by chefs of both nationalities. Those with a taste for spice can try the Thai fried crabs with curry or fried prawns with chili; otherwise, pick any seafood you like from the store next door, and the chef will prepare it to order. Steaming is highly recommended for fresh fish, as it retains the fresh taste and tender texture. ⊠ *93 Man Nin St.,* ☎ *2792–1481;* ⊠ *Seafood shop, 5 Siu Yat Bldg., Hoi Pong Sq.,* ☎ *2792–8172. MC, V.*

$$–$$$ ✕ **Tung Kee Seafood Restaurant.** Here you just order whatever you want from the deep blue ocean. Lobsters, slipper lobsters, clams, abalone, crabs, prawns, and fish of all kind are for the tasting. Crustaceans and fish are quickly cooked by steaming and wok-frying, and are presented whole, leaving no illusions as to the freshness of your food. A quick look inside the tank is better than a marine biology lesson. Pick your favorites, and leave the rest for the chef. From lobster sashimi to steamed fish, this well-established eatery will impress you a feast *de la mer.* ⊠ *96–102 Man Nin St.,* ☎ *2792–7453. AE, DC, MC, V.*

Tsim Sha Tsui

Tsim Sha Tsui, on the tip of Kowloon, is crammed with shops and with dining options, from five-star hotels to holes in the wall.

Asian

CANTONESE

$$$–$$$$ ✕ **Spring Moon.** Yes, it's like old Shanghai—antique-style teak floors with Oriental rugs, oak paneling, stained glass, elm chairs and tables, dim lighting, a traditional tea-leaf cabinet displaying some 200 miniature clay teapots, and a showcase of porcelain and old silverware. Everything at Spring Moon is très Shanghai except, funnily enough, the cuisine. This prestigious restaurant at the Peninsula has changed its look, but the kitchen still turns out first-rate Cantonese food. Waiters prepare drunken prawns right at your table, subtly infusing them with the aroma of Shaoxing wine. Braised abalone in oyster sauce, with freshly cooked vegetables, is rich in flavor and melts in your mouth. The popular roast pigeon flavored with cinnamon is another winner. Even a team of tea masters (tea sommeliers, if you will) can help you flatter your meal with one of 20 different teas. ⊠ *The Peninsula, Salisbury Rd.,* ☎ *2315–3160. AE, DC, MC, V.*

$$$ ✕ **T'ang Court.** Bedecked with golden silk drapes and contemporary sculptures, T'ang Court is one of the most elegant Chinese restaurants on the Kowloon peninsula. Spread over two floors connected by a spiral staircase, its distinctly modern look is offset by its foundation of traditional Chinese cuisine—the home-style Cantonese soups will make you feel like you're dining with a Chinese family. After covering its bases, however, the menu gets creative: baked blue-point oysters with port wine make an unfamiliar and beautiful appetizer. The baked salty chicken (half or whole) has delicately flavored meat and a gorgeously crispy skin. Desserts are just as irresistible: try the steamed pumpkin dumplings with egg-yolk cream. Lunchtime dim sum, from steamed shrimp dumplings to barbecue-pork buns, are real delicacies. ⊠ *Great Eagle Hotel, 8 Peking Rd.,* ☎ *2375–1133, ext. 2250. AE, DC, MC, V.*

$ ✕ **Happy Garden Noodle & Congee Kitchen.** For a taste of down-to-earth Hong Kong fare without the intimidation of trespassing in Chinese-only local joints, Happy Garden is the place to go. Bright and clean, with helpful waitresses and an English menu, this small place works for a typical local breakfast, an easy lunch, and even a big dinner. A popular morning combination is Cantonese congee and a glutinous rice dumpling wrapped in lotus leaf. A bowl of wonton soup or a plate of fried rice or noodles makes a simple but satisfying lunch. For dinner, the diced chicken with cashew nuts and sweet-and-sour pork are delicious Cantonese staples. ⊠ *76 Canton Rd.,* ☎ *2377–2603 or 2377–2604. No credit cards.*

SEAFOOD

$$$$ ✕ **Yü.** You're welcomed by denizens of the deep, peering out from a huge, curving aquarium. Yü is a seafood lover's dream—look elsewhere for food of terrestrial origin. Start things off with some oysters—served on ice, glazed with champagne sauce, or prepared a variety of other ways. Lobster bisque and sautéed jumping shrimp with chili and pepper are perfect hot appetizers. Moving over to the fish tank, a dozen or so fresh catches of the day are cooked to suit either Asian or Western tastes, and some specialties combine the two, such as sautéed Boston lobster with black beans and fine noodles. The atmosphere is entirely laid-back, making this a great place to enjoy a drink and fresh seafood with an unobstructed view of the harbor and, at night, the stunning light show on the island side. ⊠ *Regent Hotel, 18 Salisbury Rd.,* ☎ *2721–1211. Reservations essential. AE, DC, MC, V. No lunch.*

$$$ ✕ **Oyster & Wine Bar.** Lovers of that sensuous slippery mollusk the oyster should definitely consider a trip to the top of Sheraton Hotel & Towers. On its 18th floor, set against a romantic backdrop of Hong Kong's twinkling harbor, diners can slurp their way through 32 types of oysters freshly flown in from around the world and kept alive on ice at the huge oyster bar, ready for shucking. The current record for oysters consumed in one sitting stands at nearly 60. Besides oysters, prepared dishes include the rack of baby lamb and lobster bouillabaisse. A selection of wine from around the world is stored in wine cellars that line the walls. The friendly waiters will happily show you the day's menu on a colorfully decorated chalk board. ⊠ *Sheraton Hotel & Towers, 20 Nathan Rd.,* ☎ *2369–1111. AE, DC, MC, V. No lunch.*

SHANGHAINESE

$$ ✕ **Great Shanghai Restaurant.** Great Shanghai is not esteemed for its decor (which is old and dingy), but it's perfect for those who prefer the bold flavors of Shanghainese food to the more delicate tastes of local Cantonese fare. You may not be ready for the sea blubber or braised turtle with sugar candy, but do try one of the boneless eel dishes, the Shanghai-style yellow fish soup, the beggar's chicken, or the excellent spiced soy duck. The Peking chicken in this establishment is as good as those from any Beijing restaurant. ⊠ *26–36 Prat Ave.,* ☎ *2366–8158. AE, DC, MC, V.*

$$ ✕ **Wu Kong.** You won't miss the big sign hanging out in the air just at the intersection of Nathan Road and Peking Road, but you can easily miss the tiny entrance that leads down to this unpretentious restaurant. Nevertheless, the small entrance belies the big basement dining room where first-rate Shanghainese fare is offered at a reasonable price. The pigeon in wine sauce is an excellent appetizer to share. The subtle sauce prepared with Chinese wine adds a delicate aroma to the meat pieces arranged in the shape of the bird. Vegetarian goose with vegetables wrapped in crispy bean-curd skin is delicious and authentic. A whole fish smothered in a piquant sweet and vinegary sauce makes you want more. Leave some space for the deep-fried sweet ball whipped up with fluffy egg white stuffed with red bean and banana—a very good alternative to the doughnut you're missing. ⊠ *Alpha House, 23–33 Nathan Rd., basement (entrance on Peking Rd.),* ☎ *2366–7244. AE, DC, MC, V.*

VEGETARIAN

$–$$ ✕ **Kung Tak Lam.** Health-conscious diners will appreciate this simple Shanghainese vegetarian food. Don't turn your back when you see the no-frills decor; it's the food that makes this place so popular. Try the cold noodle plates, which come with an array of sauces to mix and match for as sweet or sour a flavor as you want. The bean-curd ravioli also gets a big thumbs up. Set-price meals are incredibly cheap. ⊠ *45–47 Carnarvon Rd., 1st floor,* ☎ *2367–7881. AE, DC, V.*

European

FRENCH

$$$$ ✕ **Gaddi's.** Gaddi's is a world unto itself. A private elevator takes you to the lobby overlooking the spacious restaurant, designed to evoke the hotel's original 1928 neoclassical elegance. The crystal chandeliers and sparkling silverware create a classical look. It's also one of the few places left where well-trained waiters carry out full service, such as dramatically flaming dishes at your table. Although Gaddi's is moving forward, it retains its exceptional quality and gracious style. The menu has eased slightly from its former classical French style, relying less on heavy sauces and concentrating more on perfecting nature's finest flavors. Raw marinated goose liver with white grapes set in Muscat aspic is sweet, rich, and verging on sinful. An intensely flavored chilled tomato soup with deep-fried scampi tails is a refreshing pre–main course pick-me-up. Bresse pigeon, a must on any self-respecting fine dining menu, is cooked two ways—the succulent red breast has the skin removed and is poached, while the leg is pan-fried with the skin intact. Bathed in a beautiful and intense duck-liver and pine-nut sauce, with mouth-puckeringly full-flavored tomatoes, it's simply delicious. End with the cheese board. ⊠ *Peninsula Hotel, Salisbury Rd.,* ☎ *2366–6251, ext. 3989. Reservations essential. Jacket and tie required for dinner. AE, DC, MC, V.*

International

CONTEMPORARY

$$$$ ✕ **Felix.** Felix sits on the 28th floor of The Peninsula and should be
★ on every traveler's list of places to go, even if only for an overpriced drink at the bar. Love it or hate it, you can't deny that both the interior and the views are stunning. Every nook and cranny in this ultramodern space was designed by the French designer Philippe Starck, from chairs bearing the faces of Starck's friends to the most celebrated bathrooms in Asia. After dark, Hong Kong Island glitters from across the harbor through a floor-to-ceiling glass wall. On busy nights there's a buzz that's hard to find anywhere else. Some find the high-tech look unsettling, but its fans hail it as a "brasserie for the 21st century." The

menu is no less adventurous; the Hawaiian chef mixes interesting ingredients in bold ways. Sautéed foie gras comes on ginger-marinated figs, tangy triangles of wrapped duck arrive with a mango salsa, and an intriguing salad of palm hearts and spinach is served with poached prawns. Grilled veal with a wasabi gratin gets the juices flowing, and unusual items such as moonfish turn up in season. Watch people's expressions when their desserts arrive. ⊠ *Peninsula Hotel, Salisbury Rd., 28th floor,* ☎ *2366–6251. DC, MC, V.*

North American

$$$ ✕ **The Bostonian American Bar & Restaurant.** It's a bit hard to find, but the Bostonian is worth the effort. Fun yet respectable, it's popular for both business and pleasure. Each table has crayons and a paper tablecloth to keep you busy, and the walls are adorned with previous diners' artworks. Seafoodies should not miss the lobster thermidor— a perfectly cooked crustacean smothered in delicious cheese sauce on a bed of mashed potatoes. Before you make up your mind, though, have a look at the flying seafood tray, piled with sumptuous seafood from sea bass to Dover sole, fresh oysters to Dungeness crabs. A wide selection of American wines ensures a match for your meal, and the staff is helpful and friendly. The bar upstairs serves sandwiches at lunchtime and tapas and cocktails in the evening. ⊠ *Great Eagle Hotel, 8 Peking Rd.,* ☎ *2375–1133, ext. 2070. AE, DC, MC, V.*

$$ ✕ **Planet Hollywood.** Come see Jackie Chan and Sylvester Stallone's handprints, grab a souvenir T-shirt, and enjoy a hilarious movie-museum tour. The food, with choices for both Eastern and Western palates, is satisfying, but it's the outrageous decor (movie pictures, props, and costumes) that packs a bigger punch. ⊠ *3 Canton Rd., Harbour City,* ☎ *2377–7888. AE, DC, MC, V.*

Tsim Sha Tsui East

European
ITALIAN

$$$ ✕ **Mistral.** You know you're on to a good thing when a customer is overheard asking for the same cheese they had when last visiting the restaurant more than a year ago. Such is the following Mistral has among its clientele, who are largely Italian nationals and expatriates in search of a true taste of home. Located in the basement, the restaurant is packed every night with diners obviously enjoying themselves. The cozy, candlelit interior buzzes with conversation and the restaurant manager is known by most of the customers as a source of knowledge as well as a friendly face. The large open kitchen serves a selection of exquisitely prepared delicacies, such as sea bass served with its skin deep-fried on an eggplant mash with rosemary, and potato soufflé and chicken livers. ⊠ *Grand Stanford Inter-Continental Harbour View, 70 Mody Rd.,* ☎ *2731–2878. AE, DC, MC, V. Closed Sun.*

$$$ ✕ **Sabatini.** Run by the Sabatini family, who also run eponymous restaurants in Rome, Japan, and Singapore, this Italian spot is unbeatable for a romantic rendezvous, with warm, rag-finished walls, wooden furnishings, impeccable service, and windows that look onto the trees and shrubbery of the Royal Garden's atrium. The pasta dishes are first-rate, particularly the lovable linguine Sabatini—cooked in a marvelous marinara sauce, fresh tomato, and garlic, and served with an array of luscious seafood. Shellfish lovers will have a hard time choosing between the lobster with lobster juice and tomato sauce, and the juicy, meaty grilled scampi. A classic mistake at Sabatini is to stuff oneself with the first two courses, leaving no room for the terrific tiramisu or refreshing wild-berry pudding. Pace yourself, and don't hesitate to ask the knowledgeable manager for advice on both food and wine. ⊠ *Royal*

Garden, 69 Mody Rd., 3rd floor, ☎ 2733–2000. Reservations essential. AE, DC, MC, V.

North American

$$–$$$ ✕ **Napa.** Perched on the top floor of the Kowloon Shangri-La, Napa gives Pacific Rim foods the full California treatment. Glittering harbor views, soft live jazz and blues, and friendly waiters create a cozy yet smart ambience. The lunch menu has a section of "lite" items; dinner focuses on fish, fowl, and meat. Seared scallops and foie gras in a sherry vinaigrette form a tantalizing starter, while crisp-skinned salmon with asparagus, Portobello mushrooms, and a cabernet reduction lives up to its promise as a main course. Succulent saddle of Australian lamb with a mushroom flan, wilted spinach, and white-cheese pesto is a good choice for carnivores. To enhance your dinner, choose from the wide selection of California wines. ⊠ Kowloon Shangri-La, 64 Mody Rd., 21st floor, ☎ 2721–2111. AE, DC, MC, V.

OUTER ISLANDS

Lamma Island

Lamma Island is relatively easy to get to, with ferries leaving Central's pier almost hourly. Yung Shue Wan, where you disembark, has a collection of local seafood restaurants, one or two Western ones, and an odd assortment of shops.

Asian

CANTONESE

$ ✕ **Lancombe.** This Cantonese seafood restaurant is Lamma's best source for no-nonsense food at no-nonsense prices. The huge English/Cantonese menu features seafood, seafood, and more seafood. Try deep-fried squid, garoupa in sweet corn sauce, broccoli in garlic, and beef with black beans. Dishes come in three sizes; the small one is generally sufficient. Go through the front of the restaurant via the kitchen (don't loiter—they're busy in there!) to the terrace out back, where you'll have a view of the sea and distant Peng Chau Island. ⊠ 47 Main St., Yung Shue Wan, ☎ 2982–0881. AE, MC, V.

International

$ ✕ **Deli Lamma.** This trendy but relaxed joint has more style than any other place on Lamma, with a designer bar made from old doors suspended from the ceiling on heavy chains and backgammon and chess boards painted on long tables along one wall, encouraging lazy afternoons with endless cups of coffee. Choose your fancy from two blackboards that will bear up to seven choices of pasta and "world" food—from Thai fish curry to British roasts and Indian curries. Your order comes with salad or yummy slabs of fresh garlic bread. Service can be a little too laid-back, but it's always friendly. ⊠ 36 Main St., Yung Shue Wan, ground floor, ☎ 2982–1583. AE, DC, MC, V.

4 LODGING

From breathtaking views, the finest service, and some of the world's top hotels to cheap and cheerful guest houses in neon-lit neighborhoods, Hong Kong has something to suit every budget and taste.

T HE DAYS OF BRITISH RULE are history, but Hong Kong's status as
a financial and business center, as well as gateway to the rest of
China, remains a strong attraction. The region's recent economic
setbacks have been offset by signs of recovery, bringing back flocks of
tourists and businesspeople.

Updated by
Toby Parker

Accommodations can be expensive here, but almost no one pays the
quoted rate. Travel agents both in Hong Kong and abroad frequently
offer huge discounts or package deals that allow you stay at a fine hotel
for a fraction of its full rate. Inquire about bargains before you reserve.
Hotels do their part, too, with such features as discounts and credits
for use in their restaurants and bars. Considering its size, Hong Kong
has more than its fair share of five-star hotels, and more often than
not these provide magnificent views over Victoria Harbour from either the Hong Kong or the Kowloon side. As they focus increasingly
on the business traveler with an expense account, hotels can charge at
least US$150 a night for rooms of a normal international standard.
These may not be in prime locations, but they offer basic and reliable
facilities—color TV, radio, telephone, same-day valet laundry service,
room service, safe-deposit box, refrigerator and minibar, air-conditioning,
and business services. Most hotels also have at least one restaurant and
bar, a travel desk, and limousine or car rental. If you pay the full rate,
many hotels will offer perks such as limousine pickup at the airport.

Of course, it's the business services that set Hong Kong apart. Most
major hotels have business centers that provide secretarial, translation,
courier, telex, fax, Internet, and printing services. Some provide PCs
in-room, while others offer support for guests' own plug-in hardware.
Executive floors or clubs have become standard in well-established hotels; these floors typically have extra concierge services, complimentary breakfast and cocktails, express check-in, personalized stationery,
and an area where guests can meet with their business contacts. Executive rooms also have enhanced business features, such as in-room
fax machines, Internet TV, and twin phone lines, though some charge
extra for their use. Of course, many hotels have ballrooms, and most
have smaller meeting and conference rooms.

For an overview of Hong Kong meeting, convention, and incentive fa-
cilities, contact the **Convention and Incentive Department** (✉ Hong Kong
Tourist Association, 10/F, Citicorp Centre, 18 Whitfield Rd., North Point,
Hong Kong Island, ☎ 2807–6543).

Book your room well in advance for a trip to Hong Kong, especially
in March and from September through early December, the high seasons for conventions and conferences. Some hotels offer attractive
seasonal packages.

The **Hong Kong Tourist Association** (HKTA,www.hkta.org) publishes
the *Hotel Guide,* which lists rates, services, and facilities for all of its
members, but the brochure comes out only once a year, making it at
least one price hike behind. The HKTA does not make hotel reservations. The Hong Kong Hotel Association (HKHA) does, and at no extra
charge, but only through its reservations office at Hong Kong International Airport.

Where to stay in Hong Kong depends on the nature of your trip.
Thanks to the three tunnels that run underneath the harbor, the Star
Ferry, and the Mass Transit Railway (MTR, or subway), it no longer
matters whether you stay "Hong Kong side" or "Kowloon side"; the
other side is only minutes away. The new airport rail link will, upon

your arrival, whisk you over the Tsing Ma Suspension Bridge through Kowloon to Central in around 25 minutes.

If you want to avoid the main tourist accommodation areas, the New Territories and Outer Islands offer a few quieter and cheaper alternatives to Hong Kong Island and Kowloon.

For price ranges, *see* the hotel chart *in* Smart Travel Tips A to Z. Our categories for hotel rates are based on the average price for a standard double room for two people; a single person in a double room will get a slightly lower rate. Prices are higher for a larger room or for a room with a view. All rates are subject to a 10% service charge and a 3% government tax, which is used to fund the activities of the HKTA. Accommodations are grouped by geographical area—Hong Kong Island, Kowloon, and New Territories and the Outer Islands—and neighborhood, and are alphabetical within each price category.

HONG KONG ISLAND

If you need to be near the city's financial hub, you'll prefer the Central or Admiralty Districts, on Hong Kong Island, but will pay for the convenience and views. Central is as busy as New York on weekdays, but, except for the Lan Kwai Fong area, it's quiet at night and on weekends. Nearby, Hong Kong's very own SoHo (South of Hollywood Road) boasts an eclectic mix of restaurants serving everything from Nepalese to modern European cuisine. Wanchai, east of Central, was once a sailor's dream of booze and Suzie Wong types. It still has plenty of nightlife, but new office high-rises and the Hong Kong Convention & Exhibition Centre—the territory's most popular venue for large-scale exhibitions and conferences—now draw businesspeople. Causeway Bay, farther east, is a brightly lit shopping district with restaurants, cinemas, and permanent crowds. Happy Valley is near the racetrack and Hong Kong Stadium, the territory's largest sports facility. Hotels and restaurants have also sprung up farther east along the MTR line, in residential North Point and Taikoo Shing.

Central

$$$$ **Mandarin Oriental.** Long acclaimed as one of the world's great ho-
★ tels, the Mandarin Oriental represents Hong Kong's high end, serving the well-heeled and the business elite since 1963. Take the opportunity to greet Robert Chan, who has been guarding the prestigious entranceway for more than two decades. The hotel has a distinctly timeless elegance: the vast lobby is decorated with Asian antiques, and the comfortable guest rooms have antique maps and prints, traditional wooden furnishings, Eastern knickknacks, and glamorous black-and-gold accents. The well-mannered staff provides extremely efficient service. Bucking the current trend, the rooms are designed for luxury rather than mere efficiency. The top floor houses Vong (☞ Chapter 3), a restaurant run by world-renowned chef Jean-Georges Vongerichten, serving French-Asian fusion cuisine in a contemporary setting overlooking the harbor. Man Wah, on the 25th floor (☞ Chapter 3), serves Cantonese cuisine in a genteel atmosphere. Centrally located beside the Star Ferry concourse, the Mandarin is the lodging of choice for many a celebrity and VIP. A live band performs in the mezzanine Clipper Lounge early in the evening. ⊠ *5 Connaught Rd.,* ☎ *2522–0111; 800/526–6566 in the U.S.,* ℻ *2810–6190. 502 rooms, 40 suites. 4 restaurants, 3 bars, indoor pool, barbershop, beauty salon, health club, business services. AE, DC, MC, V.* ✑

Lodging

Victoria Harbour

KEY

◇ Metro Stops

0 — 440 yards
0 — 400 meters

Bishop Lei International House 48

Booth Lodge 5

BP International House 13

Caritas Bianchi Lodge 6

Century 59

Cheung Chau Warwick 46

City Garden 68

Concourse 8

Conrad International 53

De Ricou–The Repulse Bay 60

Eaton 10

Emperor Happy Valley 61

The Excelsior 65

Furama 51

Garden View International House 52

Gold Coast 1

Grand Hyatt 44

Grand Plaza 62

Grand Stanford Inter-Continental . . . 36

Grand Tower 7

Great Eagle 28

Harbour Plaza 20

Harbour View International House 57

Holiday Inn Golden Mile 30

Holy Carpenter Guest House 17

Hongkong 39

Hyatt Regency 29

Island Shangri-La . . 55

J.W. Marriott 54

Kimberley 24

Kowloon 31

Kowloon Shangri-La 33

Luk Kwok 58

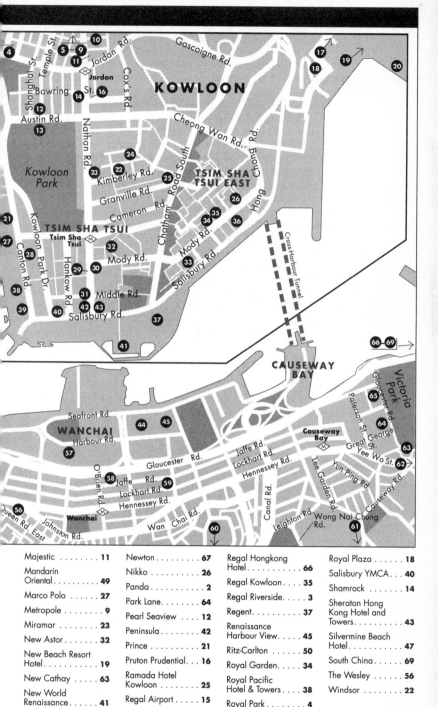

KOWLOON

Gascoigne Rd.

Jordan Rd.

Temple St.

Shanghai St.

Bowring

Jordan St.

Austin Rd.

Cox's Rd.

Nathan Rd.

Cheong Wan Rd.

Hong Chung Rd.

Kowloon Park

Kimberley Rd.

Granville Rd.

Cameron Rd.

Chatham Road South

TSIM SHA TSUI EAST

Kowloon Park Dr.

TSIM SHA TSUI

Tsim Sha Tsui

Mody Rd.

Salisbury Rd.

Hankow Rd.

Canton Rd.

Mody Rd.

Middle Rd.

Salisbury Rd.

Cross-Harbour Tunnel

CAUSEWAY BAY

Seafront Rd.

WANCHAI

Harbour Rd.

Gloucester Rd.

Jaffe Rd.

Lockhart Rd.

Hennessey Rd.

Victoria Park

Paterson St.

Gloucester Rd.

Great George St.

Yee Wo St.

Causeway Bay

O'Brien Rd.

Jaffe Rd.

Lockhart Rd.

Hennessey Rd.

Canal Rd.

Lee Garden Rd.

Yun Ping Rd.

Causeway Rd.

Queen Rd. East

Johnston Rd.

Wanchai

Wan Chai Rd.

Leighton Rd.

Wong Nai Chung Rd.

$$$$ 🏨 **Ritz-Carlton.** A rare gem of a hotel, the Ritz-Carlton couples an air
★   of refinement with superb hospitality. European antiques and repro-
      ductions mix with Asian accents, and everything from the Chippen-
      dale-style furniture to the gilt-frame mirrors is spotless and shining.
      The staff is exceptionally friendly and helpful, and the attention to de-
      tail is nonpareil. Complimentary homemade cookies and mineral water
      in the reception area hint at the level of customer care, and twin bath-
      room sinks, shoe polish, a beautiful tea and coffee cabinet, and fresh
      flowers help make you feel welcome in your own quarters. Rooms have
      colonial-style rosewood furniture and overlook either Victoria Harbour
      or Chater Garden. The main restaurant, Toscana (☞ Chapter 3),
      serves northern Italian cuisine, and a special macrobiotic menu is avail-
      able in the coffee shop and through room service. The Executive Busi-
      ness Center has Internet and E-mail access as well as computer
      workstations and color printers. ⊠ *3 Connaught Rd.,* ☎ *2877–6666;
      800/241–3333 in the U.S.,* FAX *2877–6778. 187 rooms, 29 suites. 5 restau-
      rants, bar, lounge, 13 no-smoking floors, pool, health club, shops, busi-
      ness services. AE, DC, MC, V.* 🐾

$$$ 🏨 **Furama.** Situated in the heart of Central and popular with business
      travelers, this hotel has been one of the best-known in the territory for
      over 25 years. Its excellent conference rooms can hold up to 1,000 del-
      egates, and satellite video-conferencing facilities are available. Rooms
      are spacious and functional; for views of either Chater Garden and Vic-
      toria Peak or City Hall and Victoria Harbor, ask for a room above the
      17th floor. The revolving rooftop restaurant and bar offer the ultimate
      panorama, as well as a spectacular daily lunch and dinner buffet of
      Chinese, Japanese, and Western dishes. The wine room, adjacent to
      the European Rotisserie restaurant, is stocked with hundreds of wines
      to be sampled by the bottle or glass. On the ground floor a bakery sells
      delicious snacks to famished shoppers. ⊠ *1 Connaught Rd.,* ☎ *2525–
      5111,* FAX *2845–9339. 470 rooms, 40 suites. 5 restaurants, bar, lounge,
      5 no-smoking floors, health club, shops, business services. AE, DC,
      MC, V.* 🐾

Admiralty

$$$$ 🏨 **Conrad International.** This luxurious business hotel occupies part
      of a gleaming-white, oval-shape tower rising from Pacific Place, an up-
      scale complex with a multistory mall on the edge of Central. Looking
      down from the top 21 floors of this 61-story building, the rooms have
      dramatic views of the harbor and city. On-staff masseurs can massage
      you in the comfort of your own room on request. The four floors of
      executive rooms have in-room Internet and E-mail access, fax machines,
      and even personal step machines. The restaurant Brasserie on the
      Eighth is popular for its French fare and views of the park; Nicholini's
      (☞ Chapter 3) is one of the city's top spots for Italian cuisine. ⊠ *Pa-
      cific Place, 88 Queensway,* ☎ *2521–3838; 800/445–8667 in the U.S.,*
      FAX *2521–3888. 467 rooms, 46 suites. 4 restaurants, bar, pool, health
      club, business services. AE, DC, MC, V.* 🐾

$$$$ 🏨 **Island Shangri-La.** This deluxe hotel sparkles with more than 780
★   dazzling Austrian crystal chandeliers; no matter where you go, these
      opulent creations hang overhead—in the lobby, in the restaurants,
      and in every single guest room. The world's largest Chinese landscape
      painting, *The Great Motherland of China* hangs in the atrium from
      the 39th through the 55th floors. It took the 40 artists from Beijing
      six months to paint it. Take a trip upward from the 39th floor by the
      elevator for the experience of watching the mainland's misty moun-
      tains drift by. Priding itself on Asian hospitality, the staff is friendly
      and efficient. Extra-large desks in each room are handy for business

travelers, who can also plug in notebook computers readily. You can eat very well at the renowned French eatery Petrus, the classy Lobster Bar (☞ Chapter 3), and the imperial Chinese outlet Summer Palace. The tranquil outdoor pool and health club overlook Hong Kong Park. ⊠ *Supreme Court Rd., 2 Pacific Place, 88 Queensway,* ☎ *2877–3838; 800/942–5050 in the U.S.,* 🄵🄰🄷 *2521–8742. 531 rooms, 34 suites. 4 restaurants, bar, 4 no-smoking floors, pool, barbershop, beauty salon, health club, shops, business services. AE, DC, MC, V.* 🐾

$$$$ 🏨 **J. W. Marriott.** This elegant American-style hotel was the first to open at Pacific Place. Its extravagant, glass-wall atrium lobby has a cascading waterfall and is filled with plants. Rooms have harbor and mountain views and endless amenities, including data ports for modem or fax machines, real coffee machines, and ample work space. JW's California Grill serves popular California cuisine, and the Cigar Bar has a walk-in humidor with more than 100 types of stogies. Fitness facilities include a well-equipped 24-hour gym and an outdoor pool complete with an instant spin-drier for your bathing togs. ⊠ *Pacific Place, 88 Queensway,* ☎ *2810–3000; 800/228–9290 in the U.S.,* 🄵🄰🄷 *2845–0737. 602 rooms, 25 suites. 4 restaurants, 3 bars, 14 no-smoking floors, pool, health club, business services. AE, DC, MC, V.* 🐾

Midlevels

$$ 🏨 **Bishop Lei International House.** Owned and operated by the Catholic diocese, this guest house is in a residential area of the Midlevels. Rooms are clean and functional, and half have harbor views. There's a fully equipped business center, a workout room, a pool, and a restaurant serving Chinese and Western meals. ⊠ *4 Robinson Rd.,* ☎ *2868–0828,* 🄵🄰🄷 *2868–1551. 205 rooms, 2 suites. Restaurant, pool, exercise room, business services. AE, DC, MC, V.*

$ 🏨 **Garden View International House.** This attractive, cylindrical guest
★ house on a hill overlooking the botanical gardens and harbor is run by the YWCA. Its well-designed rooms make excellent use of small, irregular shapes and emphasize the picture windows. If you want to do your own cooking, ask for a suite with a kitchenette (which will include a microwave oven); if not, the coffee shop serves European and Asian dishes. You can also use the swimming pool and gymnasium in the adjoining YWCA. Garden View is a five-minute drive (Bus 12A or Minibus 1A) from Central and just a few minutes from the Peak tram station. ⊠ *1 MacDonnell Rd.,* ☎ *2877–3737,* 🄵🄰🄷 *2845–6263. 130 rooms and suites. Coffee shop, pool, business services. AE, DC, MC, V.* 🐾

Wanchai

$$$$ 🏨 **Grand Hyatt.** "Grand" is the key word here. The Hyatt's Art Deco–
★ style lobby is topped by a ceiling hand-painted by Italian artist Paola Dindo. Artful black-and-white photographs of classic Chinese scenes lend interest to the modern backdrop of corridors and rooms. A black-and-tan color scheme and light-wood paneling in the rooms and suites resemble the airy modern apartments you might see featured in an interior-design magazine. Work space has been subtly maximized, with twin phone lines and hidden fax machines in every room. A huge Internet TV on a rotating plinth with a cordless keyboard provides entertainment. The business center features an IBM room with IBM's latest technology and software, and access to Reuters Business Briefing. The Italian Grissini restaurant (☞ Chapter 3) and the Cantonese One Harbour Road are notable—as is JJ's nightclub—and the ground-floor breakfast buffet is a decadent feast. The Grand Hyatt is close to the Wanchai Star Ferry, yet its slight removal from the main walkways assures less foot traffic than other high-profile hotels. Perhaps that's why Sir An-

drew Lloyd Webber stayed here when *Cats* came to town, and why such celebrities as Luciano Pavarotti, Cindy Crawford, Sylvester Stallone, and Bruce Willis have also signed the guest list. ⊠ *1 Harbour Rd.,* ☎ *2588–1234; 800/233–1234 in the U.S.,* FAX *2802–0677. 519 rooms, 51 suites. 4 restaurants, bar, pool, beauty salon, driving range, 2 tennis courts, exercise room, nightclub. AE, DC, MC, V.*

$$$ 🏨 **Century.** This 23-story hotel is ideal for conventioneers—it's a five-minute walk by covered overpass (a lifesaver in the steamy summer heat) from the convention center and the MTR. The hotel caters to business travelers, offering a well-equipped business center and executive floors. Rooms are modern, with wooden furniture and a color scheme of blue, green, and gray. The health club has an outdoor pool, a gymnasium, and a golf driving bay. Within the complex are a popular, independently run Shanghainese restaurant, a 24-hr coffee shop (in keeping with Wanchai's reputation for nightlife), and a karaoke lounge. ⊠ *238 Jaffe Rd.,* ☎ *2598–8888,* FAX *2598–8866. 497 rooms, 19 suites. 2 restaurants, 2 bars, no-smoking floors, pool, health club, shops, business services. AE, DC, MC, V.*

$$$ 🏨 **Luk Kwok.** This contemporary hotel and office tower designed by Hong Kong's leading architect, Remo Riva, has replaced the Wanchai landmark of the same name immortalized in Richard Mason's novel *The World of Suzie Wong.* Luk Kwok's appeal is its proximity to the Hong Kong Convention & Exhibition Centre, the Academy for Performing Arts, and the Arts Centre. Guest rooms, located between the building's 19th and the 29th floors, are clean and simple, with contemporary furniture; higher floors afford mountain or city views. It has a good Chinese restaurant. ⊠ *72 Gloucester Rd.,* ☎ *2866–2166,* FAX *2866–2622. 191 rooms, 5 suites. 2 restaurants, lounge, no-smoking floors, business services. AE, DC, MC, V.*

$$$ 🏨 **Renaissance Harbour View.** Sharing the Hong Kong Convention & Exhibition Centre complex with the Grand Hyatt is this more modest but equally attractive hotel. Guest rooms are medium-size and modern, with plenty of beveled-glass mirrors. Rooms on the executive floors are done in sophisticated dark colors and have large, no-nonsense desks. Over half of the rooms have superb views overlooking the harbor. Every room has a fax machine. Amenities include the Dynasty (☞ Chapter 3) and Scala restaurants, a cozy bar, the largest hotel outdoor pool in town, gardens, jogging trails, tennis courts, and health-club facilities on the recreation deck between the two hotels. The lobby lounge has one of the best easy-listening jazz bands in town, and is a popular rendezvous spot for local and visiting businesspeople. ⊠ *1 Harbour Rd.,* ☎ *2802–8888,* FAX *2802–8833. 807 rooms, 53 suites. 4 restaurants, 2 bars, 16 no-smoking floors, pool, barbershop, beauty salon, health club, 4 tennis courts, shops, business services. AE, DC, MC, V.*

$–$$ 🏨 **Harbour View International House.** This waterfront YMCA property offers small but clean and relatively inexpensive accommodations near the Wanchai Star Ferry pier. The best rooms face the harbor. It's well placed for travelers who want to attend cultural events in the evening: both the Arts Centre and Academy for Performing Arts are next door. Opposite Harbour View is the Hong Kong Convention & Exhibition Centre. The 16-story hostel provides free shuttle service to Causeway Bay and the Central Star Ferry. ⊠ *4 Harbour Rd.,* ☎ *2802–0111,* FAX *2802–9063. 320 rooms. Restaurant, no-smoking floors. AE, DC, MC, V.*

$–$$ 🏨 **The Wesley.** Opened in 1992 on the site of the old Soldiers and Sailors Home, this 21-story, moderately (for Hong Kong) priced hotel is a short walk from the Hong Kong Convention & Exhibition Centre, the Academy for Performing Arts, and the MTR. Rooms are small but pleasantly furnished, and the more spacious corner "suites" have alcove work areas. No health center or pool is on the premises, but you can use the facilities in Wesley's sister Grand Plaza Hotel, in Quarry Bay, for a discounted fee. A tram stop is right outside the door, and Pacific Place and the bars of Wanchai are close by. ⊠ *22 Hennessy Rd.,* ☎ *2866–6688,* 𝐅𝐀𝐗 *2866–6613. 251 rooms. 2 restaurants, no-smoking floor. AE, DC, MC, V.* ✎

Causeway Bay

$$$$ 🖭 **Regal Hongkong Hotel.** The slightly over-the-top decor in this 33-story hotel leans toward European, with marble floors and a dramatic lobby with high windows, Louis XIV furniture, and a huge mural depicting a Mediterranean scene. The reception area is small, but that doesn't affect the efficient service. Gilded elevators lead to guest rooms with maple-inlay furniture crafted by local artisans, walls and carpets in muted earth tones, brightly colored bedspreads, and spacious bathrooms with triangular tubs. The hotel has four executive floors and sumptuous dining rooms, especially the top-floor Mediterranean restaurant, which has great views of Victoria Park. The rooftop pool and terrace allow escape from the surrounding chaos. Close to the Hong Kong Stadium and the Happy Valley race course, as well as the city's most popular shopping area, this deluxe hotel is one of the most convenient in town. ⊠ *88 Yee Wo St.,* ☎ *2890–6633; 800/222–8888 in the U.S.,* 𝐅𝐀𝐗 *2881–0777. 393 rooms, 32 suites. 6 restaurants, bar, no-smoking floors, pool, health club, shops, business services. AE, DC, MC, V.* ✎

$$$ 🖭 **The Excelsior.** The Excelsior opened in 1974 and remains one of Hong
★ Kong's most popular hotels. Though a veteran, it readily adapts to the changing demands of the group and business markets. Eighty percent of the rooms enjoy splendid sea views, including the Hong Kong Yacht Club's neatly aligned yachts and boats. The spacious and clean rooms have large beds, long desks, and, according to the hotel, the cheapest minibars in town. The location is ideal for shopping and dining. At Talk of the Town (ToTT's) (☞ Chapter 3), the top-floor restaurant-bar-nightclub, you can sample a creative East-meets-West cuisine while listening to live music. The fitness-minded will appreciate the rooftop tennis courts, the well-equipped gym, and the jogging track in adjacent Victoria Park. A business center provides a plethora of services including fax machines, computer terminals, and internet access. On a historical note, the hotel sits on the first plot of land auctioned by the British government when Hong Kong became a colony in 1841. ⊠ *281 Gloucester Rd.,* ☎ *2894–8888,* 𝐅𝐀𝐗 *2895–6459. 886 rooms, 21 suites. 6 restaurants, 2 bars, no-smoking floors, 2 tennis courts, beauty salon, health club, shops, business services. AE, DC, MC, V.* ✎

$$–$$$ 🖭 **Park Lane.** With an imposing facade reminiscent of London's Knightsbridge area, this elegant hotel overlooks Victoria Park and backs onto one of Hong Kong Island's busiest shopping, entertainment, and business areas. The lobby is extraordinarily spacious, and all rooms have luxurious marble bathrooms, elegant handcrafted furniture, and marvelous views of the harbor and Victoria Park or the city. The rooftop restaurant has a panoramic view and serves international cuisine with a touch of Asian flavor. Those who can't resist retail temptations may never find time to use the well-equipped fitness center, but they'll probably get enough exercise walking the two-floor shopping arcade, whose 17 stores include such designer boutiques as agnes b, Enrico Coveri, and Perry Ellis. ⊠ *310 Gloucester Rd.,* ☎ *2890–3355,* 𝐅𝐀𝐗 *2576–7853. 759 rooms, 33 suites. 2 restaurants, bar, no-smoking floors, beauty salon, health club, shops, business services. AE, DC, MC, V.* ✎

$ 🖭 **New Cathay.** Close to Victoria Park, this Chinese-managed hotel is fairly basic and is favored by tour groups from China. The small rooms have basic amenities, such as air-conditioning and TV, and an independently run Chinese seafood restaurant is on the top floor. The hotel is just a few minutes from the bustling shopping center in Causeway Bay. ⊠ *17 Tung Lo Wan Rd.,* ☎ *2577–8211,* 🖷 *2576–9365. 219 rooms, 3 suites. 2 restaurants. AE, DC, MC, V.*

Happy Valley

$$ 🏨 **Emperor Happy Valley.** Catering mainly to business and corporate travelers, this is one of few hotels in the predominantly residential Happy Valley area. The Emperor is also the best deal in town for horse-racing fans, as it's just a few minutes' walk from the Happy Valley racetrack. It's also 5–10 minutes by taxi from the Causeway Bay shopping area. Corridors are narrow, and rooms are clean and functional. ⊠ *1A Wang Tak St.,* ☎ *2893–9406,* 🖷 *2834–6700. 157 rooms, 1 suite. 2 restaurants, bar, no-smoking floors. AE, DC, MC, V.* 🕾

North Point

$$ 🏨 **City Garden.** Although not as close to the MTR as its brochure suggests, this hotel has the advantage of being easily accessible to the Eastern Corridor Expressway, which links Causeway Bay to Taikoo Shing and the Eastern Harbour crossing. Rooms are basic and rather small. The hotel caters to Asian tour groups and has a good Cantonese restaurant. ⊠ *9 City Garden Rd.,* ☎ *2887–2888,* 🖷 *2887–1111. 611 rooms, 2 suites. 2 restaurants, bar, pool, sauna, health club, business services. AE, DC, MC, V.* 🕾

$$ 🏨 **Newton.** Housed in a boxy high-rise that is functional but largely featureless, this hotel has the advantages of proximity to the Fortress Hill MTR station and a pleasant on-site restaurant-bar with live entertainment. Rooms are small but adequate. ⊠ *218 Electric Rd.,* ☎ *2807–2333,* 🖷 *2807–1221. 362 rooms, 9 suites. Restaurant, bar, coffee shop, pool, sauna, business services. AE, DC, MC, V.* 🕾

$$ 🏨 **South China.** Managed by a mainland Chinese company and thus naturally attracting groups from mainland China, this hotel is small and functional, though it has a large Chinese restaurant and bar. It's some distance from the North Point MTR. ⊠ *67 Java Rd.,* ☎ *2503–1168,* 🖷 *2512–8698. 202 rooms, 1 suite. 2 restaurants, business services. AE, DC, MC, V.* 🕾

Quarry Bay

$$ 🏨 **Grand Plaza.** Part of a large residential-commercial-entertainment complex, the Grand Plaza is a little out of the way, but it connects to the Taikoo MTR station and has a vast recreational club with a huge pool, squash courts, a billiard room, a gymnasium, an aerobics hall, a miniature-golf course, a playground, and a jogging track. It also has an upmarket coffee shop, and plenty of shopping in the adjoining Jusco department store. ⊠ *2 Kornhill Rd.,* ☎ *2886–0011,* 🖷 *2886–1738. 208 rooms, 40 suites. 2 restaurants, indoor pool, tennis court, miniature golf, health club, squash, badminton, billiards, business services. AE, DC, MC, V.* 🕾

Repulse Bay

$$$$ 🏨 **De Ricou–The Repulse Bay.** The Repulse Bay Hotel was once a prestigious hotel overlooking a tranquil cove on the south side of Hong Kong Island. Pulled down in 1982 and built up again by The Peninsula Group, The Repulse Bay complex now provides lodging for families, or for those who want to escape the city without giving up hotel-style service. De Ricou, one of the towers, offers short-term stays in fully furnished apartments that come with most hotel perks: maid service, business services, complimentary toiletries, entertainment systems, restaurants, swimming pools, a health club with spa services, and superb sports facilities. Each apartment has two en suite bedrooms, a lounge, and a kitchen. De Ricou also breaks with the formality of a hotel by giving more privacy, space, and quiet; it's more of a home away from home. The nearby beach is one of the best on the island, with Hong Kong itself and popular Stanley a short cab ride away. Dining options on the premises include The Verandah and Spices. (☞ Chapter 3); should you wish to cook, the attached shopping and restaurant complex has a supermarket and delicatessen. Shuttle service links the hotel with Central. ⊠ *109 Repulse Bay Rd.,* ☎ *2803–1100,* FAX *2812–2176. 68 suites. 5 restaurants, bar, café, indoor and outdoor pools, beauty salon, spa, driving range, tennis court, exercise room, health club, squash, billiards, playground, shops, business services. AE, DC, MC, V.*

KOWLOON

Most of Hong Kong's hotels are on the Kowloon Peninsula, which includes Tsim Sha Tsui, Tsim Sha Tsui East, Harbour City, and the Yau Ma Tei and Mong Kok districts, just north of Tsim Sha Tsui. The fabled Golden Mile of shopping, on Nathan Road, runs through Tsim Sha Tsui, and restaurants, stores, and hotels fill the surrounding back streets.

Tsim Sha Tsui East is a grid of modern office blocks—many with restaurants or nightclubs—and luxury hotels. This area was created on land reclaimed from the harbor in the last decade, so all of the hotels are reasonably new. Hung Hom includes a noisy old residential area and a private-housing complex with cinemas and shops.

North of Tsim Sha Tsui are Yau Ma Tei and Mong Kok, which have more older, smaller, more moderately priced hotels. Most of these are on or near Nathan Road and are probably the best bets for travelers on budgets. Excellent bus service and the MTR connect these areas to the center of Tsim Sha Tsui.

Hung Hom

$$$ 🏨 **Harbour Plaza.** The opulent Harbour Plaza's slightly out-of-the-way location allows a unique perspective on the harbor—from Wanchai out to the South China Sea. Hotel buses shuttle to and from Tsim Sha Tsui all day long; the Kowloon–Canton Railway station, from which trains leave for China, is five minutes away; and ferries ply the choppy waters between Hong Kong Island and the nearby ferry terminal. The atrium lobby is spacious and well designed, with good views from lounges on two levels. Rooms are large, comfortable, and contemporary. Dining options include a Japanese *robatayaki* barbecue, a Cantonese restaurant, a grill, and a fun pub called the Pit Stop, which features actual racing cars. A scenic rooftop pool, a fitness center, and health spa are also available. ⊠ *20 Tak Fung St.,* ☎ *2621–3188,* FAX *2621–3311. 386 rooms, 30 suites. 4 restaurants, pub, pool, beauty salon, health club, shops, business services. AE, DC, MC, V.* 🐾

$ 🏨 **Holy Carpenter Guest House.** Occupying the fifth and sixth floors of a community center that also houses a church, this small hostel is a 10-minute walk from the Kowloon–Canton Railway station. Don't expect more than a humble room; lodgings here are very cheap by Hong Kong standards, and are used mainly by budget travelers who just want a place to sleep *and* can reserve at least a month in advance. Those staying for more than two weeks may get a further discount on the room rate. ⊠ *1 Dyer Ave.,* ☎ *2362–0301,* FAX *2362–2193. 14 rooms. MC, V.*

Tsim Sha Tsui

$$$$ 🏨 **Hyatt Regency.** The Hyatt Regency's modern facade, top-end shopping arcade, and dramatic, marble-and-teak lobby exude glamour. The Buddhist gods of hospitality guarding the spacious lobby's reception area are meant to give travelers warm blessings and ensure a nice stay. To that end the hotel even has its own feng shui expert. Next door to the Tsim Sha Tsui MTR station and five minutes from the Star Ferry, the hotel also has a gallery of Asian antiques and an authentic Chinese restaurant. ✉ *67 Nathan Rd.,* ☎ *2311–1234; 800/233–1234 in the U.S.,* 📠 *2739–8701. 706 rooms, 17 suites. 4 restaurants, coffee shop, 2 bars, 5 no-smoking floors, shops, business services. AE, DC, MC, V.* 🐕

$$$$ 🏨 **Peninsula.** Established in 1928, the Pen is a legend worldwide. Its
★ opulent and deluxe facilities have won over such celebrities as Charlie Chaplin, Warren Beatty, Muhammad Ali, Ronald Reagan, and the Princess of Wales. Its taste and Old World style are everywhere: colonial architecture, a columned and gilt-corniced lobby where high tea is served, a fleet of Rolls-Royces, attentive room valets, luxurious bath accessories. In 1994 the Pen added a 30-story tower with twin helipads. Classically European deep blue, gold, and ivory fabrics adorn the 132 spacious new guest rooms and suites; Chinese prints and furniture lend a subtle Eastern accent. Service is marvelously professional and always discreet. All rooms have silent fax machines and the Pen's famous shoe box (staff will retrieve the shoes through an opening from the corridor and have them cleaned). Huge corner suites allow you to wallow in your own private hot tub while looking out over Hong Kong or Kowloon. The superb spa treats you like royalty, with a pool, a sundeck, hot tub, sauna, and steam room. Restaurants include Gaddi's, one of the finest eateries in town; Chinese Spring Moon; and the hippest of the hip rooftop restaurants, Felix (☞ Chapter 3). ✉ *Salisbury Rd.,* ☎ *2366–6251,* 📠 *2722–4170. 246 rooms, 54 suites. 7 restaurants, bar, pool, beauty salon, health club, shops, business services, helipads. AE, DC, MC, V.* 🐕

$$$$ 🏨 **Regent.** The Regent is modern luxury at its most opulent. Its world-
★ class style and innovation are coupled with what may well be the best views in Hong Kong. All this has a price, but management is constantly coming up with packages that allow you to stay here without robbing a bank. The spacious, bright, and sophisticated rooms all have huge desks. Browse the Web through the TV, or plug in your own laptop and get a local high-speed connection. All rooms have sunken baths in Italian marble, and most suites have a separate steam shower. The health spa, also open to the public, is highly recommended for those who wouldn't mind feeling five years younger. The hotel's five restaurants include the high-profile Yü, serving spectacular seafood (☞ Chapter 3); Plume, with contemporary European cuisine; and The Steak House. The Regent celebrated its 20th anniversary in the year 2000; fittingly, in 1998 it was voted top Pacific Rim hotel and No. 3 hotel in the world by readers of *Condé Nast Traveler.* ✉ *18 Salisbury Rd.,* ☎ *2721–1211; 800/545–4000 in the U.S.,* 📠 *2739–4546. 510 rooms, 92 suites. 5 restaurants, pool, health club, shops, business services. AE, DC, MC, V.* 🐕

$$$$ 🏨 **Sheraton Hong Kong Hotel and Towers.** Across the street from the Space Museum at the southern end of the fabled Golden Mile, the Sheraton is contemporary, even avant-garde, its spacious, modern lobby full of arty knickknacks and paintings. Guest rooms have a choice of harbor, city, or courtyard views. Make your way to the rooftop pool and terrace via the exterior glass elevator. The sky lounge has a terrific harbor view, Someplace Else is a popular hangout at happy hour, and those needing an aphrodisiacal pick-me-up should head up to the delightful Oyster & Wine Bar (☞ Chapter 3) on the top floor. ✉ *20*

Nathan Rd., ☎ *2369–1111; 800/334–8484 in the U.S.,* ﹃ﾑ *2739–8707. 686 rooms, 94 suites. 5 restaurants, 3 lounges, 2 no-smoking floors, pool, health club, shops, business services. AE, DC, MC, V.* ✿

$$$–$$$$ ⚏ **Great Eagle.** What Great Eagle lacks in exterior presence it makes up in understated comfort. The lobby ceiling is painted with beautiful murals, and glowing backlit onyx pillars create a comfortable yet sophisticated atmosphere. Once inside, you'll find a selection of beautifully appointed rooms as well as bars, restaurants, and business services. Guest rooms are comfortable yet elegant, and all rooms on the Renaissance Club executive floors have fax machines and modem lines. The Bostonian restaurant (☞ Chapter 3) offers a great variety of seafood dishes, meats, and wines; Asian-attuned palates will love the innovative and delicately presented Chinese dishes at T'ang Court (☞ Chapter 3). ⊠ *8 Peking Rd.,* ☎ *2375–1133; 800/854–7854 in the U.S.,* ﹃ﾑ *2375–6611. 473 rooms, 27 suites. 3 restaurants, 2 bars, lounge, 4 no-smoking floors, pool, health club, shops, business services. AE, DC, MC, V.* ✿

$$$–$$$$ ⚏ **Holiday Inn Golden Mile.** Right on the Golden Mile of Nathan Road, the hub of Kowloon's business and shopping area, this business-style hotel has been popular for more than 20 years. Windows on the facade have sweeping views of Nathan Road; the Avenue restaurant serves delicious contemporary European cuisine in a fashionably decorated third-floor setting overlooking the neon sights and sounds of Tsim Sha Tsui's main artery. ⊠ *50 Nathan Rd.,* ☎ *2369–3111; 800/ 465–4329 in the U.S.,* ﹃ﾑ *2369–8016. 592 rooms, 8 suites. 3 restaurants, bar, lounge, 7 no-smoking floors, pool, health club, shops, business services. AE, DC, MC, V.* ✿

$$$–$$$$ ⚏ **Hongkong.** Lovers of things German might raise a glass to this hotel's prominent and outrageous Oktoberfest. The Hongkong holds the record for hosting the largest such gathering in the territory—up to 1,000 locals and nonlocals attend each night through the month for thigh-slapping, beer-swilling fun in a pavilion. Next to the Star Ferry, the hotel is part of the wharfside Harbour City complex, along with its sister hotels Marco Polo and Prince. The complex houses offices, shopping malls, movie theaters, and restaurants, and is near the pop-culture landmarks Hard Rock Cafe and Planet Hollywood. It has a somewhat dated feel, with key drops and coat-tailed waiters, but personal comfort gets plenty of attention. Rip Van Winkles can choose from 11 kinds of pillows, and parents are provided miniature bathrobes, mild shampoos, and rubber ducks for their tots. Rooms on the executive floor have Internet TVs with remote keyboards. ⊠ *Harbour City, Canton Rd.,* ☎ *2113–0088; 800/843–6664 in the U.S.,* ﹃ﾑ *2113–0011. 621 rooms, 44 suites. 6 restaurants, lounge, 2 no-smoking floors, pool, barbershop, beauty salon, shops, business services. AE, DC, MC, V.* ✿

$$$ ⚏ **Marco Polo.** This 16-story hotel in the shopping and commercial area along Canton Road is close to the MTR station. The brightly colored rooms and suites have large windows and comfortable beds. The most notable restaurant is La Brasserie, serving provincial French cuisine in a typical brasserie setting (long bar, dark wood, leather seats, red-checkered tablecloths). The business center is well supplied, and the staff is helpful and well trained. Guests may use the pool at the nearby Hongkong. ⊠ *Harbour City, Canton Rd.,* ☎ *2113–0088; 800/524–0500 in the U.S.,* ﹃ﾑ *2113–0022. 384 rooms, 56 suites. 3 restaurants, bar, 3 no-smoking floors, barbershop, shops, business services. AE, DC, MC, V.* ✿

$$$ ⚏ **New World Renaissance.** This popular lodging is part of a large shopping complex, and has perfect views of Hong Kong Island from the Tsim Sha Tsui waterfront. Long escalators lead from the shopping area to the hotel's large second-floor lobby. The comfortable guest rooms with pleasantly modern decor feel homey—plenty of space for working and relaxing. Greenery surrounds the outdoor pool, which stays open throughout the year. Among the three restaurants, the Panorama restaurant has one of the best harbor views in town. ⊠ *22 Salisbury Rd.,* ☎ *2369–4111,* ℻ *2369–9387. 501 rooms, 42 suites. 3 restaurants, lounge, 4 no-smoking floors, pool, beauty salon, health club, business services. AE, DC, MC, V.* ☙

$$$ 🏨 **Prince.** Like its neighbors in the Harbour City complex (the Hongkong and Marco Polo), the Prince is very convenient to upscale shops and cinemas and to the restaurants and shops of Tsim Sha Tsui. It's also near the China Hong Kong Terminal, where ferries, boats, and buses depart for China. Most rooms overlook expansive Kowloon Park, and some suites have views of Victoria Harbour. The Spice Market restaurant serves southeast Asian buffets and an international menu. Guests can use the pool at the Hongkong, a five-minute walk away. ⊠ *Harbour City, Canton Rd.,* ☎ *2113–1888; 800/924–0500 in the U.S.,* ℻ *2113–0066. 345 rooms, 51 suites. Restaurant, bar, deli, no-smoking floor, shops, business services. AE, DC, MC, V.* ☙

$$–$$$ 🏨 **Miramar.** Opened in 1948, Miramar was Hong Kong's first post–World War II hotel. It was originally owned by the Spanish Catholic Mission, which intended to use the structure as a shelter for missionaries expelled from China; as tourism blossomed here, the priests changed their plan and turned the premises into a hotel. At the top of the Golden Mile and across from Kowloon Park, the Miramar has a vast lobby with a dramatic stained-glass ceiling. New additions include a grand ballroom, meeting rooms, and an indoor pool. The adjacent Miramar Shopping Centre has two Chinese restaurants (run by the hotel) and a microbrewery. You're close to both the Jordan and Tsim Sha Tsui MTR stations. ⊠ *130 Nathan Rd.,* ☎ *2368–1111,* ℻ *2369–1788. 512 rooms, 13 suites. 3 restaurants, bar, no-smoking floor, pool, shops, business services, meeting rooms. AE, DC, MC, V.*

$$ 🏨 **BP International House.** Built by the Boy Scouts Association, this hotel next to Kowloon Park offers excellent value. A portrait of BP himself, association founder Baron Robert Baden-Powell, hangs in the spacious lobby. Despite the hotel-like cost, the small hostel-like rooms are equipped with TVs, telephones, and electronic key cards. Most rooms have panoramic views of Victoria Harbour and clear views of the busiest part of Kowloon. A multipurpose hall hosts exhibitions, conventions, and concerts, and the health club is one of the biggest in town. A major attraction for budget travelers is a self-service coin laundry. Note that you can park in the hotel's own garages—finding a parking space in Hong Kong is far more difficult than getting a room. ⊠ *8 Austin Rd.,* ☎ *2376–1111,* ℻ *2376–1333. 524 rooms, 11 suites. 2 restaurants, health club, coin laundry, business services, parking (fee). AE, DC, MC, V.* ☙

$$ 🏨 **Kimberley.** On one of the colorfully busy streets between Nathan Road and Tsim Sha Tsui East, this hotel offers plenty of bright, clean rooms. Its health spa includes masseurs to ease away the aches and pains of shopping. Golf driving nets are available for those who can't kick the habit. The two main restaurants serve Cantonese and Japanese cuisines. ⊠ *28 Kimberley Rd.,* ☎ *2723–3888,* ℻ *2723–1318. 497 rooms, 49 suites. 3 restaurants, bar, health club, business services. AE, DC, MC, V.* ☙

$$ 🏨 **Kowloon.** A shimmering, mirrored exterior and a chrome, glass, and ★ marble lobby reflect the Kowloon's efficient, high-tech orientation. Kowloon—Chinese for "nine dragons"—is the design theme here. The triangular windows and pointed lobby ceiling, made from hundreds of hand-blown Venetian-glass pyramids, represent dragons' teeth. Although the clean and functional guest rooms are small, each is equipped with a "work and entertainment center" that includes Web and E-mail access, on-line news, and a CD-ROM drive, as well as a fax machine. Airline information is displayed in the lobby *and* in each guest room. Located on the southern tip of Nathan Road's Golden Mile, the

Kowloon is next door to the Tsim Sha Tsui MTR and minutes from the Star Ferry. ✉ *19–21 Nathan Rd.,* ☎ *2369–8698,* FAX *2739–9811. 719 rooms, 17 suites. 3 restaurants, 5 no-smoking floors, beauty salon, shops, business services. AE, DC, MC, V.* ✑

$$ 🏨 **Ramada Hotel Kowloon.** The Ramada is relatively small and tries for a home-away-from-home ambience. A decorative fireplace in the lobby and comfortable rooms furnished with natural wood create a cozy atmosphere. The bar attracts many young locals for drinks and karaoke. ✉ *73–75 Chatham Rd., South Tsim Sha Tsui,* ☎ *2311– 1100,* FAX *2311–6000. 203 rooms, 2 suites. Restaurant, bar, business services. AE, DC, MC, V.* ✑

$–$$ 🏨 **New Astor.** This small, inviting, triangular hotel is on a busy corner of Old Tsim Sha Tsui across the road from the MTR. Rooms have standard dark-wood furniture and basic amenities such as minibars, hair dryers, and refrigerators. Guests tend to be groups from China and more affluent backpackers. Just a short walk away is Granville Road, where factory outlets cluster. ✉ *11 Carnarvon Rd.,* ☎ *2366– 7261,* FAX *2722–7122. 147 rooms, 1 suite. Restaurant, shops, business services. AE, DC, MC, V.* ✑

$–$$ 🏨 **Royal Pacific Hotel & Towers.** Right on the Tsim Sha Tsui waterfront, the Royal Pacific is part of the Hong Kong China City complex, which includes the terminal for ferries to China. Guest rooms—which are arranged in two blocks, the hotel and tower wings—are small but attractive and equipped with tea- and coffeemakers. The hotel connects to Kowloon Park by a footbridge and is close to shops and cinemas. ✉ *33 Canton Rd.,* ☎ *2736–1188,* FAX *2736–1212. 641 rooms, 32 suites. 3 restaurants, bar, health club, squash, business services. AE, DC, MC, V.* ✑

$–$$ 🏨 **Windsor.** This humble but smart little hotel offers clean, functional accommodations just east of the Golden Mile on Nathan Road. It has a coffee shop, a bar, and business services ranging from secretarial support to Internet access. When taking a cab here, specify your destination as the hotel, as both the Windsor Cinema and, in Causeway Bay, the Windsor House are more widely known. ✉ *39–43A Kimberley Rd.,* ☎ *2739–5665,* FAX *2311–5101. 165 rooms, 1 suite. 2 restaurants, bar, business services. AE, DC, MC, V.* ✑

$ 🏨 **Salisbury YMCA.** If you can't afford the Pen, settle at this five-star
★ Y, where you can enjoy the same magnificent harbor view at a fraction of the price. You can't compare the YMCAs in Hong Kong with the Ys in other parts of the world in terms of either price tag or amenities. The Salisbury YMCA, Hong Kong's most popular, sits on a huge, sterile-looking block opposite the Cultural Centre, Space Museum, and Art Museum—an excellent location for theater, art, and concert crawls. Thanks to a recent upgrade in mid-2000, the clean rooms are now polished up in pastels and equipped with modem lines. The superb health facilities include a fitness center, sauna, hot tub, dance studio, and even an indoor climbing wall. The Y also has a chapel, a beautiful garden, lecture rooms, a conference room with a built-in stage, and a children's library. Enjoy the free in-house movie if you have spare time. The restaurants serve good, cheap food, and the shops are very affordable. ✉ *41 Salisbury Rd.,* ☎ *2369–2211,* FAX *2739–9315. 303 rooms, 62 suites. 2 restaurants, lounge, 2 indoor pools, health club, squash, beauty salon, shops, meeting rooms. AE, DC, MC, V.* ✑

Tsim Sha Tsui East

$$$$ 🏨 **Kowloon Shangri-La.** This upscale hotel caters mainly to business
★ travelers. The business center is open 24 hours; each room has a fax machine and modem line; and global-vision teleconferencing is available on request. Remarkably, the elevator carpets are changed nightly

at midnight to indicate the day of the week, to remind you of your schedule from the moment you approach the lift. The modern, pastel rooms are large by Hong Kong standards, and daily business newspapers are delivered to your room free of charge. On-site restaurants include the Japanese restaurant Nadaman and the California-inspired Napa (☞ Chapter 3), with magnificent harbor views. The sumptuous lounge and Music Room bar provide live entertainment, including string quartets and harp and piano music. Guest rooms look out on the city or Victoria Harbour. The owners' attention to detail, the expert, highly professional staff, and the regular fine-tuning of all facilities ensure repeat business. ✉ *64 Mody Rd.,* ☎ *2721–2111; 800/942–5050 in the U.S.,* FAX *2723–8686. 705 rooms, 25 suites. 5 restaurants, bar, lounge, nosmoking floor, indoor pool, barbershop, health club, shops, business services. AE, DC, MC, V.* ✎

$$$ 🏨 **Grand Stanford Inter-Continental.** More than half the rooms in this luxury hotel (formerly the Grand Stanford Harbour View) at the east end of Tsim Sha Tsui East have an unobstructed harbor view. The elegant lobby is spacious, the staff is helpful and friendly, and the modern, comfortable rooms are decorated in warm earth tones, with fine wood fittings and expansive desks. Each room on the executive floors has a direct-line fax machine and a trouser press. The restaurants are well known locally, including Mistral (Italian; ☞ Chapter 3), Belvedere (regional French), and, particularly, Tiffany's New York Bar, which celebrates the Roaring '20s with antique furniture, Tiffany-style glass ceilings, and entertainers singing popular American songs. ✉ *70 Mody Rd.,* ☎ *2721–5161; 800/327–0200 in the U.S.,* FAX *2732–2233. 554 rooms, 25 suites. 4 restaurants, bar, pool, health club, shops, business services. AE, DC, MC, V.* ✎

$$$ 🏨 **Nikko.** Part of the Japanese Nikko chain, this luxury harbor-front hotel at the far end of Tsim Sha Tsui East attracts mostly Japanese tourists. Here you can brush up on your Japanese and learn the gracious national greeting: a smile and a bow. The spacious premises are clean but a little dated. Nearly 200 rooms enjoy harbor views, and rooms on the executive floors are equipped with additional facilities such as tea- and coffeemakers and in-room modem lines. The popular restaurant Sagano cooks with freshly imported ingredients from Japan. ✉ *72 Mody Rd.,* ☎ *2739–1111; 800/862–9354 in the U.S.,* FAX *2311–3122. 444 rooms, 17 suites. 4 restaurants, 3 bars, pool, health club, shops, business services. AE, DC, MC, V.* ✎

$$$ 🏨 **Regal Kowloon.** If you're in the mood for a French environment, check in at the Regal. The lobby has an impressive tapestry, and Louis XVI–style furniture graces the guest rooms and one of the lounges. Rooms are decorated in peach and green, with chintz bedspreads and curtains. The French restaurant Maman serves home-style French cooking in a relaxed setting. ✉ *71 Mody Rd.,* ☎ *2722–1818; 800/222–8888 in the U.S.,* FAX *2369–6950. 564 rooms, 34 suites. 4 restaurants, 2 bars, no-smoking floor, beauty salon, health club, shops, business services. AE, DC, MC, V.* ✎

$$$ 🏨 **Royal Garden.** An exquisite garden atrium with lush greenery and whispering running water rises from the ground floor to the Royal Garden's rooftop. Glass elevators, live classical music, trailing greenery, and trickling streams create a sense of serenity. All the soft, spacious, and comfortable rooms surround the atrium. Guests especially appreciate Sabatini (☞ Chapter 3), sister to the famous Roman restaurant, and the rooftop state-of-the-art health club with an indoor-outdoor pool and spa services. Fashioned after an ancient Roman bath with fountains, a colorful sun mosaic, and underwater music, the pool is heated and covered in winter by a huge bubble top. ✉ *69 Mody Rd.,* ☎ *2721–5215,* FAX *2369–9976. 374 rooms, 48 suites. 4 restaurants, bar, no-smok-*

ing floors, indoor-outdoor pool, beauty salon, spa, health club, shops, dance club, business services. AE, DC, MC, V. ✎

Yau Ma Tei and Mong Kok

$$ 🏨 **Concourse.** One of Hong Kong's nicer budget hotels, the Concourse is run by the China Travel Service. It's nicely tucked away from Nathan Road but only a minute's walk from the Prince Edward MTR station, in Mong Kok. Rooms are basic and functional, and business services are available. The hotel is well placed for a glimpse of real, day-to-day life in Hong Kong—sip coffee (or a strong mixture of tea and coffee) at a local coffee house or slurp a bowl of noodles at a neighborhood hole-in-the-wall. Loads of simple eateries dot the area, and nearby is an active nightlife scene. The hotel has both a Chinese and a pan-Asian restaurant. ✉ *22 Lai Chi Kok Rd., Mong Kok,* ☎ *2397–6683,* 📠 *2381–3768. 425 rooms, 5 suites. 2 restaurants, coffee shop, bar, business services. AE, DC, MC, V.*

$$ 🏨 **Eaton.** Housed in a brick-red shopping and cinema complex in the middle of Nathan Road, Eaton provides quick access to Hong Kong's down-to-earth street scene after dark: it's a stone's throw from Temple Street, the busy night market that bustles with vendors, fortune-tellers, and Chinese opera singers. The clean, modern rooms have all the basic necessities, and business services are available. The top floor has a swimming pool and a gym. ✉ *380 Nathan Rd., Yau Ma Tei,* ☎ *2782–1818,* 📠 *2782–5563. 458 rooms, 30 suites. 6 restaurants, bar, no-smoking floors, pool, exercise room, business services. AE, DC, MC, V.* ✎

$$ 🏨 **Grand Tower.** Above a shopping mall in the busiest part of Kowloon, the Grand Tower puts travelers near the real Hong Kong. The mall does not sell designer goods but rather ordinary consumer needs from cushion covers and knickknacks to watches, clothes, and shoes. A short walk away are Bird Street (where many Chinese walk and talk, together with their caged birds), the Women's Market, and the Mong Kok MTR. Rooms are adequately clean and functional. ✉ *627–641 Nathan Rd., Mong Kok,* ☎ *2789–0011,* 📠 *2789–1000. 539 rooms, 10 suites. 3 restaurants, barbershop, beauty salon, shops, business services. AE, DC, MC, V.* ✎

$$ 🏨 **Majestic.** This hotel is on the site of the old Majestic Cinema on upper Nathan Road. The lobby is clean and plain, and the sparsely furnished rooms have contemporary furniture, minibars, TVs, and refrigerators. All suites are equipped with fax machines. Facilities are minimal—no pool or gym, and only a coffee shop and a bar for dining and imbibing. But the complex holds shops and a cinema, and plenty of restaurants—running the gamut from Chinese food to Malaysian cuisine—are nearby, as well as the Jordan MTR. ✉ *348 Nathan Rd., Yau Ma Tei,* ☎ *2781–1333,* 📠 *2781–1773. 387 rooms, 9 suites. Bar, coffee shop, no-smoking floor, shops, cinema, business services. AE, DC, MC, V.* ✎

$$ 🏨 **Pearl Seaview.** Reclamation of the harbor front and the subsequent construction have taken away most of this slender hotel's sea view, but it has compensatory features. Convenient to the Yau Ma Tei MTR, it's located on Shanghai Street, where traditional Hong Kong lives on, with shops selling handmade kitchenware, temple offerings, and wedding dresses. Temple Street, a must-see for Hong Kong's street nightlife, is nearby, as is the territory's art house cinema, Broadway Cinematheque (☞ Chapter 5). The restaurant has bargain-priced buffets, especially for lunch. Guest rooms are very small. The hotel attracts mainly tour groups from Europe and Asia. ✉ *268 Shanghai St., Yau Ma Tei,* ☎ *2782–0882,* 📠 *2388–1803. 254 rooms, 3 suites. Restaurant, bar, lounge. AE, DC, MC, V.* ✎

$$ 🏨 **Pruton Prudential.** Rising from a busy corner on upper Nathan Road, above the Jordan MTR station, this hotel is a find if you're on a modest budget. The spacious rooms have views of bustling Nathan Road, with the neon-lit shop signs and banners. The hotel shares a building with a lively shopping mall and has its own pool. Rooms on the five executive floors have tea- and coffeemakers. ⊠ *222 Nathan Rd., Yau Ma Tei,* ☎ *2311–8222,* FAX *2311–1304. 415 rooms, 17 suites. Bar, coffee shop, pool, shops, business services. AE, DC, MC, V.*

$–$$ ⊞ **Metropole.** Just north of Nathan Road's major shopping area, the Metropole is a Yau Ma Tei delight. To start, its facade is adorned with a 150-ft steel mural titled *Magnificent China,* depicting the country's scenic attractions. The modern, clean rooms have simple decor, a harmonious mélange of East and West. The rooftop pool and health club offer a relaxing atmosphere. The on-site Chinese restaurant, House of Tang, serves authentic Szechuan and Cantonese food. ⊠ *75 Waterloo Rd., Yau Ma Tei,* ☎ *2761–1711,* FAX *2761–0769. 479 rooms, 8 suites. 3 restaurants, bar, pool, health club, business services. AE, DC, MC, V.* 🕭

$–$$ ⊞ **Royal Plaza.** One of the newest additions to Hong Kong's long list of lodgings, the Royal Plaza is easily accessible from either the adjacent Kowloon–Canton Railway station or the nearby Mong Kok MTR station. As part of the massive New Century Place shopping complex, it's a consumer's paradise. The hotel itself offers a mix of restaurants, bars, and leisure facilities, including a ballroom and a 40-m pool with underwater music. The garden allows seekers of solitude to contemplate the true meaning of Hong Kong in peace and quiet. ⊠ *193 Prince Edward Rd. W, Mong Kok,* ☎ *2928–8822,* FAX *2606–0088. 419 rooms, 50 suites. 3 restaurants, bar, indoor pool, spa, health club, business services. AE, DC, MC, V.* 🕭

$ ⊞ **Booth Lodge.** This pleasant contemporary retreat near the Jade Market is operated by the Salvation Army. But contrary to the image that might conjure up, everything in this renovated lodge is clean, bright, and new, from freshly painted walls to starched sheets on the double beds. The lobby is a study in minimalism and has an officelike atmosphere, but the Booth is a good value. The coffee shop serves mainly buffets. The Yau Ma Tei MTR is nearby. ⊠ *11 Wing Sing La., Yau Ma Tei,* ☎ *2771–9266,* FAX *2385–1140. 54 rooms. Coffee shop. AE, MC, V.*

$ ⊞ **Caritas Bianchi Lodge.** This clean and friendly lodge with simple, modern decor has basic facilities including TVs, minibars, air-conditioning, and private bathrooms. Just around the corner from busy Nathan Road, it's also close to the Jade Market and the nightly Temple Street Market. ⊠ *4 Cliff Rd., Yau Ma Tei,* ☎ *2388–1111,* FAX *2770–6669. 88 rooms, 2 suites. Restaurant. AE, DC, MC, V.*

$ ⊞ **Shamrock.** With rooms that are more spacious than elegant and an atmosphere best described as old-fashioned (the hotel is more than 40 years old), the Shamrock is still a good bargain. It's just north of Kowloon Park and steps from the Jordan MTR. ⊠ *223 Nathan Rd., Yau Ma Tei,* ☎ *2735–2271,* FAX *2736–7354. 128 rooms, 19 suites. Restaurant. AE, DC, MC, V.* 🕭

THE NEW TERRITORIES AND THE OUTER ISLANDS

Although lodging options are limited outside the cities of Hong Kong and Kowloon, some are worth considering, especially if you're traveling to or from China on the Kowloon–Canton Railway. You're also closer to the airport out here. Some islands, such as Cheung Chau, do a booming business in rooms for rent, with agents displaying photographs of available rentals on placards along the waterfront opposite the ferry pier.

The New Territories

$$$ 🖭 **Regal Riverside.** This large, modern hotel in the foothills of Shatin overlooks the Shing Mun River. Rooms have river and garden views. The 8,000-square-ft health club has a full range of facilities, from an aerobics room to a hot tub to Hong Kong's only float capsule—purported to soothe away the day's pressures. You can also join the healthy horde of people jogging or cycling along the river, or just watch rowers at practice. The hotel is a few minutes from the busiest shopping center in Hong Kong, the New Town Plaza; shuttle service leaves every hour for the plaza and every half hour for Tsim Sha Tsui. ⊠ *Tai Chung Kiu Rd., Shatin,* ☎ *2649–7878; 800/222–8888 in the U.S.,* 𝖥𝖠𝖷 *2637–4748. 789 rooms, 41 suites. 5 restaurants, bar, no-smoking floors, pool, barbershop, beauty salon, health club, shops, dance club, business services. AE, DC, MC, V.* 🕭

$$–$$$ 🖭 **Panda.** You can't miss the huge panda mural on the side of the largest hotel in the western New Territories; its 30 stories dominate the skyline of bustling Tsuen Wan. Decor in this hotel recalls hotels in Tokyo's Ginza district, with lots of open-plan lounges and ultramodern rooms in warm and natural tones. Some rooms have harbor views. On the premises are a pool, a health club, business and meeting facilities, a variety of restaurants, and a department store. Executive guests in the Mega Club also get in-room Nintendo and Internet access. Complimentary bus service runs to and from Tsim Sha Tsui and Mong Kok, and the MTR is nearby. The Panda is one of the closest hotels to Hong Kong International Airport. ⊠ *3 Tsuen Wan St., Tsuen Wan,* ☎ *2409–1111,* 𝖥𝖠𝖷 *2409–1818. 971 rooms, 55 suites. 4 restaurants, 2 bars, no-smoking floor, pool, health club, shops, business services, meeting rooms. AE, DC, MC, V.* 🕭

$–$$$ 🖭 **Royal Park.** Right next to New Town Plaza, the busiest shopping mall in the territory, this 16-story hotel is far from the city yet easily accessed by train and buses. It's also the nearest hotel to the Shatin Racecourse. The lobby is decorated in deep colors, and rooms have bay windows with panoramic views of Shatin. Four rooms are specially designed for the disabled. ⊠ *8 Pak Hok Ting St., Shatin,* ☎ *2601–2111,* 𝖥𝖠𝖷 *2601–3666. 436 rooms, 12 suites. 4 restaurants, lounge, no-smoking floor, pool, tennis court, exercise room, jogging, business services. AE, DC, MC, V.* 🕭

$$ 🖭 **Gold Coast.** Opened in 1994, the Gold Coast is Hong Kong's first conference resort. Its vast complex on Kowloon's western harbor front is well connected to the city center by public bus, and the hotel runs shuttle buses to the MTR and the airport. Inside, the decor is extravagant, with acres of marble, miles of wrought-iron balustrades, a grand ballroom, and palm-court atriums. Facilities include a large marina, a water-sports area, tennis courts, volleyball and soccer fields, pitch-and-putt golf, a full-service spa, and even an archery range. The resort is known among conference planners for facilities that can accommodate over 1,000 people. All guest rooms face the sea over a beautiful beach. Last, but not necessarily least, this is the only hotel in Hong Kong with equipment for Outward Bound courses. ⊠ *1 Castle Peak Rd., Tuen Mun, New Territories,* ☎ *2452–8888,* 𝖥𝖠𝖷 *2440–7368. 440 rooms, 10 suites. 4 restaurants, bar, pool, beauty salon, spa, putting green, 2 tennis courts, archery, health club, soccer, volleyball, boating, business services. AE, DC, MC, V.* 🕭

$–$$ 🖭 **New Beach Resort Hotel.** Look no further if you're into water sports. Though the beach isn't particularly impressive, the water-sports facilities are—sailing, windsurfing, canoeing, speed boats, water scooters, rowing dinghies, pedal boats, aqua bikes . . . you name it. Beginners can ask for coaching while experienced players can rent equipment and head out to sea. Athletic landlubbers can check out the archery and beach volleyball grounds. On the waterfront of Saikung, the New Beach is only 10 minutes' walk from the town and its sumptuous seafood restaurants. The hotel's restaurant serves Thai, Chinese, and Western cuisines. ⊠ *Tai Mong Tsui Rd. (off Hiram's Hwy., 1 mi past Saikung town), New Territories,* ☎ *2791–1068,* ℻ *2792–7102. 24 rooms, 8 suites. 3 restaurants, bar, picnic area, pool, tennis court. AE, DC, MC, V.*

Cheung Chau Island

$ 🔲 **Cheung Chau Warwick.** Miles from the fast-paced city, this six-story beachfront nook aims to assure you a carefree and relaxed stay—a nice pool and a sandy beach take the place of business services and executive floors. An hour by ferry from Hong Kong Island, it's a popular getaway for Hong Kong families. There are no cars on the leisurely island, but the hotel is just a 10-minute walk from the pier. ⊠ *East Bay, Cheung Chau,* ☎ *2981–0081,* ℻ *2981–9174. 71 rooms. 2 restaurants, pool, beach. AE, DC, MC, V.*

Lantau Island

$ 🔲 **Silvermine Beach Hotel.** This bayside resort in Mui Wo steers entirely clear of Hong Kong's sound and fury. It's an hour by ferry from Hong Kong Island, then a five-minute walk from the pier. A pool is open in summer, and a tennis court, exercise room, and sauna are open year-round. The island of Lantau has plenty of sights of its own, including the bronze statue Tin Tan Buddha, the Po Lin Monastery, and Tai O fishing village; and you'll thank yourself for hiking a section of the Lantau Island trail—the scenery is unexpectedly beautiful. ⊠ *D.D. 2, Lot 648 Silvermine Bay, Mui Wo, Lantau Island,* ☎ *2984–8295,* ℻ *2984–1907. 128 rooms, 2 suites. 2 restaurants, pool, exercise room. AE, DC, MC, V.* 🐾

Hong Kong International Airport

$$$ 🔲 **Regal Airport.** Ideal for transit passengers, or those who want to visit Hong Kong without staying near the city, this modern hotel does not suffer from the size restrictions found elsewhere in the territories. It's some distance from the city itself, but the efficient high-speed rail system can have you on Hong Kong Island in around 25 minutes. Connected directly to the passenger terminal by an air-conditioned moving walkway, the brand-new Regal Airport is aimed at leisure and business travelers alike. Its size makes it Hong Kong's largest hotel and one of the largest airport hotels in the world. Some rooms have terrific views of planes landing from afar. For a more resortlike feel, rooms with balconies and outdoor furniture overlook the hotel's two swimming pools. The Grand Ballroom is the largest hotel ballroom in Hong Kong, with space for up to 1,000 people and simultaneous translation, video-conferencing capability, and a built-in stage. ⊠ *Chek Lap Kok,* ☎ *2286–8888,* ℻ *2286–8686. 1,100 rooms, 25 suites. 7 restaurants, 2 lounges, bar, 2 no-smoking floors, indoor-outdoor pool, exercise room, shops, business services. AE, DC, MC, V.* 🐾

5 NIGHTLIFE AND THE ARTS

Hong Kongers play as hard as they work. With cabaret and wine bars giving way to dance clubs and avant-garde theater, the work-weary have no shortage of diversions to choose from.

NIGHTLIFE

Updated by
Lara Wozniak

HONG KONG'S nightlife districts announce themselves with a riot of neon, heralding frenetic after-hours action. Hectic workdays make way for an even busier night scene. Clubs and bars fill to capacity nightly, evening markets pack in shoppers looking for bargains, restaurants welcome hearty diners, cinemas pop corn as fast as they can, and theaters and concert halls prepare for full houses. Hong Kong has sophisticated piano bars, elegant lounges, superstrobe discos, rowdy pubs, smoky jazz dens, hostess clubs, cabarets, and, of course, karaoke bars.

All premises licensed to serve alcohol are supposedly subject to stringent fire, safety, and sanitary controls, although at times this is hard to believe, given the overcrowding at the hippest places. True clubs, as distinct from public premises, are even less strictly controlled, and wise travelers should think twice before succumbing to the city's raunchier hideaways. If you stumble into one, check out cover and hostess charges *before* you get too comfortable. Pay for each round of drinks as it's served (by cash rather than credit card), and never sign any blank checks. Hong Kong is a surprisingly safe place, but as in every tourist destination the art of the tourist rip-off has been perfected. If you're unsure, visit places signposted as members of the Hong Kong Tourist Association (HKTA). You can pick up the association's free membership listing (that is, approved restaurants and nightspots) at any HKTA information office.

Take note, too, of Hong Kong's laws. You must be over 18 to buy alcohol. Drugs, obscene publications, and unlicensed gambling are ostensibly illegal. There is some consumer protection, but the generally helpful police, many of whom speak English, expect everyone to know the meaning of *caveat emptor* (let the buyer beware).

Note that many of Hong Kong's smarter nightspots are in hotels. Fast-paced, competitive Hong Kong is a world of change where buildings seem to vanish overnight and new fads emerge weekly; don't be surprised if some places have changed their decor, changed their name, or closed altogether since this book went to press.

Bars

Hong Kong has its share of licensed designer bars that provide some diversion from the staid pubs. Whether it's because of the transient nature of the city or hardworking lifestyles that leave little time for relationships, there's a rampant singles scene here, with lots of people out looking for that special someone or even that special someone just for the night.

Many Westerners and "chuppies," or Chinese yuppies, meet in crowded comfort in the Lan Kwai Fong area, a hillside section around Central's D'Aguilar Street, with many appetizing bistros and bars.

Singles mix happily at the ultramodern **California** (⊠ 32–34 D'Aguilar St., Lan Kwai Fong, Central, ☎ 2521–1345), which has a late-night disco most nights and is still one of the trendiest places to be seen if you have a beautiful body. The tiny bar **La Dolce Vita** (⊠ G/F, 9 Lan Kwai Fong, Central, ☎ 2810–9333)—beneath its sister restaurant **Post 97** and next to its other sibling **Club 97**—often spills onto the pavement. With sleek decor and a crowd to match, this chic, name-dropping, land of people is a place to be seen. The latest in place is **Insomnia** (⊠ 38–44 D'Aguilar Street, Lan Kwai Fong, Central, ☎ 2525–0957), which is so crowded with perfumed women and suited men on weekend nights you have to fight your way to the back to the bathrooms. If you stay up at the front bar, by the arched windows, you might have some breathing room.

When the late-night pub-crawl rumbles strike, go to **Al's Diner** (⊠ 39 D'Aguilar St., Lan Kwai Fong, ☎ 2869–1869), which is open 'til 3 AM, serving up hamburgers and fry-ups, along with good bagels and coffee, all to the tunes of '50s bebop in a neon-lit, chrome-plated diner atmosphere. For those who have a bit of a frat-boy spirit, try a vodka-spiked Jell-O shot at US$6 a go; or for the ultra-insane: a tequila worm Jell-O, with the worm, at a mere US$8 a round.

The arts-minded mingle at the **Fringe Club** (⊠ 2 Lower Albert Rd., Lan Kwai Fong, Central, ☎ 2521–7251), in a historic redbrick building that also houses the members-only Foreign Correspondents Club. The Club is HQ for Hong Kong's alternative arts scene and normally stages live music twice a week. Writers, artists, bankers, and travelers gravitate toward the unpretentious environs of **Club 64** (⊠ 12–14 Wing Wah Lane, Lan Kwai Fong, Central, ☎ 2523–2801), where you can get a reasonably priced drink in a humble and cozy, if a little run-down setting. For a gregariously cosmopolitan ambience, the trendy **Le Jardin** (⊠ 10 Wing Wah Lane, Lan Kwai Fong., Central, ☎ 2526–2717) has a lovely outdoor terrace overlooking a not-so-lovely alley.

Straddling Lan Kwai Fong and SoHo is **Petticoat Lane** (⊠ 2 Tun Wo La., Central, ☎ 2973–0642), with rich red walls and large gilt-framed oil paintings. Tucked discreetly away in an alley near the Midlevels escalator between Lyndhurst Terrace and Hollywood Road, it's a little hard to find, but definitely worth the wander.

Hong Kong is proud of its own *très* chic SoHo, a small warren of streets between Central and Midlevels. This area is filled with commensurately priced cosmopolitan restaurants ranging from Middle Eastern and Portuguese to Vietnamese and Cajun, as well as a handful of bars. **Club Cubana** (⊠ 47B Elgin St., Central, ☎ 2869–1218) stays open 'til late and has a smallish dance floor and small courtyard in back. Adjacent to Hong Kong's famous outdoor escalator is the hip bistro-style **Staunton's Wine Bar & Cafe** (⊠ 10–12 Staunton St., Central, ☎ 2973–6611). Partly alfresco, it's the perfect place to people-watch and attracts crowds at night to drink and by day to sip coffee or take in a meal. It's a Sunday morning favorite for many expats nursing hangovers over brunch. Affectionately known by locals as the Vodka Bar, the **V 13** (⊠ 13 Old Baily St., SoHo, ☎ 8208–1313) teems with locals and expats who enjoy hearty libations. Once the bartenders start pouring the vodka, they don't stop until they reach the rim. Then they add the tonic.

Solo businessmen can always find someone to talk to in hotel bars, frequented by both locals and expats. The **Mandarin Oriental** (⊠ 5 Connaught Rd., Central, ☎ 2522–0111) is home to the **Chinnery Bar** and **Captain's Bar,** where the smart, Cohiba-cigar set meets to discuss the day's business or to enjoy a post-meeting drink. The **Hyatt's Chin Chin** and **Nathan's** (⊠ 67 Nathan Rd., Tsim Sha Tsui, ☎ 2311–1234) both appeal to the executive set.

Cabarets and Nightclubs

The biggest and best old-fashioned nightclub-restaurants are Chinese, where both the cuisine and the singers are Cantonese. Big-name local balladeers and stars perform nightly, singing both Chinese classics and Cantopop. The massive **Ocean City Restaurant & Night Club** (⊠ New World Centre, Tsim Sha Tsui, ☎ 2369–9688) hosts modest Las Vegas–style entertainment.

Ocean Centre's **Ocean Palace Restaurant & Night Club** (⊠ Harbour City, Canton Rd., Tsim Sha Tsui, ☎ 2730–7111) is a favorite for Hong Kong family and wedding parties, which can be shows in themselves.

Club 97 (⊠ 9–11 Lan Kwai Fong, Central, ☎ 2810–9333 or 2186–1819) is a small, glitzy, often crowded nightclub that draws mobs of beautiful people. It started out as a members-only club; a rule that has been selectively enforced, seemingly depending upon how busy business is that night. If any foreign celebrities are in town, from rock stars to supermodels, this is where they'll be partying. The club is open from 9 PM to 4 AM or later, as long as there are customers. The nightly entrance fee is appropriately HK$97.

Propaganda (⊠ 1 Hollywood Rd., lower ground floor, Central, ☎ 2868–1316), off a quaint but steep cobblestone street, is one of the most popular gay clubs in the territory. (It's known as PP to the locals, Props to the expatriate lot.) The Art Deco bar area is stylish, with elegant booths and tables surrounded by soft lighting; at the other end of the aesthetic spectrum, the dance floor has lap poles on either side for go-go boys who willingly flaunt their wares. Crowds don't arrive until well after midnight, and the entrance fee varies from HK$70 to HK$160 depending on the time and day.

Cocktail and Piano Bars

Sophisticated and elegant cocktail bars are the norm at Hong Kong's luxury hotels. They offer live music (usually Filipino trios with a female singer; occasionally international acts) in a gleaming setting. Some venues have a small dance floor. Hong Kong's happy hours typically run from late afternoon to early evening, with two drinks for the price of one.

In all the following hotels, request a window seat when making reservations. High-altitude harbor gazing is the main attraction at the Island Shangri-La's 56th-floor music lounge **Cyrano** (⊠ 2 Pacific Pl., 88 Queensway, Hong Kong, ☎ 2820–8591), which draws a chic, hip, young crowd. The Peninsula's **Felix** (⊠ Salisbury Rd., Tsim Sha Tsui, ☎ 2366–6251) is a must for visitors; it not only has a brilliant view of the island, but the impressive bar and disco were designed by the visionary Philippe Starck. Don't forget to check out the padded disco room. Ride the bubble elevator to the Sheraton's **Sky Lounge** (⊠ 20 Nathan Rd., 18th floor, Tsim Sha Tsui, ☎ 2369–1111) in time for sunset, and you won't be disappointed. At the Excelsior's **Talk of the Town** (⊠ 281 Gloucester Rd., Causeway Bay, ☎ 2837–6786), or Tott's, you're treated to a 270-degree vista of Hong Kong Harbour.

With spectacular harbor views from the ocean-liner level and a central bar modeled after a high-class London pub, **Gripps** (⊠ Harbour City, Tsim Sha Tsui, ☎ 2113–0088), in the Hong Kong hotel, draws the executive set with its nightly entertainment by visiting pianists and touring cover bands. The Renaissance Harbour View's **Oasis Bar** (⊠ 1 Harbour Rd., Wanchai, ☎ 2802–8888) has a unique glass roof and harbor scenery, albeit slightly obstructed by the Convention & Exhibition Centre's extension.

Feeling pampered is your pleasure at **The Bar** in the Peninsula hotel (⊠ Salisbury Rd., Tsim Sha Tsui, ☎ 2366–6251). Society watchers linger in the Peninsula's lobby; sit to the right of the hotel entrance to better observe the crème de la crème. The lobby lounge at **The Regent** (⊠ 18 Salisbury Rd., Tsim Sha Tsui, ☎ 2721–1211) is a place to see and be seen; be ready to chat about the fashion industry with a parade of Armani-clad and Chanel-scented men and women. The Regent's **Club Shanghai** is an elegant after-dinner spot, decorated in 1930s Chinese style. You won't be out of place if you don your newly purchased long, tight-fitting *cheongsam* here. Before 9:30 the resident band performs love songs, but later you can hear jazzier, more upbeat tunes.

Pubs

Lively pubs proliferate in Hong Kong. Some serve cheap drinks in a modest setting, while others are pricier and more elegant. They help ease homesickness for the expats by serving up fish-and-chips while airing rugby and football matches. As is the rage in the U.K. these days, the trivia quiz games have taken many of the Hong Kong pubs by storm.

In Central, the business folk flock to the British-managed, oak-beam **Bull & Bear** (⊠ 10 Harcourt Rd., Central, ☎ 2525–7436), which attracts all types—a large share of them British—serves standard pub fare, and is known to get a little rowdy on weekends. Several connecting walkways lead to one of the island's most popular shopping malls, Pacific Place, which houses **Pomeroy's** (⊠ The Mall, Pacific Place, Level 3, Admiralty, ☎ 2523–4772). Crowds gather in this congenial, if rather noisy, spot, especially at happy hour.

Cheery Western crowds gather at the wood-paneled pubber's pub **Mad Dogs** (⊠ Basement, Century Sq., 1 D'Aguilar St., Central, ☎ 2810–1000), in the Lan Kwai Fong area. This drinking establishment has been open since 1985, albeit in different locations; current theme nights include Trivial Pursuit. Knock back a beer or two with down-to-earth folks at the **Globe** (⊠ 39 Hollywood Rd., Central, ☎ 2543–1941).

Both branches of the pioneer of Hong Kong Irish pubs, **Delaney's** (⊠ Basement, 71–77 Peking Rd., Tsim Sha Tsui, ☎ 2301–3980; ⊠ 2/F 1 Capital Place, 18 Luard Rd., Wanchai, ☎ 2804–2880) have interiors that were made in Ireland and shipped to Hong Kong, and the atmosphere is as authentic as the furnishings. There are Guinness and Delaney's ale (a specialty microbrew) on tap, corner snugs (small private rooms), and a menu of Irish specialties, plus a happy hour that runs from 3 to 8 PM daily. A more recent addition to the Irish lineup is **Dublin Jack** (⊠ 37 Cochrine St., Central, ☎ 2543–0081), which also serves Guinness and Irish ales while airing the latest football games. This pub just off the Midlevels outdoor escalators stands out with a fetching, bright-red exterior.

Pub-hopping in Wanchai is best enjoyed by the energetic and the easy-to-please or those trying to immortalize Suzie Wong. The **Horse & Groom** (⊠ 161 Lockhart Rd., ☎ 2507–2517) is down-at-the-heels but certainly a true pub. The **Old China Hand Tavern** (⊠ 104 Lockhart Rd., ☎ 2527–9174) has been here since time immemorial and the decor suffers accordingly, but the pub atmosphere is intact. It's something of an institution for those wishing to sober up with greasy grub after a long night out. The **Flying Pig** (⊠ 2/F, Empire Land Commercial Bldg., 81–85 Lockhart Rd., ☎ 2865–3730) has amusing and original decor. For a reasonably priced hotel drinking hole, try the Excelsior's **Dickens Bar** (⊠ 281 Gloucester Rd., ☎ 2837–6782), which offers live music most nights.

If it's not too hot, relax at an outdoor table at Causeway Bay's **King's Arms** (⊠ Sunning Plaza, 1 Sunning Rd., ☎ 2895–6557), one of Hong Kong's few city-center beer gardens. The convivial outdoor area is a great place to meet fellow travelers.

A Wanchai favorite bar is the **Jump** (⊠ Causeway Bay Tower 2, 7th floor, 463 Lockhart Rd., Wanchai, ☎ 2832–9007). This pub actually flies in professional bartenders from around the world, who skillfully flare (toss bottles) to concoct some strange brews—consider the FBI, a combination of ice cream and vodka. Beware the dentist's chair, however, unless you like to imbibe your margaritas upside-down. Wednesday nights ladies drink for free.

Over in Tsim Sha Tsui a diverse, happy crowd frequents the Aussie-style **Kangaroo Pub** (⊠ 35 Haiphong Rd., ☎ 2376–0083), which has good pub food and interesting views of Kowloon Park.

Rick's Cafe (⊠ 4 Hart Ave., Tsim Sha Tsui, ☎ 2367–2939), a local hangout, is a restaurant-pub decorated à la *Casablanca,* with potted palms, ceiling fans, and posters of Bogie and Bergman (there's also a branch on Lockhart Road in Wanchai). We guess the curiously named **Just "M"** (⊠ Shop 5, Podium Plaza, 5 Hanoi Rd., Tsim Sha Tsui, ☎ 2311–9188) stands for either "men" (but don't mistake it for a gay bar) or "money," but the owners playfully refuse to give up the goods. The minimalist industrial design gives it a laid-back feel, and the small mezzanine level has large black couches to sink into. **Ned Kelly's Last Stand** (⊠ 11A Ashley Rd., Tsim Sha Tsui, ☎ 2376–0562) is an institution, with Aussie-style beer tucker (pub grub), and rollicking live jazz in the evening.

A trendy place in Tsim Sha Tsui is an out-of-the-way strip called Knutsford Terrace. You'll find tropical rhythms at the Caribbean-inspired **Bahama Mama's** (⊠ 4–5 Knutsford Terr., ☎ 2368–2121), where world music plays and the kitsch props include a surfboard over the bar and the silhouette of a curvaceous woman showering behind a screen over the rest room entrance. You wouldn't think that **Chasers** (⊠ 2–3 Knutsford Terr., ☎ 2367–9487), fitted with genuine English antiques including chairs, lamps, and prints, would be as groovy as it is, but with live pop music most evenings it draws a regular and bustling crowd.

Wine Bars

For an intimate encounter, try **Le Tire Bouchon** (⊠ 45A Graham St., Central, ☎ 2523–5459), where fine wines by the glass accompany tasty bistro meals.

Tiny, classy **Juliette's** (⊠ 6 Hoi Ping Rd., Causeway Bay, ☎ 2882–5460) provides a cozy ambience for chuppie (Hong Kong's Chinese yuppies) couples and corporate types.

Pacific Wine Cellars (⊠ Basement, Seibu, Pacific Place, 88 Queensway, Central, ☎ 2971–3897) is tucked away behind tall shelves of vintage wines in Seibu's magnificent basement grocery store. Wandering shoppers delight in stumbling upon this secret.

Jazz and Folk Clubs

The appropriately named **Jazz Club** (⊠ 2/F, California Entertainment Bldg., 34–36 D'Aguilar St., Central, ☎ 2845–8477) offers a wide selection of excellent local jazz, R&B, and soul acts as well as top-notch international acts every month, including harmonica player extraordinaire Carey Bell and bluesmen Georgie Fame and Joe Louis Walker.

Ned Kelly's Last Stand (☞ Pubs, *above*) is an Aussie-managed haven for pub meals and, oddly enough, Dixieland, courtesy of Ken Bennett's Kowloon Honkers. Get here before 10 PM to get a comfortable seat.

Wanchai's unpretentious alternative to the topless bar scene is **The Wanch** (⊠ 54 Jaffe Rd., ☎ 2861–1621), which features live local folk and rock performances. The Hong Kong–theme decor (remember *Love Is a Many Splendored Thing?*) is worth a visit in itself.

Discos

Hong Kong's discos are diverse in style and clientele, not to mention price, so there's something to suit everyone. The thriving youth culture is best exemplified in these houses of dance, where young folks prance about in the latest fashions. Cover charges are high by U.S. standards; entrance to the smarter spots can be HK$100 or more (much more on the eves of major holidays), though this usually entitles you to two drinks. If you prefer dance parties to discos, look for posters in Lan Kwai Fong and Wanchai that scream about the latest international DJ (usually very well known) arriving in town to play for one night only. Some bars and restaurants also hold weekly or monthly club nights, where music ranges from drum-and-bass to happy house.

The perennial favorite is **JJ's** (⊠ Grand Hyatt, 1 Harbour Rd., Hong Kong, ☎ 2588–1234), the Grand Hyatt's entertainment center. The comfortable upstairs lounge area has a dartboard and a bar that screens major sporting events, but JJ's is most revered for its flashy disco lights and resident band in the music room, where wall-to-wall businessmen and their escorts lounge.

Both branches of **Rick's Cafe** (⊠ 4 Hart Ave., Tsim Sha Tsui, ☎ 2367–2939; ⊠ 78–82 Jaffe Rd., Wanchai, ☎ 2311–2255) are practically disco institutions, and despite being among the oldest, they remain popular. If you arrive after midnight on a weekend, be prepared to stand in line.

In the basement of the Park Lane Hotel is **Stix** (⊠ 310 Gloucester Rd., Causeway Bay, ☎ 2839–3397), which has a large dance floor that fills up with groovers enjoying the house band's latest pop covers.

Joe Bananas (⊠ 23 Luard Rd., Wanchai, ☎ 2529–1811) is the mainstay of Wanchai nightlife, its reputation for all-night partying and general good times unchallenged. This disco-cum-bar strictly excludes the military and people dressed too casually: no shorts, sneakers, or T-shirts. Arrive before 11 PM to avoid the queue.

The dance floor at the **Big Apple Pub and Disco** (⊠ Basement, 20 Luard Rd., Wanchai, ☎ 2529–3461) gets going in the wee hours—and keeps going. There is a sleaze factor here, but this is one of the best places to dance and is beloved by the club and dance-party crowds. **Neptune Disco II** (⊠ 98–108 Jaffe Rd., Wanchai, ☎ 2865–2238) is another late-night haunt for the dance-till-you-drop set.

Hostess Clubs

These are clubs in name only. Hong Kong's better ones are multimillion-dollar operations with hundreds of presentable hostess-companions of many races. Computerized time clocks on each table tabulate companionship charges in timed units; the costs are clearly detailed on table cards, as are standard drink tabs. The clubs' dance floors are often larger than those at discos, and they have one or more live bands and a scheduled lineup of both pop and cabaret singers. They also have dozens of luxuriously furnished private rooms, with partitioned lounges and the ubiquitous karaoke setup. Local and visiting businessmen adore these rooms—and the multilingual hostesses; business is so good that the clubs are willing to allow visitors *not* to ask for companionship. The better clubs are on a par with music lounges in deluxe hotels, though they cost a little more. Their happy hours start in the afternoon, when many have a sort of tea-dance ambience, and continue through to mid-evening. Peak hours are 10 PM–4 AM. Be aware that many hostess-oriented clubs, whether modest or posh, are also prostitution fronts.

Club BBoss, in Tsim Sha Tsui East's Mandarin Plaza (☎ 2369–2883), is the grandest and most boisterous hostess club, tended by a staff of more than 1,000. Executives, mostly locals, provide the entertainment. If your VIP room is too far from the entrance, you can hire an electrified vintage Rolls-Royce and purr around an indoor roadway. Be warned that this is tycoon territory—a bottle of brandy can cost HK$18,000. Along the harbor, in New World Centre, is **Club Deluxe** (☎ 2721–0277), a large, luxurious dance lounge.

Club Kokusai (✉ 81 Nathan Rd., Tsim Sha Tsui, ☎ 2367–6969), as its name applies, appeals to visitors from the Land of the Rising Yen. Karaoke dominates.

Mandarin Palace (✉ 24 Marsh Rd., ☎ 2575–6551) is a grand yet comfortable Wanchai nightclub where clients can indulge their singing aspirations in karaoke duets with hostesses until the wee hours.

THE ARTS

The most comprehensive calendar of cultural events is *HK Magazine,* a free weekly newspaper distributed each Friday to many restaurants, stores, and bars. You can also read daily reviews in the Life section of the *Hong Kong Standard* and its weekend *Hong Kong Life* magazine. The other English-language newspaper, the *South China Morning Post,* lists events and has an entertainment pullout every Friday called WE. Highlights of other weekly happenings are listed in the *TV Times,* which comes out every Thursday.

City Hall (✉ By Star Ferry, Hong Kong Island, ☎ 2921–2840) has posters and huge bulletin boards listing events and ticket availability. You can buy tickets for cultural events held in government centers from booths on the ground floor by the main entrance. **URBTIX** (☎ 2734–9009) outlets are the easiest places to buy tickets for most performances; you'll find a branch at the **Hong Kong Arts Centre** (☎ 2582–0232) in addition to the one at City Hall. The free monthly newspaper *City News* lists City Hall events.

Dance

Hong Kong Dance Company. Since 1981, this ensemble has been promoting the art of Chinese dance and choreographing new works with historical themes. The 30-odd members are experts in folk and classical dance: Sponsored by the Urban Council, they perform about three times a month throughout the territory. ☎ 2853–2642.

Hong Kong Ballet. This is Hong Kong's first professional ballet company and vocational ballet school. Western-oriented in both its classical and its contemporary repertoires, it performs at schools, auditoriums, and festivals. ☎ 2573–7398.

City Contemporary Dance Company. Dedicated to contemporary dance, this group presents innovative programs with Hong Kong themes at various venues both indoors and outdoors. ☎ 2326–8597.

Drama

Chung Ying Theatre Company. This professional company of Chinese actors stages plays—most of them original and written by local playwrights—mainly in Cantonese. The group also organizes exchanges with theater companies from overseas, often inviting international directors to head productions. Sites vary. ☎ 2521–6628.

Fringe Club. The Fringe presents an enormous amount of alternative theater, ranging from one-person shows to full dramatic performances. It's the only club of its kind to offer facilities to amateur drama, music, and dance groups. Short-run contemporary plays by American and English writers are also presented, as well as shows by independent local groups. ⊠ *2 Lower Albert Rd., Central,* ☎ *2521–7251.*

Zuni Icosahedron. The best-known avant-garde group in Hong Kong stages multimedia drama and dance, usually in Cantonese, at various locations. ☎ *2893–8419.*

Film

With only two main studios (one of them owned by sweet-faced action hero Jackie Chan), Hong Kong reins as the film capital of Asian martial arts/Triad-themed movies. Unlike western shoot-'em-ups, the camera work in martial-arts flicks emphasizes the ricochet choreography of physical combat.

If you want to experience a true Hong Kong Canto-flick, you'll have plenty to choose from. If a Jackie Chan or Chow Yun Fatt film is in release, you can be sure nearly every cinema in town will be showing it. Other movies are mostly B-grade, centering around the cops-and-robbers and slapstick genres; locals love these because they star popular Hong Kong actors. Wong Kar Wai, Ann Hui, and John Woo, all international award–winning filmmakers, have helped draw attention to Hong Kong film with their visionary and dynamic direction. For show times and theaters, check the listings in *HK* magazine, the *South China Morning Post,* and the *Hong Kong Standard.*

If you're looking for more than just a visual feast (that is, you want to see something in English or with subtitles), visit **Broadway Cinematheque** (⊠ Prosperous Garden, 3 Public Square St., Yau Ma Tei, ☎ 2388–3188; 2384–6281 for ticket reservations). The train-station design of this art house has won awards; the departure board displays foreign and independent films (local films are rare). Here you can read the latest reel-world magazines from around the globe in a minilibrary, view laser discs, and access the Internet. A shop sells new and vintage film paraphernalia, and there's a coffee bar as well. To get here, use the Temple Street exit at the Yau Ma Tei MTR.

Before the Broadway Cinematheque, cinephiles in search of alternative and independent films from Japan and the West had only two options. The **Cine-Art House** (⊠ Ground floor, Sun Hung Kai Centre, Wanchai, ☎ 2827–4778) is a quaint two-theater complex. **The Hong Kong Arts Centre** (☞ *below*) screens some of the best independent, classic, and documentary films from around the world as well as local products, often with themes focusing on a particular country, period, or director.

Performance Halls

Hong Kong Island

City Hall (☞ *above*). Classical music, theatrical performances, films, and art exhibitions are presented in this complex's large auditorium, recital hall, and theater.

Hong Kong Academy for Performing Arts. This arts school has two major theaters, each seating 1,600 people, plus a 200-seat studio theater and a 500-seat outdoor theater. Performances include local and international theater, modern and classical dance, and concerts. E 1 Gloucester Rd., Wanchai, P 2584–8500.

Hong Kong Arts Centre. Several floors of auditoriums, rehearsal halls, and recital rooms spotlight both local and visiting groups. E 2 Harbour Rd., Wanchai, P 2582–0232.

Hong Kong Fringe Club. Some of Hong Kong's most innovative entertainment and art exhibits play here. Shows range from the blatantly amateur to the dazzlingly professional. Entertainment also includes good jazz, avant-garde drama, and many other events. E 2 Lower Albert Rd., Central, P 2521–7251.

Queen Elizabeth Stadium. Though it's basically a sports stadium, this 3,500-seat venue frequently presents ballets and orchestral and pop concerts. E 18 Oi Kwan Rd., Wanchai, P 2591–1346.

Kowloon

Hong Kong Coliseum. This 12,000-plus-seat stadium presents everything from basketball to ballet, from skating polar bears to local and international pop stars. E 9 Cheong Wan Rd., Hung Hom railway station, Hung Hom, P 2355–7234.

Hong Kong Cultural Centre. This conference and performance facility contains the Grand Theatre, seating 1,750, and a concert hall seating 2,100. The center is used by both local and visiting artists for operas, ballets, and orchestral concerts. E 10 Salisbury Rd., P 2734–2009.

University Hall. Baptist University owns this modern auditorium, which usually hosts pop concerts but also offers dance and symphony concerts. The odd headline act plays here, such as the legendary Tom Jones, but the space usually caters to local talent, which is worth checking out. E 224 Waterloo Rd., P 2339–5182.

The New Territories

Shatin Town Hall. Attached to New Town Plaza, an enormous shopping arcade, this impressive building is a five-minute walk from the KCR station at Shatin. Its cultural events include dance, drama, and concert performances. E 1 Yuen Wo Rd., Shatin, P 2694–2511.

Tsuen Wan Town Hall. It's off the beaten path, but this auditorium gets a constant stream of local and international performers. Acts include everything from the Warsaw Philharmonic to Chinese acrobats. The hall seats 1,424 and probably has the best acoustics of any performance hall in Hong Kong. E 72 Tai Ho Rd., Tsuen Wan, P 2414–0144; Tsuen Wan MTR station.

Orchestras

Hong Kong Philharmonic Orchestra. Almost 100 musicians from Hong Kong, the United States, Australia, and Europe perform everything from classical to avant-garde to contemporary music by Chinese composers. Past soloists have included Vladimir Ashkenazy, Rudolf Firkusny, and Maureen Forrester. Performances are usually held Friday and Saturday at 8 PM in City Hall or in recital halls in the New Territories (☎ 2721–2030).

Hong Kong Chinese Orchestra. Created in 1977 by the Urban Council, this group performs only Chinese works. The orchestra consists of bowed strings, plucked instruments, wind, and percussion. Each work is specially arranged for each concert (☎ 2853–2622).

Chinese Opera

Cantonese Opera. There are 10 Cantonese opera troupes in Hong Kong, as well as many amateur singing groups. These groups perform "street opera" in, for example, the Temple Street Night Market almost every night, while others perform at temple fairs, in City Hall, or in playgrounds under the auspices of the Urban Council (☎ 2922–8008). Visitors unfamiliar with the form are sometimes alienated by the strange sounds of this highly complex and extremely sophisticated art form. Every gesture has its own meaning; in fact, there are 50 gestures for the hand alone. Props attached to the costumes are similarly intricate and are used in exceptional ways. For example, the principal female often has 5-ft-long pheasant-feather tails attached to her headdress; she shows anger by dropping the head and shaking it in a circular fashion so that the feathers move in a perfect circle. Surprise is shown by what's called "nodding the feathers." One can also "dance with the feathers" to show a mixture of anger and determination. Orchestral music punctuates the singing. It's best to have a local acquaintance translate the gestures, since the stories are so complex that Wagner and Verdi librettos begin to seem basic in comparison.

Peking Opera. This highly stylized variety of opera employs higher-pitched voices than Cantonese opera. Peking opera is an older form, more respected for its classical traditions; the meticulous training of the several troupes visiting Hong Kong from the People's Republic of China each year is well regarded. They perform in City Hall or at special temple ceremonies. Call the Urban Council (☎ 2922–8008) for further information.

6 SPORTS AND OUTDOOR ACTIVITIES

Hong Kong's international reputation as a fast-paced metropolis doesn't prepare most travelers for its athletic and outdoor offerings. While here you can test your luck at a racetrack, hike a well-developed network of trails, learn a martial art, or just loaf on a lovely beach.

Updated by
Lara Wozniak

S WEAT IN HONG KONG spills beyond the floors of the stock exchange and dance clubs. If you're in town during the horse-racing season, don't miss the spectacle when gambling-mad punters stake a huge part of their incomes on stallions and mares. Rugby and soccer tournaments draw enthusiastic fans, and the annual dragon boat races are highly entertaining. Check weekly activity schedules at a HKTA information booth for listings of spectator-sport events. Although most activities require a little advance planning, they're well worth the effort.

If you want to participate in local activities, you can join the elderly men and women who rise when the roosters crow to perform their ritual morning tai chi in public parks before they head off for a light breakfast of *yum cha* or dim sum. And of course this is the place to study martial arts from karate to tae kwon do. Hong Kongers are also partial to hiking in the mountains, sailing beyond Victoria Harbour into the the South China Sea, golfing with co-workers, and playing tennis with friends on weekends.

PARTICIPANT SPORTS

Perhaps because of its British legacy, Hong Kong has long been known as a club-oriented city: whether you're into golf, sailing, squash, or tennis, you'll find that members-only clubs have the best facilities. And several clubs have reciprocal privileges with clubs outside Hong Kong. The Hong Kong Jockey Club offers members of such affiliates free entry to its members' enclosure during racing season (though not use of club recreational facilities). Visitors with reciprocal privileges at the Hong Kong Golf Club are allowed 14 free rounds of golf each year. Other clubs with reciprocal policies are the Hong Kong Yacht Club, Hong Kong Cricket Club, Kowloon Cricket Club, Hong Kong Football Club, Hong Kong Country Club, Kowloon Club, Hong Kong Club, and Ladies' Recreation Club.

Before you leave for Hong Kong, check with your club to see if it has an arrangement with one there. If so, you'll need to bring your membership card, a letter of introduction, and often your passport when you visit the affiliated establishment in Hong Kong. Call when you arrive to book facilities, or ask your hotel concierge to make arrangements.

Golf

Locals generally head up to nearby Shenzhen, China's Special Economic Zone, to enjoy a round or three of golf on the weekends, but some of Hong Kong's clubs allow visitors to play their courses.

The **Clearwater Bay Golf and Country Club,** in the New Territories, has five outdoor and two indoor tennis courts, three indoor squash courts, and two indoor badminton courts as well as an outdoor pool and health spa in addition to its 18-hole golf course. Together with the Hong Kong Tourist Association (HKTA), the club sponsors a Sports and Recreation Tour, which allows visitors to tour the facilities and play golf. ⊠ *139 Tai Aumum Rd., Causeway Bay, New Territories,* ☎ *2719–1595; 2335–3885 for booking office; 2807–6543 for HKTA tour.* ☜ *Tours range from HK$380 to HK$430 and include transfers, lunch, and greens fees.*

The **Discovery Bay Golf Club,** on Lantau Island, has an 18-hole course open to visitors on Monday, Tuesday, and Friday. You must reserve two days in advance. ⊠ *Take Discovery Bay ferry from Star Ferry pier in Central, then catch bus to course (call club for current bus-line info),* ☎ *2987–7273.* ☜ *Greens fees HK$1,400, club rental HK$160, golf-*

cart rental HK$190, and shoe rental HK$50; ½-hr lesson HK$400. Non-members can play Mon., Tues., and Fri.

The **Hong Kong Golf Club** allows visitors to play on its three 18-hole courses at Fanling, in the New Territories. ⊠ *Just off Fanling Hwy.,* ☎ *2670–1211 for bookings; 2670–0647 for club rentals (HK$250).* ▣ *Greens fees HK$1,400 for 18 holes; ½-hr lesson HK$300.*

The **Tuen Mun Golf Centre** is a public center with 100 driving bays and a practice green. ⊠ *Lung Mun Rd., Tuen Mun,* ☎ *2466–2600.* ▣ *HK$12 per bay, HK$12 per club, and HK$12 per hr per 30 balls.* ☉ *Daily, including public holidays, 8 AM–10 PM.*

Health Clubs

Most Hong Kong health clubs require membership; the person behind the desk will look at you blankly if you try to explain that your health club at home might have a reciprocal arrangement. The majority of first-class hotels have health clubs on their premises, and the first two below will let you enter for a reasonable day rate.

The **California Fitness Center** (⊠ 1 Wellington St., Central, ☎ 2522–5229; ⊠ 99 Percival St., Causeway Bay, ☎ 2577–0004; ⊠ 88 Gloucester Rd., Wanchai, ☎ 2877–7070) has guest passes for HK$300 per day.

Tom Turk Fitness Club (⊠ Asia Pacific Finance Tower, 3 Garden Rd., 3rd floor, Central, ☎ 2521–4541; ⊠ HK Scout Centre, 8 Austin Rd., Tsim Sha Tsui, ☎ 2736–7188) charges HK$200 for a weekday visit before 5 PM, HK$250 after 5 and on weekends.

Situated alongside the Midlevels outdoor escalator, **New York Fitness** (⊠ 32 Hollywood Rd., Central, ☎ 2543–2280) sells a 10-day pass for HK$2,000.

Hiking

Lush lowlands, bamboo and pine forests, rugged mountains with panoramas of the sea, and secluded beaches are the little-known alter ego of Hong Kong. In fact, about 40 percent of Hong Kong is protected in 23 parks, three marine parks, and one marine reserve. A day's hike (or two days if you're prepared to camp out) takes a bit of planning, but you'll see the best of Hong Kong. You'll see farther than you really are from the buildings below, which seem almost insignificant from this perspective.

Don't expect to find the wilderness wholly unspoiled, however. Few upland areas escape Hong Kong's relentless plague of hill fires for more than a few years at a time. Some are caused by dried-out vegetation; others erupt from small graveside fires set by locals to clear the land around ancestors' eternal resting spots. Partly because of these fires, most of Hong Kong's forests, except for a few spots in the New Territories, support no obvious wildlife other than birds—and mosquitoes. Bring repellent.

Gear

Basic necessities include sunglasses or hat, bottled water, day pack, and sturdy hiking boots. Wear layered clothing; weather in the hills tends to be very warm during the day and colder toward nightfall. The cliffsides get quite windy. Of course, if you're planning to camp, carry a sleeping bag and tent.

Great Outdoor Clothing Company (⊠ 2/F Silvercord Bldg., 30 Canton Rd., Tsim Sha Tsui, ☎ 2730–9009) doesn't sell the same range of camping equipment, backpacks, sleeping bags, and clothes you'd find in the United States or in the United Kingdom, but it'll do in a pinch.

Timberland (⌧ Shop 212, Pacific Pl., 88 Queensway, Admiralty, ☎ 2868–0845) sells hiking boots, backpacks, and appropriate clothing.

World Sports Co. Ltd. (⌧ 83 Fa Yuen St., 2/F, Mong Kok, ☎ 2396–9357) is probably comparable to your favorite camping store back home, catering to your every outdoor need with a very helpful staff. It stocks everything from pocket knives and woolly socks to gas burners and tents.

Maps

Before you go, pick up trail maps at the **Government Publications Centre** (⌧ Pacific Pl., Government Office, ground floor, 66 Queensway, Admiralty, ☎ 2537–1910). Ask for blueprints of the trails and the Countryside Series maps. The HM20C series comprises handsome four-color maps, but it's not very reliable.

Trails

You can hike through any of the territory's country parks and around any of the accessible outlying islands. Here are two short, one-day hikes and two camping treks on the most popular trails.

Dragon's Back. This is a relatively easy, half-day, meandering walk with lots of straightaway sections on southeastern Hong Kong Island, which boasts some surprisingly wild country a world away from the urban bustle. You start out walking through woodland, but this soon gives way to wind-pruned grass and bamboo jungle along the ridge that is the spine of the dragon. The foliage grows over the path, so you are shaded. At about the halfway mark you reach a great place to stop, take a drink of your bottled water, and absorb the scenery. On a clear day the trail affords tremendous views over the south of the island, **Shek O,** and the **South China Sea.** If it is windy, you may see daredevils paragliding and children of all ages (usually of the adult variety) flying remote-control airplanes from the cliffside middle point of the trail. From here you walk down a sandy path that at times looks like it is cutting through the hills of the Highlands in Scotland, although the trail is more rambling than rugged. Follow it to the main road to catch one of the frequent well-marked buses to Shek O, where you can mingle with the villagers and day trippers as you stroll along the soft white beach that affords some interesting rocks and the occasional shell or two. You can take a bus or taxi home from Shek O. Distance: 4 km (3 hours hiking, 60 to 90 minutes traveling). While you could easily do this on your own, contact Martin Williams (☎ 2981–3523) for a guided tour.

Lantau Island. Take a ferry ride from Central on Hong Kong Island to **Lantau Island,** then take a scenic bus ride along Lantau's southern coast and up to **Ngong Ping,** below the summit of **Lantau Peak,** Hong Kong's second-highest mountain. Here, you can see **Big Buddha,** visit **Po Lin Monastery,** and stroll through the old Tea Gardens to a vantage point with stunning views of **Shek Pik reservoir** and the **South China Sea** beyond. Then you can hike a path that drops, levels, and takes you to the road leading toward **Kwun Yam Temple.** Named after the Goddess of Mercy, this beautiful Taoist temple is set on a wooded hillside from where you can see more temples. Enjoy a break at this temple before heading along a quiet level road. Distance: 7 km (3½ hours hiking, expect about 2½ hours traveling). Longer stretches of uphill walking, however, make this trek more strenuous than the Dragon's Back hike. You can hike on your own, or contact Martin Williams (☎ 2981–3523) for a guided tour.

McLehose Trail. Named after an ex-governor of Hong Kong, this trail is the course for the annual McLehose Trailwalker, an international run/walk for charity. This grueling event covers 97 km (60 mi) and must essentially be completed nonstop; teams winning first place have finished the walk in an astonishing 15 hours. The average hiker can tackle sections of the McLehose trail in one day; otherwise, it's a four- or five-day trip from beginning to end. This splendidly isolated path through the New Territories starts at **Tsak Yue Wu,** beyond Sai Kung, and circles the **High Island Reservoir** before breaking north. Climb through **Sai Kung Country Park** to a steep section of the trail, up the mountain called **Ma On Shan.** Turn south for a high-ridge walk through **Ma On Shan Country Park.** From here you walk west along the ridges of the eight mountains, also known as the Eight Dragons, that gave Kowloon its name. (The last emperor of the Sung dynasty is thought to have named the peninsula Nine Dragons, for these eight peaks plus himself.) You may see wild monkeys on the trail near Eagles Nest; they are, in fact, very tame. After you cross Tai Po Road, the path follows along ridge tops toward **Tai Mo Mountain,** 3,161 ft above sea level. This is the tallest mountain in Hong Kong and is sometimes capped with snow. Continuing west, the trail drops gradually to **Tai Lam Reservoir** and then to **Tuen Mun,** where you can catch public transportation.

Wilson Trail. Hong Kong's newest major trail is 78 km (48 mi) long, from Stanley Gap on Hong Kong Island to Nam Chung in the northeastern New Territories. You have to cross the harbor by MTR at Quarry Bay to complete the entire walk. The trail is smoothed by steps paved with stone, and footbridges aid with steep sections and streams. Clearly marked with signs and information boards, this popular walk is divided into 10 sections, and you can easily take just one or two; traversing the whole trail takes about 31 hours. It begins at Stanley Gap Road, on the south end of Hong Kong Island, and takes you through rugged peaks that offer a panoramic view of Repulse Bay and the nearby Round and Middle islands. This first part, Section 1, is only for the very fit. Much of the trail requires walking up steep mountain grades. For an easier walk, try Section 7, which takes you along a greenery-filled, fairly level path that winds past the eastern shore of the Sing Mun Reservoir in the New Territories and then descends to Tai Po, where there's a sweeping view of Tolo Harbour. Other sections will take you through the monkey forest at the Kowloon Hill Fitness Trail (Section 5), over mountains, and past charming Chinese villages.

Jogging

The best stretch of land for jogging is **Bowen Road.** It's a 8-km (5-mi) run back and forth on a wooded street that's closed to vehicular traffic. **Victoria Park** at Causeway Bay also has an official jogging track.

The **Hong Kong Running Clinic** is open to all levels of ability, including those training for marathons, and meets every Sunday morning at 7 from April through December. There is no charge for visitors. Doctor Dan Neisner, who runs the club, recommends shorter runs in the oppressively hot summer months. ✉ *Meet at the parking lot in front of Adventist Hospital, 40 Stubbs Rd., Happy Valley,* ☎ *2835–0555 (Health Promotions Department).*

Junking

Dining on the water aboard large pleasure craft—which also serve as platforms for swimmers and water-skiers—is a boating style unique to Hong Kong. Junking has become so popular that there is now a fairly large junk-building industry producing highly varnished, plushly appointed, air-conditioned junks up to 80 ft long. After a day out on a junk, sailing by the shimmering lights of Hong Kong Island on the ride back into town is spectacular.

These floating rumpus rooms serve a purpose, especially for denizens of Hong Kong Island who suffer from "rock fever" and need to escape for a day on the water. Also known as "gin junks" because so much alcohol is consumed, these junks are commanded by "weekend admirals." If anyone so much as breathes an invitation for junking, grab it.

You can also rent a junk. The pilot will take you to your choice of the following outer islands: Cheung Chau, Lamma, Lantau, Po Toi, or the islands in Sai Kung Harbour. **Simpson Marine Ltd.** (⊠ Aberdeen Marina Tower, 8 Shun Wan Rd., Aberdeen, ☎ 2555–7349) is an established charter operator whose crewed junks can hold 35–45 people. Prices begin at HK$2,800 for an eight-hour day trip or a four-hour night trip during the week, HK$4,500 on summer weekends. The price goes up on holidays. You need to reserve in advance; half of the fee is required upon receipt of a signed contract, the remaining half at least five days prior to departure. **Jubilee International Tour Centre** (⊠ Far East Consortium Building, 121 Des Vouex Rd., Central, ☎ 2530–0530) is another established charter outfit recommended by the HKTA.

Martial Arts

C. S. Tang at the **Hong Kong Chinese Martial Arts Association** (⊠ Sports House, 1 Stadium Patch, Room 1008, So Kon Po, Causeway Bay, ☎ 2394–4803, 2504–8164) can advise you on where to find short-term martial-arts instruction, with courses that last from 10 days to a few months.

The **Martial Arts School** (⊠ 446 Hennessy Rd., 3/F, Causeway Bay, ☎ 2891–1044) of master Luk Chi Fu uses the white-crane system of internal-strength training. This method is one of the schools of *chi kung* or *noi kung,* the names for internal-strength kung fu, as opposed to the more violent type seen in the movies. This gentler version is said to be the forerunner of yoga. It relies on quick thinking, controlled breathing, and an instant grasp of the situation at hand; at the advanced level, a student can absorb blows and use spears and knives as if they were an extension of his or her body. Now run by the master's son, Luk Chung Mau, the school is open to anyone who will be around Hong Kong long enough to take an ongoing class.

Paragliding

The **Hong Kong Paragliding Association** (⊠ Union Commercial Bldg., 12–16 Lyndhurst Terrace, Room 202, Central, ☎ 2543–2901) will recommend an instructor. Weather permitting, you can soar over Hong Kong at an altitude rarely experienced by the populace. Paragliders are usually sighted over the scenic Shek O Peninsula. (If you just want to watch, you can spy take-offs and landings from the hike along Dragon's Back.) A tandem flight costs around HK$600.

Sailing

To sail here, you must belong to a yacht club that has reciprocal privileges with one in Hong Kong. Contact the **Hong Kong Yacht Club** (☎ 2832–2817) to make arrangements. Sometimes members need crews for weekend races, so experienced sailors can check the "crew wanted" board in the club's Course Room.

Scuba Diving

Bunn's Divers Institute (⊠ 2 Johnston Rd., Wanchai, ☎ 2893–7899) runs outings for qualified divers to areas like Sai Kung. The cost of a day trip runs HK$340 if you bring your own equipment, HK$520 if

118

Close-Up

MARTIAL ARTS GOES HOLLYWOOD

ALTHOUGH A POPULAR CULT favorite around the globe, martial-arts films in Hong Kong are no less than a phenomenon—their actors no less than superstars. Walk into a Hong Kong shop, visit a tourist office, step into an office atrium, and who do you see? Jackie Chan. Not the man, but his image. A life-size, cut-out figure of the humorous martial-arts superstar with a thousand-watt smile.

Chan has been called a "physical genius" and "the world's greatest action star." After years of international fame and accolades, this ultraflexible stuntman extraordinaire finally broke into the American market with 1996's *Rumble in the Bronx.* Two years later, Chan solidified his fame in the West with his first exclusively U.S. production, *Rush Hour.*

But in Hong Kong he's been a god, a crutch during economic hard times, when he was routinely asked to step in, support, sing praise, and bring up the people. He's the man who's guaranteed to draw the crowds every time a new movie is released. When he's on the silver screen, Hong Kongers know they can kick back and forget about their troubles for a while.

Of course Chan is not the first, or only, martial-arts golden son of Hong Kong. Recent heroes include John Woo, who created such bullet-ridden cult classics as *A Better Tomorrow, The Killer,* and *Hard-Boiled.* He was also responsible for launching Chow Yun-Fat's movie career. Chow Yun-Fat, who was born on the small island of Lamma and moved to Hong Kong in 1965, is the ultratough, cut martial artist who worked with Woo on *A Better Tomorrow,* which propelled both men into the limelight of the action-movie genre. Both men are best known for the slick Hollywood flick *The Replacement Killers,* which Woo produced and Chow Yun-Fat starred in.

While their Hollywood films do well in the United States, both Chow Yun-Fat and Jackie Chan are equally famous in the Hong Kong film industry for their locally filmed slapstick and heroic bloodshed films. Like the godfather of the genre, Bruce Lee, both are quickly becoming more than just home boys made good—they're international stars.

But it was Lee who broke the ground and still shines as the martial artist to live up to in life and on the screen. Martial artists still talk about Lee and his muscular physique. Lee and his style.

Just after moving to America in the 1960s, Lee was challenged to a fight by Cantonese experts in Oakland's Chinatown because he was teaching Chinese "secrets" to non-Chinese individuals. This was perceived as treason among some members of the martial-arts community. Lee won the challenge, and nowadays students around the world study such techniques. In part they can thank Lee for their schooling.

Unlike other areas in the region, this isn't a city where you're likely to get into a bar fight with a local who thinks he is Jackie Chan or Bruce Lee. But you are likely to see some of the cheesiest, funniest, most artistically and athletically amazing movies here if you just pop into a movie theatre, turn on your local television station, or visit a friend with a home-viewing/video system. It's a Hong Kong experience without parallel.

you need to rent gear. You must bring or rent a tank (HK$70 each; you'll need one each for morning and afternoon).

Mandarin Divers (⊠ Aberdeen Marina Tower, 8 Shun Wan Rd., Aberdeen, ☎ 2554–7110) offers two-week open-water training for a cost of HK$4,250, including boat rental, equipment, and certification (medical certificate required).

Skating

Cityplaza II, on Hong Kong Island, has a first-class ice-skating rink. ⊠ *1111 Kings Rd., Taikoo Shing,* ☎ *2885–4697.* ➣ *HK$45 morning session, HK$55 afternoon session.* ☉ *Weekdays 8–noon, 12:30–10 PM; Sat. 7–9 AM, 12:30–2, 3–5, 5:30–7:30, and 8–10; Sun. 7–noon, 12:30–2:30, 3–5, 5:30–7:30, and 8–10.*

The Glacier is part of Festival Walk, an extensive entertainment complex in Yau Yat Tsuen, next to the Kowloon Tong KCR station. It's the largest ice-skating rink in Hong Kong. You can rent figure skates that fit larger feet (up to a man's 11½). ☎ *2265–8888.* ➣ *HK$60 weekdays, HK$55 weekends.* ☉ *Daily 8:30 AM–10 PM.*

Squash

The **Hong Kong Urban Council** runs many public squash courts in the Territory and provides a **central booking service** (☎ 2927–8080 or 2922–8008). You can reserve courts up to 10 days in advance, and should do so as early as possible. Bring a passport for identification. Most courts are open from 7 AM to 10 or 11 PM and cost HK$27 for 30 minutes, HK$54 for an hour. The Urban Council can give directions, or you can contact the court directly.

Harbour Road Indoor Games Hall (⊠ 27 Harbour Rd., Wanchai, ☎ 2827–9684).
Hong Kong Squash Centre (⊠ Cotton Tree Dr., across from Peak Tram Terminal, Central, ☎ 2521–5072).
Laichikok Park (⊠ 1 Lai Wan Rd., Kowloon, ☎ 2745–2796).
Victoria Park (⊠ Hing Fat St., Causeway Bay, ☎ 2570–6186).

Swimming

Public swimming pools close in winter but fill to capacity in summer. With no lane ropes, swimmers must weave past other bodies, and the congestion can sometimes be as bad as in the streets. Most travelers use the clearer and more relaxing pools in their hotels. (☞ Beaches, *below*).

Tennis

Public tennis courts are usually booked far in advance. To reserve one you'll need identification, such as a passport. Most courts open from 7 AM to 10 or 11 PM and cost HK$42 in the daytime and HK$57 in the evening. For further information, contact the Hong Kong Urban Council (☞ Squash, *above*) or the **Hong Kong Tennis Association** (⊠ Sports House, 1 Stadium Path, Room 1021, So Kon Po, Causeway Bay, ☎ 2504–8266). The following courts are open to the public:

Bowen Road Courts (⊠ 7 Kennedy Rd., Wanchai, ☎ 2528–2983) has four courts; no nighttime tennis available.
Hong Kong Tennis Centre (⊠ Wongneichong Gap, Happy Valley, ☎ 2574–9122) has 17 courts.
Kowloon Tsai Park (⊠ 13 Inverness Rd., Kowloon Tong, ☎ 2336–7878) has eight courts.
Victoria Park (⊠ Hing Fat St., Causeway Bay, ☎ 2570–6186) offers 14 courts.

Waterskiing

Patrick's Waterskiing & Windsurfing (✉ Stanley Main Beach, Stanley, ☎ 2813–2372) is run by the friendly, laid-back man himself. Patrick will take you to the best waters in the Stanley Beach area and give you pointers on your waterskiing or wakeboarding technique. The fee— HK$700 per hour—includes a range of equipment and life jackets. To rent a speedboat, equipment, and the services of a driver, contact the **Waterski Club** (✉ Pier at Deep Water Bay Beach, ☎ 2812–0391) or ask your hotel for the names and numbers of other outfitters. The cost is usually about HK$580 per hour. Some junk-hiring companies also provide speedboats for waterskiing for an extra charge. (☞ Junking, *above*.)

Windsurfing

The popularity of this sport was declining until Hong Kong's native daughter Lee Lai-shan sailed off with the gold medal in the 1996 Summer Olympics in Atlanta. Now windsurfing centers at Stanley Beach, on Hong Kong Island, and Tun Wan Beach, on Cheung Chau Island, will gladly start you on the path to glory with some lessons. Patrick's Waterskiing & Windsurfing (☞ Waterskiing, *above*) offers a full-day course for HK$880; the more experienced can rent windsurfing boards for HK$70–$120 a day. For more windsurfing information, contact the Government Sports Centre (✉ St. Stevens Beach, Water Sports Centre, Wong Ma Kok Path, Stanley, ☎ 2813–5407).

SPECTATOR SPORTS

Horse Racing and Gambling

Horse racing is the nearest thing in Hong Kong to a national sport. It is a multimillion-dollar-a-year business, employing thousands of people and drawing crowds that approach insanity in their eagerness to rid themselves of their hard-earned money. Even if you're not a gambler, it's worth going to one of Hong Kong's two tracks just to experience the phenomenon. If you exclude the stock market, which is by far the territory's largest single gambling event, the only legalized forms of gambling are horse racing and the lottery. Nearby Macau (☞ Chapter 8) is another story—there you can get your fill of casino gambling.

The "sport of kings" is run under a monopoly by the Hong Kong Jockey Club, one of the most politically powerful entities in the territory. Profits go to charity and community organizations. The racing season runs from September through June. Some 65 races are held at one or the other of the two courses, most often on Saturday and Sunday at Shatin and Happy Valley, with an occasional Wednesday-night session at Happy Valley. The **Hong Kong Tourist Association** (☎ 2508–1234 hot line) organizes tours to the club and track. Costs range from HK$245 to HK$490 and can include transfers, lunch, and tips on picking a winner. Alternatively, you can watch the races from the public stands, where the atmosphere is lively and loud—this is highly recommended for a truly local experience, and the cost is only HK$10. Both courses have huge video screens at the finish line so that gamblers can see what's happening every foot of the way.

The **Happy Valley Race Track** (✉ Hong Kong Jockey Club, 1 Sports Rd., Happy Valley, ☎ 2966–8111 or 2966–8364), on Hong Kong Island, is one of Hong Kong's most beloved institutions. It holds most of the night races, which are usually held on Saturday or Sunday.

The **Shatin Racecourse** (✉ Tai Po Rd., Shatin, next to Racecourse KCR station, ☎ 2966–6520), in the New Territories, is newer than Happy Valley—one of the most modern racecourses in the world, in fact. Most of its races are run during the day on Saturday or Sunday. The easiest way to get here is by KCR train; on race days, the KCR detours to the Racecourse stop, between Sha Tin and University. A walkway from the station takes you directly to the racetrack. By car, take the exit marked RACECOURSE from Tai Po Road, just past central Shatin.

Rugby

One weekend every spring (usually in March), Hong Kong hosts the international tournament of Sevens-a-Side teams, otherwise known as the Rugby Sevens or simply "the Sevens," at the Hong Kong Stadium. The whole town goes half mad. To avoid camping outside the stadium all night to buy tickets, you can purchase them in advance from an overseas agent; for a list of agents contact the **Hong Kong Rugby Football Union** (✉ Sports House, 1 Stadium Path, Room 2001, So Kon Po, Causeway Bay, ☎ 2504–8300, FAX 2576–7237).

BEACHES

Hong Kong is not known for its beaches, but it's surrounded by hundreds of them and has a thriving sunbathing culture. About 40 of the beaches around Hong Kong and its outlying islands are "gazetted"—cleaned and maintained by the government, with services that include lifeguards, floats, and swimming-zone safety markers.

The scenery is often breathtaking, but pollution is a problem in Hong Kong waters, so before you embark on a day out, check the *South China Morning Post* for pollution ratings of the more popular beaches. Moreover, the occasional shark has been spotted in the waters of the New Territories. We restrict our recommendations to the beaches that offer a variety of activities in addition to swimming. Check with the HKTA before taking the plunge, and don't swim if a red flag—indicating either pollution or an approaching storm—is hoisted. The red flag flies often at Big Wave Bay (on the south side of Hong Kong Island) because of the rough surf. Check with the HKTA or listen to announcements on the radio or TV before heading out there.

Swimming is extremely popular with Hong Kongers, which means locals pack most beaches on summer weekends and public holidays. The more popular beaches, such as Repulse Bay, are busy day and night throughout the summer.

Almost all beaches can be reached by public transportation, but knowing which bus to catch and where to get off can be difficult. Pick up bus maps at a HKTA information booth before you start out. You can also take a taxi, but it will cost around HK$150 or more depending on where you're staying. Beaches on outlying islands connect to Central by the Hong Kong Ferry, and are often a short walk from the pier.

Hong Kong Island

Big Wave Bay, Hong Kong's most accessible surfing beach, lives up to its name and is frequently closed for swimming as a result. The beach has kiosks, barbecue pits, a playground, changing rooms, showers, and toilets. ✉ *From Shau Ki Wan take Bus 9 to the roundabout; walk about 20 mins along the road, which is usually lined with cars on weekends.*

At **Deep Water Bay** the action starts at dawn every morning, all year long, when members of the Polar Bear Club go for a dip. The beach is

TAI CHI

WHEN YOU ARRIVE in Hong Kong, chances are you'll be suffering from jet lag. If you wake up at 4 AM raring to go, you can wander down to any public park and watch Hong Kongers indulge in their morning tai chi ritual.

Just before dawn it's not unusual to see young businessmen and retired grandparents practicing tai chi: slowly stretching, breathing deeply, and moving in ways most Western teenagers can't manage. There's no better advertising for tai chi than seeing someone balance on one leg, with the other outstretched and held high for a long moment before gracefully swinging into another pose that requires balance, coordination, and strength.

More than 100,000 people are said to practice tai chi in Hong Kong each morning. If you're polite and ask permission, you could easily capture an award-winning photo of people performing this balletlike sport at dawn.

The art of tai chi consists of slow, steady, flowing movements with moderate postures—suitable for people of all ages, flexibility, and fitness levels to practice. It offers physical and mental benefits and may give you insights into the philosophical path followed by thousands throughout the centuries. While that may be common knowledge, few people know that tai chi is also a subtle, sophisticated, and scientific method of self-defense.

The founder of tai chi was Chang San Feng, a Taoist, who was born in AD 1247. His accomplishments were such that during the Ming Dynasty news of his fame reached the ears of the Emperor. Titles and honors were showered on Chang, and a magnificent mansion was built for him on Wutan Mountain as a special gift from the provincial governor.

One of the greatest tai chi masters was Yang Lu Chan (1799–1872) who, during the Ching Dynasty, served as the chief combat instructor to the Imperial Guard. He practiced tai chi for many years, and his fighting ability earned him the nickname "Invincible Yang."

To follow in their footsteps you need to study under an accomplished master. Only a good master can correctly demonstrate techniques, identify faults, and give proper advice and guidance that will help you progress. You will also experience a more calming feeling when studying under an accomplished master.

If you want to try tai chi while you're in Hong Kong, contact the Hong Kong Tourist Association (☎ 2508-2134). Under the guidance of a tai chi master, you can learn simple breathing and relaxation exercises. Free classes are offered at Hong Kong Park every Tuesday, Friday, and Sunday from 8:15 to 9:15 AM.

packed in summer, when there are lifeguards, swimming rafts, and safety-zone markers, plus a police reporting center. Barbecue pits, showers, and rest rooms are open year-round. A taxi from Central will take about 20 minutes. ⊠ *Take Bus 6A from Exchange Sq. Bus Terminus; or, for a scenic route, take Bus 70 from Exchange Sq. to Aberdeen and change to Bus 73, which passes the beach en route to Stanley.*

Repulse Bay has changing rooms, showers, toilets, swimming rafts, swimming safety-zone markers, and playgrounds. Several Chinese restaurants dot the beach, and kiosks serve light refreshments. The Lifesaving Club is at the east end and resembles a Chinese temple, with large statues of Tin Hau, Goddess of the sea, and Kwun Yum, Goddess of mercy. ⊠ *Take Bus 6, 6A, 64, 260, or 262 from Exchange Sq., or Bus 73 from Aberdeen.*

Shek O, not far from Big Wave Bay, is almost Mediterranean in aspect. A wide beach with shops and restaurants nearby, it has refreshment kiosks, barbecue pits, lifeguards, swimming rafts, playgrounds, changing rooms, showers, and toilets. The views are magnificent as the bus begins its descent toward the heart of the small village. ⊠ *Take the MTR from Central to Shau Ki Wan (there is a bus from Central to Shau Ki Wan, but it takes hours), then Bus 9 to the end of the line.*

Stanley Main, a wide sweep of sand, is popular with the windsurfing crowd and has a refreshment kiosk, swimming rafts, changing rooms, showers, and toilets, plus a nearby market. It also hosts the annual dragon boat races, usually held in June, in which friendly teams paddle out into the sea, turn around, and, at the sound of the gun, race ferociously back to the beach. It's a great day out, but head out early to claim a spot along the beach, as it gets chaotically crowded. Contact the HKTA for more details. ⊠ *Take a taxi from Central; or Bus 6, 6A, or 260 from Exchange Sq.; or Bus 73 from Aberdeen.*

Turtle Cove, isolated but scenic, has lifeguards and rafts in summer, barbecue pits, a refreshment kiosk, changing rooms, showers, and toilets. ⊠ *From Central take the MTR to Sai Wan Ho and change to Bus 14; get off at Tai Tam Rd. after passing the dam of Tai Tuk Reservoir.*

The New Territories

Expansive Sai Kung Peninsula has some of Hong Kong's most beautiful beaches, and many of these are easily reached by public transportation. Here are the three most popular:

Pak Sha Chau is a gem of a beach, with brilliant golden sand. Located on a grassy island near Sai Kung Town, it can only be reached by sampan. (Go to a pier to look for sampans. A driver will probably approach you. You must negotiate a fee, but you can expect to pay about HK$100.) Amenities include barbecue pits and toilets. ⊠ *Take MTR to Choi Hung, then Bus 92 to Sai Kung.*

Sha Ha's waters are sometimes dirty, but because they remain shallow far from shore, this beach is ideal for beginning windsurfers. You can take lessons or rent a board at the Kent Windsurfing Centre. Facilities include refreshment kiosks, a coffee shop, and a Chinese restaurant in the adjacent Surf Hotel. ⊠ *Take MTR to Choi Hung, then Bus 92 to the end of the line at Sai Kung, and walk or take a taxi for about a mile.*

Silverstrand is always crowded on summer weekends. Though a little rocky in spots, it has soft sand and all the facilities, including changing rooms, showers, and toilets. ⊠ *MTR to Choi Hung, then Bus 92 or taxi.*

The Outer Islands

A day trip to one of Hong Kong's islands is a terrific way to spend some time outside the city. If you take a morning ferry to Lamma, Lantau, or Cheung Chau, you can combine a beach trip with a sightseeing tour of the island (☞ The Outer Islands *in* Chapter 2).

Cheung Sha is a popular beach, only a short taxi or bus ride from the Silvermine Bay ferry pier. Its mile-long sandy expanse is excellent for swimming. All of the standard facilities are available. ⊠ *Take the ferry from Central to Silvermine Bay. Buses meet the ferry every half hr on weekdays; on Sun. and holidays buses leave when full, which is often on a sunny day.*

Hung Shing Ye, on Lamma Island, is popular with young locals. It is known as Power Station Beach because a massive plant is clearly visible from the beach, but that doesn't deter sunbathers, who materialize whenever the rays smile down. There are showers, toilets, changing rooms, barbecue pits, and a kiosk, but no swimming rafts. ⊠ *Take the ferry from Central to Yung Shue Wan and walk through the village, then over a low hill.*

Lo So Shing, also on Lamma Island, is popular with local families. It's an easy hike on a paved path from the fishing village of Sok Kwu Wan. Facilities include a kiosk, barbecue pits, swimming rafts, changing rooms, showers, and toilets. ⊠ *Take the ferry from Central to Sok Kwu Wan, then walk for 20–30 mins.*

Tung Wan is the main beach on Cheung Chau Island. On weekends its wide sweep of golden sand is so crowded with sunbathers that it's barely visible. You'll see it from the ferry as you approach the dock—at one end of the beach is the Warwick Hotel. Plenty of restaurants along the beach offer refreshments, seafood, and shade. Amenities include changing rooms, showers, and toilets. ⊠ *Take the ferry from Central to Cheung Chau ferry pier and walk 5 mins through the village to the beach.*

7 SHOPPING

Hong Kong is not the mercantile paradise it once was, but many practiced shoppers still swear by it, returning year after year for such items as Chinese antiques, Chinese porcelain, pearls, watches, cameras, eyeglasses, silk sheets and kimonos, tailor-made suits, and designer clothes at outlet prices.

Updated by
Lara Wozniak

RENT INCREASES, unstable economies in the rest of the region, and a tendency for manufacturers to open outlets elsewhere in the world have put a damper on the megabargains for which Hong Kong was once known. Although the lack of sales tax helps cut prices, you might still find that clothes, computers, and many electronic items cost about the same as they do in the United States, or even slightly more. But this is not to say you won't find some good values; you just have to know when and where to look.

We've divided this chapter into two handy sections for mastering the the art of shopping in Hong Kong: the first is divided into regions, the second into categories. To many Hong Kongers, especially women, shopping is a sport, a pastime. When Hong Kong women shop they don't go out to buy a blouse or a pair of trousers, they go out to *shop*. They scout areas and scour markets carrying designer shopping bags advertising previous scores. If you ask one of these shopaholics where to buy a specific item, the answer will not be a specific shop, but a whole section of town. If you want to shop as the experts do, you should learn the regions. The Western tendency, however, is to shop for specifics. Given short visits to Hong Kong, sometimes this style of shopping is unavoidable, which is why the second half of the chapter is divided into categories of potential purchases such as carpets or womens' clothing.

If you are coming to Hong Kong just to shop, you should plan your visit for the end-of-season sales (January–February and July–August). This is when prices are slashed anywhere from 50% to 90% in major department stores and boutiques. Many major boutiques are in malls or shopping complexes in the basement of office buildings and hotels. It might seem incongruous to mall crawl in Hong Kong—the land of bargain alleys and outdoor markets—but the advantage is air-conditioning and big-name designers all piled on top of one another. Still, some of the best deals are found in the local boutiques and in the freestanding designer shops.

Although shopping in Hong Kong can be a thrilling adventure, you need to be careful. Electronics shops selling the ever-popular photographic and hi-fi gear in Tsim Sha Tsui have a fearsome—and, regrettably, well-earned—reputation. Watch out for absurd discounts (to get you in the door), the switch (after you've paid, they pack a cheaper model), and the heavy, and sometimes physical, push to get you to buy a more expensive item than you want. It is also not uncommon for jewelers in the midprice range to offer you a discount of 10%–20% if you look at a few items and seem moderately interested. Be wary if a salesperson tries to drop the price much lower, however; you might go home to find you've purchased an inferior or defective item. Know, too, that in spite of the credit-card decals on the door (every card you could possibly imagine and more), most stores will insist on cash or add 3%–5% to the total. Shopping at stores with the Hong Kong Tourist Association (HKTA) decal on the window buys you some protection, since the shop belongs to the organization, but if you have troubles, head for the police, the Consumer Council, or the HKTA itself.

If you're really determined to shop till you drop, **Asian Cajun Ltd.** (✉ 12 Scenic Villa Dr., 4th floor, Pokfulam, ☎ 2817–3687) leads customized shopping tours for visitors seeking good buys in antiques, art, jewelry, designer clothes, and specialty items. Escorted tours, which include hard-to-find shops and private dealers, are US$100 per hour (not including transportation), with a three-hour minimum, for up to four people.

When it Comes to Getting Local Currency at an ATM, Same Thing.

Whether you're in Yosemite or Yemen, using your Visa® card or ATM card with the PLUS symbol is the easiest and most convenient way to get local currency. For example, let's say you're in France. When you make a withdrawal, using your secured PIN, it's dispensed in francs, but is debited from your account in U.S. dollars. This makes it easy to take advantage of favorable exchange rates. And if you need help finding one of Visa's 627,000 ATMs in 127 countries worldwide, visit **visa.com/pd/atm**. We'll make finding an ATM as easy as finding the Eiffel Tower, the Pyramids or even the Grand Canyon.

It's Everywhere You Want To Be.®

SEE THE WORLD
IN FULL COLOR

Fodor's Exploring Guides bring all the great sights vividly to life with hundreds of photographs, fascinating historical background, and colorful anecdotes. Detailed maps and practical information keep you headed in the right direction.

Pair a **Fodor's** Exploring Guide with your trusted Gold Guide for a complete planning package.

MAJOR SHOPPING AREAS

Hong Kong Island

Hong Kong Island shopping districts are listed here from west to east. All of them are easily accessible by MTR stations. Visiting them all in one day is conceivable but would likely be exhausting. Try working in two or at most three regions per shopping day.

If you are interested in everything from antiques to clothing to furniture, consider shopping in Western and nearby Central together. Start with the streets behind Western Market for some traditional Chinese atmosphere, where spices, herbs, and aphrodisiacs are sold amid old, walk-up buildings. Majhong shops, tea-sellers and packed Dim Sum restaurants abound. Then head up the main thoroughfare **Des Voeux Road** if you want to quickly work your way over to the department stores and boutiques in Central. More interesting, though, is a walk along **Hollywood Road,** renowned for its plethora of antiques and curio shops. Once you've reached Central, Hollywood turns into **Wyndham Street,** which also has antiques, statuary and ceramic shops, and carpet shops. Depending on how many of the small antiques shops you wander in and out of, shopping in both Central and Western will most certainly take a full day. If you walk, wear comfortable shoes and remember to buy bottled water along the way.

Western District

The Western District is one of the oldest and most typically Chinese areas in Hong Kong. (Take the MTR to Sheung Wan or the tram to Western Market.) Here you'll find craftsmen making mah-jongg tiles, opera costumes, fans, and chops (seals carved in stone with engraved initials); Chinese-medicine shops selling ginseng, snake musk, shark's fin, and powdered lizards; rice shops and rattan-furniture dealers; and cobblers, tinkers, and tailors. You'll also come across alleyways where merchants have set up stalls filled with knickknacks and curios.

The Victorian redbrick structure of **Western Market** (✉ Des Voeux Rd., Sheung Wan), similar to London's Covent Garden, was built in 1906 as a produce market. The first two floors are filled with shops selling crafts, toys, jewelry, collectibles, and fabrics, but it's certainly not worth a special trip. You can find these goods elsewhere in town.

Shun Tak Centre (✉ 200 Connaught Rd.), attached to the **Macau Ferry Terminal**, offers a selection of boutiques selling clothing, handbags, toys, and novelties. If you're waiting for the Macau Ferry, have a look around; otherwise, a special trip is not required since most of the stores here are chain stores and can be found all over Hong Kong.

The streets behind Western Market are some of the best places to soak up some of Hong Kong's traditional Chinese atmosphere. **Wing Lok Street** and **Bonham Strand West** are excellent browsing areas, with shops selling herbs, rice, tea, and Chinese medicines. Visit **She Wong Yuen** (✉ 89–93 Bonham Strand) for a taste of snake's-gall-bladder wine. Heading uphill, don't miss the stalls selling bric-a-brac on **Ladder Street,** which angles down from Queen's Road in Central to Hollywood and Caine roads. **Hollywood Road** is lined with Chinese antiques and collectibles; it turns into **Wyndham Street** in Central.

Two of Hong Kong's largest Western-style department stores, **Sincere** and **Wing On**, are technically in Central but you will pass them as you are walking from Western to Central. The **Sincere Company**, which celebrated it's 100th anniversary last year, is run by the third generation of the Ma family, grandchildren of the founder Ma Ying-piu. Sin-

128

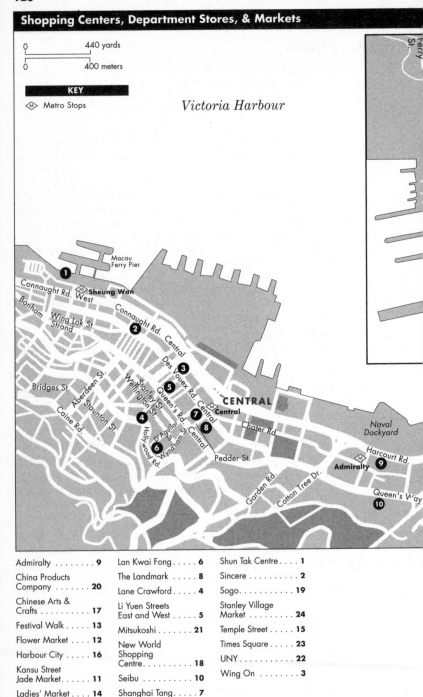

0   440 yards

0   400 meters

KEY

Metro Stops

Victoria Harbour

Macau
Ferry Pier

Connaught Rd. West   Sheung Wan

Bonham   Wing Lok St.   Connaught Rd. Central

Strand

Des Voeux Rd. Central

Bridges St.   Aberdeen St.   Wellington St.   Stanley St.   Queen's Rd. Central

Staunton St.   **CENTRAL**

Caine Rd.   Hollywood Rd.   D'Aguilar St.   Wyndham St.   Central

Chater Rd.

Naval
Dockyard

Pedder St.

Harcourt Rd.

Garden Rd.   Cotton Tree Dr.   **Admiralty**

Queen's Way

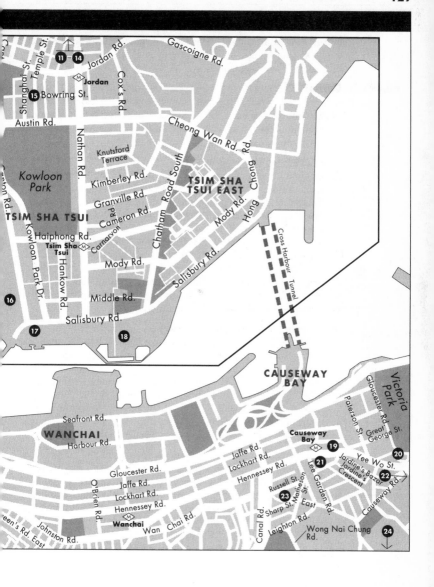

TSIM SHA TSUI EAST

TSIM SHA TSUI

Kowloon Park

Gascoigne Rd.

Shanghai St.
Temple St.
Jordan Rd.
Cox's Rd.
(11)–(14)
Jordan
(15) Bowring St.
Austin Rd.
Nathan Rd.
Knutsford Terrace
Kimberley Rd.
Granville Rd.
Cameron Rd.
Carnarvon Rd.
Haiphong Rd.
Tsim Sha Tsui
Kowloon Park Dr.
Hankow Rd.
Mody Rd.
Middle Rd.
Salisbury Rd.
(16)
(17)
(18)
Cheong Wan Rd.
Chatham Road South
Mody Rd.
Hong Chong Rd.
Salisbury Rd.

Cross Harbour Tunnel

CAUSEWAY BAY

Victoria Park

WANCHAI
Seafront Rd.
Harbour Rd.
Gloucester Rd.
O'Brien Rd.
Jaffe Rd.
Lockhart Rd.
Hennessey Rd.
Wanchai
Wan Chai Rd.
Johnston Rd.
een's Rd. East

Jaffe Rd.
Lockhart Rd.
Hennessey Rd.
Canal Rd.
Russell St.
Sharp St.
Leighton Rd.
Matheson St.
Lee Garden Rd.
Causeway Bay
(19)
(21)
(23)
Jardine's Bazaar
Jardine's Crescent
Yee Wo St.
Paterson St.
Gloucester Rd.
Great George St.
(20)
(22)
Causeway Rd.
Wong Nai Chung Rd.
(24)

cere was the first store to give paid days off to employees, the first to showcase newly arrived imported merchandise in store windows, the first to hire women in sales positions—beginning with the founder's wife and sister-in-law—and the first to establish a fixed-price policy backed up by the regionally novel idea of issuing receipts.

Central District
Otherwise known as Hong Kong's financial and business district, Central has an extraordinary mixture of designer boutiques, department stores and narrow lanes full of vendors selling inexpensive clothing and knockoffs of designer goods.

Lane Crawford (⊠ 70 Queen's Rd. Central, ☎ 2118–3388), east of the Chinese Merchandise Emporium, is one of Hong Kong's premier department stores. Other exclusive shops are housed in Central's major office buildings and shopping complexes. For example, the **Landmark,** on Des Voeux Road, **Prince's Building,** on 10 Chater Road, and **The Galleria at Nine Queen's Road** (MTR: Central) are all connected by elevated walkways. If couture labels are what you are after, don't miss shopping here. While absorbing the piped music, golden hues, and spacious settings of these interconnected shopping arcades, you will find Christian Dior, the internationally renowned fashion designer; Coach, makers of fine leather handbags, purses, and belts; giftware from Lalique; and a whole range of designer boutiques.

In the **Shanghai Tang Department Store** (⊠ 12 Pedder St., Central, ☎ 2525–7333), you will find fine silk Mandarin jackets for men and women, as well as an exciting array of silks and cashmeres in brilliant colors. Custom-made suits start around US $666. You can also have a *cheongsam* (a slit-skirt dress with a Mandarin collar) made for about US $400, including fabric. Ready-to-wear Mandarin suits and unisex kimonos are all in the US $200 to US $300 range. Among the Chinese souvenirs are novelty watches with miniature dim sum servings instead of numbers or fluffy Teddy bears wearing silk pajamas.

If you are visiting from Britain, **Marks & Spencer,** at 28 Queen's Road Central, features classic clothing, including large sizes that may be harder to find in other department stores in Hong Kong. However, you may find the discounts here aren't much better than you will find at home. In the **Jardine House,** at Connaught Place, across from the Central Post Office, check out the **Oxfam Hong Kong** shop in the basement. Even if you are not a secondhand shopper, it's worth a look for all the designer labels selling for a fraction of their original cost.

You can hunt for bargains on clothing, shoes, woolens, handbags, and accessories in the stalls that fill **East and West Li Yuen streets,** between Queen's Road and Des Voeux Road. Watch out for pickpockets in these crowded lanes. On **Wyndham Street** you'll find art, antiques, and carpets, and nearby **Lan Kwai Fong** has art galleries and clothing boutiques in its small office buildings.

Admiralty
Bounded by Central on the west and Wanchai on the east, Admiralty is another mall-crawler's dream world. If you plan on a full-day of shopping, consider taking a tai chi class in nearby Hong Kong Park in the morning (Sunday, Tuesday, and Friday, ☎ 2509–1234) to limber up before starting your day.

The **Admiralty** complex (⊠ Queensway, Central, MTR: Admiralty) comprises four shopping centers connected by elevated walkways: United Centre, Admiralty Centre, Pacific Place, and Queensway Plaza. The **United Centre** houses several furniture shops. It is worth visiting just for

Tequila Kola (☞ Furniture and Furnishings, *below*), which sells upscale, handcrafted bedroom sets, couches, fabrics, and gifts. **Admiralty Centre** has reasonably priced optical shops and men's tailors, a chop maker, and an excellent carpet shop. **Queensway Plaza** is dominated by smaller, lesser-name boutiques, which are worth checking out if you want one-of-a-kind buys without having to scour the street markets.

The glitziest of the four shopping arcades and perhaps the most popular shopping mall in Hong Kong is **Pacific Place,** with four floors of upscale shops and restaurants; its flagship Japanese department store, **Seibu,** has upmarket products and a vast and varied food department in the basement. **Lane Crawford** (☞ Central, *above*), another upscale emporium, has a branch here. For a break in your shopping, stop by at the multiplex cinema, which screens international releases, or dine at one of the dozens of restaurants. The Marriott, the Island Shangri-La and the Conrad hotels are all connected to this shopping plaza.

Wanchai District

More famous for its Suzie Wong–style nightlife than for daytime shopping, Wanchai has some interesting holdings for the curious or adventurous shopper. Tattoos, for example, are available on **Lockhart Road** (MTR: Wanchai stop for the Lockhart Road exit), traditional Chinese bamboo birdcages on **Johnston Road**. Wandering through vegetable and fruit markets in the lanes between Johnston Road and Queen's Road East, you'll see dozens of stalls selling buttons and bows and inexpensive clothes. **Queen's Road East** (near the junction with Queensway) is known for shops that make blackwood and rosewood furniture and camphor-wood chests. There are more furniture shops on **Wanchai Road,** off Queen's Road East.

Causeway Bay

Causeway Bay is a major shopping point for Hong Kongers precisely because you can get just about anything here, from electronics to shoes to clothes. It is dominated by two large Japanese department stores: **Mitsukoshi** and **Sogo,** which are directly across the street from one another on Hennessy Road, so it's easy to visit both. **Hennessy Road** is filled with smaller shops selling jewelry, watches, stereos, cameras, and electronic goods, and parallel **Lockhart Road** has several good shoe stores featuring brands from Nine West to Rockport.

The boutiques of **Vogue Alley,** at the intersection of Paterson and Kingston streets, feature the best of Hong Kong's own fashion designers. Just behind the Excelsior is the **In Square** (**Windsor House**), toward Victoria Park opposite the Park Lane Hotel on Gloucester Road, with a mall plus two floors of computer supplies. The **Chinese Resources Center (CRC)** (✉ 19–31 Yee Wo St., Causeway Bay, next to Victoria Park, ☎ 2890–8321) has a vast selection of goods made in China, including everything from chopsticks to fanciful porcelain vases to quilted Mandarin jackets.

Behind Sogo (away from the waterfront) are two streets: **Jardine's Bazaar,** which has stacks of Chinese restaurants, and **Jardine's Crescent,** which is an alley of bargain-basement clothes and accessories. This market, a traditional favorite for inexpensive clothing, is geared toward Chinese shoppers, so you're not likely to find too many Western sizes. At the end of the alley, you'll experience a bustling "wet market" (so called because the vendors are perpetually hosing down their produce), where Chinese housewives shop for fresh produce and for fresh chickens, which are slaughtered on the spot.

Times Square, on Russel Street (on the site of the old Causeway Bay tram station), is a megamall with 12 floors of shopping, from boutiques to department stores such as **Lane Crawford** and **Marks & Spencer.** It's more crowded than Central's **Landmark,** but less congested than some of the other Chinese emporiums. An indoor atrium hosts entertainment—ranging from heavy-metal bands and fashion shows to local movie-star appearances—a cinema complex, and a dozen or so eateries. The streets around Time Square feature some of the most interesting boutique shopping in Hong Kong. These shops go in and out of business with some frequency, and they cater to Hong Kong womens' sizes; if you fit the clothes, you're likely to find some real one-of-a-kind deals.

Eastern District

If you're shopping with children, you might want to shop in the Eastern District, which includes North Point, Quarry Bay, and Shaukiwan.The best shopping is in Quarry Bay's huge **Cityplaza** (⊠ 1111 Kings Rd., Taikoo Shing, Quarry Bay, MTR: Taikoo Shing), which houses Hong Kong's largest department store, **UNY,** as well as more than 400 shops (including toy stores), an ice-skating rink, a bowling alley, and weekly cultural shows.

Stanley Market

Most people visit popular Stanley Market as part of a tour. You should allot at least a half day for this market. If you dine here, it can be an all-day outing. The area around **Main Street** has a trendy, artsy ambience. On the way to Stanley Market, stop at **Repulse Bay**'s shopping arcade, in which several stores sell fine reproductions of traditional Chinese furniture.

Stanley Village Market (Bus 6, 6A, or 260 from Central Bus Terminus, Hong Kong Island, or 260 from the Star Ferry; in Kowloon, Bus 973 from Tsim Sha Tsui) is not quite the bargain trove it used to be, but you can still find some good buys in sportswear and casual clothing if you comb through the stalls. Dozens and dozens of shops line a main street so narrow that awnings from each side meet in the middle. Stores open early, at about 10, but close between 5 and 6. **China Town** (⊠ 39 Stanley Main St.) has well-priced cashmere sweaters. **Sun and Moon Fashion Shop** (⊠ 18A–B Stanley Main St.) sells casual wear, with bargains on such familiar names as L. L. Bean, Yves St. Laurent, and Talbots. **Allan Janny Ltd.** (⊠ 17 Stanley New St.) has antique furniture and porcelain. Stanley Market is also a good place to buy linens; **Tong's Sheets and Linen Co.** (⊠ 55–57 Stanley St.) has sheets, tablecloths, and brocade pillow covers, as well as silk kimonos and pajamas. The market is most enjoyable on weekdays, when it's less crowded.

Kowloon

Kowloon is home to famous Nathan Road, which is a bright-lights, full-on neon experience for tourists. Locals usually don't shop on Nathan Road and tourists usually get ripped off here. But when it comes to outdoor markets, Kowloon draws the locals and the in-the-know tourists who are willing to bargain for their bargains. In addition to good sales at outdoor vending areas such as Temple Street market and Ladies Market, cultural shopping experiences abound in places such as the Bird Market or the Jade Market.

Visiting all the outdoor markets in Kowloon in one day may be exhausting. You're better off picking three sites you want to spend some time in rather than rushing through them all.

Tsim Sha Tsui District

Known for its Golden Mile of shopping along **Nathan Road,** Tsim Sha Tsui is popular with tourists for its hundreds of stereo, camera, jewelry, cosmetics, fashion, and souvenir shops. Branching off Nathan Road are narrow streets lined with shops crowded with every possible type of merchandise. Explore **Granville Road,** with its embroidery and porcelain shops and clothing factory outlets (not as plentiful as they were a few years ago, but worth a look for serious bargain hunters), and **Mody Road,** for souvenir shops.

Unfortunately, the shopkeepers on Nathan Road are known to take advantage of unsuspecting shoppers. It's best to be absolutely sure of the quality and price you should be paying before shopping on Nathan Road. Stick to the places we list or those displaying HKTA stickers. At **Chinese Resources Center** (✉ 44 Nathan Rd., Tsim Sha Tsui, ☎ 2739–3839) you can buy reasonably priced goods made in China.The **Chinese Products Company** (✉ 54 Nathan Rd., Tsim Sha Tsui, ☎ 2739–3839) has a fairly wide and good-quality selection of household items.

Yue Hwa Chinese Products Emporium (✉ 143–161 Nathan Rd., Tsim Sha Tsui, ☎ 2739–3888; ✉ 54–64 Nathan Rd., Tsim Sha Tsui, ☎ 2368–9165; ✉ 301–309 Nathan Rd., Yau Ma Tei, ☎ 2384–0084) carries a broad selection of Chinese goods and has a popular medicine counter. At **Joyce** (✉ 23 Nathan Rd., Tsim Sha Tsui, ☎ 2367–8128) you can find chic housewares and clothes by such designers as Issey Miyake and Prada.

Harbour City (✉ Canton Rd., Tsim Sha Tsui, next to the Star Ferry Pier; MTR or Star Ferry to Tsim Sha Tsui) is the largest shopping complex in Hong Kong, and one of the largest in the world; if you can't find it here, it probably doesn't exist. Harbour City houses **Ocean Terminal, Ocean Centre, Ocean Galleries,** and the Hong Kong, Marco Polo and Prince Hotels. At last count there were some 50 restaurants and 600 shops, including 36 shoe stores and 31 jewelry and watch stores. The complex contains a vast **Toys "R" Us** (✉ Ocean Terminal, ☎ 2730–9462) and a large branch of **Marks & Spencer** (✉ Ocean Centre, ☎ 2926–3318). Note that this mall caters to cruise-ship passengers with limited time and a need to shop, so you are not likely to get the best bargains here.

New World Shopping Centre (✉ 18 Salisbury Rd., Tsim Sha Tsui; MTR: Tsim Sha Tsui) is a harborfront shopping center (next to the New World Hotel) with four floors of fashion and leather boutiques, jewelry stores, restaurants, optical shops, tailors, stereo stores, arts and crafts shops, and the Japanese **Tokyu** department store. The **Regent Hotel Shopping Arcade** (✉ Salisbury Rd., Tsim Sha Tsui), with mostly designer boutiques, is adjacent to the New World Shopping Centre. The **Palace Mall** is an underground mall between the Regent Hotel and the Space Museum (you enter from the promenade between the hotel and the Star Ferry Pier). Although it's just the place to go when it's pouring rain, these sites also cater to the time-crunched cruise shoppers.

Hung Hom District

Travel east of Tsim Sha Tsui to Hung Hom, the center of Hong Kong's jewelry and textile industries, for a tremendous selection of bargains in both designer boutiques and factory outlets. **Man Yue Street** is a good nexus.

Yaumatei and Mongkok

North of Jordan Road, Tsim Sha Tsui's bright lights and big-city world give way to tenements and overcrowding. You could visit this area in conjunction with Nathan Road. But if you're planning a day of hunting and gathering, skip Nathan Road shops and start here. Here street signs revert to Chinese, retirees gather to play checkers and mah-jongg in the park, and outdoor markets abound. You can find great deals as well as fakes, pickpockets, and hawking shopkeepers with no-return policies. Truly a place to enjoy the bargaining and the chaos of it all.

Temple Street (⊠ Kowloon, near Jordan MTR station) becomes an open-air market at night, filled with a colorful collection of clothes, handbags, electrical goods, gadgets, and all sorts of household items. By the light of lamps strung up between stalls, hawkers try to catch the eyes of shoppers by flinging clothes up from their stalls; Cantonese opera competes with pop music; and a constant chatter of vendors' cries and shoppers' haggling fills the air. The market stretches for almost a mile and is one of Hong Kong's liveliest nighttime shopping experiences. You can go as early as 5 PM and leave by 10 PM. It's best to hire a local guide to take you. Some of the surrounding neighborhoods may be unsafe at night.

Kansu Street Jade Market (⊠ Kansu St. off Nathan Rd., Yau Ma Tei) displays jade in every form, color, shape, and size. The market is full of traders conducting intriguing deals and keen-witted sellers trying to lure tourists. Some trinkets are reasonably priced, but unless you know a lot about jade, don't be tempted to buy something pricey. ☉ *Daily 10–4.*

The **Ladies' Market** (⊠ Tung Choi St., take Nelson St. exit from the Mongkok MTR station, walk two blocks east to Tung Choi Street) features the same clothing you find in the Temple Street night market, except you can go by daylight. Despite it's name, men's and children's clothing is also sold. ☉ *Daily noon–11.*

The **Bird Market** (⊠ Hong Lok St.) is one of the most exotic markets in Asia. Two long alleys are nearly covered over with bamboo bird cages with tropical birds that are tenderly fed live worms via chopsticks poked through the bars by their owners. You'll also find old men taking their own caged birds out for walks through the market. (Take the MTR to Mongkok, exit on Nelson St.: Hong Lok Street is two blocks west.)

The **Flower Market** (⊠ Flower St., near Prince Edward MTR station) in Mongkok is a collection of street stalls selling cut flowers and potted plants, with a few outlets specializing in plastic plants and silk flowers.

New Kowloon and New Territories

Kowloon proper ends at Boundary Street, which in the 19th century served as the border with China marked by bamboo pole. As the New Territories develop, Kowloon, New Kowloon, and the New Territories continue to blend together. The key difference is the farther out you travel from Kowloon the less densely populated the area becomes. High rises still abound in many pockets, but give way to trees, rolling hills, and seaside views. Most of the shopping experience in this region is in malls.

New Kowloon
Festival Walk (⊠ 80 Tat Chee Ave., Kowloon Tong, MTR and KCR: Kowloon Tong) is the fanciest mall in Hong Kong and very easy to reach, albeit slightly off the beaten path. Hong Kong's largest **Marks & Spencer** and a very large **Esprit** serve as anchors; the mall also has the largest ice rink in Hong Kong, perfect if you're shopping with kids who want a respite from the sometimes scorching-hot weather.

New Territories
Maritime Square (⊠ 33 Tsing King Rd., Tsing Yi, MTR: Tsing Yi) is Hong Kong's newest mall. On fast-growing Tsing Yi Island, it's full of shops and restaurants.

New Town Plaza in Shatin (KCR: Shatin) is Hong Kong's largest mall, with 350 shops. It's anchored by a Japanese department store called Seiyu.

NEED A BREAK?	Check out the **Pacific Coffee Company Ltd.** for a cup of strong, freshly brewed coffee. Sip, relax, and read a gratis international newspaper before heading back to the shops. The stores are located in malls, by the ferries, and in office buildings throughout Hong Kong. For the nearest locale, call ☎ 2805–1617.

SPECIALTY SHOPPING

Time is a valuable entity in Hong Kong, and you may be limited to the amount necessary to scour the districts. If you're looking for something specific, below is a list of shopping items and places where you can find them.

Antiques

China has laws against taking items more than 120 years old out of the country, but Hong Kong's antiques dealers can, at least officially, sell whatever they want to. So ancient porcelain, textiles, and specialty furniture are still available. Everyday furniture and pottery are not considered national treasures and are not affected by the export laws.

Auction Houses

Hong Kong auctions are interesting even if you don't go in with a particular goal. The international houses **Christie's** and **Sotheby's** carry fine, expensive pieces. The two local houses, **Lammert Brothers** and **Victoria Auctioneers,** cater more to locals with less-expensive goods. Watch for auction announcements in the classified section of the *South China Morning Post.*

Christie's (⊠ 2203 Alexandra House, 22nd floor, 16–20 Chater Rd., Central, ☎ 2521–5396, FAX 2877–1709).
Lammert Brothers (⊠ Union Commercial Bldg., 12–16 Lyndhurst Terr., mezzanine floor, Central, ☎ 2545–9859).
Sotheby's (⊠ 4–4A Des Voeux Rd., Central, ☎ 2822–8100, FAX 2810–6239).
Victoria Auctioneers (⊠ Century Sq., 1–13 D'Aguilar St., 16th floor, Central, ☎ 2524–7611).

Shops

HOLLYWOOD ROAD AND WYNDHAM STREET
Hollywood Road and Wyndham Street, which is one long lane that runs from Central to Western, is undeniably the best place for poking about in shops and stalls selling antiques from many Asian countries. Treasures are hidden away among a jumble of old family curio shops, sidewalk junk stalls, slick new display windows, and dilapidated warehouses. You will also find great furniture here.

C. L. Ma Antiques (⊠ 43–55 Wyndham St., Central, ☎ 2525–4369) has Ming Dynasty–style reproductions, especially large carved chests and tables made of unlacquered wood.
Dynasty Furniture Co. (⊠ 68A Hollywood Rd., Central, ☎ 2369–6940) has small netsukes skillfully carved out of tagua, a rain-forest nut that looks a lot like ivory.
Eastern Dreams (⊠ 47A Hollywood Rd., Central, ☎ 2544–2804; ⊠ 4 Shelley St., Central, ☎ 2524–4787) has antique and reproduction furniture, screens, and curios.
Honeychurch Antiques (⊠ 29 Hollywood Rd., Central, ☎ 2543–2433) is known especially for antique silver jewelry from Southeast Asia, China, and England.

A SHOPPER'S PARADISE

NO **MATTER** why you come to Hong Kong, and whether or not you're a shopper by nature, it's highly unlikely that you'll leave here without having bought something. Hong Kong does a roaring trade in bargain-priced luggage simply because so many travelers run out of space in their suitcases.

There are good reasons for this: Hong Kong's status as a free port, where everything other than alcohol, tobacco, perfumes, cosmetics, cars, and some petroleum products comes in without import duty; access to a skilled and still relatively inexpensive labor force just across the border in China; and the highly competitive retail business, the result of a local free-trade policy that encourages shopkeepers to try to undercut one another.

What else makes Hong Kong special? Because it's small and heavily populated, Hong Kong has had to grow upward and downward rather than outward. There are shops and small businesses in all sorts of unexpected places—a boutique might be up a back staircase of a scuffy building in the alleyway; in the basement of a lighting shop; on the 13th floor of an office building. Space is limited and precious in Hong Kong, so don't confine yourself to the main roads if you're really bargain-hunting. This is the land of free trade; shopping around is a prerequisite to any successful purchase.

The pressure from salespeople can be exasperating. If you're just browsing, make this very clear; don't be pushed into a purchase. While you are looking around, note ballpark prices and descriptions on the shop's business card. Even if you're not the first customer, always ask for discounts—you might get deeper ones for multiple purchases. Expect 10% to 50% off; you'll likely get deeper discounts in the outdoor markets. Everywhere, except in Japanese department stores and

some of the larger boutiques, discounts abound. Don't be shy. Bargain. This is the accepted and expected way of conducting business all over Asia. Don't take the salesman's word for it when he assures that his price is the "very best": shop around. Once you've looked around at other places and have a good idea how much you should pay, go back to the shop of choice first thing the next morning. Remind the salesperson that you are the first customer; it's a superstition that works in your favor. Local shopkeepers believe if they sell to the first customer who walks into their store, they will have a good business day.

If you plan to shop in the outdoor stalls and alleys, don't dress up; being well dressed will not help your bargaining position. Inspect the goods you buy very carefully; many are seconds. When you buy clothing, inspect the actual item handed to you; if you've chosen it based on a hanging sample, you might end up taking home a different, seriously flawed item. Having made your selection and struck the right price for it, you're ready for the exchange of money. Although credit cards and traveler's checks are widely accepted, surcharges are common, so you may get a better price if you pay cash. Make sure you get the worldwide guarantee that carries the name or logo of the relevant sole agent in Hong Kong, and, for electronics, make sure there's a service center in your home country. Lastly, get a fully itemized receipt for any major purchase.

Whether you're drifting about in the comfort of an air-conditioned shopping mall, exploring the factory outlets of Hung Hom, or poking through alleys and backstreets, you're getting a look at the life and guts of Hong Kong. It's as much a cultural experience as a shopping expedition, and that's the best bargain of all.

Schoeni Fine Arts (✉ 27 Hollywood Rd., Central, ☎ 2542–3143) sells Japanese, Chinese, and Thai antiques, Chinese silverware, such as opium boxes, and rare Chinese pottery.

Teresa Coleman (✉ 79 Wyndham St., Central, ☎ 2526–2450) carries antique embroidered pieces, including magnificent must-see kimonos.

The Tibetan Gallery (✉ 55 Wyndham St., Central, ☎ 2530–4863) sells antique *Thangkas,* or meditation paintings, incense holders, and prayer rugs from Tibet.

True Arts & Curios (✉ 89 Hollywood Rd., ☎ 2559–1485) is a cluttered shop with good buys in embroidered items (including slippers for bound feet), silver, porcelain, and snuff bottles.

Yue Po Chai Antique Co. (✉ 132–136 Hollywood Rd., Central, ☎ 2540–4374) is one of Hollywood Road's oldest shops, and it has a vast and varied stock.

Zitan Oriental Antiques (✉ 43-55 Wyndham St., ground floor, Central, ☎ 2523–7584) sells antique furnishings only from mainland China. Look for traditional wood wedding beds or intricately carved armoires.

CAT STREET

Cat Street (or Upper Lascar Row), once famous for its thieves' market of secondhand stolen goods, now has almost as many small antiques shops as Hollywood Road itself. They're lined up behind the outdoor stalls selling old—or at least old-looking—jewelry, curios, and assorted bits of junk.

Cat Street Galleries (✉ 38 Lok Ku Rd., Sheung Wan, Western, ☎ 2541–8908) is a ground-floor cluster of shops selling porcelain and furniture.

China Art (✉ 15 Upper Lascar Row, Western, ☎ 2542–0982) has fine furnishings, mostly from the Suzhou area of China, and leads tours roughly once a month to its warehouse in southern China.

OTHER AREAS

Altfield Gallery (✉ 248–249 Prince's Bldg., 10 Chater Rd., Central, ☎ 2537–6370) carries furniture, fabrics, and collectibles from all over Asia.

Charlotte Horstmann and Gerald Godfrey (✉ Ocean Terminal, Tsim Sha Tsui, ☎ 2735–7167) is good for wood carvings, bronzeware, and furniture.

Eileen Kershaw (✉ Peninsula Hotel, Tsim Sha Tsui, ☎ 2366–4083) sells fine Chinese porcelain and jade carvings.

Art

Like other major cosmopolitan cities around the world where the monied-class is looking for aesthetic investment, Hong Kong has a lively contemporary gallery scene, much of it concentrating on the best work coming out of China and Southeast Asia.

Galleries

Asian Art News, a bimonthly magazine, sold at bigger newsstands for HK$50, is a good guide to what's happening in galleries around the region. If you want a firsthand look at the latest trends in Asian art, plan to spend a day gallery-hopping in Central and in Lan Kwai Fong.

Alisan Fine Arts Ltd. (✉ Prince's Bldg., Central, ☎ 2526–1091) was one of the first galleries in Hong Kong to promote Chinese artists living abroad. It shows a wide range of contemporary art with an East-meets-West flavor.

Fringe Gallery (✉ 2 Lower Albert Rd., Central, ☎ 2521–7251), part of the Fringe Club, is a showcase for young, not-yet-famous Hong Kong artists, both Chinese and expat.

Galeriasia (✉ 1 Lan Kwai Fong, 6th floor, Central, ☎ 2529–2598) promotes artists from Asia, with exhibits from Myanmar and Vietnamese artists.

Galerie La Vong (✉ 1 Lan Kwai Fong, 13th floor, Central, ☎ 2869–6863) highlights the works of today's leading Vietnamese artists, many of whose creations reveal an intriguing combination of French impressionist and traditional Chinese influences.

Hanart TZ Gallery (✉ Room 202, Henley Bldg., 2nd floor, 5 Queen's Rd. Central, ☎ 2526–9019) shows contemporary Chinese artists from the mainland, Taiwan, Hong Kong, and abroad.

Plum Blossoms Gallery (✉ Coda Plaza, 51 Garden Rd., 17th floor, Central, across from Botanical Gardens, ☎ 2521–2189) shows Chinese and Western art, along with antique textiles and Tibetan carpets.

Sandra Walters (✉ 501 Hoseinee House, 69 Wyndham St., Central, ☎ 2522–1137) runs a public showroom with a wide range of late-19th-century to contemporary Western and Chinese art; call for an appointment.

Schoeni Art Gallery (✉ U.G. Floor, 21–31 Old Bailey St., Central, ☎ 2869–8802) exhibits a dramatic mix of abstract, realist, and political paintings by contemporary mainland-Chinese artists. Once a year Schoeni mounts a show of European masters.

Wagner Art Gallery (✉ Lusitano Bldg., 4 Duddell St., 7th floor, Central, ☎ 2521–7882) is owned by an Australian couple who make it their mission to introduce Hong Kong to the best Australian artists. From time to time there are shows of major contemporary names.

Wattis Fine Art (✉ 20 Hollywood Rd., 2nd floor, Central, ☎ 2524–5302) specializes in 18th- to 20th-century European paintings and the work of contemporary artists living in Hong Kong, both Chinese and expat.

Zee Stone Gallery (✉ Yu Yuet Bldg., 43–55 Wyndham St., Central, ☎ 2810–5895) displays a combination of contemporary Chinese paintings and antique Tibetan silver and carpets. It sells Chinese furniture as well.

Framers

It may be worth having your artwork framed in Hong Kong, as prices are much lower than in Europe and the United States. The following framers are reputable and centrally located:

Man Fong (✉ 1 Lyndhurst Tower, Lyndhurst Terr., Central, ☎ 2522–6923).

Po Shu Frame & Glass Co. (✉ 255 Queen's Rd. E, ground floor, Wanchai, ☎ 2891–4030).

Wah Cheong (✉ 174 Wai Yip St., ☎ 2523–1900).

Cameras, Lenses, and Binoculars

Many of Hong Kong's thousands of camera shops are clustered in the Lock Road–lower Nathan Road area of Tsim Sha Tsui, in the back streets of Central, and on Hennessy Road in Causeway Bay. If in doubt about where to shop for such items, stick to HKTA shops. (Pick up the HKTA shopping guide at any of the association's visitor centers.) All reputable dealers should give you a one-year worldwide guarantee. If you want to buy a number of different items in one camera shop (most also stock binoculars, calculators, radios, and other electronic gadgets), you should be able to bargain for a good discount. You may find good bargains at unauthorized (but legal) dealers, but these shops will most likely not provide a guarantee.

Always be on the lookout for con jobs, as tourists are frequent targets. Quite often merchandise is physically switched so that you select one type of camera only to discover back in your hotel room that you've been given another. Another ploy is to lure you in with word of a great deal, tell you that particular model is out of stock, and begin an aggressive campaign to sell you a more expensive model. **Don't be rushed; compare prices in several shops.** If a shop will not give you a written quote, you don't want to do business with them. Be advised that paying by credit card may increase the final bill by 3%–5%, regardless of what the card companies say.

Photo Scientific Appliances (⌧ 6 Stanley St., Central, ☎ 2522–1903) is where local photographers shop for equipment. Expect good prices on both new and used cameras, lenses, video cameras, and accessories. **Williams Photo Supply** (⌧ 341 Prince's Bldg., 10 Chater Rd., Central, ☎ 2522–8437) stocks an array of photography needs.

Carpets and Rugs

Regular imports from elsewhere in China and from Iran, India, Pakistan, Afghanistan, and Kashmir make carpets and rugs a very good buy in Hong Kong. Plenty of carpets are also made locally. Though prices have increased in recent years, carpets are still cheaper in Hong Kong than in Europe and the United States.

Chinese Carpets

Carpet World Ltd. (⌧ 46 Morrison Hill Rd., Wanchai, ☎ 2893–0202; ⌧ Shop 271 Ocean Terminal, Harbour City, 3 Canton Rd., Tsim Sha Tsui, ☎ 2730–4275) has a wide selection.

Branches of **China Products Company** (⌧ 54 Nathan Rd., Tsim Sha Tsui, ☎ 2739–3839) and **China Arts & Crafts** (⌧ 26 Harbour Rd., Wanchai, ☎ 2827–6667 for list of other outlets) provide some of the best selections and price ranges.

Tai Ping Carpets Ltd. (⌧ 816 Times Square, 1 Matheson St., Causeway Bay, ☎ 2522–7138; ⌧ Wing On Plaza, 62 Mody Rd., Tsim Sha Tsui East, ☎ 2369–4061) is highly regarded for locally made carpets, especially custom-made rugs and wall-to-wall carpets. The store takes 2½–3 months to make specially ordered carpets; you can specify color, thickness, and even the direction of the weave. Tai Ping's occasional sales are well worth attending; check the classified section of the *South China Morning Post* for dates.

Other Asian Carpets

On Upper Wyndham Street, in Central, several shops sell Central Asian, Persian, Turkish, Indian, Pakistani, Tibetan, and Afghan rugs— just don't expect miraculously low prices. Note: because of customs regulations, American citizens are rarely allowed to import Persian rugs into the United States (☞ Customs and Duties *in* Smart Travel Tips).

Chine Gallery (⌧ 42A Hollywood Rd., Central, ☎ 2543–0023) specializes in Mongolian rugs and carpets.
Mir Oriental Carpets (⌧ 52 Wyndham St., Central, ☎ 2521–5641) is one of the most appealing of the Wyndham shops for its service and large stock. New selections arrive frequently.
Oriental Carpet (⌧ 41 Wyndham St., Central, ☎ 2523–9502) has a large stock of carpets from Iran (Persia), Pakistan, Afghanistan, and China (Persian designs only). The staff is extremely helpful and friendly.
Oriental Carpets Gallery (⌧ 44 Wyndham St., ground floor, Central, ☎ 2521–6677) specializes in hand-knotted carpets and rugs from Iran, Afghanistan, Pakistan, and Russia.
Tribal Rugs Ltd. (⌧ Admiralty Centre, 18 Harcourt Rd., 2nd floor, ☎ 2529–0576), a bit out of the way in a run-of-the-mill shopping mall, sells a variety of rugs from many countries.

Ceramics

For a full range of ceramic Chinese tableware, visit the various China Products Company stores (☞ Chinese Carpets, *above*), which also have fantastic bargains on attractively designed vases, bowls, and table lamps. Inexpensive buys can also be had in the streets of Tsim Sha Tsui, the shopping centers of Tsim Sha Tsui East and Harbour City, the Kowloon City Market, and the shops along Queen's Road East in Wanchai.

Antiques and Reproductions

Sheung Yu Ceramic Arts (✉ Vita Tower, 29 Wong Chuk Hang Rd., Aberdeen, ☎ 2845–2598) carries good reproductions.

Yue Po Chai Antique Co. (✉ 132–136 Hollywood Rd., ground floor, Central, next to Man Mo Temple, ☎ 2540–4374) is the best place for antique ceramic items.

Factory Outlets

Ah Chow Factory (✉ Hong Kong Industrial Centre, 489–491 Castle Peak Rd., Block B, 7th floor, Laichikok, ☎ 2745–1511) is a popular place to score deals. Take the MTR to the Laichikok station and follow exit signs to Leighton Textile Building/Tung Chau West.

Overjoy Porcelain (✉ 10–18 Chun Pin St., 1st floor, Kwai Chung, New Territories, ☎ 2487–0615) has good bargains. Take the MTR to the Kwai Hing station, then grab a taxi.

Clothing (Children's)

Plenty of stores in Hong Kong sell Western-style ready-to-wear children's clothing. You can also shop for adorable traditional Chinese-style clothing for tots in two Central clothing alleys—Li Yuen Street East and West.

Crocodile Garments Ltd. (✉ The Mall, Pacific Pl., Central, ☎ 2524–3172; ✉ Ocean Terminal, Tsim Sha Tsui, ☎ 2735–5136; and other locations all over town) sells Western-style children's clothes.

Mothercare (✉ Windsor House, 311 Gloucester Rd., Causeway Bay, ☎ 2882–3468; ✉ Prince's Bldg., Central, ☎ 2523–5704; ✉ Ocean Terminal, Tsim Sha Tsui, ☎ 2735–5738), a British firm, carries baby clothing and maternity wear.

Clothing (Tailor-Made)

Along with Hong Kong's multitude of ready-to-wear clothing stores, you can still find Chinese tailors to make suits, dresses, and evening gowns. Unfortunately, many of the next generation in tailors' families are leaving the business, so don't wait too long to visit their shops. All tailors keep records of clients' measurements so that satisfied customers can make repeat orders by mail or telephone. Keep a copy of the original measurements in case you need to change them. Here are some other do's and don'ts:

For a suit, overcoat, or jacket, give the tailor plenty of time—at least three–five days—and allow for a minimum of two proper fittings plus a final one for finishing touches. Shirts can be made in a day, but you'll get better quality if you allow more time.

Tailors in hotels or other major shopping centers may be more expensive, but they're conveniently located and will be more accustomed to Western styles and fittings.

Have a good idea of what you want before you go to the tailor. Often the best plan is to take a suit you want copied. Go through the details carefully, and make sure they're listed on the order form, together with a swatch of the material ordered (the swatch is essential).

When you pay a deposit (which should not be more than 50% of the final cost), make sure the receipt includes all relevant details: the date of delivery, the description of the material, and any special requirements.

For Men

A-Man Hing Cheong Co., Ltd. (⊠ Mandarin Oriental Hotel, Central, ☎ 2522–3336) is known for European-cut suits and custom shirts and has a list of distinguished clients.

Ascot Chang Co. Ltd. (⊠ Shop 130, Prince's Bldg., 10 Chater Rd., Central, ☎ 2523–3663; ⊠ Peninsula Hotel, Salisbury Rd., Tsim Sha Tsui, ☎ 2366–2398; ⊠ Regent Hotel Arcade, 18 Salisbury Rd., Tsim Sha Tsui, ☎ 2367–8319) has specialized in custom-made shirts for men since 1949. Clients have included George Bush and Andy Williams.

David's (⊠ Mandarin Oriental Hotel, 5 Connaught Rd., Central, ☎ 2524–2979; ⊠ Wing Lee Bldg., 33 Kimberley Rd., Tsim Sha Tsui, ☎ 2367–9556) is an excellent shirtmaker.

Jimmy Chen Co. Ltd. (⊠ Peninsula Hotel, Tsim Sha Tsui, ☎ 2536–6333) can make suits, shirts, and whatever else you need.

Sam's Tailor (⊠ Shop K, Burlington Arcade, 94 Nathan Rd., Tsim Sha Tsui, ☎ 2721–8375) is one of the most famous of all Hong Kong's custom tailors, having outfitted everyone from European royal families to American and British politicians and, of course, your average tourist looking for a bargain.

W. W. Chan & Sons (⊠ Burlington House, 92–94 Nathan Rd., Tsim Sha Tsui, ☎ 2366–9738) is known for top-quality classic cuts and has bolts and bolts of fine European fabrics. Chan will make alterations for the lifetime of the suit, which should be about 20 years. Tailors also travel to the United States several times a year to fill orders for their customers; if you have a suit made here and leave your address, they'll let you know when they plan to be in town.

For Women

Hong Kong tailors do their best work on tailored suits, coats, and dresses, performing less well with more fluid styles or knit fabrics. Tailors are the place to order a traditional Chinese cheongsam. As for patterns, you can bring in an item to be copied or choose a style from one of the tailor's catalogs; you can also bring in a photo from a magazine or, if you're skilled with pencil and paper and sure of what you want, bring in a sketch.

A good tailor has a wide selection of fabrics, but you can also bring in your own. Visit Chinese Arts & Crafts (☞ Chinese Carpets, *above*) for beautiful Chinese Brocades. **Western Market** (☞ Western District, *above*) has fabrics on the second floor. One detail often overlooked by the customer is buttons; your tailor will probably provide buttons made of the suit fabric at no extra charge.

Bobby's Fashions (⊠ Mirador Mansion, 3A Carnarvon Rd., Tsim Sha Tsui, ☎ 2724–2615) is a favorite of local expats.

Irene Fashions (⊠ Burlington House, 92–94 Nathan Rd., Tsim Sha Tsui, ☎ 2367–5588) is the women's division of W. W. Chan.

Jimmy Chen Co. Ltd. (☞ For Men, *above*) makes suits, dresses, evening dress, outerwear, you name it.

Linva Tailors (⊠ 38 Cochrane St., Central, ☎ 2544–2456) is one of the best of the old-fashioned cheongsam tailors. Prices begin at around HK$2,200 (including fabric and labor) and go up, up, and up if you want special brocades or beautifully embroidered fabrics.

Mode Elegante (⊠ Peninsula Hotel, Tsim Sha Tsui, ☎ 2366–8153) is known for its high-fashion suits for the executive woman.

Sam's Tailor (☞ For Men, *above*) serves women as impeccably as it serves men.

Shanghai Tang (⊠ 12 Pedder St., Central, ☎ 2525–7333) can make conservative or contemporary versions of the cheongsam. Men can also have a Chinese *tang* suit made to order.

Clothing Factory Outlets

Hong Kong used to be the factory-outlet center of the world, the place where European and American labels were manufactured and the overruns sold at near-wholesale prices. Those days are long gone, but because many garments manufactured elsewhere in China and in other developing countries still come through Hong Kong's duty-free port, you can find samples and overruns in the territory's many outlets. Discounts generally run a mere 20%–30% off retail, but if you comb through everything, more often than not you'll bag at least one fabulous bargain. A word of caution, however: check garments carefully for damage and fading. Outlets do not accept returns.

Pedder Building

The Pedder Building (⊠ 12 Pedder St., Central), just a few feet from a Central MTR exit, contains five floors of small shops. The number of shops offering discounts of around 30% off retail—and sometimes more—seems now to be growing, after a few years of an upscale trend. The **Anne Klein Shop** (☎ 2521–2547), however, is the building's first full-fledged retail store, so don't pass through that particular door in search of discounts. **Blanc de Chine** (☎ 2524–7875) has beautiful Chinese clothes, in styles similar to those at the more famous Shanghai Tang but in subtler colors, plus reproductions of antique snuffboxes as well as silver mirrors and picture frames. **Cascal** (☎ 2613–1066) has Celine, Dior, and Prada bags at about 20% off retail. **Ca Va** (☎ 2537–7174) has fabulous knitwear, along with suits and designer casual wear. **Labels Plus** (☎ 2521–8811) has some men's fashions as well as women's daytime separates. **La Place** (☎ 2868–3163) has youthful fashions, Prada bags, and a large selection of Chanel jackets at about 20% off retail. **Shopper's World–Safari** (☎ 2523–1950) has more variety than most outlets and a small upstairs department with men's fashions. **Swatow Linen Lace Co.** (☎ 2522–8547), which carries embroidered sheets, tablecloths, and doilies from the Swatow region of China.

Lan Kwai Fong Area

The small area of Central called Lan Kwai Fong is another good place to outlet-shop. Ask passersby for directions if you have trouble finding this neighborhood; it's three streets tucked away, but locals know its nightlife well.

Anna's Collection (⊠ Grand Progress Bldg., 15–16 Lan Kwai Fong, 3rd floor, Central, ☎ 2501–4955) sells casual clothing, swimwear (up to size 16) and Italian shoes for women that fit American sizes 7 to 11½. The outside entrance to this building is under the huge, neon Carlsberg sign.

Evelyn B Fashion (⊠ Grand Progress Bldg., 15–16 Lan Kwai Fong, 3rd floor, Central, ☎ 2523–9506) is next door, and co-owned by the owner of Anna's Collection. Business wear, cocktail dresses, and full gowns are its mainstays.

Gat (⊠ Cosmos Bldg., 8–11 Lan Kwai Fong, 7th floor, ☎ 2524–9896) carries Kenar, sometimes at as much as 40%–50% off U.S. retail prices. There have been reports, however, of rayon sweaters from Gat coming unraveled and the store refusing to give refunds or exchanges, so shop carefully.

IN Fashion (⊠ 9A Grand Progress Bldg., 15–16 Lan Kwai Fong, ☎ 2877–9590) carries career wear and casual clothes by Ann Taylor, Laura Ashley, Next, Talbots, and an occasional item designed for Nordstrom, as well as designer ball gowns.

Pot Pourri (⊠ Wong Chung Ming Commercial Bldg., 16 Wyndham St., 12th floor, ☎ 2525–1111) has Talbots, Emanuel Ungaro, and Fenn Wright & Manson.

Ricki's (⊠ Cosmos Bldg., 8–11 Lan Kwai Fong, Room 8–11, ☎ 2877–1552) from time to time carries Emanuel Ungaro, Episode, Donna Karan, Tahari, Jaeger, Ellen Tracy, and Just Cotton.

Zeno Fashions (⊠ Man Cheung Bldg., 15–17 Wyndham St., Block B, ☎ 2868–4850) stocks mostly career wear, from labels such as Ellen Tracy, Emmanuel Ungaro, Episode, Krizia, Banana Republic, and Country Road.

Other Outlets

Coast 2 Coast Design Warehouse (⊠ Hing Wai Centre, 7 Tin Wan Praya Rd., Room 1904, Aberdeen, ☎ 2518–3100) has clothes, crystal, linens, and ceramics at up to 50% off retail prices.

Diane Freis Factory Outlet (⊠ Kaiser Estate, Phase I, 41 Man Yue St., Hung Hom, ☎ 2362–1760) has discounts of around 30% on Hong Kong–based designer Diane Freis's daywear concoctions and elaborate cocktail dresses. Ask your hotel concierge about the bus to the outlets in Hung Hom. Many other outlets here have branches in Central, so you may decide it's not worth the trip.

Fair Factor (⊠ 44 Granville Rd., ☎ no phone) has plenty of uninteresting items, but you may be rewarded with some real finds—such as items by GAP, Adrienne Vittadini, Villager, and Victoria's Secret for a mere HK$50 to HK$100.

The Joyce Warehouse (⊠ 34 Horizon Plaza, 2 Lee Wing St., Ap Lei Chau, ☎ 2814–8313) has taken local shopaholics by storm: it's an outlet for women's and men's fashions in the ritzy Joyce Boutiques in Central and Pacific Place, with labels by such major designers as Jil Sander and Giorgio Armani. Prices for each garment are reduced by about 10% each month, so the longer the piece stays on the rack the less it costs. The outlet is open Tuesday to Saturday 10–6 and Sunday noon–6. Take Bus 90 from Exchange Square and get off at Ap Lei Chau; from there it's easiest to get a taxi to Horizon Plaza, a three- to four-minute ride.

Le Baron (⊠ Flat B Yeung Chung, No. 6, Industrial Bldg., 19 Cheung Shun St., 4th floor, ☎ 2722–0581) has some of the best cashmere buys in the territory, which makes the trouble of finding this building worth it. Get off at Kowloon's Laichikok station. Near the end of Cheung Shun Street, enter through the garage and use the single elevator on the far right. You'll see an office with a sign that says HEYRO DEVELOPMENT CO. LTD. Go into the office, then enter the showroom through the second door on the right.

Timothy Fashion Co. (⊠ Kaiser Estate, Phase I, 41 Man Yue St., Hung Hom, Kowloon, ☎ 2362–2389) has classic wool sweaters for men and women at good prices. Silk garments for men and women and lingerie are also good buys, but you can find a similar selection in Tsim Sha Tsui, so don't go all the way to Hung Hom if these are all you want.

TSL Jewelry Showroom (⊠ Summit Bldg., 30 Man Yue St., Hung Hom, ☎ 2764–4109; ⊠ Wah Ming Bldg., 34 Wong Chuk Hang Rd., Aberdeen, ☎ 2873–2618) has fairly good prices on diamonds and other precious stones in unique settings, and both locations have on-site workshops where you can see the jewelry being made.

Computers

All the big names sell in Hong Kong. If you plan to buy, make sure the machine will work on the voltage in your country—a PC sold in Hong Kong works on 220 volts, while the identical machine in the United States works on 110 volts. Servicing is another major concern. The real computer bargains are the locally made versions of the most popular brands. Several malls specialize in computers, peripherals, and electronic equipment, each containing hundreds of shops ranging from small local enterprises to branches of the international brand names. The individual shops usually don't have retail phone numbers.

Check out **One Take Computer Store** (⌗ Block B, New Capital Computer Plaza, 608 Castle Peak Rd., Rm. 104, Kowloon, ☎ 2728–0045) if you're looking for Apple Computers and software.

Star Computer City (⌗ Ground Floor, Star House, 3 Salisbury Rd., Tsim Sha Tsui), conveniently located near the Star Ferry Pier in Kowloon, has some good deals on office equipment and desktop computers.

Wanchai Computer Centre (⌗ 130 Hennessy Rd., Wanchai) has honest to goodness bargains on computer goods and accessories in its labyrinth of shops.

Furniture and Furnishings

Hong Kong has seen a tremendous boom in the home-decor market in recent years, and manufacturers of furniture and home furnishings have been quick to increase production. Rosewood furniture is a very popular buy in Hong Kong, as are several other specialty woods. A number of old-style shops specialize in the rich-looking blackwood furniture that originated in southern China at the turn of the century; look for chairs, chests, couches, and other pieces at the west end of Hollywood Road, near Man Mo Temple. Queen's Road East and nearby Wanchai Road are good sources for camphor-wood chests, as is Canton Road in Kowloon.

Reproductions are common, so "antique" furniture should be inspected carefully. Traits of genuinely old pieces are: a mature sheen on the wood, slight gaps at joints as a result of natural drying and shrinking of the wood, signs of former restorations, and signs of gradual wear, especially at leg bottoms. Keep in mind, too, that blackwood, rosewood, and teak must be properly dried, seasoned, and aged to prevent pieces from cracking in climates that are less humid than Hong Kong's. Even in more humid areas, the dryness of winter heating systems can be harmful.

Definitely look on Wyndham Street and Hollywood Road (☞ Antiques, *above*), but also consider shopping in Hong Kong but buying in Macau. Prices in Macau are often considerably cheaper for the exact same item sold in Hong Kong; Macau stores will ship to Hong Kong for free.

The Banyan Tree (⌗ Prince's Bldg., Central, ☎ 2523–5561; ⌗ Repulse Bay Shopping Arcade, Repulse Bay, ☎ 2592–8721; ⌗ Ocean Terminal, Harbour City, Tsim Sha Tsui, ☎ 2730–6631; ⌗ Times Square, 1 Matheson St., Causeway Bay, ☎ 2506–3850) has furniture and bric-a-brac, both old and new, from Europe, India, and Southeast Asia. Its **warehouse outlet** (⌗ 18/F Horizon Plaza, 2 Lee Wing St., Ap Lei Chau, ☎ 2555–0540) has some discounted items; a Chinese birdcage was recently spotted here for HK$700, an excellent buy. (Lesser-quality birdcages go for more than HK$800 at Stanley Market.) You can arrange to visit Banyan Tree's **warehouse** by calling its office (☎ 2877–8303). You won't get a discount if you buy from the warehouse, but you will have the chance to see—and buy—pieces that have just arrived.

Cathay Arts (⌗ Ocean Centre, ☎ 2730–6193) is one of many rosewood-furniture dealers in the Harbour City complex at Tsim Sha Tsui.

Horizon Plaza (⌗ 2 Lee Wing St., Ap Lei Chau, near Aberdeen) has several furniture outlets including Shambala, G.O.D. Warehouse, Tequila Kola, Resource Asia, E&H, Antique Express, Inside, Banyan Tree, Dynasty Antiques, and Elmwood.

Luk's Furniture (✉ 52–64 Aberdeen Main Rd., Aberdeen, ☎ 2553–4125) is a bit out of the way, but it has two floors of rosewood and lacquer furniture, as well as Korean chests, at warehouse prices, and makes furniture to order.

Queen's Road East, in Wanchai, the great furniture retailing and manufacturing area, sells everything from full rosewood dining sets in Ming style to furniture in French, English, and Chinese styles. Custommade orders are accepted in most shops here. **Choy Lee Co. Ltd.** (✉ 1 Queen's Rd. E, ☎ 2527–3709) is the most famous.

Tequila Kola (Main showroom: ✉ United Centre, Admiralty, ☎ 2520–1611) has reproductions of antique wrought-iron beds, one-of-a-kind furniture, home accessories, and jewelry from various corners of Asia. It's like a cross between IKEA and an Asian boutique.

Handicrafts and Curios

China's traditional crafts include lanterns, temple rubbings, screen paintings, paper cuttings, seal engravings, and wooden birds.

The Banyan Tree (☞ Furniture and Furnishings, *above*) carries a pricey but attractive selection of items from several Asian countries.

Kinari (✉ Anson House, 61 Wyndham St., Central, ☎ 2869–6827) sells crafts and antiques from all over Southeast Asia.

Mountain Folkcraft (✉ 12 Wo On La., Central, ☎ 2525–3199) has a varied collection of fascinating curios. From Queen's Road Central walk up D'Aguilar Street past Wellington Street, then turn right onto Wo On Lane.

Vincent Sum Designs Ltd. (✉ 15 Lyndhurst Terr., Central, ☎ 2542–2610) carries Indonesian silver, crafts, and batiks.

The Welfare Handicrafts Shop (✉ Jardine House, 1 Connaught Pl., Shop 7, basement, Central, ☎ 2524–3356; ✉ Salisbury Rd., next to the YMCA, Tsim Sha Tsui, ☎ 2366–6979) stocks a good collection of inexpensive Chinese handicrafts for both adults and children. All profits go to charity.

Jewelry

Jewelry is the most popular item with visitors to Hong Kong. It is not subject to any local tax or duty, so prices are normally much lower than in most other places. Turnover is fast, competition is fierce, and the selection is fantastic.

Settings for diamonds and other gems will also cost less here than in most Western cities, but check your country's customs regulations, as some countries charge a great deal more for imported set jewelry than for unset gems. Hong Kong law requires all jewelers to indicate on every gold item displayed or proffered for sale both the number of carats and the identity of the shop or manufacturer—make sure these marks are present. Also, check current gold prices, which most stores display, against the price of the gold item you are thinking of buying. For factory outlets, see the HKTA's *Factory Outlets for Locally Made Fashion and Jewellery.*

Gems

DIAMONDS

As one of the world's largest diamond-trading centers, Hong Kong sells these gems at prices at least 10% lower than world market levels. When buying diamonds, remember the four "C"s: color, clarity, carat (size), and cut. Shop only in reputable outlets—those recommended by someone who lives in Hong Kong or listed in the Hong Kong Tourist Association's shopping guide (available at HKTA visitor centers). For information or advice, call the **Diamond Importers Association** (☎ 2523–5497).

Pearls, another good buy, should be checked for color against a white background. Shades include white, silvery white, light pink, darker pink, and cream. Cultured pearls usually have a perfectly round shape, semibaroque pearls have slight imperfections, and baroque pearls are distinctly misshapen. Check for luster, which synthetics never have. Freshwater pearls from China, which look like rough grains of rice, are inexpensive and look lovely in several twisted strands. Jewelry shops with a good selection of pearls include the following:

K. S. Sze & Sons (⊠ Mandarin Oriental Hotel, ☎ 2524–2803) is known for its fair prices on pearl necklaces and other designs.

Po Kwong (⊠ 82 Queen's Rd., Central, ☎ 2521–4686) specializes in strung pearls from Australia and the South Seas and will add clasps to your specifications.

Trio Pearl (⊠ Peninsula Hotel, Tsim Sha Tsui, ☎ 2367–9171) has beautiful one-of-a-kind designs in pearl jewelry.

Hong Kong's most famous stone, jade comes not only in green but in shades of purple, orange, yellow, brown, white, and violet. Although you'll see trinkets and figurines purported to be made of jade throughout Hong Kong, high-quality jade is rare and expensive. Translucency and evenness of color and texture determine jade's value; translucent, deep-emerald-green Emperor's jade is the most expensive. Be careful not to pay jade prices for green stones such as aventurine, bowenite, soapstone, serpentine, and Australian jade.

Many of the pieces for sale at the **Kansu Street Jade Market** (☞ Yaumatei and Mongkok, *above*) are made of these impostors; but the endless sea of stalls brimming with trinkets of every size, shape, and color makes a visit worthwhile. If you are wary of spending any money on Kansu Street, visit the following:

Chow Sang Sang (⊠ 229 Nathan Rd., Tsim Sha Tsui, ☎ 2730–3241, and 17 smaller branches around town) has jade necklaces, bracelets, and brooches in traditional Chinese designs.

Chow Tai Fook (⊠ 29 Queens Rd., Central, ☎ 2523–7128, and 15 branches) is a good place to shop for fine jade.

Jewelers

Chan Che Kee (⊠ 18 Pottinger St., Central, ☎ 2524–1654) has fist-size 14- to 18-carat gold Chinese zodiac animals, a unique gift. Smaller versions can be worn as charms. Other stores on Pottinger Street also carry these animals.

China Handicrafts & Gem House (⊠ 25A Mody Rd., Tsim Sha Tsui East, ☎ 2366–0973) sells loose gemstones.

Just Gold (⊠ 47 Queen's Rd. Central, ☎ 2869–0799; ⊠ 27 Nathan Rd., Tsim Sha Tsui, ☎ 2312–1120; and 14 other branches) specializes in delicate gold jewelry, a favorite with the Hong Kong Chinese. Prices rarely go past HK$5,000.

Kai-Yin Lo (⊠ The Mall, Pacific Place, Admiralty) has fabulous modern jewelry with an Asian influence.

The Showroom (⊠ Central Bldg., Pedder St., Room 1203, 12th floor, Central, ☎ 2525–7085) specializes in creative pieces using various gems and diamonds.

Leather Bags and Belts

Italian bags, belts, and briefcases are popular status symbols in Hong Kong, but you'll pay top dollar for them. Locally made leather bags are clearly of inferior quality—the leather isn't as soft, and the smell isn't nearly as luxurious as that of fine European leather. But if you're looking for bargains, check out the locally produced designer knockoffs on Li Yuen streets East and West, in Central, and in other shopping lanes. The leather-garment industry is a growing one, and although most of the production is for export, you can find some good buys in the factory outlets of Hung Hom, Kowloon. Medium-quality bags and belts from the local manufacturer Goldlion are sold at Chinese Arts & Crafts.

For top-name international products, visit department stores such as **Lane Crawford, Wing On,** and **Sincere** and the Japanese stores in Causeway Bay, **Mitsukoshi** and **Sogo**; all carry leather by such names as Nina Ricci, Cartier, Lancel, Il Bisonte, Comtesse, Guido Borelli, Caran d'Ache, Franco Pugi, and Christian Dior. You may, however, find the prices higher than they are at home.

Linens, Silks, Embroideries

Pure silk shantung, silk and gold brocade, silk velvet, silk damask, and printed silk crepe de chine are just some of the exquisite materials available in Hong Kong at reasonable prices. China Products Company, Chinese Arts & Crafts (☞ Chinese Carpets, *above*), and **Yue Hwa Chinese Products Emporium** (☞ Yaumatei and Mongkok, *above*) have the best selections. Ready-to-wear silk garments, from mandarin coats and cheongsams to negligees, dresses, blouses, and slacks, are good buys at Chinese Arts & Crafts.

Irish linen, Swiss cotton, Thai silk, and Indian, Malay, and Indonesian fabric are among the imported cloths available here. Vincent Sum Designs specializes in Indonesian batik; there's also a small selection in **Mountain Folkcraft** (☞ Handicrafts and Curios, *above*). Thai silk is about the same price in Hong Kong as it is in Bangkok.

The best buys from China are hand-embroidered and appliquéd linen and cotton. You'll find a magnificent range of tablecloths, place mats, napkins, and handkerchiefs in the **China Products Company** and **Chinese Arts & Crafts** stores and in linen shops in Stanley Market. Try, too, the various shops on Wyndham and On Lan streets in Central. When buying hand-embroidered items, be certain the edges are properly overcast, and beware of machine-made versions being passed off as handmade.

Martial Arts Supplies

There are hundreds of martial-arts schools and supply shops in Hong Kong, especially in the areas of Mong Kok, Yau Ma Tei, and Wanchai, but they're often hidden away in back streets and up narrow stairways.

The most convenient place to buy your drum cymbal, leather boots, sword, whip, double dagger, studded wrist bracelet, Bruce Lee *kempo* gloves, and other kung-fu exotica is **Kung Fu Supplies Co.** (✉ 188 Johnston Rd., Wanchai, ☎ 2891–1912).

Miscellaneous Chinese Gifts

If you're really stuck for a gift idea, think Chinese. Some of the most unusual gifts are often the simplest. How about an embroidered silk kimono or a pair of finely painted black-lacquer chopsticks? Or a Chinese chop, engraved with your friend's name in Chinese? These are available throughout Hong Kong. For chop ideas, take a walk down **Man Wa Lane,** in Central (⊠ Opposite Wing On department store, 26 Des Voeux Rd.).

For those who live in cold climates, wonderful *mien laps* (padded silk jackets) are sold in the alleys of Central or in the various shops featuring Chinese products. Another unusual item for rainy weather—or even as a decorative display—is a hand-painted Chinese umbrella, available very inexpensively at **Chinese Arts & Crafts** and **China Products Company.** Chinese tea, packed in colorful traditional tins, is sold in the teahouses in Bonham Strand and Wing Lok Street in Western. A bit more expensive, but novel ideas, are padded tea baskets with teapot and teacups, and tiered bamboo food baskets, which also make good sewing baskets.

Optical Goods

Hong Kong has a vast number of optical shops and some surprising bargains. Soft contact lenses, hard lenses, and eyeglass frames—in all the latest styles and of the highest quality—are sold in leading optical shops at prices generally much lower than those in Europe and the United States.

The Optical Shop (Main branch: ⊠ 117 Prince's Bldg., 10 Chater Rd. Central, ☎ 2523–8385) is probably the most reliable optical store and has branches throughout Hong Kong. Eye tests using the latest equipment are given free of charge.

Shoes

The best place to buy shoes in Hong Kong is on Wong Nai Chung Road, in Happy Valley, next to the racetrack. Here a variety of shops sell inexpensive locally made shoes; Japanese-made shoes; and copies of European designer shoes, boots, and bags. If you have small feet, these shops can offer excellent buys; if you wear a women's size 8 or larger, you'll probably have trouble finding shoes that fit well. The merchants are also particularly good at making shoes and bags, covered with silk or satin, to match an outfit. If you leave your size information, you can make future purchases through mail order. Top-name Italian and other European shoes are sold in Hong Kong's department stores and shopping centers, but prices for designer shoes will be similar to those back home.

Kow Hoo Shoe Company (⊠ Prince's Bldg., 1st floor, Central, ☎ 2523–0489) has great cowboy boots in knee-high calfskin.
Luen Fat Shoe Makers (⊠ 19–21B Hankow Rd., Tsim Sha Tsui, ☎ 2376–1180) custom-makes shoes for both men and women and is renowned for its skill in copying specific styles at reasonable prices.
Mayer Shoes (⊠ Mandarin Oriental Hotel, Central, ☎ 2524–3317) has an excellent range of styles and leathers for men and women.

Sporting Goods

Hong Kong is an excellent place to buy sports gear, thanks to high volume and reasonable prices.

Bunns Diving Equipment (⊠ 2 Johnston Rd., Wanchai, ☎ 2572–1629; ⊠ 217 Sai Yee St., Mongkok, Kowloon, ☎ 2380–5344) is the biggest dive shop in Hong Kong.
Marathon Sports (⊠ Tak Shing House, Theatre La., 20 Des Voeux Rd., Central, ☎ 2810–4521; ⊠ Pacific Place, Admiralty, ☎ 2524–6992; with another dozen stores on both sides of the harbor) carries a good range of equipment and clothing for tennis players and golfers.

Po Kee Fishing Tackle Company (✉ 6 Hillier St., Central, ☎ 2543–7541) has everything the fisherman needs.

World Top Sports Goods Ltd. (✉ 49 Hankow Rd., Tsim Sha Tsui, ☎ 2376–2937) has a comprehensive range of sports equipment.

Stereo Equipment

Hennessy Road in Causeway Bay has long been the center for stereo gear, although many small shops on Central's Queen Victoria and Stanley streets and on Tsim Sha Tsui's Nathan Road sell a similar variety of goods. Be sure to compare prices before buying, as they can vary widely. Make sure also that guarantees are applicable in your own country. It helps to know exactly what you want, since most shopkeepers don't have the space or inclination to let you test and compare sound systems. Some major manufacturers do, however, have individual showrooms where you can test equipment before buying; the shopkeeper will be able to direct you. Another tip: though most of the export gear sold in Hong Kong has fuses or dual wiring that can be used in any country, it pays to double-check.

Tea

Cha (Chinese tea) falls into three categories: green (unfermented), black (fermented), and oolong (semifermented). The various flavors include jasmine, chrysanthemum, rose, and narcissus. Loong Ching green tea and jasmine green tea are among the most popular, and are often sold in attractive tins that make inexpensive and unusual gifts. If you wanted to buy a ton of tea, you could probably do so in the Western district, Hong Kong's most famous tea area. Walk down Queen's Road West and Des Voeux Road West and you'll see dozens of tea merchants and dealers. You can also buy packages or small tins of Chinese tea in Western tea shops or at various Chinese-product stores and leading supermarkets, such as Park 'n' Shop and Wellcome.

Cheng Leung Wing (✉ 526 Queen's Rd. W, ☎ no phone) is a longstanding tea purveyor in the heart of the tea district.
Fook Ming Tong Tea Shop (✉ Prince's Bldg., Central, ☎ 2521–0337; other branches at Mitsukoshi and Sogo stores in Causeway Bay, Ocean Terminal, Harbour Centre, and Tsim Sha Tsui) is dreamland for the sophisticated tea shopper. You can get superb teas in beautifully designed tins or invest in some antique clay teaware.
Tea Zen (✉ House for Tea Connoisseurs, 290 Queen's Rd., ground floor, Central, Sheung Wan, ☎ 2544–1375) offers a range of teas in a simple atmosphere.

TVs and VCRs

Color TV systems vary throughout the world, so it's important to be certain the TV set or videocassette recorder you find in Hong Kong has a system compatible to the one in your country. Hong Kong, Australia, Great Britain, and most European countries use the PAL system; the United States uses the NTSC system; and France and Russia use the SECAM system. Before you buy, tell the shopkeeper where you'll be using your TV or VCR; you'll generally be able to get the right model without a problem.

Watches

You'll have no trouble finding watches in Hong Kong. Street stalls, department stores, and jewelry shops overflow with every variety, style, and brand name imaginable, many with irresistible gadgets. Just remember Hong Kong's remarkable talent for imitation. A super-bargain gold "Rolex" may have hidden flaws—cheap local mechanisms, for instance, or "gold" that rusts. Stick to officially appointed dealers carrying the manufacturers' signs if you want to be sure you're getting the real thing. When buying an expensive watch, check the serial number against the manufacturer's guarantee certificate and ask the salesperson to open the case to check the movement serial number. If the watch has an expensive band, find out whether it comes from the original manufacturer or is locally made, as this will dramatically affect the price (originals are much more expensive). Always obtain a detailed receipt, the manufacturer's guarantee, and a worldwide warranty.

City Chain Co. Ltd. (⊠ Times Square, 1 Matheson St., Shop 609–610, Causeway Bay, ☎ 2506–4217), with locations all over Hong Kong, has a wide selection of watches for various budgets, including Swatch.

8 SIDE TRIP TO MACAU

Now in Chinese hands after almost 450 years of Portuguese rule, Macau was both the first and last major European colony in Asia. It remains one of the most uniquely hybrid societies on earth: pastel-color churches share narrow alleys with Chinese wet markets, while diners drink hearty Portuguese wines with their Beijing roast duck.

Updated by
Sean Rocha

IF YOU ASK PEOPLE in Hong Kong what they think of Macau, the former Portuguese colony an hour away by jetfoil, they'll probably concede that it has good food and wine, maybe a little gambling, but not much else. This obscurity is highly undeserved. To see what makes Macau special, you have to walk through the Old Town square and up a small hill to where two narrow, winding alleys called Travessa de Don Quixote and Travessa de Sancho Pança meet at a corner marked by a Buddhist temple. Such cultural juxtapositions are commonplace in Macau. At every turn in this intriguing, densely populated city of 450,000 you'll see evocative street names, Baroque buildings, and sidewalk cafés that reflect long, intimate ties to Europe. The connection changed but did not break when Macau was handed over to China in December 1999, ending almost 450 years of Portuguese rule.

It is the Buddhist temple, with its swaying red lanterns and faint scent of joss sticks, that reminds you that, for all the Portuguese influence here, you're in Asia, not Europe. The people, the culture, the way of life is predominantly Chinese—or, more accurately, a uniquely Macanese fusion of East and West. Macau's cuisine is legendary within the region, drawing on both Chinese cooking techniques and flavors from throughout Portugal's onetime globe-spanning empire. Historic architecture also exhibits mixed traditions; a pink colonial building might house a traditional Chinese herbal medicine shop.

Above all, Macau's unique culture is seen in the faces of the Macanese themselves, in particular the thousands of Eurasian families who consider themselves neither Portuguese nor Chinese but something in between. Some can trace the intermarriage of their ancestors back a century or two, and in many ways they form the bridge between Macau's two identities. Many of the mixed-blood Macanese are from old, established families, and count among their numbers Stanley Ho—Macau's biggest taipan, whose business interests include the boat that brings you here from Hong Kong, the hotel you stay in (if it's the *Lisboa, Sintra,* or one of a host of others), and the casino where you gamble (no matter which one, since he runs them all).

And it is gambling that essentially keeps Macau afloat, providing almost half the government's tax revenues and countless jobs. (The casinos rely mainly on Chinese bettors, as most Westerners find them drab compared to, say, Las Vegas.) Hidden below Macau's calm, communal surface are gambling's inevitable sister industries: pawn shops, cabarets, and prostitution. Fortunately, this seedy side of Macau is almost invisible unless you set out to find it.

Macau's past was very different. Settled in 1557 by the Portuguese, Macau was Europe's first colony in east Asia, and for a time its richest. For a century it thrived as the main intermediary in the trade between Asia and the rest of the world: ships filled with Chinese silk and tea, Japanese crafts, Indian spices, African ivory, Brazilian gold, and European technological inventions all sought refuge in Macau's small harbor.

Portuguese dominance over global trade didn't last long, however. Early in the 17th century the Dutch emerged as the most powerful empire in southeast Asia, repeatedly attacking Macau without successfully capturing it. But it was the rise in the mid-19th century of Portugal's former ally, Great Britain, that finally ended Macau's prosperous role as an entrepôt. The British victory over China in the Opium War of 1841 led to the founding of Hong Kong, which—with its deepwater port, free-trade rules, and British protection—forever changed the balance of power in the region.

Today Macau is very much the poor relation to wealthy Hong Kong, but in the last few decades it has rebuilt a position (in tandem with its neighbor, the booming Chinese Special Economic Zone of Zhuhai) as an exporter of textiles, toys, furniture, and electronics. And for all its status as a relative backwater, Macau is no stranger to Hong Kong–style property speculation and handover frenzy, a fact that will become obvious the moment you step off the ferry. The Portuguese administration launched a staggering number of public works in the run-up to the handover: a new airport, a cultural center, several massive land-reclamation projects, a new bridge to China, the construction of two artificial lakes along the Praia Grande and a related off-shore highway, numerous sculpture installations, and too many new office buildings to count. Whether this flurry of activity was an effort by the Portuguese to get money out of the colony before the Chinese took over (as many locals think) or part of a bold vision of Macau's future, the effect has been to give wide swaths of the city the feel of a boomtown.

Indeed, the Portuguese departure from Macau was so sordid—scarred by rumors of widespread corruption and wasteful public spending—that most Macau residents (unlike their Hong Kong counterparts) welcomed Chinese rule, hoping it would bring with it a return to law and order. And thus far, to China's credit, it has. As a result, probably the most obvious impact of the handover has been the reduction in the size of the Portuguese expatriate community, many of whom returned home once their comfy government jobs disappeared. Some remain, of course, as do most of the mixed-blood Macanese, but since all Macau residents were given the option of taking a Portuguese (and thus, European Union) passport, they may elect to leave if the situation changes. If that happens, we may look back on Macau in the 20th century much as we now look at Córdoba or Toledo before the Christian Reconquest: an improbable convergence of peoples, languages, and cultures that will never be replicated. For now, though, there is much in Macau to persuade people to stay: despite all the soulless construction in the newer areas, the city remains, at heart, a tranquil, romantic place, with a community that reflects its special history.

Pleasures and Pastimes

Architecture

Architecture in Macau is not merely a matter of having a few old buildings: it represents the visual legacy of almost 450 years of European rule and cultural exchange. Little wonder, then, that in the run-up to the handover the Portuguese administration engaged in a furious last-minute preservation program, hoping to secure their cultural heritage before the Chinese arrived. You can now see the fruits of their efforts throughout Macau, where vibrantly colored Baroque churches sit cheek-by-jowl with Chinese merchant shops and Buddhist temples.

A decade or two ago, however, it looked like Macau might go the way of Hong Kong, which has torn down almost every building over thirty years old. The Macau government faced the classic problem of having a collection of traditional buildings too beautiful to tear down but too decrepit to use. Fortunately, it hit upon an innovative solution: build modern buildings within the walls of old ones. The results are most visible on Largo do Senado, Macau's Old Town square, where the colorful, carefully restored facades hide modern, fully functioning interiors. Not all of Macau has survived unscathed: the Outer Harbour district, near the ferry terminal (and thus your first impression on arrival), is particularly unlovely, and the Rua da Praia Grande, once one of the most romantic seaside walks in all of Asia, now fronts two artificial ponds enclosed by reclaimed land.

Casinos

You can easily visit Macau and never set foot in a casino, but the city would not survive without them. Sociedade de Turismo e Diversoes de Macau (STDM), the syndicate that runs the casinos, provides more than 40% of the government's total tax revenues and still makes enough to earn a hefty profit. But if you've ever been to Las Vegas or Monte Carlo, Macau's casinos will disappoint: they're sparsely decorated, unglamorous places where the serious business of losing money is not disturbed by free drinks or entertainment. The Hong Kong and mainland Chinese who crowd around the tables don't seem to mind, as they're indulging a passion largely barred to them at home. The amount of money bet is staggering, though this won't be obvious at first glance, as most gamblers maintain an inscrutable stoicism. However, if you tap someone on the shoulder in the middle of a game—a gesture the Chinese consider very bad luck for the player so disturbed—that stoicism will disappear in a flash.

Dining

Macau makes much of its position at the crossroads of East and West, but nowhere is that more evident than in the distinctive local cuisine. Indeed, the Portuguese first conquered Macau in the 16th century to get control of the spice trade with China and the legendary Spice Islands (in what is now Indonesia), once the world's only source of nutmeg, mace, and cloves. In return, the Portuguese imported foods from the rest of their empire, which extended from Brazil and Mozambique to Goa and Malacca. You can see the results of this exchange today in uniquely Macanese dishes such as prawns *piri-piri*, which fuses shrimp sautéed in a wok with a fiery red pepper from Mozambique; or "African chicken," baked in a sauce of tomatoes, coconut, curry, and saffron (it's more subtle than it sounds).

That is just the beginning of what Macau offers the gourmand. In addition to its fusion cuisine, Macau has a host of traditional Portuguese restaurants serving the best *caldo verde* (a filling blend of kale and potatoes) and stewed rabbit this side of Lisbon. There are even a few bakeries that make the Portuguese specialty *bolo de arroz* (a sort of rice muffin with a hint of lemon), always wrapped in its signature blue-and-white ribbon of wax paper and delicious with a morning coffee.

Wandering

Having few monumental sights, Macau doesn't lend itself to heavily planned itineraries but is, instead, best seen spontaneously, by catching a glimpse down an alley and just following it. What you discover en route to your destination will probably be the most memorable— the little Mediterranean café down a blind alley, or the Chinese antique furniture store hidden behind a street stall. The history of Macau is literally embedded in the urban landscape, and the only way to unearth it is to wander with a keen eye.

EXPLORING

Almost all of the territory's residents live in peninsular Macau, as the two nearby islands of Taipa and Coloane have only recently developed beyond their old villages. On today's maps, huge tracts of land (especially along the Outer Harbour and between Taipa and Coloane) are marked off with diagonal lines, indicating areas that have been reclaimed from the sea—these tend to be brutally functional and, for the traveler, largely uninteresting. Thus, the historic areas are mostly in the interior rather than on the coast, occupying the parts of peninsular Macau that have been above water for more than 20 years. Largo do Senado, the Old Town square, is still the center, and you can take interesting walks through the skein of small streets running north to the Kun Iam Temple and south to the A-Ma Temple. Because the streets are so irregular, getting lost is common (indeed, part of the pleasure), even though streets are generally well marked.

Numbers in the text correspond to numbers in the margin and on the Macau and Taipa and Coloane Islands maps.

Downtown

Most visitors to Macau arrive at the ferry terminal, which offers easy access to buses and taxis (just exit the terminal and turn right) but is a 40-minute walk from the town center. Alas, the district you see first—the Outer Harbour—is one of Macau's least charming, and the only nearby sights of real interest are the Grand Prix Museum and the Wine Museum, both in the Macau Forum. You'll do better to go straight to the historic area around Avenida Almeida Ribeiro (more commonly known by its Chinese name, Sanmalo) and circle back to see the museums before you return to Hong Kong.

A Good Walk

Avenida Almeida Ribeiro (Sanmalo) runs from the Avenida da Praia Grande, on the eastern shore, to the Inner Harbour, on the west. Starting at the eastern end, the buildings are a mix of new glass-and-marble towers and old merchants' shops, their ground floors modernized but their upper floors still intriguing. The weathered neon Coca-Cola and Fanta signs are particularly striking. The handsome gray-stone building on the right as you walk west is the **General Post Office** ①, and the historic town square is called the **Largo do Senado** ②. The buildings around the square have all been carefully restored and form an explosion of pastels. The most important is the Senate, **Leal Senado** ③, on the south side; also interesting are the whitewashed House of Charity **Santa Casa da Misericordia** ④ and the church of **São Domingos** ⑤. The main tourist office is in the yellow **Ritz Building** ⑥. Continue down Sanmalo, past jewelers and pawn shops, and turn left on Travessa do Mastro to reach **Rua da Felicidade** ⑦, once a red-light district and now lovingly restored as a traditional China Coast merchants' street. You can either follow Rua da Felicidade to the end or return to Sanmalo to get to the Inner Harbour, which teems with workers unloading ships and ducking in and out of decaying warehouses.

TIMING

This walk does not cover much distance, so you could complete it in about an hour, but there's so much to discover just off the route that two or three hours is a better estimate. An exhibit in Leal Senado might distract you even further.

Sights to See

❶ **General Post Office.** Built in 1931, this is the newest of the old buildings on Largo do Senado, with an attractive stone facade that complements its colorful neighbors. Like most historic buildings in Macau, it's been restored with an eye toward practicality and still functions as a post office and telephone center. ⊠ *Largo do Senado at Av. Almeida Ribeiro,* ☎ *396–8516.*

★ ❷ **Largo do Senado** (Senate Square). The heart of old Macau and one of the most charming squares in Asia, the Largo is surrounded by an exquisite collection of brilliantly colored colonial buildings. In 1994 it was repaved with black-and-white stone tiles arranged in a very Por

Macau

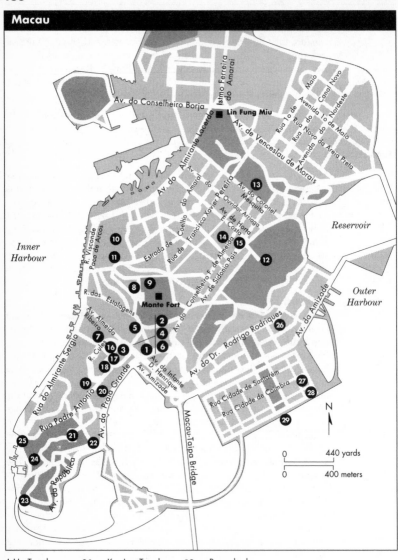

Lin Fung Miu

Monte Fort

Inner Harbour

Reservoir

Outer Harbour

Av. do Conselheiro Borja

Istmo Ferreira do Amarai

Av. de Venceslau de Morais

Av. do Almirante Lacerda

Estrada de Coelho do Amaral

Av. do Conselheiro F. de Almeida

Av. de Sidonia Pais

Av. do Coronel Mesquita

Av. de Ovidor Arriaga

Av. da Horta e Costa

Rua de Francisco Xavier Pereira

Maio

Avenida 1o de Maio

Rua 1o de Maio

Canal Novo

Avenida 1o de Nordeste

Rua Novo da Areia Preta

R. Visconde Paço de Arcos

R. das Estalagens

Av. Almeida Ribeiro

R. Cuba

Rua da Praia Grande

Av. de Infante D. Henrique

Av. Amizade

Av. do Dr. Rodrigo Rodriques

Av. da Amizade

Rua do Almirante Sergio

Rua Padre Antonio

Av. da República

Macau-Taipa Bridge

Rua Cidade de Santarém

Rua Cidade de Coimbra

N

0   440 yards
0   400 meters

tuguese wave pattern and furnished with benches, plants, and a fountain. Residents appropriated the space immediately, and it now functions as a town square should: as a communal meeting place where old women gather to gossip and children run free. At night the buildings are lit by spotlights, and the square becomes even more alluring, as locals of all generations meet and socialize. ✉ *Av. Almeida Ribeiro.*

❸ Leal Senado. A superb example of colonial architecture, the Loyal Senate anchors the southern end of Largo do Senado. It was built in the late-18th century to house the senate of leading citizens—which was, at the time, far more powerful than the governors, who usually served their appointed time and then promptly returned to Portugal. Today the senate has both elected and appointed members and acts as the municipal government, with its president holding the same power as a mayor. Inside the building, a beautiful stone staircase leads to wrought-iron gates that open onto a charming garden. Note the blue-and-white tilework (such tiles are called *azulejos*), a typical Portuguese craft originally perfected by the Moors of North Africa. The attractive garden in the back has cast busts of two great Portuguese men of letters: the 16th-century poet Luis de Camões and the 19th-century writer João de Deus. The foyer and garden are open during business hours, and there are frequent art and historical exhibitions in the foyer and gallery.

The Leal Senado also houses the **Macau Central Library**. A superb copy of the classic Portuguese library in Mafra, it holds what may be the world's best collection of books in English about China. (Many were inherited from the British- and American-managed Chinese Customs House.) The library also has rare books from the early days of the Portuguese empire and bound copies of old Macau newspapers. Scholars and others are welcome to browse or study; there's also a nice view of the square. ✉ *Largo do Senado at Rua Dr. Soares, 2nd floor,* ☎ *558–049,* FAX *318–756.* ☺ *Mon.–Sat. 1–7.*

❻ Ritz Building. Home of the Macau Government Tourist Office, this building looks like an old colonial three-story from the outside. As you step inside, however, you realize that only the walls of the original remain; a new building stands within the old, squeezing in five stories where there were once only three. ✉ *Largo do Senado (opposite Santa Casa da Misericordia).* ☺ *Daily 8–5.*

NEED A BREAK? | For a slightly out-of-the-ordinary refreshment, step into the **Leiteria i Son milk bar** (☎ 573–638) at Largo do Senado 7—look for the small cow sign overhead. The decor is cafeteria-style spartan, but the bar whips up frothy glasses of fresh milk from its own dairy and blends them with all manner of juices: papaya, coconut, apricot . . . there's even a mysterious "steamed milk in two films." But the highlight is the series of almost pornographic photos of cows, their udders on the verge of bursting.

❼ Rua da Felicidade. This street was once the heart of Macau's red-light district. That trade has since moved from Rua da Felicidade, leaving it to a respectable existence as a street of inexpensive guest houses, tailors, laundries, and restaurants. In 1996 the Cultural Institute of Macau decided to restore the appearance of the old China Coast and fitted traditional facades to all the buildings on this street—the result is stunning, with red wooden lattices over the windows, retractable red canopies, and gray-stone gateways to shrine-filled courtyards. The new look has helped local business, especially in the evening, when food stalls with stools and tiny tables emerge. It's a charming area, albeit not one likely to appeal to animal lovers: the restaurants do a brisk trade in giant fish, which lie motionless in small tanks, and furry creatures, which are cooped up in cages until mealtime. ⊠ *Off Av. Almeida Ribeiro at Travessa do Mastro.*

④ Santa Casa da Misericordia. Founded in 1569, Portugal's Holy House of Mercy is the oldest Christian charity on the China Coast. This handsome Baroque building with a blindingly white facade houses its headquarters on Largo do Senado. Look inside if you can (it's not normally open to the public), as the interior was rebuilt in an attractive modern style that contrasts starkly with the timeless exterior. The Casa's offices administer homes for the elderly, kitchens for the poor, clinics, and a leprosarium, and its president is by tradition the senate president. A reception room on the second floor (also generally closed to the public) contains paintings of benefactress Marta Merop and Macau's first bishop, Dom Belchior, along with the latter's cross and skull. ⊠ *Largo do Senado, next to the GPO.*

⑤ São Domingos. Following an ambitious restoration, St. Dominick's is once again the most beautiful church in Macau. The stunning cream-and-white nave leads to a filigreed altar intricately carved in the Mannerist style. São Domingos was originally a convent founded by Spanish Dominican friars in 1587, but was rebuilt as a church in the 17th century. When convents were banned in Portugal in 1834, this church became a repository for sacred art. The works now form the basis of the collection in the **Museum of Sacred Art,** which is on the upper floors, accessible via a small staircase to the right of the altar. Indeed, the church itself has had a stormy history: in 1644 a Portuguese officer was murdered at the altar by a mob during mass; in 1707 the church was besieged by the governor's troops when the Dominicans sided with the Pope against the Jesuits on the question of whether ancestor worship should be permitted among Chinese Christian converts. After three days the soldiers broke down the doors and briefly imprisoned the priests. ⊠ *Rua de São Domingos at Largo do Senado.*

The Old Citadel

The most remarkable early buildings in Macau were on or around the centrally located **Monte Hill,** and those that have survived are eloquent reminders of Portugal's golden age.

A Good Walk

Approach the old citadel from the Largo do Senado by following the black-and-white tiles. Take Rua da São Domingos, to the right of the church, then turn left on Rua da Palha—look for the design of concentric circles in the paving. This street runs into Rua de São Paulo and leads you to the dramatic, freestanding facade of **São Paulo** ⑧. Go up the steps, visit the Museum of Sacred Art, then cross the road to view the remains of the **Monte Fort,** which holds the new **Museum of Macau** ⑨. Return down the stone staircase and turn right onto Rua de São Paulo. Pass the antiques and souvenir shops and arrive at the Praça Luís Camões Park. People-watch in the **Camões Grotto and Garden** ⑩ and relax in the shade of giant banyan trees. Finally, go next door to visit the graves of early American and British pioneers in China now buried in the **Old Protestant Cemetery** ⑪.

TIMING

The walk should take about two hours, depending on how much time you spend in the museums.

Sights to See

⑩ Camões Grotto and Garden. Macau's most popular public park is frequented from dawn to dusk by tai chi enthusiasts, young lovers, students, and men huddled over Chinese chess boards with their caged

ONE LAST TRAVEL TIP:

Pack an easy way to reach the world.

Wherever you travel, the MCI WorldCom Card℠ is the easiest way to stay in touch. You can use it to call to and from more than 125 countries worldwide. And you can earn bonus miles every time you use your card. So go ahead, travel the world. MCI WorldCom℠ makes it even more rewarding. For additional access codes, visit **www.wcom.com/worldphone**.

EASY TO CALL WORLDWIDE

1. Just dial the WorldPhone® access number of the country you're calling from.

2. Dial or give the operator your MCI WorldCom Card number.

3. Dial or give the number you're calling.

China (A)	108-12
Hong Kong	800-96-1121
Indonesia ◆	001-801-11
Japan ◆	00539-121▶
Korea	00729-14
Malaysia ◆	1-800-80-0012
Philippines ◆	105-14
Singapore (A)	8000-112-112
Taiwan ◆	0080-13-4567
Thailand (A) ★	001-999-1-2001
Vietnam (A) ⁝ ●	1201-1022

(A) Calls back to U.S. only. ◆ Public phones may require deposit of coin or phone card for dial tone.
▶ Regulation does not permit intra-Japan calls. ★ Not available from public pay phones. ⁝ Limited availability.
● Local service fee in U.S. currency required to complete call.

EARN FREQUENT FLIER MILES

Bureau de change

Cambio

外国為替

In this city, you can find money on almost any street.

NO-FEE FOREIGN EXCHANGE

The Chase Manhattan Bank has over 80 convenient
locations near New York City destinations such as:

    Times Square
    Rockefeller Center
    Empire State Building
    2 World Trade Center
    United Nations Plaza

Exchange any of 75 foreign currencies

THE RIGHT RELATIONSHIP IS EVERYTHING.®

Exploring 159

songbirds nearby. The garden houses the Orient Foundation and was originally the private grounds of the Camões Museum, which later became the headquarters of the British East India Company. In 1785 it was used by French cartographer La Perouse as a small observatory aimed at China. The garden was taken over by the city in 1886 and a heroic bronze bust of Camões, Portugal's greatest poet and 16th-century Macau resident, was installed in a rocky niche. Nearby, a wall of stone slabs is inscribed with poems by various contemporary writers praising Camões and Macau. At the entrance to the grotto a bronze sculpture honors the friendship between Portugal and China. Some rooms in the Orient Foundation contain historical and art exhibits; the basement houses an art gallery. ⊠ *13 Praça Luis de Camões,* ☎ *554–699.* ⊡ *Free.* ☉ *Gardens daily dawn–dusk, house weekdays 9:30–6.*

★ ➒ **The Museum of Macau.** Brilliantly constructed within the base of Monte Fort, this new museum is the ideal place to learn about the rich cultural layering that shaped the development of Macau. The exhibition begins with a comparison, dating back to the 16th century, of the dress, religious icons, ships, and writing instruments of Macau's two dominant civilizations: China and Portugal. This theme of exchange—rather than competition—runs through the rest of the museum, where there are displays of Chinese and Portuguese architectural facades, markets, traded goods, sacred art, and printing presses. The cumulative effect is very powerful: East and West have been meeting (and learning from each other) for far longer than many imagine. ⊠ *Praceta do Museu de Macau, base of Monte Fort,* ☎ *357–911.* ⊡ *15 patacas.* ☉ *Tues.–Sun. 10–5:30.* ⊛

Monte Fort. On the hill overlooking St. Paul's, this recently renovated fort was built by the Jesuits in the early 17th century and, in 1622, became the site of Macau's most legendary battle. At the time, the Dutch, jealous of Portugal's power in Asia, were attempting to invade Macau, which was guarded by a small force of soldiers, priests, and African slaves. As the Dutch closed in on Monte Fort, a lucky cannon shot (fired by one of the priests) hit the enemy's powder supply. In the ensuing confusion the Dutch were driven back to sea. Soon after the victory, the first full-time governor of Macau evicted the Jesuits from the fort, and for the next 150 years it served as the residence and office of Macau's governors. The interior buildings were destroyed by fire in 1835, but the great walls remain, along with the cannon. The fort has since become a popular park and is a soothing place to sit, enjoy the breeze, and survey the city.

➒ **Old Protestant Cemetery.** Through the cream-colored entrance to the right of the Camões Garden lies the tranquil resting place of more than 150 Americans and British, whose tombstones recall the triumphs and troubles of Westerners in 19th-century China. Some of the names are familiar: George Chinnery; Captain Henry Churchill, great-granduncle of Sir Winston; Joseph Adams, grandson of John Adams, the second U.S. president; and Robert Morrison, who translated the Bible into Chinese. It is for Morrison that the small whitewashed chapel on the grounds was named. This was the first Protestant church on Chinese soil and dates from the early 1800s (although it was rebuilt in 1922). The Chinese characters in the stained-glass window read: "In the beginning there was the Word." When the sun is down they cheat and use an electric light to illuminate the window. ⊠ *22 Praça Luis Camões.* ☉ *Daily 9–6.*

➑ **São Paulo.** The church of St. Paul, which occupies an imposing site at the top of a long flight of steps, has long since been adopted as Macau's symbol, even though the only thing that remains of the once spectacular structure is its facade. Built under the direction of the Jesuits by exiled Japanese Christians and local craftsmen between 1602 and 1627, St. Paul's has always been tied to the struggle to preserve a Christian presence in Asia. The story of the church is told on its carved-stone facade and in the excavated crypt, which contains the tomb of the church's founder, Alessandro Valignano, and the bones of Japanese and Indo-Chinese martyrs. St. Paul's also served as part of the first Western-style university in Asia, attended by such scholars as Matteo Ricci and Adam Van Schall, who studied here before going to the emperor's court in Peking. The college, along with the body of the church and most of Monte Fort, was destroyed in the disastrous fire in 1835. Behind the facade, in an underground site beneath the onetime body of the church, is the **Museum of Sacred Art,** which holds statues, crucifixes, chalices, and other sacramental objects dating from the 17th through the 18th centuries and borrowed from local churches. The 17th-century paintings by exiled Japanese artists depict the crucified martyrs of Nagasaki and the Archangel Michael in the guise of a samurai. ⊠ *Rua de São Paulo at Largo da Companhia,* ☎ *358–444.* ⊡ *Free.* ☉ *Daily 9–6.*

Restoration Macau

One of the most endearing aspects of Macau is the fact that traditional Chinese temples and gardens—many of them restored in the last few decades—continue to flourish in the modern, European-influenced heart of the city.

A Good Tour

Begin with a taxi ride to **Guia Hill** ⑫ for an overview of the city, then walk around the hill to take the cable car to Avenida de Sidonio Pais—alternatively, you can reach the avenue by walking down the steps that lead through the Flora Gardens. Turn right (north) on Sidonio Pais and then left (west) to get to the **Kun Iam Temple** ⑬, on Avenida do Coronel Mesquita, where the first Sino-American treaty was signed. If you're up for the walk, continue along the avenue until you pass Mong Ha hill and then turn right (north) on Avenida do Almirante Lacerda, which becomes Avenida de Barbosa (on your left see the Canidrome, where greyhound dog races are run three or four nights a week), to find the little-visited Temple **Lin Fung Miu,** with its statue of the opium-burning Commissioner Lin. From there, catch a taxi to the charming **Lou Lim Ioc Garden** ⑭. Exit left from the gardens and then take your second left to find the neo-Moorish **Memorial Home of Dr. Sun Yat-sen** ⑮, which is between Rua de Antonio Basto and Rua de Leoncio Ferreira, across from the police station. Nearby on Avenida do Conselheiro Ferreira de Almeida is the Dutch quarter with a series of restored red-and-ocher 1920s mansions now housing the government archives, the public library, and the Health Department.

TIMING

This walk should take around four hours, depending on how long you linger in the gardens and temples.

Sights to See

⑫ **Guia Hill.** Studded with new homes, a convent, and a hospital, Guia (Guide) Hill is topped with a fort that dates from the 1630s. It also has the oldest lighthouse on the China Coast (built in 1865) and a small white-stone chapel built in 1707. You need permission from the **Macau Marine Department** (☎ 573–409) to enter the lighthouse, but the chapel is usually open; inside are crumbling frescoes that depict an unorthodox mix of Christian angels and Chinese dragons. One of the old guardhouses is a café, and there is also a small tourist information office. From the fort you can see all of Macau, its islands, the airport, and the surrounding Chinese seascape—a much easier way to catch a

glimpse of China than making the trek up to Portas do Cerco. ✉ *Est. do Engenheiro Trigo.* ⊙ *Daily 9–5:30.*

OFF THE
BEATEN PATH

Lin Fung Miu. The Temple of the Lotus, dedicated to both Buddhist and Taoist deities, was built in 1592 and used for overnight lodging by mandarins traveling between Macau and Canton. It's best known for the facade's 19th-century clay bas-reliefs depicting mythological and historical scenes, and for an interior frieze of colorful writhing dragons. One famous visitor was Commissioner Lin Zexu, who spent some hours here soon after burning the foreign traders' opium in 1839. His statue stands in the courtyard, outside a small museum that describes his battle against the opium traders. ✉ *Av. do Artur Tamagnini Barbosa at Est. do Arco.* ⊙ *Daily dawn–dusk.*

⓭ Kun Iam Temple. This Buddhist temple dedicated to the Goddess of Mercy was founded in the 13th century. The present 17th-century buildings are richly filled with carvings, porcelain figurines, statues, old scrolls, antique furniture, and ritual objects—note the three exquisite statues of Buddha that grace the entry chamber. The temple is best known among Western visitors as the place where the first Sino-American treaty was signed by the viceroy of Canton and the United States envoy, Caleb Cushing, on July 3, 1844. The temple has a large number of funeral chapels, with offerings of paper cars, airplanes, luggage, and money that are burned in order to accompany the souls of the dead. ✉ *Av. do Coronel Mesquita at Rua do Almirante Costa Cabral.* ⊙ *Daily dawn–dusk.*

⓮ Lou Lim Ioc Gardens. This classic Chinese garden, modeled on those of old Suzhou, was built in the 19th century by a wealthy Chinese merchant named Lou. With the decline of the Lou family fortunes early in the 20th century, the house was sold and turned into a school. The gardens had fallen into ruin before the city restored them in 1974. Now they're a haven of tranquillity in an increasingly hectic city. Enclosed by a wall, the gardens are a miniaturized landscape, with miniforests of bamboo and flowering bushes, a mountain of sculpted concrete, and a small lake filled with lotuses and golden carp. A traditional nine-turn bridge (to deter evil spirits, which can move only in straight lines) zigzags across the lake to a colonial-style pavilion with a wide veranda. The pavilion is used for exhibitions and concerts. ✉ *Est. de Adolfo Loureiro at Av. do Conselheiro Ferreira de Almeida.* 🎫 *1 pataca.* ⊙ *Daily dawn–dusk.*

⓯ Memorial Home of Dr. Sun Yat-sen. Father of the 1911 Chinese revolution, Sun lived in Macau from 1892 to 1894 while working as a physician. The memorial home was built in the 1930s in a strange mock-Moorish style and was occupied by some of his family members following his death. It was renovated by Sun admirers from Taiwan—hence the preponderance of Taiwanese flags hanging about. It now contains interesting photographs, books, and souvenirs of Sun and his long years of exile in different parts of the world. ✉ *1 Rua Ferreira do Amaral, between Rua de Antonio Basto and Rua de Leoncio Ferreira,* ☎ *574–064,* 📠 *523–799.* 🎫 *Free.* ⊙ *Wed.–Mon. 10–5.*

Peninsular Macau

Macau's narrow, hilly peninsula is one of the oldest districts in the city and is full of colonial churches, landmark hotels, restaurants, and shopping streets. It's bordered on the east by the Rua da Praia Grande and the Avenida da República, both tree-shaded promenades on a bay from which land is now being reclaimed to make way for new construction. (This was once a favorite place for residents to stroll, fish, or play chess.) On the west side, the Inner Harbour's Rua do Almi-

rante Sergio and Rua das Lorchas still retain the bustle of an Asian port with their traditional Chinese shop houses—ground floors occupied by ships' chandlers, net makers, ironmongers, and shops selling spices and salted fish.

A Good Walk

Begin at the Leal Senado and take the steep Rua Dr. Soares, which climbs up to the left. Branch left on Calçada Tronco Velho and arrive in the peaceful Largo Santo Agostinho. Visit the little-known **Sir Robert Ho-tung Library** ⑯ in the former home of one of the most prominent Macanese families; on the same square are the church of **St. Augustine** ⑰ and the **Dom Pedro V Theater** ⑱. The Rampo do Teatro will lead you down to Rua Central. Continue to the right, and on the block-long Rua de São Lourenço you'll find **St. Lawrence's Church** ⑲. Take the Travessa Padre Narciso down to the Praia Grande, and the **Government Palace** ⑳ will be on your left. Go right along the waterfront—less picturesque than it once was, due to the huge land-reclamation project—and make a detour up Calçada do Bom Parto to **Penha Hill** ㉑ for some great views. On the way back to the waterfront you'll pass the **Bela Vista** ㉒, once the city's most luxurious hotel and now the home of the Portuguese consul-general. Continue along Avenida da República and stop for a drink on the terrace of the **Pousada de São Tiago** ㉓, a small hotel built into an old fortress; just offshore is the *Monument of Understanding,* a massive arched sculpture rising out of the bay, celebrating Sino-Portuguese friendship. Walk around the tip of the peninsula to the **A-Ma Temple** ㉔ and finish with a visit to the unique **Maritime Museum** ㉕.

TIMING

This walk should last most of the day, with a leisurely lunch at an Inner Harbour or Praia Grande restaurant, drinks at the São Tiago, and plenty of time in the museum and temple. If you're brisk, however, you can cover it in four or five hours.

Sights to See

㉔ **A-Ma Temple.** Properly called Ma Kok temple but known to everyone as A-Ma, this is thought to be the oldest building in Macau, dating from sometime in the Ming Dynasty (1368–1644). Its origins are obscure, but it was here when the Portuguese first landed in Macau just beneath it. The rocks are inscribed with red calligraphy telling the story of A-Ma (also known as Tin Hau); a favorite goddess of fishermen, she is purported to have saved a humble junk from a storm. One of the many Chinese names for this area was A-Ma Gau (Bay of A-Ma), and the Portuguese transformed this name into Macau. The temple is the territory's most picturesque, with ornate prayer halls and pavilions among the giant boulders of the waterfront hillside. On Sunday morning you can catch performances of the traditional lion dance, in which a long line of dancers huddle under a painted lion's body led by a dancer wearing a colorful lion's head with a hinged jaw. ⊠ *Largo do Pagode da Barra opposite the Maritime Museum.* ☉ *Daily dawn–dusk; lion dances Sun. 10–10:30 AM.*

㉒ **Bela Vista.** The Bela Vista was built in the 1870s as the private home of a prosperous merchant, but became the city's grandest hotel around the turn of the century. It had a brief golden age but then followed Macau's waning fortunes into a long, steady decline. In 1992 the building was magnificently resurrected by local architects Bruno Soares and Irene O, who transformed it into a luxurious eight-suite hotel that reclaimed its rightful place in the city's social universe. Sadly, it closed to the public in 1999 and now, following the handover to China, serves as the official residence of the Portuguese consul-general. ⊠ *8 Rua do Comendador Kou Ho Neng.*

⑱ Dom Pedro V Theater. The oldest Western theater on the China Coast, the Dom Pedro V was built in 1859 in the style of a European court theater. It was in regular use until World War II, and since its recent renovation by the Orient Foundation it now hosts concerts, plays, and recitals once again. You can sometimes look inside when performances are not scheduled, though the rather bare interior may come as a disappointment after the striking green-and-white facade. ⊠ *Largo do Sto. Agostinho at Rampa do Teatro.*

⑳ Government Palace. This pink-and-white colonial building on the Praia Grande has deep verandas and a handsome portico. For a long time it was Lisbon's seat of power in Macau, housing the offices of the governor and his cabinet, but with the departure of the Portuguese it has lost some of its symbolic importance, although it still retains its architectural grace. It is not open to the public. ⊠ *Av. de Praia Grande between Travessa do Padre Narciso and Travessa da Paiva.*

★ ㉕ Maritime Museum. Ideally situated on the waterfront **Barra Square**, this gem of a museum has been a favorite since it opened in 1987. The four-story building resembles a sailing ship and contains one of the foremost maritime museums in Asia. The adjacent dock was restored as a pier for a tug, a dragon boat, a sampan, and working replicas of a South China trading junk and a 19th-century pirate-chasing *lorcha* (a wooden sailing ship). Inside the museum is a breathtaking series of detailed models of local and foreign ships, with illustrations of how each one catches fish or captures the wind. There are also light-box charts of great voyages by Portuguese and Chinese explorers, a relief model of 17th-century Macau, the story of the A-Ma Temple in slide-show style, navigational aids such as a paraffin lamp once used in the Guia Lighthouse, and all manner of touch screens and videos. The museum also operates a 30-minute pleasure junk (10 patacas extra per person) around the Inner and Outer harbors daily except Tuesday and the first Sunday of the month. ⊠ *Largo do Pagode da Barra, opposite A-Ma Temple,* ☎ *307–161.* ⊡ *10 patacas.* ⊘ *Wed.–Mon. 10–5:30.* ⊗

㉑ Penha Hill. The Bishop's Palace, on Penha Hill, overlooks the entire city and islands, and you can take in some of the best views of Macau from its courtyard. The chapel is dedicated to the patroness of seafarers and was originally built in 1622. The current structure (along with the adjacent palace, which is closed to the public) was completely rebuilt in 1837. ⊠ *Est. de D. João Paulino.* ⊘ *Daily 9–5:30.*

㉓ Pousada de São Tiago. There's no more tranquil place to linger over a drink than on the terrace of this Portuguese inn (☞ *Lodging, below*). Built into the ruined foundations of a 17th-century fort, the hotel has a magnificent view of the harbor. ⊠ *Fortaleza de São Tiago da Barra, Av. da República.*

⑰ St. Augustine. This church dates from 1814 and feels like a real colonial outpost: grand but slightly worn, with a high wood-beam ceiling and a drafty interior. The stone altar has a recessed scene of Christ on his knees bearing the cross, with small crucifixes in silhouette on the hill behind him. The statue, called *Our Lord of Passos,* is carried through the streets on the first day of Lent. ⊠ *Largo do Sto. Agostinho at Calçada do Tronco Velho.*

⑲ St. Lawrence Church. What is arguably Macau's most elegant church stands in a pleasant garden, shaded by palm trees. Always a fashionable place, it looks the part with elegant wood carvings, an ornate Baroque altar, and stunning crystal chandeliers. Concerts are held here during the Macau International Music Festival. ⊠ *Rua de São Lourenço at Travessa do Padre Narciso.* ⊡ *Free.* ⊘ *Daily 10–4.*

⑯ **Sir Robert Hotung Library.** In a small garden hidden behind wrought-iron gates, this was once the private home of the Hotung family. The ground floor is a functioning library, and on the second floor you'll find a traditional-style study (ask someone to open the door if it's locked) with classical Chinese furniture, scrolls, family portraits, and large cabinets filled with old texts. The smell of lacquered wood and musty books is intoxicating—so, too, the way the light on the enclosed balcony shimmers on a sunny day. ⊠ *3 Largo do S. Agostinho.* 🖾 *Free.* ☾ *Mon.–Sat. 1–7.*

New Macau

The newly developed districts along the Outer Harbour may have been built on an inhuman scale that is more functional than charming, but they also house most of the city's most important contemporary cultural institutions.

A Good Tour

Take a taxi to the **Macau Forum** ㉖, near the base of Guia Hill, to visit the **Wine Museum**, with its focus on Portuguese regional wines, and the superb **Grand Prix Museum**, which is interesting even to those not particularly fanatical about cars. From the Forum take a taxi to the **Handover Pavilion** ㉗, which (like the Eiffel Tower) was intended to be a temporary building but will now be kept indefinitely. Just behind it is the new **Cultural Centre** ㉘, which often has excellent exhibitions. From there, you can walk along the water on Avenida Dr. Sun Yat-sen to reach the **Kun Iam Ecumenical Center** ㉙, which has a lovely view out to Taipa Island.

TIMING
This walk should take about four hours, although some may want to spend that long in the Grand Prix Museum alone.

Sights to See

㉘ **Cultural Centre of Macau.** This building, easily identifiable by the giant swooping curve gracing the roof, serves as an all-purpose cultural forum, hosting dance, music, theater, films, and art and photography exhibitions. Some shows are free but most require tickets, with opening hours depending on the event. ⊠ *Av. Xian Xing Hai,* ☎ *797–7418.*

㉗ **Handover Pavilion.** Built in haste for the 1999 handover, this translucent-skinned pavilion was slated for dismantling, but the public outcry—over its historic importance and, conversely, the epic waste of money involved—has kept it open. It's extremely popular with mainland tourists, but other visitors will find it looks like a convention center. The interior is decorated with enormous Chinese and Portuguese flags and cases holding the tributes sent to celebrate the handover. ⊠ *Av. Xian Xing Hai.* 🖾 *Free.* ☾ *Weekdays 10–6, weekends 10–10.*

㉙ **Kun Iam Ecumenical Center.** This elegant 65-ft-high (20-m-high) bronze statue of the Buddhist Goddess of Mercy was designed by Portuguese architect Cristina Rocha Leiria. It rests on an artificial islet and houses an ecumenical center that aims to spread the peaceful teachings of Buddhism, Taoism, and Confucianism. So far, however, it has sown mostly strife. The center was installed just before the handover amid much local grumbling about the exorbitant cost and supposed Portuguese efforts to fleece the territory before leaving town. To make matters worse, it fails to adhere to the appropriate *feng shui* principles, which would have the statue facing out to sea rather than toward land. ⊠ *Av. Dr. Sun Yat-sen.* ☾ *Sat.–Thurs. 10:30–1 and 2:30–5:45.*

㉖ **Macau Forum.** This multipurpose facility has a 4,000-seat stadium for sports events and pop concerts and a 350-seat auditorium for operas and plays. The adjoining Tourism Activities Centre—usually known by its Portuguese initials, CAT—has two museums. ⊠ *Rua Luís Gonzaga Gomes.*

The **Grand Prix Museum** tells the story of the races that were first run in Macau in 1953. It's a required stop for all racing fans, with an exquisite collection of winners' cars, among which pride of place is given to Eduardo de Carvalho's gorgeous Triumph TR-2 "long door," which won the first Grand Prix. In the background you hear the suitably frenzied voices of English announcers, and around you are videos, photos, memorabilia, and two simulators, one interactive, in which you can experience the sensation of driving in the Grand Prix. ☎ 798–4126. ⅏ *10 patacas (20 patacas for the simulator).* ⊙ *Daily 10–6.*

The **Wine Museum** illustrates the history of winemaking with photographs, maps and paintings, antique wine presses, Portuguese wine fraternity costumes, and 750 different Portuguese wines. Admission includes a glass of wine. ☎ 798–4108. ⅏ *15 patacas.* ⊙ *Daily 10–6.*

Taipa Island

Although the Portuguese presence on Macau peninsula dates from the mid-1500s, they did not occupy Taipa until the mid-1800s, when it was actually two separate islands. Taipa remained a military garrison and pastoral retreat—albeit one that was also home to a number of fireworks factories—until the 1970s, when it was linked to the city by a bridge. Since then it has evolved in two different directions: parts retain the quiet, charming feel of village life while others have been transformed into a local version of Hong Kong, with block after block of soulless high-rise apartment buildings. Highlights of Taipa's past are the village's narrow alleys and many restaurants and the seafront promenade of the Taipa House Museum; the newer areas have the Macau Jockey Club and the airport.

A Good Walk

Take a bus or taxi over one of the bridges to **Taipa Village** ㉚ and explore the narrow lanes. Take the main Rua Direita Carlos Eugenio to Calçada do Carma and walk up to the small square in front of the Church of Our Lady of Carmel. Continue down to the old seafront to visit the **Taipa House Museum** ㉛. To see other parts of Taipa, take a bus or taxi to the Hyatt Regency Hotel and walk around the back road, Estrada de Almirante Joaquim Marques Esparteiro, to the **Pou Tai Un Temple** ㉜.

TIMING

The walk around Taipa Village and the house museum can take as little as one hour, but a visit to Taipa is incomplete without lunch at one of its many restaurants.

Sights to See

㉜ **Pou Tai Un Temple.** This temple is famed for its restaurant, which serves a large selection of fresh, reasonably priced vegetarian dishes. Thanks to donations from devotees, it has a series of prayer halls, including an impressive yellow-tile pavilion, and a statue of Kun Iam, the Buddhist Goddess of Mercy. ⊠ *Est. de Almirante Joaquim Marques Esparteiro, behind Hyatt Regency Hotel.*

㉛ **Taipa House Museum.** This area has long been one of the most charming stretches of Macau: five colonial mansions along a tree-lined cobblestone path look out over the ocean. Until recently only one of the mansions was open to the public, but following a recent renovation three others are now accessible. Unfortunately, the interiors were gutted, leaving unexpectedly large exhibition spaces (showing Chinese artifacts, Portuguese folk costumes, and an illustrated history of the

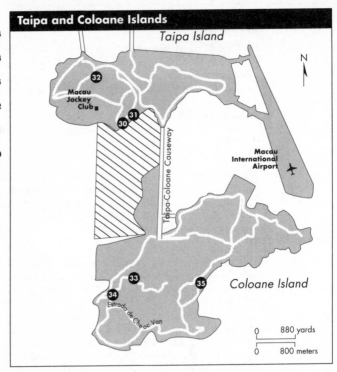

islands) that do little to re-create the feel of colonial domestic life. Just up the hill is the small, boxy Church of Our Lady of Carmel, across from which is an antiquated *biblioteca* (library). ⊠ *Taipa Praia off Largo do Carmo.* ☎ *Free.* ⊙ *Daily 10–8.*

30 Taipa Village. Despite the recent addition of new homes and such modern conveniences as banks, this tight maze of streets and shops retains much of the feel of an old China Coast fishing village. There are small well-kept temples and restored colonial buildings that house the municipal council for the islands. Occasionally you can still see racks of fish lying out in the sun to dry. But the village is, today, most treasured for its numerous restaurants, which in good weather spill out of the two- and three-story shop houses and fill the quiet back alleys.

Coloane Island

The 1½-mi causeway that once separated Coloane from Taipa has been bridged by a massive land reclamation project. But the larger, less populated island of Coloane still retains a distinctive feel, with a village that's quieter and more intimate than the comparatively bustling Taipa. Coloane is also popular for its parks, beaches, and golf club.

A Good Walk

Take a bus or taxi to **Coloane Park** ㉝ any day but Monday and see the aviary, the forest, and the **Natural History Museum.** Continue by bus along Estrada de Seac Pai Van to Coloane Village and visit the **Chapel of St. Francis Xavier** ㉞. Continue on to **Hac Sa Beach** ㉟, a black-sand beach adjoining the marvelous bluff-side Westin Resort.

TIMING

Try to spend a day on Coloane, taking it easy with the walk and stopping for a leisurely lunch. The walk alone takes about three hours.

Sights to See

㉞ Chapel of St. Francis Xavier. This charming little village chapel, with a blue-and-white facade and bell tower, was once the site of a Christian mission established to educate the local Chinese. It was built in 1928 to house a reliquary containing an arm bone of the eponymous saint (other body parts were kept in Goa and Rome) who died on an island south of Macau while waiting to enter China. Since then the relic has been moved, as have the bones of Japanese and Vietnamese martyrs once enshrined here. The square outside is paved with colored Portuguese tiles, landscaped with gardens, and marked by a monument commemorating the local defeat of a pirate band in 1910—Macau's last encounter with old-style buccaneers. ⊠ *Largo do Sto. Francisco Xavier, Coloane Village.*

㉝ Coloane Park. On the west coast of Coloane Island, this park is one of Macau's most interesting natural preserves, though parts of it have been paved over to provide visitor facilities. Its walk-in aviary has more than 200 species of birds, including the rare Palawan peacock and the crested white pheasant. Nearby are a playground, a pond with black swans, the Balichão restaurant, a picnic area, and a nature trail around the hillside, which now ends at a giant A-Ma statue carved out of white jade and weighing 1,000 tons. It was installed to celebrate the handover, and it faces north to protect the city. The park also has a small **Natural History Museum,** which contains traditional farm implements, clay statues illustrating rice cultivation, and displays of traditional herbal medicines. ⊠ *Est. de Seac Pai Van.* 🖾 *Free.* ☉ *Park Tues.– Sun. 10–6; museum Tues.–Sun. 10:30–4:30.*

㉟ Hac Sa Beach. This black-sand beach is the biggest and best in Macau. Despite its ocher color, created by the silt carried by the Pearl River from the delta, the water is clean and safe for swimming and water sports. It draws a crowd in the summer, many of whom grill food at the barbecue pits in the nearby picnic area. Also nearby is **Fernando's** (☞ Dining, *below*), the one Macau restaurant known to everyone in Hong Kong. ⊠ *Praia da Hac Sa, Est. de Hac Sa.*

DINING

Macau is legendary in the region for the diversity of its cuisine, which reflects the range of influences on its long history. There are a number of excellent Chinese restaurants, particularly Cantonese and Chiu Chow; but since there is no shortage of those in the neighboring countries, Macau has earned its reputation for its more distant cuisines.

Portuguese food is the most common, of course. Most restaurants serve the beloved *bacalhau* (salt cod), either baked, boiled, grilled, deep-fried with potato, or stewed with onion, garlic, and eggs. You'll also find Portuguese sardines, country soups such as *caldo verde* and *sopa alentejana,* and various rabbit dishes. Some kitchens prepare baked quail, curried crab, and the delectable Macau sole, as well as giant prawns in spicy sauce, one of Macau's special dining pleasures. There are, as well, dishes drawn from throughout Portugal's once-mighty empire: from Brazil come *feijoadas,* stews of beans, pork, spicy sausage, and vegetables; and from Mozambique comes African chicken, baked or grilled in fiery *piri-piri* (a type of chili pepper).

The Macanese have their own signature cuisine that is, like the city, a blend of East and West. For years this food was difficult to find outside private homes, but a few restaurants (such as Balichão and Litoral) have filled this gap. One of the most distinctive Macanese ingredients is *balichão,* a flavorful shrimp paste for which every family traditionally had its own recipe. Another Macanese staple is *minchi*, a blend of ground pork or beef sautéed with onion, garlic, a bit of soy, and diced potatoes.

After Chinese, Portuguese, and Macanese cuisine, there are a few superb Italian and French places. Regardless of cuisine, however, almost every restaurant in Macau has at least a bottle or two of delicious Portuguese wine—usually a hearty red from the Dão region or the slightly sparkling *vinho verde*. Some Western restaurants have wine lists as long as small phone books.

Prices for both food and wine are, on the whole, very reasonable, and a drinkable Portuguese wine often costs little more than a bottle of mineral water. Outside Chinese restaurants, the service trade is almost completely run by Filipinos, so ordering in English is rarely a problem—indeed, many Macanese have to order in English to make themselves understood. Meals are on a southern European schedule: that is, long, leisurely affairs with lunch from 1 to 3 and dinner after 8, though it's usually possible to eat earlier. Dress is casual, and most restaurants are open daily year-round with perhaps a few days off around Chinese New Year (in late January or early February). Reservations are rarely necessary except at the very finest restaurants, and even then only on weekends. The tourist-office brochure "Eating Out in Macau" has an exhaustive listing of local dining spots.

CATEGORY	COST*
$$$	over $20
$$	$10–$20
$	under $10

per person including service but excluding wine

Chinese

$$ ✕ **Chiu Chau.** This is probably the best—and certainly the most sumptuous—restaurant in Macau serving the Chiu Chow cuisine of Chaozhou (formerly known as Swatow), in eastern Guangdong. Many Hong Kong and Thai Chinese (i.e., many of Macau's gamblers) are Chiu Chow, and they love this rich cuisine, with its thick, strong shark's fin soup, chicken in hot *chinjew* sauce, oyster omelet, and crabs in chicken sauce. ⊠ *Hotel Lisboa,* ☎ 577–666, ext. 83001. AE, DC, MC, V.

$$ ✕ **Four Five Six.** Lovers of Shanghainese food flock here for the house specialties: lacquered duck, braised eel, and chicken broiled in rice wine, plus steamed crabs during the winter. The atmosphere is generally cheerful, noisy, and welcoming. ⊠ *Hotel Lisboa, mezzanine of new wing,* ☎ 388–404. AE, DC, MC, V.

$$ ✕ **Long Kei.** One of the oldest and most popular Cantonese restaurants in Macau, Long Kei has a huge menu. Daily specials are printed only in Chinese, so ask the waiter to translate. Like all good Chinese restaurants in this part of the world, this one is noisy and chaotic, and makes no attempt at glamour or sophistication. The focus is the food, and it rarely disappoints; be sure to sample the shrimp toast. ⊠ *7B Largo do Senado,* ☎ 573–970. No credit cards.

$$ ✕ **Portas do Sol.** Despite its Portuguese name, this is a great place for a dim sum lunch. You get a menu with almost endless options: Shanghainese pork buns, chicken feet, rice-flour rolls, dumplings with shark's fin or minced beef . . . just pick a few that sound good and wait for the steaming bamboo containers to arrive. There's no need to make all your decisions at the beginning; you can add more as you go along. Desserts tend to be very sweet Chinese favorites, such as sago pudding and double-boiled papaya with snow fungus, which is less interesting than you'd think. ⊠ *Hotel Lisboa, Av. de Amizade,* ☎ 377–666. AE, MC, V.

$$ ✕ **Royal Canton.** This large, attractively decorated Cantonese restaurant in the Royal Hotel is very popular with both locals and Hong Kong or Chinese visitors, who use it for family parties and celebrations as well as for breakfast and morning dim sum. The menu is extensive and the service friendly and efficient. ⊠ *2-4 Est. da Vitorio,* ☎ *378–633. AE, DC, MC, V.*

Contemporary

$$$ ✕ **Fresco.** This new open-air restaurant is part of the Mandarin resort and makes for a relaxing summer evening. The food is billed as "MediterAsian," but it's less elaborate than it sounds: dishes range from pasta to salads and wood-fired pizzas to steak and roasted vegetables, many of them with an Asian touch. At press time, the chef was still working out the balance of flavors for many of the dishes, but he has the desserts nailed: delights such as the lime ice parfait and the star-anise crème brûlée are as exquisite to look at as they are to eat. ⊠ *Mandarin Oriental, Av. da Amizade,* ☎ *567–888. MC, V.*

Continental

$$$ ✕ **Os Gatos.** The setting is the main reason to dine here, since the restaurant is part of the Pousada de São Tiago (☞ Lodging, *below*), a traditional Portuguese inn built into a 17th-century fortress. Os Gatos (The Cats) integrates the original bar, café, and large terrace into a casually smart restaurant, with indoor and outdoor sections separated by sliding glass doors. The outdoor area has huge linen umbrellas and patio furniture, while the interior has hand-carved mahogany furniture, blue-and-white wall tiles, and terra-cotta tile floors. A vibrant mural depicts Macau in the past, present, and future. The food, though enjoyable, is not quite the equal of the setting. The menu is heavy on Italian dishes (at twice the price of Pizzeria Toscana but only half as good), with others from Portugal, Spain, Provence, and Greece. Specialties include seafood paella, baked crab with saffron and sage, and chicken piri-piri. ⊠ *Pousada de São Tiago, Av. da República,* ☎ *781– 111. AE, DC, MC, V.*

Italian

$$ ✕ **Pizzeria Toscana.** Don't be put off by the "pizzeria" in the name or
★ the strange location in the middle of a parking lot opposite the ferry terminal: this is one of the best restaurants in the city. In fact, it's sometimes difficult to think of a good reason to eat anywhere else. Owned by a Macanese family with roots in Pisa, Toscana turns out consistently good Italian food, from appetizers straight through entrées and pizzas to desserts. Try the *bresaola involtini* (air-cured beef with shredded Parmesan) or the delicate salmon carpaccio to start; then move on to grilled king prawns in a garlic-and-tomato sauce or tortellini with porcini mushrooms. End with the melt-in-your-mouth tiramisu and a strong espresso. The owner is one of the biggest wine importers in the region, so the wine list is superb and the prices very reasonable. ⊠ *Av. da Amizade, opposite the ferry terminal,* ☎ *726–637. MC, V.*

Macanese-Portuguese

$$$ ✕ **A Galera.** Probably the city's priciest restaurant, A Galera is a trea-
★ sure. The atmosphere is that of an elegant men's club, with cut-crystal glasses and Christofle silverware on the table and dark wood and blue-and-white azulejos on the walls. The wine menu alone is 25 pages long. The food ranges from seafood to grilled food to distinctive Macanese dishes; specialties include crispy-fried Kobe beef, a rare del-

icacy, and local favorites such as bacalhau, but there is nothing quite like the steamed lobster served with a rich, slightly sweet Sauterne sauce. For dessert, don't miss the chocolate soufflé with warm chocolate sauce, which is, mercifully, lighter than it sounds. ⊠ *Hotel Lisboa, new wing, 3rd floor, Av. de Amizade,* ☎ *577–666, ext. 3151. AE, MC, V.*

$$$ ✕ **Military Club.** When the exclusive Military Club restored its headquarters (which date from 1870) a few years ago, it appeared the beautiful dining hall might remain off-limits to the public. But despite lingering confusion about the issue, it is, in fact, open to all and well worth the visit. The languid old-world atmosphere is a rare treat and the extensive Portuguese menu—with such specialties as partridge pie, cold stuffed crab, grilled venison, and a range of egg puddings—is excellent. ⊠ *795 Av. Praia Grande,* ☎ *714–009. No credit cards.*

$$ ✕ **A Lorcha.** Ask people in town to name their favorite Portuguese restau-
★ rant and odds are they'll mention A Lorcha. It's not a fancy place—although the stone archways, white stucco, and terra-cotta tile floors make for a soothing environment—but they get everything just right. The menu leans towards traditional stalwarts such as *bacalhau* and grilled seafood or meat, but the dishes are always prepared with fresh ingredients and lots of care. The service is efficient and knowledgable (feel free to ask what is best that day), and the prices are quite reasonable—all told, a combination that will bring you back again and again. ⊠ *289 Rua do Almirante Sergio,* ☎ *313–193. Reservations essential. MC, V. Closed Tues.*

$$ ✕ **Afonso III.** After some years at the Hyatt Regency, Afonso decided to open his own place and cook the way his grandmother did. The result is this modest café in the heart of downtown, with a small, cozy downstairs decorated in wood and stucco and a larger, less intimate upstairs. The food is nothing complicated—just simple, hearty Portuguese dishes served up to homesick expatriates who work nearby. Most choose the daily specials, which usually include codfish, braised pork, and beef stew prepared as nowhere else in Macau. The wine list is equally unusual, and the prices are low. ⊠ *11A Rua Central,* ☎ *586–272. No credit cards.*

$$ ✕ **Balichão.** This Macanese restaurant is best seen in the summer, when it takes maximum advantage of its location in Coloane Park between a small pond and an aviary. The decor features birdcages (some with resident birds), brass pots, and rattan furniture. The restaurant was started by mother-daughter team Maria and Isabel Eusébio with the goal of bringing real Macanese food out of the confines of the family kitchen. The food is an interesting combination of innovative dishes available only as daily specials, and old Macanese favorites such as casserole of pork and tamarind in balichão, curry crab, and chicken Macau. This is a great place for private parties; it's huge and you'll be well looked after. ⊠ *Est. Seac Pai Van Granja, Coloane,* ☎ *870–098. AE, DC, MC, V.*

$$ ✕ **Fernando's.** You may have to look long and hard to find this country-style Portuguese restaurant next to Hac Sa Beach; the entrance looks like that of a typical Chinese café. Your guiding light is the fact that everyone from Hong Kong comes here, and the owner aggressively promotes the place with tourists. It has a pleasant open-air setting (covered with a roof) and serves satisfying seafood that's not altogether worthy of the hype. Fernando personally reigns over the dining room, and he is without a doubt the restaurant's greatest selling point. ⊠ *Hac Sa Beach 9, Coloane,* ☎ *882–264. No credit cards.*

$$ ✕ **Litoral.** Litoral has long been one of the most popular local restau-
★ rants, serving Portuguese and Macanese dishes that are relatively humble but invariably delicious. Be warned that the Portuguese favor cuts of meat for which others need to acquire a taste: pig's ear and ox tripe, to name just two. From time to time the owner, Manuela Ferreira, re-

moves the better dishes—such as the braised duck in a complex sweet-soy sauce—from the menu; it's worth asking if it's available. For dessert, try the *bebinca de leite,* a coconut-milk custard, or the traditional egg pudding, *pudim abade de priscos.* Although it's set in a boxy modern building, the interior looks like a traditional Portuguese restaurant installed in a Chinese shop house, all to brilliant effect. ✉ *261 Rua Almirante Sergio,* ☎ *967–878. AE, MC, V.*

$$ ✕ Montanha Russa. In the northern suburbs of Macau there is a quiet park on a hill shaped like a snail shell. It's a great retreat, and the perfect spot for Macau's only real outdoor restaurant, which accounts for its popularity among the people who work nearby. Operated by Filipinos, Montanha Russa is very much a family-style place, with a daily choice of soups, fish, and meats. Service comes with a smile, and the bill is a pleasant surprise. ✉ *Est. Ferreira de Amaral,* ☎ *302–731. No credit cards.*

$$ ✕ O Porto Interior. The focus at this restaurant, named for its location on the Inner Harbour (but separated from the water by warehouses), is on beautifully presented upmarket Macanese dishes. It has a daily set menu that is one of the best deals in town. It's the design, however, that makes the place so special. The elegant two-story facade has colonnades and Iberian arches; inside, the walls are covered with azulejos and intricately carved wooden grilles. To enter, you cross a marble bridge. ✉ *259 Rua Almirante Sergio,* ☎ *967–770. AE, MC, V.*

$$ ✕ Praia Grande. Wonderfully situated on the Praia Grande, this classic Portuguese restaurant was cleverly created from a prefab corner building. The decor is simple—white arches, terra-cotta floors, and wrought-iron furniture. The menu presents such imaginative fare as Portuguese dim sum, African chicken, mussels in white wine, and clams *cataplana* (in a stew of pork, onions, tomatoes, and wine). The esplanade, with a serving kiosk and umbrella-shaded tables, is ideal for drinks and snacks. ✉ *10A Lobo d'Avila, Praia Grande,* ☎ *973–022. AE, MC, V.*

$$ ✕ Sol Nascente. This modest restaurant on the main road at the entrance to Taipa Village has proved a real winner. It's furnished simply, with homemade chairs and a nice mural to illustrate the name ("Rising Sun"), but what's special is the menu, where you're bound to find clams in coriander sauce; mussels stuffed with bread crumbs, spring onions, and garlic; Goan prawn curry; and beef rice with chestnuts as well as the usual Macanese favorites—all for 90 patacas or less. Wine is available for as little as 60 patacas a bottle, and the servers are friendly and helpful. ✉ *Av. Dr. Sun Yat-sen, Edificio Chun Leong Garden, ground floor, Taipa Island,* ☎ *836–288. MC, V.*

LODGING

Although Macau's landmark colonial hotel, the luxurious Bela Vista, is now the residence of the first Portuguese consul-general, the territory still has an impressive range of lodging options for such a small city. The most charming are the *pousadas,* such as the São Tiago, a modern hotel within an old Portuguese fort; others, such as the Mandarin, are modern and blissfully efficient. Only the cheaper and more modest guest houses occupy old buildings in the historic heart of the city, but even the Westin Resort, on the distant island of Coloane, is just a 15-minute taxi ride from the main square—and heaven knows it compensates, with extensive sports facilities, including access to a golf course and a black-sand beach.

In general, hotels listed in the $$$$ and $$$ categories are of the highest international standard, with swimming pools and health clubs, meeting rooms for conferences and parties, fine restaurants, elaborately designed public areas, business centers, and guest rooms with all the modern comforts and conveniences. Those in the $$ category are efficient, clean, and comfortable, with air-conditioning, color TV (showing English and Chinese programs from Hong Kong as well as the local channel), room service, and restaurants. They cater primarily to gamblers, regular Hong Kong visitors, and budget tour groups. Hotels in the $ category tend to be old and spartan and are used mostly by mainland Chinese travelers, so their staffs generally speak little English. They are, however, usually clean and inexpensive and sometimes even offer private bath and TV. Rooms in all other categories listed below will have private baths.

Bear in mind that Macau relies heavily on weekend traffic, so reservations are difficult to come by on Saturday night. You can save up to 40% off the published rate (and have the hotel virtually to yourself) by coming to Macau during the week.

The Macau Government Tourist Office (☞ Macau A to Z, *below*) has details.

CATEGORY	COST*
$$$$	$230–$350
$$$	$105–$230
$$	$40–$105
$	under $40

Per room, not including 10% service charge and 5% tax.

$$$$ 🏨 **Mandarin Oriental.** The Mandarin has always been luxurious—with
★   an opulent lobby, beautifully appointed rooms, and service that is second to none—but the recent addition of a 49,000-sq-ft (15,000-sq-m) Mediterranean-style spa makes it irresistible. After a grueling day of sightseeing, pop into the sauna and then ease into the heat of the hot tub before heading outdoors to the large tropical swimming pool. And if that doesn't get rid of the knots and kinks of real life, sit under the miniature waterfall and let the warm cascade pound your shoulders. Amid such pleasures, it's easy to forget that the office towers and frenzied traffic of urban Macau lie just beyond the hotel's entrance. ⌧ *Av. da Amizade,* ☎ *567–888; 2881–1988 in Hong Kong; 800/526–6566 in the U.S.;* ⅢÄ *594–589. 435 rooms. 4 restaurants, bar, cafe, 2 pools, beauty salon, massage, sauna, spa, 2 tennis courts, exercise room, squash, casino. AE, DC, MC, V.* 🐾

$$$$ 🏨 **Westin Resort.** The Westin is designed for those primarily interested
★   in getting away from it all. Occupying a magnificent site on a headland overlooking the black-sand beach of Hac Sa, the resort is surrounded by open water and total silence. It's only a fifteen-minute taxi ride from the city center, but from the moment you enter the lobby the pace slows to that of a tropical island, where a day spent by the pool or out on the golf course counts as reasonably ambitious. The comfortable rooms are large and the terraces even larger, while the sports and recreational facilities are the best in Macau—guests even have course and clubhouse privileges at the adjacent Macau Golf and Country Club (☞ Outdoor Activities and Sports, *below*). ⌧ *Hac Sa Beach, Coloane Island,* ☎ *871–111; 2803–2015 in Hong Kong; 800/228–3000 in the U.S.;* ⅢÄ *871–122. 208 rooms. 4 restaurants, 2 bars, 2 pools, golf course, 8 tennis courts, health club, squash, shops. AE, DC, MC, V.* 🐾

$$$ 🏨 **Grandeur.** Owned and operated by CTS (Hong Kong), this hotel in the Outer Harbour boasts Rotunda, Macau's first revolving restaurant, with great views and nightly entertainment. Other restaurants serve Chinese and Italian meals. Each room has a window bay with a table and chairs, and furnishings are brightly floral. Hair dryers are provided.

The hotel is an efficient, businesslike place, without the grand lobby favored by most other hotels; but you can relax in its indoor pool and health club. The Grandeur caters to Japanese and mainland tour groups, Hong Kong businesspeople, and Western tourists. ⊠ *Rua de Pequim,* ☎ *781–233; 2857–2846 in Hong Kong;* ℻ *781–211. 350 rooms. 3 restaurants, bar, indoor pool, health club, business services. AE, DC, MC, V.*

$$$ 🏨 **Hotel Lisboa.** Despite its split personality, the Lisboa is an unexpectedly appealing place to stay. The exterior of the hotel has, out of sheer eccentricity, become a popular symbol of Macau: a gaudy mustard-and-white confection with a roof of giant balls on spikes that is said to resemble a roulette wheel. The lobby is more tasteful but still a little ostentatious, littered with baubles such as an intricately carved 2-ton piece of jade borrowed from the art collection of local taipan (and Lisboa owner) Stanley Ho. But after all that, the rooms, especially in the new tower, come as a delightful surprise: large, comfortable, wedge-shaped spaces that have been decorated with a thoughtful (and restrained) hand. And geographically speaking, the Lisboa is like Rome: all roads (and many buses) lead here, making this an exceptionally convenient option. On the premises are a large shopping center, a casino, the Mona Lisa Theater (☞ Nightlife, *below*), the superb restaurant A Galera (☞ Dining, *above*), a children's game room, and a billiards hall. Men shouldn't be too flattered if they attract the attention of the bevy of young women who prowl the shopping center—it's their job. ⊠ *Av. da Amizade,* ☎ *377–666; 2546–6944 in Hong Kong;* ℻ *567–193. 1,050 rooms. 12 restaurants, 3 bars, coffee shop, pizzeria, pool, sauna, bowling, casino, dance club, theater, video games. AE, DC, MC, V.* 🐾

$$$ 🏨 **Hotel Ritz.** This handsome hotel is a series of low-rise blocks built into the hillside opposite the Bela Vista, so many of its rooms have balconies that look out over the Outer Harbour—and, unfortunately, the construction that goes along with the new Nam Van Lakes project. The huge, marble-clad, chandelier-lighted lobby opens onto a café, a French restaurant, and a large health center containing two pools, a squash court, a gym, and a sauna. The restaurant Lijinxuan, which serves dishes from many parts of China, is over-the-top opulent, with enormous chandeliers and masses of gilded wood. Guests include VIPs from the mainland and five-star tour groups from Japan. ⊠ *Rua Comendador Kou Ho Neng,* ☎ *339–955; 2739–6993, 2540–6333, or 2367–3043 in Hong Kong;* ℻ *317–826. 162 rooms and suites. 3 restaurants, bar, 2 indoor pools, sauna, 2 tennis courts, health club, squash, business services. AE, DC, MC, V.* 🐾

$$$ 🏨 **Hyatt Regency and Taipa Island Resort.** The Hyatt was the originator of the resort concept in Macau but in the last few years it has been trumped by its rivals: the Mandarin has a newer resort closer to downtown and the Westin has its unique, secluded location. Nevertheless, the Hyatt is a pleasant place to stay, with rooms that have been much improved by a recent renovation. And it still has superb resort facilities, including a health spa, huge outdoor swimming pool, and a hot tub that looks like a modern take on the Turkish bath. The service can be spotty, however; the front desk feels chronically understaffed. The racetrack is nearby, and the hotel operates a shuttle-bus service to the wharf and to the Lisboa. The Hyatt is particularly popular with Hong Kong families. ⊠ *Taipa Island,* ☎ *831–234; 2559–0168 in Hong Kong; 800/233–1234 in the U.S.;* ℻ *830–195. 326 rooms. 3 restaurants, 2 bars, pool, barbershop, beauty salon, 4 tennis courts, health club, squash, casino. AE, DC, MC, V.* 🐾

$$$ 🏨 **New Century.** Between the university and the Hyatt Regency, this opulent hotel tends to appeal more to mainland Chinese than to Westerners, who may find the shininess of all the decorations a little over the top. The atrium lobby really is breathtaking, however, and the huge pool terrace has splendid views of the city and Taipa. Rooms are somewhat more tastefully furnished, and there's a wide range of dining options, including a wooden deck with Caribbean-style cabanas for parties. The Prince Galaxie is an excellent entertainment center, with a pub, a disco, and karaoke rooms. ✉ *Est. Almirante Marques Esparteiro, Taipa Island,* ☎ *831–111; 2581–9863 in Hong Kong;* FAX *832-222. 599 rooms. 4 restaurants, bar, pub, pool, 2 tennis courts, bowling, health club, squash, casino, dance club. AE, DC, MC, V.*

$$$ 🏨 **Pousada de São Tiago.** With the closing of the Bela Vista, the São
★ Tiago now has the monopoly on charm among Macau's hotels. It was ingeniously built into a 17th-century Portuguese fortress that once guarded the southern tip of the peninsula, and the entrance alone is worth a visit, with a staircase that runs through an old lichen-covered tunnel through which water seeps in soothing trickles. In the hallways, bedrock has been allowed to protrude through the floor tiles, while the rooms have been decorated with unusual mahogany furnishings and azulejos that enhance the general old-world atmosphere. Ancient trees that had taken over the fort were also incorporated into the design; the positions of their roots, for example, dictated the shape of the coffee shop and terrace, and are now a part of the casual Mediterranean restaurant, Os Gatos (☞ Dining, *above*). The only shortcoming is that the service can be a little lethargic, so be prepared to carry your own bags upstairs to the reception desk. Book well in advance for weekends and holidays. ✉ *Av. da República,* ☎ *378–111; 2739-1216 in Hong Kong;* FAX *552–170. 23 rooms. Restaurant, bar, pool, chapel. AE, DC, MC, V.* 🍴

$$$ 🏨 **Royal.** The Royal has an excellent location, on a small hill with fine views of Guia, the city, and the Inner Harbour. The marble-clad lobby has a marble fountain, a lounge, and some fine shops, and the basement hides sports facilities and a karaoke bar. Upstairs are the glass-roof swimming pool and three restaurants: the Royal Canton for Chinese food, the Vasco da Gama for Portuguese-Continental, and a coffee shop. The hotel runs shuttle buses to the casinos. ✉ *Est. da Vitoria,* ☎ *552–222; 2540–6333 in Hong Kong;* FAX *563–008. 380 rooms. 3 restaurants, bar, indoor pool, sauna, health club, squash, shops. AE, DC, MC, V.*

$$ 🏨 **Beverly Plaza.** Located on the reclaimed land behind the Lisboa, this hotel is managed by the China Travel Service and is a fairly standard China-run operation, with disco and karaoke, sauna and massage, a large Chinese banquet room, and a Western coffee shop. The hotel shop sells bargain-price stereos, television sets, microwave ovens, and other goods that local Chinese buy for their relatives in China and ship home. The rooms are clean, air-conditioned, and equipped with television, minibar, and flasks of hot water for tea and coffee. Devoid of frills, it's a good budget option. ✉ *Av. Dr. Rodrigo Rodrigues,* ☎ *782–288; 2739–9928 in Hong Kong;* FAX *780–684. 300 rooms. Restaurant, bar, coffee shop, shops. AE, DC, MC, V.*

$$ 🏨 **Kingsway.** This moderately priced hotel on the Outer Harbour has small rooms, but all have phones with international direct-dial capability, minibars, and in-house movies. The casino caters mostly to gambling junketeers from Southeast Asia. ✉ *Rua Luis Gonzaga Gomes,* ☎ *702–888; 2571–1886 in Hong Kong;* FAX *702–828. 410 rooms. 2 restaurants, sauna, casino. AE, DC, MC, V.*

$$ 🏨 **New World Emperor.** In the Outer Harbour district, this hotel is near casinos and the wharf and is a smart value. Rooms are furnished with potted plants, desks, TV consoles, and pastel drapes and bedspreads. There's a fine Cantonese restaurant and a nightclub with disco and karaoke, and the lobby bazaar sells clothes and accessories. ✉ *Rua de*

Xangai, ☎ *781–888; 2733–0399 in Hong Kong;* FAX *782–287. 405 rooms. 2 restaurants, bar, sauna, dance club, nightclub. AE, DC, MC, V.* 🐾

$$ 🏨 **Presidente.** The Presidente has an excellent location a block from the Lisboa casino, on the Outer Harbour Road between the ferry terminal and the bridge to Taipa Island. It's very popular with Hong Kongers and has an agreeable lobby lounge, European and Chinese restaurants, the best Korean food in town, and a disco. ⊠ *Av. da Amizade,* ☎ *553–888; 2857–1533 in Hong Kong;* FAX *552–735. 340 rooms. 3 restaurants, sauna, dance club. AE, DC, MC, V.*

$$ 🏨 **Sintra.** Hands down, this is the best value option in its price range. There's nothing fancy here: the furnishings are simple and the facilities don't extend much beyond a sauna and a not-very-appetizing European restaurant. But where it counts most, the Sintra gets it right: the rooms are exceptionally comfortable and the location is arguably the best of any hotel, within easy walking distance of both the Old Quarter and the new ones. ⊠ *Av. Dom João IV,* ☎ *710–111; 2546–6944 in Hong Kong;* FAX *566–7749. 236 rooms. 2 restaurants, sauna. AE, DC, MC, V.* 🐾

$ 🏨 **Central.** In the heart of town just off the Old Town square, this was once the tallest building in the city. It was also the home of Macau's only legal casino—and doubled as a brothel. All that is long gone, and it's now a budget hotel with clean, basic rooms and an excellent Chinese restaurant. ⊠ *Av. Almeida Ribeiro,* ☎ *378–888,* FAX *332–275. 160 rooms. Restaurant. AE, MC, V.*

$ 🏨 **Holiday.** This budget hotel is behind Monte Fort and St. Paul's. Rooms are basic one-star, with small, hard beds, TVs, telephones, air-conditioning, and bathrooms with tubs and showers. The staff does not speak English but is friendly and helpful. ⊠ *36 Est. de Repousa,* ☎ *361–696. 40 rooms. Restaurant, nightclub. AE, MC, V.*

NIGHTLIFE

According to old movies and novels about the China Coast, Macau was a city of opium dens, wild gambling, international spies, and slinky ladies of the night. While this image is not far from the truth today (albeit shorn of any romantic mystique), it's kept so well hidden that most visitors will be unaware such an underbelly exists. The tacky hostess nightclubs, karaoke lounges, and so-called sauna parlors that abound are popular with Asian men, but unfortunately, nightlife that does not involve gambling or live girls is hard to come by here; many travelers find themselves simply enjoying long dinners that run late into the night. The city is trying to develop the Outer Harbour waterfront into a cluster of pubs and music bars, but it's too early to tell whether or not this will catch on.

Mona Lisa Theater (Hotel Lisboa). The Lisboa's *Crazy Paris Show* was first staged in the late 1970s and has become a popular fixture. The stripper-dancers are artists from Europe, Australia, and the Americas who put on a highly sophisticated and cleverly staged show. They shed their clothes, but the performance is not lewd; in fact, half the audience is likely to be made up of female tourists. The acts change every few months. Tickets are available at hotel desks, Hong Kong and Macau ferry terminals, and the theater itself. ⊠ *Hotel Lisboa, 2nd floor, Av. da Amizade,* ☎ *377–666, ext. 3195.* 🎫 *HK$200–HK$250.* ☉ *Shows Sun.–Fri. at 8 and 9:30, Sat. at 8, 9:30, and 11.*

Nightclubs & Pubs

Many nightspots are staffed with hostesses from Thailand, the Philippines, or Russia and are merely thinly veiled covers for the world's oldest profession. The legitimate clubs that do exist tend not to survive for very long. Check with the Macau Government Tourist Office to find out about interesting spots that are currently open.

Pubs and music bars open and close with astonishing speed and are mostly known only to locals by word of mouth. You can inquire at the tourist office or, better still, spot the coolest-looking person on staff at your hotel and ask where they go out at night. For some time the government has been promoting the area on the reclaimed land near the Hotel Lisboa as the city's new entertainment district (billing it as the "Lan Kwai Fong of Macau," after Hong Kong's popular nightlife district). Although the comparison to Hong Kong is still a bit of a stretch, there is finally a critical mass of bars, live music spots, and restaurants. It's somewhat desolate by day but comes alive at night. The main street here is Rua Cidade de Tavira, and most of the hot spots are gathered on the southwestern block.

Casinos

There are nine casinos in Macau: the **Lisboa, Mandarin Oriental, New Century, Kingsway, Holiday Inn,** and **Hyatt Regency** hotels, and the **Jai Alai Stadium,** the **Kam Pek,** and the **Palacio de Macau,** usually known as the Floating Casino. The busiest is the two-story operation in the Lisboa, where the games are roulette, blackjack, baccarat, *pacapio,* and the Chinese games called fan-tan and "big-and-small." There are also hundreds of slot machines, which the Chinese call "hungry tigers."

The solid mass of players in the casinos might look rather unsophisticated, but they are as knowledgeable as any gamblers in the world. They are also more single-minded than most, eschewing alcohol and all but essential nourishment while at the tables. (Small bottles of chicken essence are much in evidence!) And they are extremely superstitious, which leads to gambles that may confuse Westerners.

There are few limitations to gambling in Macau. No one under 18 is allowed in, but identity cards are not checked. Although there are posted betting limits, high rollers are not discouraged by such formalities. A credit card can get you cash in either patacas or Hong Kong dollars from the automatic teller machines, and there are also 24-hour currency exchanges. Bets are almost always placed in Hong Kong dollars. There are a few games that might not be familiar:

Baccarat has, in recent years, become a big-status game for well-heeled gamblers from Hong Kong, who brag as much about losing a million as about winning one. The baccarat tables occupy their own special corners and are usually surrounded by an admiring, envying crowd. Minimum bets are HK$1,000 to HK$30,000. In Macau the player cannot take the bank, and the fixed rules on drawing and standing are complex, making this completely a game of chance.

Big and small is a traditional game in which you bet on combinations of numbers for big or small totals determined by rolled dice. The minimum bet is HK$50.

Fan-tan is an ancient Chinese game that has somehow survived Western competition—"somehow," because it's so incredibly simple. A pile of porcelain buttons is placed on the table, and the croupier removes four at a time until one, two, three, or four are left. Players wager on the result, and some are so experienced they know the answer long before the game ends.

Pacapio has replaced the similar game of keno: players choose between 4 and 25 numbers from 1 to 80. Winning numbers are chosen by computer and appear every half hour or so on screens in the Lisboa and the Jai Alai Stadium.

Pai kao has been a popular Chinese game since the 19th century. It's played with dominoes and a revolving banker system, both of which make it all but impossible for novices to understand. The minimum bet is either HK$100 or HK$200.

Roulette is based on the European system, with a single zero, but has some American touches. Players buy colored chips at an American-style table, and bets are collected, rather than frozen, when the zero appears. Roulette has been steadily losing popularity and is now played only in the Lisboa and Mandarin Oriental casinos. The minimum bet is HK$50.

OUTDOOR ACTIVITIES AND SPORTS

For most regular visitors to Macau, the sporting life means playing the casinos, but there are plenty of other sports here, albeit often with gambling on the side. The Macanese are keen on team sports, and perform quite creditably in soccer and field hockey. In addition to traditional annual events, such as the Grand Prix auto race, there are international championships in volleyball and table tennis (a.k.a. Ping-Pong, which, played professionally, is a completely different animal from the game you played in your basement). Major indoor events, such as the World Volleyball Championships, are held in the **Macau Forum,** while the new venue for outdoor events is the **Taipa Stadium.** Participatory sports activity has increased in recent years, with some excellent routes for joggers and more fitness facilities in hotels.

Dragon Boat Racing

This newest of international sports derives from the ancient Chinese dragon boat festivals, during which fishing communities competed, paddling long, shallow boats with dragons' heads and tails in honor of a poet who drowned himself to protest official corruption. At the time, about 2,000 years ago, his friends took boats into the water and pounded their oars and beat drums to scare away the fish who would have eaten the poet's body. The festival and races have been revived in many parts of Asia, with teams competing from Hong Kong, Japan, Singapore, Thailand, Malaysia, and Macau, plus crews from Australia, the United States, Europe, and China's Guangdong Province. The races are held alongside the waterfront, which provides a natural grandstand for spectators. The Dragon Boat Festival takes place on the fifth day of the fifth moon (usually sometime in June) and is attended by a flotilla of fishing junks decorated with silk banners and by fishing families beating drums and setting off firecrackers.

Go-Cart Racing

On reclaimed land opposite Coloane Park is Macau's new go-cart track, the **Kartodromo,** where you can hire a vehicle for go-cart racing. It's basically headquarters for local carters and is usually open only on Sunday (sometimes on Saturday). There are floodlights for night racing. ⊠ *Seac Pai Van, Coloane,* ☎ *688–6886 (rental) or 882–126 (competition).* ▣ *100 patacas for 10 mins, 200 patacas for 25 mins.* ☉ *Weekends 10–6.*

Golf

The **Macau Golf and Country Club** is affiliated with the **Westin Resort,** beside Hac Sa Beach. The 18-hole, par-71 course is built into the wooded headland above the hotel; an elevator leaves you a few yards from the first tee. The clubhouse has a pro shop, a pool, a sauna, massage rooms, steam baths, and restaurants. Only hotel guests and members of affiliated clubs can play. ☎ 871–111. ✉ *Greens fees for 18 holes: HK$700 weekdays, HK$1,400 weekends.*

Greyhound Racing

The dogs are very popular with both residents and Hong Kong gamblers, who flock to races in the scenic, open-air **Macau Canidrome,** near the old Chinese border. Most dogs are imported from Australia; some come from Ireland and the United States. The 10,000-seat stadium has rows and rows of betting windows and stalls for food and drink. Multimillion-dollar purses are not unheard of, and special events, such as Irish Nights, are held frequently. Races start at 8 PM (there are usually eight) and finish at about 11 PM. ✉ *Av. do Artur Tamagnini Barbosa at Av. General Castelo Branco.* ✉ *2 patacas for public stands, 5 patacas for members' stand, 80 patacas for 6-seat box.* ☉ *Tues., Thurs., and weekends.*

Horse Racing

The **Macau Raceway,** originally built as Asia's first trotting track, occupies 50 acres of reclaimed land near the Hyatt Regency Hotel. Trotting did not catch on with local gamblers, so the **Macau Jockey Club** was formed and the facility converted, with no expense spared, into a world-class racecourse, with grass and sand tracks, floodlighting, and the most sophisticated computerized betting system available. The five-story grandstand can accommodate 15,000 people, 6,000 of them in air-conditioned comfort; members have boxes where five-star meals can be catered. There are several public restaurants, bars, a small casino, and a huge electronic screen to show the odds, winnings, and races in progress. Races are held throughout the year on weekends (usually in the afternoon) and midweek (at night), timed not to clash with events at the Hong Kong Jockey Club. The Hotel Lisboa runs free bus service to the racecourse. Ask your hotel desk for more details. ✉ *Est. Governador Albano de Oliveira.* ✉ *20 patacas.*

Ice-Skating

The **Future Bright Amusement Park** has a small, crowded rink and a highly qualified teaching staff. The park also houses a bowling alley, a food court, a video arcade, and a children's playground. Don't bother calling ahead unless you speak Chinese. ✉ *Praça Luis de Camões,* ☎ *953–399.* ✉ *40 patacas, including skate rental for unlimited time between 9 AM and 10 PM.*

Motor Racing

The **Macau Grand Prix** takes place the third or fourth weekend of November. From the beginning of the week, the city is pierced with the sound of supercharged engines testing the 6-km (4-mi) Guia Circuit, which follows the city roads along the Outer Harbour to Guia Hill and around the reservoir. The route is as challenging as that of Monaco, with rapid gear changes demanded at the right-angle Statue Corner, the Doña Maria bend, and the Melco hairpin.

The Grand Prix was first staged here in 1953, and the standard of performance has now reached world class. Today cars achieve speeds of 224 kph (140 mph) on the straightaways, with the lap record approaching 2 minutes, 20 seconds. The premier event is the Formula

Three Championship, with cars competing from around the world in what is now the official World Cup of Formula Three racing, where winners qualify for Formula One licenses. There are also races for motorcycles and production cars.

Room reservations for the week of the Grand Prix should be made months in advance, and anyone not interested in motor racing should avoid coming to Macau that weekend. Tickets are available from tourist offices or from agents in Macau and Hong Kong; prices vary.

Running

The 42-km (26-mi) **Macau International Marathon** has been run since 1980. Held in early December, it challenges runners with a course that includes both of Macau's bridges, the airport, and a circuit of peninsular Macau. If you'd like a shorter challenge, try the trails on Coloane. Guia Hill has an exercise trail. For more information contact the **Sports Institute** (☎ 510–426).

Stadium Sports

Since the opening of the **Macau Forum,** with its 4,000-seat multipurpose hall, sporting events have been much easier to stage in these parts. The world table-tennis, volleyball, and roller-hockey championships have been held in Macau, as have regional basketball, soccer, and badminton matches. The new 15,000-seat **Taipa Stadium** (✉ Av. Olimpica, adjacent to the racetrack) has facilities for soccer and track-and-field contests. Ask your hotel what's on while you're here.

Tennis and Squash

The Hyatt Regency, Mandarin Oriental, New Century, and Westin all have tennis and squash courts for use by guests only. The Hyatt also supplies a tennis coach.

SHOPPING

At first glance, Macau is a poor country cousin to Hong Kong in the retail business. So why bother to shop here at all? First, the shopping areas are much more compact and navigable. Second, the sales staffs are on the whole more pleasant and relaxed here, even if their command of English is less impressive. And most important, many goods are cheaper. Like Hong Kong, Macau is a duty-free port for almost all items; but commercial rents, unlike those in the former British territory, are reasonable, and wages are low, reducing the overhead and hence the prices shopkeepers need to charge.

Except for family-run businesses, which take a short holiday after the Chinese New Year, Macau's shops are open 365 days a year. Opening hours vary according by type of shop, but usually extend into mid-evening, around 8 or so. Most shops accept major credit cards, except on those items with the deepest discounts. Friendly bargaining is expected and is done by asking for the "best price," which produces discounts of 10% or more. Discounts larger than that on expensive items should be treated with suspicion. Macau has its share of phony antiques, fake name-brand watches, and other rip-offs. Be sure to shop around, check the guarantee on name brands (sometimes fakes come with misspellings), and get receipts for expensive items.

Macau's major shopping districts are its main street, Avenida Almeida Ribeiro (commonly known by its Chinese name, Sanmalo); Mercadores and its side streets; Cinco de Outubro; and Rua do Campo. Shop names reflect Macau's dual heritage; for example, Pastelarias Mei Mun (pastry shops), Relojoaria Tat On (watches and clocks), and Sapatarias João Leong (shoes).

Antiques

The days of discovering treasures from the Ming among the Qing (pronounced Ching) chinoiserie in Macau's antiques shops are long gone, but there are still plenty of old and interesting pieces lying about. Collectors of old porcelain can find some well-preserved bowls and other simple Ming ware once used as ballast in trading ships. Prices for such genuine items run into the hundreds or thousands of dollars. Far cheaper are the ornate vases, stools, and dishes from the late Qing period (concurrent with England's Victorian era). This style of pottery is still very popular among the Chinese, and a lot of so-called Qing is faithfully reproduced today in China, Hong Kong, and Macau. Many of these copies are excellent and hard to distinguish from their antique cousins. For the best selection of traditional Chinese furniture, scroll paintings, porcelain, figurines, fans, dragon robes, lacquerware, and other collectibles, troll the area around St. Paul's, particularly Rua do São Antonio and Rua de São Paulo.

Interesting antique furniture is the focus of a store called **Asian Artifacts** (⌧ 25 Rua dos Negociantes, Coloane, ☎ 881–022), on a side street in Coloane Village. The owner keeps her shop and its extension filled with valuable old tables, screens, chests, and wardrobes as well as some high-quality reproductions. Other antiques shops that have earned excellent reputations over the years include **Hong Hap** (⌧ 170 Cinco de Outubro) and **Wing Tai** (⌧ 1A Av. Almeida Ribeiro).

Clothing

Many Macau stores sell casual and sports clothes for men and women at bargain prices. Most items are made here in Macau and carry brand-name labels—in some cases these are fakes, but more often they're genuine overruns or rejects from local factories that are licensed manufacturers for **Yves Saint Laurent, Cacharel, Van Heusen, Adidas, Gloria Vanderbilt,** and many others. You can also buy padded jackets, sweaters, jogging suits, windbreakers, and a wide range of clothes for children and infants at very low prices. The best shopping areas are on **Rua do Campo** and around **Mercadores.** For the very best bargains, visit the street markets of **São Domingos** (off Largo do Senado), **Rua Cinco de Outubro,** and **Rua da Palha.** There are also a growing number of designer and name-brand boutiques, such as the two-story **Emporio Armani** at 61 Avenida Almeida Ribeiro, where prices are usually much lower than in Hong Kong. Credit cards are accepted at most larger shops.

Crafts

Many traditional Chinese crafts are made in Macau. The best places to watch the craftspeople at work are **Tercena** and **Estalagens**; these old streets are lined with three-story shop houses with open-front workshops on the ground floor, living quarters and offices above. Some shops produce beautifully carved chests and furniture made of mahogany, camphor wood, and redwood, some inlaid with marble or mother-of-pearl; others make bamboo birdcages with tiny porcelain bowls to go in them, door plaques thought to bring luck, and family altars. To find these two small streets, turn left off the path to St. Paul's church at the intersection of Rua da Palha and Rua São Paulo and then take your first right. Follow the cream and black paving tiles that the government uses to indicate the route to many of Macau's major sights. Macau also produces lacquer screens, modern and traditional Chinese pottery, and ceremonial items such as lion-dance costumes, giant incense coils, and temple offerings.

Department Stores

In 1994, the Japanese chain **Yaohan** opened Macau's first major department store, next door to the Jai Alai Stadium. It is now called New Yaohan following an obscure bankruptcy and trademark battle but still offers a one-stop arena for everything from linen tablecloths to clothing, jewelry, housewares, shoe repair, a bakery, a fully stocked food hall, and several dining options. Other popular stores are the two branches of **Nam Kwong**—at 95 Avenida Almeida Ribeiro and at 9 Ria Pequim, next door to the Holiday Inn—which specialize in products made in China.

Gold and Jewelry

Macau's jewelry shops are not as lavish as those in downtown Hong Kong, but they charge a much lower premium for workmanship, resulting in markedly lower prices for the finished piece. The price of the gold itself fluctuates with trading on the Hong Kong Gold Exchange and each store will have an electronic display showing the current price of gold per *tael,* which is 1.2 troy ounces. Some counters display 14- and 18-karat jewelry, such as chains, earrings, pendants, brooches, rings, and bangles; however, the best-seller is 24-karat (pure) gold in the form of jewelry, coins, and tiny bars, which come with assays from a Swiss bank. Since prices for gold items are based on the established international price of gold plus a rate for workmanship and a small percentage profit, there is only limited scope for bargaining.

Among the best-known shops are **Chow Sang Sang** (⊠ 360 Av. Almeida Ribeiro), **Pou Fong** (⊠ 453 Av. Almeida Ribeiro), **Sheong Hei** (⊠ 275 Av. Almeida Ribeiro), and **Tai Fung** (⊠ 446 Av. Almeida Ribeiro). Salespeople at all four speak English and are friendly and helpful.

Wine

Because of Macau's long connection to Europe, wines—and little-known Portuguese wines in particular—are a real bargain. You can buy them everywhere, from the corner convenience store to the largest grocery, but the basement wine cellar at **Pavilions** (417–425 Av. da Praia Grande) has one of the best selections. And if you've developed a taste for port wine, consider loading up (just be aware that Hong Kong customs technically allows only one bottle per passenger); prices are much cheaper in Macau than anywhere else except Oporto itself.

MACAU A TO Z

Arriving and Departing

By Boat

The Hong Kong–Macau route is one of the world's easiest border crossings. Ferries run every fifteen minutes and take just under an hour, with no more than five minutes for immigration control on either side (be sure to bring your passport). Only on weekend evenings and major public holidays is it necessary to reserve in advance (☎ 2895–6596 or 2183–8138); at all other times, just show up and take the next boat. Of course, service can be disrupted when typhoons sweep in.

The majority of ships to Macau leave Hong Kong from the Macau Terminal in the **Shun Tak Centre** (✉ 200 Connaught Rd.), which has its own marked exit from the Sheung Wan MTR station. From Macau, ferries use the modern three-story ferry terminal. There is also limited service to and from the China Hong Kong Terminal, on the Kowloon side of Hong Kong Harbour.

The Shun Tak Centre houses the Macau Government Tourist Office, booking offices for all shipping companies, and offices of most Macau hotels, travel agents, and excursions to China.

Following the merger of **Far East Jetfoil Company** and **CTS-Parkview**, there is now a unified service of **Turbojets**, which run every fifteen minutes around the clock, with slightly less frequent sailings from 3 AM to 6 AM. The Turbojets are larger and more comfortable than the old Jetfoils and make the 64-km (40-mi) trip in about an hour. Beer, soft drinks, and snacks are available on board, as are duty-free cigarettes and Macau's instant-lottery tickets. There is no smoking on board. First-class seats are available for a small premium, but there is no discernible difference in quality save for a free box of unappetizing snacks.

There are three classes of tickets—economy, first, and super—as well as VIP cabins for four or six people. The prices, depending on class, are HK$130–HK$232 on weekdays, HK$141–HK$247 on weekends and holidays, and HK$161–HK$260 at night (after 6 PM). The return trip from Macau is HK$1 more per ticket. People over 60 years of age get a HK$15 discount. Boats are so frequent that you don't really have to reserve in advance unless you want to return late Saturday night, when gambling addicts race home to their wives.

HK Ferries (✉ Shun Tak Centre, ☎ 2516–9581; 726–301 in Macau) also runs catamaran service, with 12 round-trips daily from the China Terminal in Kowloon. Fares are HK$119 weekdays, HK$140 weekends, and HK$160 at night.

TICKETS

Travel agents and most Hong Kong hotels can arrange tickets. Eleven of Hong Kong's major MTR stations have computer-booking outlets that sell Turbojet tickets up to 28 days in advance. You can get your return ticket at the same time, though it's easy to get it in Macau except at very busy periods. If you decide to return earlier than the date on your ticket, you can sail standby at the terminal. **Turbojet tickets** can also be booked in Hong Kong by phone (☎ 2859–6596) using American Express, Diners Club, and Visa credit cards, but they must be picked up at least a half hour before the boat leaves.

By Helicopter

East Asia Airlines runs helicopter service from the Macau Terminal, with departures every 30 minutes 9:30–5:30. The 20-minute flight costs HK$1,205 weekdays, HK$1,309 weekends from Hong Kong, and HK$1,206 and HK$1,310, respectively, from Macau, including taxes. This is mostly a perk for big gamblers; it's not much quicker than the Turbojets. Book through the **Shun Tak Centre** (☎ 2859–3359) or the **Macau Terminal** (☎ 790–7240).

By Plane

The **Macau International Airport** opened in late 1995 and has established itself as a busy regional hub. Built on reclaimed land, the airport is 15–20 minutes by road from downtown Macau and the Chinese border. The handsome glass-clad passenger terminal is connected by the gracefully arched Friendship Bridge to the Ferry Terminal and the Chinese border. At press time there were daily flights to and from Beijing, Shanghai, and Taiwan, with regular services from other Chinese cities, major capitals of Southeast Asia, and Japan, Korea, and Portugal. Air Macau is the local carrier. Departure tax for Chinese destinations is 80 patacas; otherwise it's 130 patacas. ⊠ *Est. da Ponte da Cabrita,* ☎ 861–111 *for airport information; 396–5555 for Air Macau reservations.*

Currency

One U.S. dollar is worth about 8 Macau patacas, making the pataca marginally weaker than the Hong Kong dollar (which is pegged at 7.75 to the U.S. dollar). You'll get roughly 5.5 patacas to the Canadian dollar and 12.5 to the pound sterling. The Hong Kong dollar is accepted everywhere in Macau at parity with the pataca, so it is not really necessary to change money at all for short trips (☞ Money *in* Smart Travel Tips A to Z). No one in Hong Kong will accept patacas, however, so be sure to change it back before you leave Macau.

Getting Around

Walking is the best way to get around the old parts of town and in shopping areas because the streets are narrow, often under repair, and invariably crowded with vehicles weaving between sidewalk vendors and parked cars. Other forms of transport, however, are varied, convenient, and often fun.

By Bicycle

You can rent bikes for about 10 patacas an hour at shops near the Taipa bus station. This can be a pleasant way to get around the island, which operates at a fairly civilized pace, but don't try to ride into town—the bridge to Macau is a lot longer than it looks and insane traffic awaits you on the other side.

By Bus

Public buses in Macau are cheap—2.50 patacas within the city limits—and convenient. Services from the terminal are most useful for visitors; itineraries are posted at bus stops. There are several services to Taipa, for 3 patacas, and Coloane, for 5 patacas. For 6 patacas, Minibus 1A provides service between the airport, the Hotel Lisboa, and the ferry terminal. All other buses in town are chartered and are replicas of 1920s London buses, known as Tour Machines. Their depot is at the terminal, and you can hire one for a party of up to nine people for 200 patacas an hour. They're also often used to transfer groups to and from hotels.

By Hired Car

Macau is the land of counterintuitive directions, where roundabouts and detours often require you to turn left in order to go right, so you might think twice about driving yourself around. Still, you can rent *mokes,* little Jeep-like vehicles that are fun to drive and ideal for touring. Drive on the *right* side of the road. International and most national driver's licenses are valid here. Rental rates are HK$380 for 24 hours on weekdays and HK$500 on weekends, plus HK$50 insurance and a deposit of HK$1,000. Hotel packages often include special moke-rental deals. Contact **Happy Mokes** (☎ 2523–5690 in Hong Kong; 831–212 or 439–393 in Macau) for rental details. Along with mokes, Avis rents cars for HK$500–HK$700 weekdays and HK$700–HK$900 weekends; contact **Avis Rent-a-Car** (☎ 336–789 in Macau; 2541–2011 in Hong Kong).

By Pedicab

Tricycle-drawn two-seater carriages have been in business as long as Macau has had bicycles and paved roads. They cluster at the ferry ter-

minal and near hotels around town, their drivers hustling for customers
and usually offering to serve as guides. It used to be a pleasure to hire
a pedicab, but heavy traffic and vast construction projects now detract
from the experience. Macau's city center is not a congenial place for
pedicabs, and the hilly districts are impossible. If you decide to take
one, you'll have to haggle, but don't pay more than HK$30 for a trip
to a nearby hotel.

By Taxi

Taxis are inexpensive and plentiful. The black cabs with cream-color
roofs can be flagged on the street; the yellow cabs are call taxis. All
are metered, and most are air-conditioned and reasonably comfortable.
Drivers often speak limited English and may not recognize English or
Portuguese place names, so you're strongly advised to carry a bilingual map or name card in Chinese. The base charge is 10 patacas for
the first 1,500 meters (about 1 mi) and 1 pataca for each additional
250 meters. Drivers don't expect more than small change as a tip. Trips
to Taipa incur a 5-pataca surcharge; trips to Coloane, 10 patacas. Expect to pay about 15 patacas for a trip from the terminal to downtown.

Guided Tours

Two basic tours of Macau are available. One covers mainland Macau,
with stops at the Chinese border, Kun Iam Temple, St. Paul's, and Penha
Hill; this lasts about 3½ hours. The other typical tour consists of a two-
hour trip across the bridge to the islands to see old Chinese villages,
temples, beaches, the Jockey Club, and the new airport. Tours travel
by bus or car, and prices vary between operators.

The most comfortable way to tour is by chauffeur-driven luxury car.
A car with a maximum of four passengers goes for HK$100 an hour.
You can also rent a regular taxi for touring, though few drivers speak
English or know the place well enough to be good guides. Depending
on your bargaining powers, the cost will be HK$60 or more per hour.

Most travelers to Macau book tours with Macau agents while in Hong
Kong or with travel agents before leaving home. If you prearrange in
this way, you'll have transportation from Hong Kong to Macau all set,
with your guide waiting in the arrival hall. There are many licensed
tour operators in Macau; among those with offices in Hong Kong and
a focus on English-speaking visitors are **Able Tours** (⊠ 179 Rua do
Campo, ☎ 566–939), which also operates Grayline tours; **Macau
Tours** (⊠ 35 Av. Dr. Mario Soares, ☎ 710–003; ⊠ 91 Des Voeux Rd.,
Hong Kong, ☎ 2542–2338); and **Sintra Tours** (⊠ Sintra Hotel, ☎ 710–
361; ⊠ Shun Tak Centre, Hong Kong, ☎ 2540–8028).

Visas

No visa is required for Portuguese citizens or nationals of the United
States, Canada, Australia, New Zealand, all European countries, and
most Asian countries for visits of up to 20 days, or for Hong Kong
residents for up to 90 days. Other nationals need visas, which can be
obtained on arrival: these cost 100 patacas for individuals, 200 patacas for family groups, and 50 patacas for tour group members.

Important Addresses and Numbers

Visitor Information

The **Macau Government Tourist Office (MGTO)** runs an excellent Web
site (✍), which provides information on the latest exhibitions and festivals, as well as cultural sights, restaurants, and hotels. The site also
has an interactive city map.

In Macau, the main office of the **MGTO** is in Largo do Senado (☎ 315–566). They're exceptionally helpful and have brochures (in a host of languages) on almost every aspect of Macau, as well as the usual maps and general information. They also have offices at the ferry and airport terminals, both of which are open daily 9–6, but for some reason the staff there are not as nice.

Hong Kong has a **MGTO** in Shun Tak Centre (✉ 200 Connaught Rd., Central, ☎ 2559–0147), open Tuesday–Saturday 10–1 and 2–5, and at Hong Kong airport (☎ 2769–7970), open daily 8 AM–10 PM.

Business visitors to Macau can get trade information from the **Macau Trade and Investment Promotion Institute.** ✉ *World Trade Centre, 5/ F, Av. da Amizade, Macau,* ☎ *712–660,* FAX *590–309.*

9 SIDE TRIPS TO SOUTH CHINA

Although the Pearl River Delta region is best known as one of Asia's new "little tigers" thanks to its booming economy, it preserves a heritage of traditional temples, arts, crafts, and the beloved Cantonese cuisine.

By Shann
Davies

Updated by
Lara Wozniak

MAINLAND CHINA IS STILL a world apart from Hong Kong's glitz, high finance, and conspicuous consumerism. Hong Kong may be a part of China, but it's not until you cross the border into Guangzhou that you can say you've visited China proper.

Ever since the 7th century, foreign traders from Southeast Asia, India, and Arabia have come to the "tradesmen's entrance" at Guangzhou (Canton) at the mouth of the Pearl River Delta. Because of the city's comparative isolation, local merchants didn't feel bound to obey the imperial ban on trade with Japan (according to the government, China needed nothing that any foreign "barbarian" had to offer). In the mid-16th century, when Portuguese trading adventurers arrived and offered to act as intermediaries between Guangzhou and the merchants of southern Japan (whose government had similarly banned trade with China), Cantonese businessmen were delighted to accept.

With Guangzhou's approval, the tiny peninsula of Macau was settled by the Portuguese and quickly became a great international port, eventually attracting traders from Europe and America. By the early 19th century, the Macau-based foreigners had gained a virtual monopoly on China's overseas trade.

Opium became the predominant commodity here, and the Chinese government's attempts to stamp it out only provoked the Opium War with Great Britain. Defeated by the British, the Chinese were forced to open up several coastal ports to Western merchants and cede to Britain nearby Hong Kong, which displaced Guangzhou as the mercantile hub of the delta.

In the 1980s, China signed the agreements with Britain and Portugal that established the return to China of Hong Kong in 1997 and Macau in 1999. During the same period, investment poured across the borders into China as industrialists and property developers from Hong Kong and Macau transformed former farmland into booming new economic zones. History comes full circle: the fates of the two territories are once more bound up with that of South China.

Today, visitors find that South China's cities are developed, with luxury hotels, good restaurants, generally reliable transportation, and efficient communications. At the same time, this is an area in transition, with old buildings—however historic—succumbing to glass-and-steel skyscrapers, streets being dug up for new power lines, and growing industrial pollution that is quite visible.

So what of the countryside, the "timeless China" promised in tour brochures? Sadly, a vast majority of the region has been converted into industrial suburbs, dormitory towns, and highways. You can still get an idea of the way it used to be, however, with glimpses of rural life off the main roads or in selected villages that are paid by the tour companies to preserve their traditional appearance and atmosphere.

A delta excursion is thus an opportunity to see China's past, present, and future at the same time. It's also a chance to experience Cantonese cuisine in Canton itself, and to visit the Shenzhen Bay theme parks that bring Chinese civilization into brilliant (if somewhat idealized) focus. Golfers can tee off at any one of the delta's dozen challenging courses, which are a main attraction for Hong Kong expats.

Pleasures and Pastimes

Dining

When people outside China talk about Chinese food, they're usually referring to the cuisine of the Cantonese, who comprised the majority of migrants to the Americas, Australia, and Europe during the 19th and early 20th centuries.

Forced to use their ingenuity to survive centuries of feudal repression and natural disasters, the Cantonese made use of roots, fungi, and every creature found on land and sea, developing what is arguably the most varied and imaginative cooking in the world. The results are at their most authentic in Guangdong, where eating is the favorite activity and restaurants are hubs of society. It's possible to have a Cantonese meal for two or four people, but ideally you'll have 12 or at least 8, so everyone can share the traditional 8–10 courses.

The table is never bare, from opening courses of pickles, peanuts, and cold cuts to the fresh fruit signaling the end of the meal. Between the two you'll have mounds of steamed green vegetables (known rather vaguely as Chinese cabbage, spinach, and kale), braised or minced pigeon, bean curd that can be steamed or fried, luscious shrimp, mushrooms in countless forms, bird's-nest soup (a delicacy made from the congealed saliva of sea swallows), egg-drop soup, fragrant pork or beef, and a large fish steamed in herbs, all accompanied by steamed rice, beer, soft drinks, and tea.

The restaurants of the Pearl Delta vary in atmosphere, but from the alleyway café to the banquet hall of a five-star hotel, all make use of only the freshest produce. Prices, of course, vary accordingly, but generally are much lower than in Hong Kong. A six-course meal in one of the hotels used by tour operators will cost the equivalent of US$10 per person, including unlimited beer and soft drinks. At top-ranked Guangzhou hotels the cost is about US$20.

Golf

Since the 1980s, golf has become a popular elite sport in China and nowhere more than in the Pearl River Delta, where a dozen all-service golf clubs with internationally recognized first-class courses have opened. The first clubs were built by and for golfers, but their success has given developers visions of big profits from corporate memberships. How many will be able to rely on well-heeled members remains to be seen, but for now there are quite a few that welcome nonmembers.

Lodging

Tourists on arranged excursions to the Pearl Delta cannot choose their own hotels, but those chosen are always among the best available. The growing number of independent travelers are usually businesspeople or golfers. If you are an independent traveler, be aware that although major hotels meet most international first-class standards, staff members do not always speak English, so it's advisable to make reservations through a travel agent or hotel office in Hong Kong. In recent years there has been a large oversupply of rooms, and hotels have offered generous discounts. All the hotels listed below have rooms with private baths. Restaurants in hotels and resorts are, by and large, the best in the region.

CATEGORY	COST*
$$$	over $70
$$	$40–$70
$	under $40

Rates are for double occupancy, not including 10% service charge.

EXPLORING

Zhongshan

Zhongshan, the county across the border from Macau, was originally known as Heungshan (Fragrant Mountain). The name was changed to Chung Shan (Central Mountain) in honor of Sun Yat-sen—Chung Shan was his pen name. Zhongshan is the pinyin transliteration of its name (pinyin is the system now most commonly used to romanize Chinese ideograms). The county covers 1,786 square km (687 square mi) of the fertile Pearl River Delta and supports about 1.3 million people, many of whom are wealthy farmers who supply Macau with much of its fresh produce.

With substantial help from overseas Chinese investors, many new industries have been developed here in recent years. The new prosperity contrasts starkly with Zhongshan's situation a century ago, when mandarins benefited from nature's bounty but the peasants who harvested it were kept in abject poverty. This was true in much of China, but in Zhongshan the downtrodden had a way out—crossing the border to Macau and taking a coolie ship to the railroads of California and the gold mines of Australia.

Tens of thousands of peasants left. Zhongshan's city fathers boast of the half-million native sons now living in lands around the globe. Quite a number came back, though, either from a sense of patriotism or to show off their newly acquired wealth. Among these was Sun Yat-sen, born in Cuiheng, who led the movement to overthrow the Manchus and became known as the "father of the Chinese Republic."

Cuiheng, where Sun Yat-sen was born in 1866, has a memorial park containing the town's attractions. The house that Sun built for his parents during a visit in 1892 is here; it's a fine example of China Coast architecture, with European-style verandas facing west. Next door is the **Sun Yat-sen Museum,** in which rooms arranged around a patio contain exhibits on Sun's life and times (labels are in English, Chinese, and Japanese). There are also videos about Sun and Zhongshan. ☎ 760/550–1691. ⊙ *Daily 8:30–4:45.*

Shiqi (formerly spelled Shekkei) is the capital of Zhongshan County and has been an important market center and inland port for 800 years. Today it's a convenient stopover on excursions to the delta.

A decade ago, Shiqi was a picturesque port where a cantilever bridge over the Qi River was raised twice a day to allow small freighters to pass; but the old town has been all but obliterated by modern highrises, and farms that once surrounded it are now covered with factories. Still, the **Sun Yat-sen Memorial Hall** and **Xishan Temple,** restored in 1994, are worth a visit—and the food here is exceptionally good.

Dining and Lodging

$$ ✕⊞ **Chung Shan Hot Springs Resort.** This vast complex consists of a charming compound of villas, which have pagoda roofs and Chinese antiques in some rooms. Villas are built around a traditional Chinese garden landscaped with classical pavilions and willow-screened ponds filled with carp and lotus blossoms. The English-speaking staff is helpful, and there is a large Chinese restaurant (popular with tour groups) and a smaller Western restaurant. Outside, extensive grounds contain a swimming pool, horseback-riding ring, shopping center, and four baths fed by nearby hot springs. The hotel is 15 mi (24 km) from Macau. ⊠ *Macau-Shiqi Hwy. near Sanxiang, Zhongshan, 519015,* ☎ *760/668–*

190

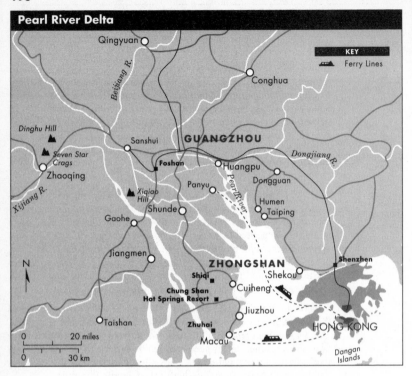

Pearl River Delta

3888, FAX 760/668–3333. 230 rooms. 2 restaurants, pool, 2 18-hole golf courses, 4 tennis courts, shops. AE, MC, V.

$$ ✕⊞ **Zhongshan International Hotel.** Topped with a revolving restaurant, this 20-story tower has become a landmark of downtown Shiqi. Rooms have unremarkable hotel furniture, but its suites, at least, are spacious. The staff is friendly and will go out of their way to help you. ⊠ 142 Zhongshan Rd., Shiqi, 528400, ☎ 760/862–0600, FAX 760/863–3368. 369 rooms. 3 restaurants, pool, sauna, bowling, billiards. AE, MC, V.

$ ✕⊞ **Cuiheng Hotel.** Opposite the Sun Yat-sen Memorial Park, this hotel consists of low-rise wings and bungalows of an elegant contemporary design. There are gardens around the pool, a riding school next door, and a statue of Sun out front. ⊠ Cuiheng Village, Zhongshan 528454, ☎ 760/550–2668, FAX 760/550–3333. 220 rooms. 3 restaurants, pool, dance club. AE, V.

Outdoor Activities and Sports

GOLF

The **Chung Shan Golf Club** was the first course in China and is still considered one of the best. A half hour north of Macau, the par-72 course was designed by Arnold Palmer's company and opened in 1984, with Palmer among the first to try it out. A second 18-hole course of rolling hills and streams, designed by Jack Nicklaus, was added a few years ago. The clubhouse, with gleaming mahogany paneling and elegant rattan furniture, has a bar, restaurant, sauna, and granite-walled pool, plus a pro shop with everything you'd expect to find in an American or Japanese club. Greens fees for visitors are HK$500 for 18 holes during the week, HK$1,200 on weekends. Caddies cost HK$160 a round, and club rentals cost HK$110. Bookings, transport (via Macau or Jiuzhou), and visas can be arranged through the club's office in Hong Kong. ⊠ Bank of China Bldg., 38th floor, 1 Garden Rd., ☎ 2521–0377, FAX 2868–4642.

Zhuhai

In 1980 Zhuhai was set up as one of China's first Special Economic Zones, which have special liberal laws to encourage foreign investment. The zone has been extended from an original 13 square km (5 square mi) to 121 square km (46 square mi), complete with a long coastline and many small off-shore islands. Zhuhai has the highest standard of living anywhere in China. It's also one of the cleanest and most congenial areas thanks to its high-tech industrial base.

Every day, hundreds of Western travelers come from Macau and observe hundreds of Chinese travelers, often from remote provinces, who observe them in return. Domestic tourists come to Zhongshan to pay their respects to Sun Yat-sen, and then they explore Zhuhai's shops and restaurants, from which you can gaze across at Macau.

Dining and Lodging

$$$ ✕⚎ **Grand Bay View Hotel.** Sumptuously furnished, the rooms at this handsome hotel have soft beds and couches and a homier style—with colorful quilts and soft lighting—than you'll find in most South China hotels. It also has some of the zone's best nightlife and dining, as well as imaginative function areas that include a balcony overlooking the water and Macau. In addition to a disco, the Stargazer Nightclub has 20 private rooms for video karaoke. ⊠ *Shui Wan Rd., Gongbei 519020,* ☎ *756/887–7998,* ℻ *756/887–8998. 238 rooms. 4 restaurants, pool, massage, sauna, exercise room, billiards, nightclub. AE, DC, MC, V.*

$$$ ✕⚎ **Paradise Hill.** Looking like a Belle Epoque palace on the French Riviera, this hotel has a stunning white-and-cream stone facade, with balconies overlooking a garden that's terraced around fountains. A marble-clad atrium lobby and a grand marble staircase complete the rich touches. The rooms are tastefully decorated with glass-top coffee tables, potted flowers, and floor-to-ceiling windows. The health center is state-of-the-art. ⊠ *1 Shichingshan, Zhuhai 519015,* ☎ *756/333–7388,* ℻ *756/ 333–3508; 853/552–739, ext. 406, in Macau. 211 rooms. 4 restaurants, 2 pools, beauty salon, 2 tennis courts, health club. AE, DC, MC, V.*

$$ ✕⚎ **Zhuhai Holiday Resort Hotel.** Expect modern, clean facilities in this new resort with 87 villas that offer extra privacy. Set on a peaceful lake, every room has an excellent waterfront view. The service is attentive and friendly. ⊠ *Shichingshan, Zhuhai 519015,* ☎ *756/333– 3838,* ℻ *756/333–2036. 459 rooms. 2 restaurants, bar, pool, bowling alley, business services, meeting rooms. AE, DC, V.*

Outdoor Activities and Sports

GOLF/LODGING

The lakeside **Zhuhai Wansheng Sports & Country Club** covers more than 700 acres with its shooting range, game farm, clubhouse, and new 18-hole golf course. The Moosehead Lounge occupies the main clubhouse along with 72 guest rooms, a restaurant, a bar, a pool, and a health club. Most activities and amenities are priced individually. Other facilities include tennis (2 courts), badminton, squash, boating, and fishing. ⊠ *Zhuhai Doumen County, Wushan Town, Sanli Village, Zhuhai 519175,* ☎ *756/557–3888; 2827–8307 in Hong Kong,* ℻ *756/ 557–3388; 2827–7654 in Hong Kong. AE, DC, MC, V.*

Guangzhou

Guangzhou is still better known as Canton, an English corruption of the Portuguese version of the Chinese name. The city has always benefited from its strategic location on the South China coast, where it has been a major trading port for almost 2,000 years. Guangzhou received cargo from the Spice Islands (in what is now Indonesia), India, and the Middle East long before Europe knew China existed, and it was the point of export for silk—centuries ago the city began holding semiannual fairs at which silk was bartered for spices, silver, and sandalwood. From the time the Portuguese settled Macau, Guangzhou was the prime meeting place of East and West. During the 19th century it was a business home for British, American, and European traders.

Guangzhou has long had a rebellious streak, and the Cantonese have frequently been at odds with the rulers in the north. Exposure to foreign ideas made them more independent, and it was no surprise that the 1911 revolution and the organization of the Chinese Communist Party both started here.

Shamian (Sandbank Island) appeals to those who know something of its history: Western traders set up shop here when the island was a sand spit in the Pearl River, linked to the city by bridges that closed at night. The traders built fine mansions, churches, and even a cricket pitch. Most buildings have been renovated to house government and business offices, hotels, and shops.

Yuexiu Gongyuan (Yuexiu Park) has an array of Krupp cannons and the 14th-century Zhenhai Tower. The park contains the **Guangzhou Museum** (☎ 020/8354–1035, ☉ daily 9–5), which, founded in 1929, is one of the oldest museums in China. It features exhibitions on Guangzhou history. Nearby is a modern statue of five goats with sheaves of grain in their mouths, which have been adopted as the city's symbol; legend has it that the goats were sent from heaven with gifts of cereals. Sun Yat-sen is, of course, honored in the city where he studied medicine and later celebrated the birth of the Chinese republic: the **Sun Zhongshan Jinian Tang** (Sun Yat-sen Memorial Hall), built in 1925, contains a 5,000-seat auditorium. It stands at the foot of Yuexiu Mountain and is linked by stone steps with the Dr. Sun Yat-sen Monument at the top of the mountain. Records of Dr. Sun's political career are exhibited in a building complex to the west of the hall. ⊠ *Jiefang Beilu.* ☉ *Daily 9–5.*

The **Nongmin Yundong Jiangxi Suo** (Peasant Movement Institute) is a monument to an early communist organization. In 1924 Mao Zedong and his comrades set up a school in a Ming Dynasty Confucian temple to teach their doctrine to peasant leaders from around the country. The classroom and Mao's Spartan bedroom are preserved. ⊠ 42 *Zhongshan Silu.* 🎫 *Free.* ☉ *Daily 10–6*

The **Chen Jia Ci** (Chen Family Institute) was built by the Chen clan late in the 19th century. It's an architectural masterpiece, with some magnificent porcelain friezes depicting the *Romance of Three Kingdoms* on the pavilion ridgepoles, and some intricately carved stone balustrades. ⊠ 7 *Zhongshan Xilu.* ☉ *Daily 8:30–5.*

The 11th-century Zen Buddhist **Liu Rong Si Hua Ta** (Temple of Six Banyans) is famous for its 184-ft pagoda, whose carved wooden roofs earned it the name "Flowery Pagoda." ⊠ *Haizhu Beilu.* ☉ *Daily 8–5.*

The 7th-century **Huaisheng Si Guang Ta** (Huaisheng Mosque) was the first mosque built in China, erected during the Tang dynasty. Its white-wall minaret was for centuries a beacon for ships. ⊠ *Guangta Lu.* 🎫 *Free.* ☉ *Sat.–Thurs. 8–5, except holy days.*

The **Nan Yue Wang Mu** (Museum and Tomb of the Southern Yue Kings) was uncovered in 1983 behind the China Hotel. Excavated treasures from the tomb include jade armor, pearl pillows, gem-encrusted crossbows, a bronze orchestra, and gold crowns buried with the king 2,000 years ago. ⊠ *Jiefang Beilu.* 🎫 *Free.* ☉ *Daily 9:30–5:30.*

Nestled among some of the city's newest and splashiest condo complexes, northwest of Ersha Island, the new **Guangdong Museum of Art** is billed as the largest museum of its kind in China. Specializing in contemporary Chinese art, the museum has 12 massive exhibition halls, including one devoted entirely to sculpture. The displays center on the recent works of Chinese painters (working both here and overseas). ⊠ *Wenming Lu.* 🖾 *Free.* ☉ *Tues.–Sun. 9–5.*

Dining and Lodging

$$$ ✕🖾 **China.** This vast complex opposite the Trade Fair Exhibition Hall, with office and apartment blocks, is favored by business travelers. It has a convenient location, a multitude of restaurants, executive floors with business-center services, and plenty of entertainment options. The hotel also has Guangzhou's only Hard Rock Cafe, a hot spot for the city's night owls. ⊠ *Liuhua Rd., 510015,* ☎ *020/8666–6888; 2724–4622 in Hong Kong;* ＦＡＸ *020/8667–7014; 2721–0741 in Hong Kong. 1,017 rooms. 6 restaurants, pool, bowling, health club, shops, theater, business services. AE, DC, MC, V.*

$$$ ✕🖾 **Dong Fang.** This luxury complex is across from Liuhua Park, which has the largest artificial lake in the city. The modern and spacious rooms are done in mauves and light pastels, in Chinese or Western decor. The elegant, golden-hue lobby has an interesting selection of Chinese antiques and carpets in its shopping concourse. The restaurants serve a variety of Chinese regional cuisines as well as Western and Southeast Asian dishes. ⊠ *120 Liuhua Rd., 510016,* ☎ *020/8666–9900; 2528–0555 in Hong Kong;* ＦＡＸ *020/8666–2775; 2510–0991 in Hong Kong. 1,300 rooms. 5 restaurants, beauty salon, shops, recreation room, business services, meeting rooms. AE, DC, MC, V.*

$$$ ✕🖾 **Garden Hotel.** Set in Guangzhou's upmarket northern section, this place has some spectacular gardens, including an artificial hill with a waterfall and pavilions. Antiques and modern artwork both decorate this complex, which includes apartments, offices, and a convention center. The excellent Western and Eastern dining options include Carousel, a revolving restaurant on the 30th floor. ⊠ *368 Huanshi Dong Lu, 510064,* ☎ *020/8333–8989,* ＦＡＸ *020/8335–0467. 1,112 rooms. 8 restaurants, pool, 2 tennis courts, health club, squash, shops, dance club, business services. AE, DC, MC, V.*

$$$ ✕🖾 **GITIC Plaza.** This urban landmark is a spectacular 63-story complex with a hotel on top—next to a complex with 14 restaurants and lounges, shops, and banquet halls. The rooms here have some of the best views in Guangzhou; obviously the higher you go the better the vista. There are extensive recreation facilities. ⊠ *339 Huanshi Dong Rd., 510098,* ☎ *020/8331–1888; 2865–7371 in Hong Kong;* ＦＡＸ *020/ 8331–1666; 2865–1705 in Hong Kong. 402 rooms, 300 suites. 14 restaurants (5 in the hotel), pool, health club, tennis court, shops, bowling, business services. AE, DC, MC, V.*

$$$ ✕🖾 **Ramada Pearl.** In the eastern part of the city, on the Pearl River, the Ramada Pearl is a full-service deluxe hotel. Ask for a room overlooking the Pearl River. It benefits from its proximity (5 km/3 mi) to the East Railway Station, a terminus for Hong Kong trains. ⊠ *9 Ming Yue Yi Rd., 510600,* ☎ *020/8737–2988,* ＦＡＸ *020/8737–7907. 331 rooms. 5 restaurants, pub, pool, driving range, tennis court, dance club, meeting rooms. AE, DC, MC, V.*

$$$ ✕🖾 **White Swan.** The first international hotel in town occupies a marvelous site on historic Shamian Island, beside the Pearl River. The luxury complex is surrounded by banyan trees, with a landscaped pool and a jogging track nearby. Rooms have replicas of Chinese antique furniture and porcelain. Even if you don't stay here, pop into the lobby to see the spectacular indoor waterfall. The hotel also offers a Pearl

River dinner cruise on Friday and Saturday nights for 180RMB. ✉ *1 South Shamian St., 510133, ☎ 020/8188–6968; 2524–0192 in Hong Kong;* FAX *020/8186–1188; 2877–0811 in Hong Kong. 843 rooms. 9 restaurants, 2 pools, health club, driving range, 10 tennis courts, squash, shops, dance club, business services, meeting rooms, travel services. AE, DC, MC, V.*

$$ ✕▥ **Holiday Inn Guangzhou City Centre.** You'll feel at home in the familiar setting of this Holiday Inn, conveniently located in the financial district. The rooms are done in subdued neutral colors, with soft headboards, comfortable sitting areas, and wooden bureaus like those in Holiday Inns worldwide. There's an adjoining exhibition center and an 800-seat cinema. ✉ *Huanshi Donglu, 510095, ☎ 020/8776–6999,* FAX *020/8775–3126. 431 rooms. 5 restaurants, pool, health club, shops, airport shuttle. AE, DC, MC, V.*

Outdoor Activities and Sports

GOLF

The **Guangzhou Luhu Golf & Country Club** occupies 180 acres of Luhu Park. Forty minutes from the Guangzhou East train station and twenty minutes from Baiyun Airport, it's a convenient diversion for golfing visitors. The 6,820-yard, 72-par course was designed by Dave Thomas, and the club has a 75-bay driving range and fully equipped clubhouse. Members' guests and those from affiliated clubs pay HK$600 greens fees (visitors without affiliation pay HK$800) for 18 holes on weekdays, HK$800 on weekends (HK$1,200 for visitors). The club is managed by Hong Kong–based CCA and is a member of the International Associate Club network. ✉ *Luijing Road, Luhu Park, ☎ 020/8350–7777; 2317-1933 in Hong Kong,* FAX *8359–6698.*

Foshan

Once a town of artisans, Foshan (Buddha Mountain) has a venerable history of more than 1,200 years. Today, you can still find ceramics and statues here, but the 30-minute drive along the expressway from Guangzhou is no longer lined with artisans but instead new housing estates and high-rise factories. Given its proximity to Guangzhou there is no compelling reason to stay overnight in Foshan.

Foshan might seem in danger of becoming a concrete extension of the great port, but happily the legacy of the past is preserved in the **Zu Miao,** with its brilliantly decorated prayer halls and ridgepole frieze containing thousands of figures, birds, animals, and tiny pavilions. The complex contains the **Wanfutai Chinese Opera** theater, which has the oldest surviving wooden stage in China. Figurines and other craft items are sold in the spacious courtyard. ✉ *Zumiao Lu.* ☯ *Daily 8–6.*

You can browse and buy crafts at the **Renshou Si** (Folk Art Center), where intricate paper cutouts are made by hand. Chinese lanterns, fishbone carvings, and other handicrafts are also produced here and sold at extremely reasonable prices. ✉ *Renmin Lu St.* ☯ *Daily 8–6.*

Shenzhen

Shenzhen (Shumchun in Cantonese) was just a farming village across the border from Hong Kong until it was designated a Special Economic Zone in the late 1970s and became the first "instant China" excursion for foreign travelers. As one of the fastest-growing towns in China, it jumped from a population of 20,000 in 1979 to 2.5 million today and is aspiring to become the next Hong Kong by 2010. It has its own stock exchange, one of the highest gross domestic products in China, and a tightly packed garden of skyscrapers—but it also has all the attendant pollution. Most visitors to Shenzhen are Hong Kong Chinese on business or family holidays, golfing and relaxing in lavish but moderately priced resorts. Foreigners are drawn to Shenzhen's series of theme parks, which provide a condensed tour of the great sights of China and an introduction to the country.

Jin Xiu Zhong Hua (Splendid China) replicates the major historical and geographical sights of China on a scale of 1:15. Beautifully sculpted scenery peopled by 50,000 pottery figures is laid out along winding paths. ⊠ ☎ *0755/660–0626,* ⊙ *Daily 8:30–5:30.*

The adjoining half of the park holds **Zhong Hua Minzu Wen Hua Cun** (China Folk Culture Villages), where China's different ethnic minorities are represented by people in traditional costumes making local crafts and performing songs and dances. There is a grand stage show and parade at night. ☞ *150RMB combined ticket for Splendid China and China Folk Culture Villages.* ⊙ *Weekdays 10:30–9, weekends and holidays 11–10.*

Dining and Lodging

$$$ ✕⌸ **The Landmark Hotel.** Close to the train station, the Landmark is popular with Hong Kong business travelers. The four-story atrium gives the lobby a spacious, opulent feeling typical of China's flashiest five-star hotels. The Fu Yuan Seafood Restaurant serves excellent dim sum, while the Chao Zhou Restaurant specializes in such delicacies as shark's-fin soup and bird's nest. The hotel's nightspot, Hollywood, is a glitzy combination of a pub, a disco, and a karaoke lounge. ⊠ *3018 Nanhu Rd., 518001,* ☎ *0755/217–2288; 2375–6580 in Hong Kong;* FAX *0755/229–0473; 2730–6871 in Hong Kong. 351 rooms. 3 restaurants, pool, exercise room, nightclub. AE, DC, MC, V.*

$$$ ✕⌸ **Shangri-La Hotel.** Next to the train station, in the busiest section of Shenzhen, the Shangri-La is the plushest hotel in town. The rooms are large, the beds exceptionally soft and comfortable, and the lighting is subtle and gentle. The restaurants—including a revolving buffet, Tiara—are some of the best in town, serving Japanese, Cantonese, and Continental cuisine. Henry J. Bean's Bar & Grill is a hangout for homesick Western expatriates. ⊠ *East Side, Railway Station, Jianshe Rd., 518001,* ☎ *0755/233–0888,* FAX *0755/233–9878. 553 rooms. 6 restaurants, bar, pool, massage, sauna, concierge floor, business services. AE, DC, MC, V.* ✎

$$ ✕⌸ **Holiday Inn Donghua Shenzhen.** This new Holiday Inn is a solid, reasonably priced option. About 40 minutes from the border, within minutes of the Shekou Ferry Pier and high-tech zone (an official designation meant to attract computer and Internet firms), it's a good choice for travelers catching flights at Shenzhen's busy international airport. Book a room with a bay view in the 28-story shiny glass tower. ⊠ *Nanyou Rd., Nanshan District, 518052,* ☎ *0755/664–9699; 800/ 968868 in Hong Kong;* FAX *0755/664–5282. 288 rooms. 3 restaurants, Western coffee shop, pub, indoor pool, sauna, health club, billiards, travel services. AE, DC, MC, V.*

Outdoor Activities and Sports

GOLF

Mission Hills Golf Club, in Shenzhen, scored a signal success when it hosted the World Cup of Golf in 1995. It has two 18-hole championship courses, with another 36 holes planned. Adjoining the clubhouse are a 228-room resort, courts for basketball tournaments as well as tennis and squash courts, a variety of restaurants, and an indoor-outdoor pool. The courses are not open to nonmembers except for resort guests, for whom greens fees are HK$700 weekdays and HK$1,200 weekends; caddies are HK$100 and caddie carts HK$200. For more details contact the club's Hong Kong office. ✉ *9 Queen's Rd., 29/F, Central,* ☎ *2973–0303; 2826–0288 for reservations,* FAX *2869–9632.*

Just across the border between Hong Kong and Shenzhen, the **Sand River Golf Club** can be the quickest to reach if there's no delay at immigration. Next door to the Window of the World park, it offers courses designed by Gary Player, one of which has nine holes and is floodlit. It also offers a large driving range, a fishing lake, and various resort facilities. Greens fees for visitors are HK$800 weekdays and HK$1,200 weekends; caddies are HK$180. For details contact the Hong Kong office. ✉ *SPA Centre, 19/F, 55 Lockhart Rd., Wanchai,* ☎ *800/ 938079,* FAX *800/938080.*

SOUTH CHINA A TO Z

Arriving and Departing

Although there is no shortage of transportation options in and out of Guangdong, you may have trouble finding travel operators who speak English. Ask your hotel concierge for the latest schedules and prices or call the **China Travel Service** (CTS; ✉ Main office, G/F, CTS House, 78–83 Connaught Rd., Central, ☎ 2853–3533 for general information). CTS is the most convenient place to book tickets to China, though you'll pay a service charge.

The Chinese arrival points have currency-exchange counters and sell duty-free liquor and cigarettes at bargain prices.

All fares quoted are one-way only.

Hong Kong–Zhuhai
Fast, modern **catamaran ferries** make eight round-trips daily to the pier at Jiuzhou, with five departures from the **China Hong Kong City (CHKC) Terminal** (✉ Canton Rd., Kowloon) at 7:45, 9:30, and 11 AM, 2:30 and 5 PM, and six from the **Macau Ferry Terminal** (✉ Shun Tak Centre, 3f, Connaught Rd., Central ☎ 2546–3528, FAX 2559–4976) at 8:40 and 10 AM, noon, 4, 7:30, and 9:30 PM. The trip takes 90 minutes. 🚢 *HK$187 1st class, HK$177 economy.*

Hong Kong–Zhongshan
Catamarans make six round-trips daily to Zhongshan Harbor, close to Shiqi, with five departures from the CHKC Terminal and one from Shun Tak Centre on Hong Kong Island. The trip takes approximately 80 minutes and costs HK$251, HK$231, or HK$221, depending on class.

Hong Kong–Guangzhou
Four express trains depart from the **Kowloon–Canton Railway (KCR) Station** daily (✉ Cheong Wan Rd., Hung Hom, Kowloon) at 8:50 AM and 12:05, 1:23, and 4:08 PM, plus there is an additional peak-season train at 7:53 AM. The trip takes about an hour and 45 minutes. The last train back to Hong Kong leaves at 5:25 PM. The trip costs HK$230 premium class, HK$190 first class.

A **ferry** makes the journey every day, departing CHKC Terminal at 9 PM; it arrives at dawn, and passengers disembark at 7 AM. Cabins and restaurants come in different classes; fares start at HK$202 for a four-berth cabin.

Turbo Cat ferries depart CHKC Terminal daily at 7:30 AM and 2 PM. The journey takes about two hours and costs HK$293 first class, HK$198 economy.

CAAC, the Chinese airline, has frequent flights between Hong Kong and Guangzhou Airport; the trip takes about 20 minutes. The fare is HK$920 round-trip (plus a departure tax of HK$100 from Hong Kong, 90RMB from Guangzhou).

Citybus (☎ 2873–0818 in Hong Kong) has five round-trips a day between Hong Kong and Guangzhou on new vehicles that have toilets, reclining seats, and individual air-conditioning and lighting controls. Snacks and drinks are provided. The trip takes 3½ hours and costs HK$150. Buses depart from CHKC, Admiralty, and occasionally City One Shatin in the morning, and return from Guangzhou's Garden Hotel in the early afternoon.

Among other bus services, **China Travel Service** (CTS) makes numerous round-trips daily, with pickup and return at major Guangzhou hotels. The cost from Hong Kong is HK$170; the return leg costs 130RMB and can be purchased at the transportation desks in large hotels.

Hong Kong–Shenzhen

The KCR runs an **electric commuter train service** throughout the day (first train 6:08 AM; last train back to Hong Kong 12:08 AM) from Kowloon Station to Lo Wu, at the border. The trip takes about 40 minutes, but expect to spend up to an hour at border checkpoints. The fare is HK$66 first class, HK$31 economy.

Citybus (☎ 2873–0818) makes five round-trips daily to Shenzhen, with four continuing on to the Shenzhen Bay theme parks. Buses depart Admiralty Station, CHKC Terminal, and City One Shatin. Another route makes eight trips from Hong Kong to Dongguan, Shenzhen's international airport. Fares depend on the destination and day: HK$65 one way to Shenzhen City weekdays, HK$85 weekends; HK$75 one way to Shenzhen Bay weekdays, HK$95 weekends.

Turbo Cat ferries make a pleasant one-hour trip to Shekou six times daily, with departures between 7:30 AM and 7 PM from the Macau Ferry Terminal. The fare is HK$289 first class, HK$189 economy class.

Currency

You can easily change foreign currency at hotels and banks in Guangdong, but the Hong Kong dollar is widely accepted as a second currency here, so you probably won't even need Chinese RMB.

Guided Tours

The vast majority of travelers on side trips to other parts of southern China take a guided tour of one or two days. Although transportation in the region has greatly improved, it is still much easier for foreigners to get around this part of China with a guide. Tours offered by CTS and Hong Kong travel agents are designed to fit into any reasonable schedule.

By far the most popular tour option is **Zhongshan** via Macau, a full and diverse (if rather tiring) day trip. All one-day Zhongshan tours begin with an early departure from Hong Kong to Macau and a bus transfer to the border at Gongbei, in the Zhuhai Special Economic Zone. From here itineraries vary, but all spend time in Cuiheng. A six-course lunch, with free beer and soft drinks, is taken in Shiqi, at the Chung Shan resort, or in one of the faux Ching Dynasty hotels of Zhuhai. Completing the itinerary is a visit to a "typical" farming village (kept traditional for tourists). Tours return to Hong Kong in the late afternoon via Zhongshan Harbor, taking about 10 hours total. The cost is HK$880–HK$895 per person.

Another well-established day trip takes in **Shenzhen,** immediately across the border from Hong Kong. This begins with a coach trip to Shenzhen and the Splendid China theme park or the adjoining China Folk Culture Villages. This tour also includes visits to a Hakka village, a kindergarten, and a market. ✉ *HK$660–HK$720.*

Visas

Tourists can get visas on arrival in Shenzhen and Zhuhai, but the office is often overrun on the weekends, so it may be easier to get a visa either in your home country before you leave or in Hong Kong. At the Lo Wu border in Shenzhen, a three-day visa restricting travel to Shenzhen is HK$100, and a photo is not necessary. The cost for a standard visa depends on how quickly you have it issued. A single-entry visa with a two-day wait costs HK$160; a same-day visa costs between HK$310 and HK$560, depending on the time of application. Visas are available in Hong Kong from the CTS and from most travel agents (expect a service charge), and require one passport-size photo. Mainland China has recently stopped issuing individual traveling permits to journalists, who must now travel on package tours. Before you go, contact the consulate of the People's Republic of China to see how strict the current mood is.

10 PORTRAITS OF HONG KONG

IMPACTS AND IMAGES

HONG KONG IS in China, if not entirely of it, and after 150 years of British rule the background to all its wonders remains its Chineseness—98% if you reckon it by population, hardly less if you are thinking metaphysically.

It may not look like it from the deck of an arriving ship, or swooping into town on a jet, but geographically most of the territory is still rural. The empty hills that form the mass of the New Territories, the precipitous islets and rocks, even some of the bare slopes of Hong Kong Island itself, rising directly above the tumultuous harbor, are much as they were in the days of the Manchus, the Mings, or the Neolithic Yaos. The last of the leopards has indeed been shot (1931), the last of the tigers spotted (1967, it is claimed), but that recondite newt flourishes still as *Paramesotriton hongkongensis*. There are still civets, pythons, barking deer, and porcupines about and the marshlands abound with seabirds. The predominant country colors are Chinese colors: browns, grays, tawny colors. The generally opaque light is just the light one expects of China, and gives the whole territory the required suggestion of blur, surprise, and uncertainty. The very smells are Chinese smells—oily, laced with duck-mess and gasoline.

Thousands of Hong Kong people still live on board junks, cooking their meals in the hiss and flicker of pressure lamps among the riggings and the nets. Thousands more inhabit shantytowns, made of sticks, canvas, and corrugated iron but bustling with the native vivacity. People are still growing fruit, breeding fish, running duck farms, tending oyster beds; a few still grow rice and a very few still plow their fields with water buffalo. Village life remains resiliently ancestral. The Tangs and the Pangs are influential. The geomancers are busy still. Half-moon graves speckle the high ground wherever feng shui decrees, sometimes attended still by the tall brown urns that contain family ashes. Temples to Tin Hau, the Queen of Heaven, or Hung Shing, God of the Southern Seas, still stand incense-swirled upon foreshores.

But the vast majority of Hong Kong residents live in towns, jam-packed on the flatter ground. They are mostly squeezed in gigantic tower-blocks, and they have surrounded themselves with all the standard manifestations of modern non-Communist chinoiserie: the garish merry signs; the clamorous shop-fronts; the thickets of TV aerials; the banners; the rows of shiny hanging ducks; the washing on its poles; the wavering bicycles; the potted plants massed on balconies; the canvas-canopied stalls selling herbs, or kitchenware, or antiques, or fruit; the bubbling cauldrons of crab-claw soup boiling at eating stalls; the fantastic crimson-and-gold facades of restaurants; the flickering television screens in shop windows; the trays of sticky cakes in confectionery stores; the profusion of masts, poles, and placards protruding from the fronts of buildings; the dragons carved or gilded; the huge elaborate posters; the tea shops with their gleaming pots; the smells of cooking, spice, incense, oil; the racket of radio music and amplified voices; the half-shouted conversation that is peculiar to Chinese meeting one another in the street; the ceaseless clatter of spoons, coins, mah-jongg counters, abaci, hammers, and electric drills.

It can appear exotic to visitors, but it is fundamentally a plain and practical style. Just as the Chinese consider a satisfactory year to be a year in which nothing much happens, so their genius seems to me fundamentally of a workaday kind, providing a stout and reliable foundation, mat and bamboo, so to speak, on which to build the structures of astonishment.

What the West has provided, originally through the medium of the British Empire, later by the agency of international finance, is a city-state in its own image, overlaying that resilient and homely Chinese style with an aesthetic far more aggressive. The capitalists of Hong Kong have been terrific builders, and have made of the great port, its hills and its harbors, one of the most thrilling of all metropolitan prospects—for my own tastes, the finest sight in Asia. More than 6 million people, nearly twice the population of New Zealand, live here on less than 400 square mi of land, at least half of which is rough mountain country. They are necessarily packed tight, in urban forms as startling in the luminous light of Hong Kong as the upper-works of the clippers must have been when they first appeared along its waterways.

T HE TANGS AND the Lius may still be in their villages, but they are invested on all sides by massive New Towns, started from scratch in starkly modernist manner. All over the mainland New Territories, wherever the hills allow, busy roads sweep here and there, clumps of tower-blocks punctuate the skyline, suburban estates develop and blue-tiled brick wilts before the advance of concrete. Even on the outlying islands, as Hong Kong calls the rest of the archipelago, apartment buildings and power stations rise above the moors. Flatland in most parts of Hong Kong being so hard to find, this dynamic urbanism has been created largely in linear patterns, weaving along shorelines, clambering up gullies or through narrow passes, and frequently compressed into almost inconceivable congestion. Some 80% of the people live on 8% of the land, and parts of Kowloon, with more than a quarter of a million people per square mile, are probably the most crowded places in all human history. An amazing tangle of streets complicates the topography; the architect I. M. Pei, commissioned to design a new Hong Kong office block in the 1980s, said it took nine months just to figure out access to the site.

There is not much shape to all this, except the shape of the place itself. Twin cities of the harbor are the vortex of all Hong Kong, and all that many strangers ever see of it. On the north, the mainland shore, the dense complex of districts called Kowloon presses away into the hills, projecting its force clean through them indeed by tunnel into the New Territories beyond. The southern shore, on the island of Hong Kong proper, is the site of the original British settlement, officially called Victoria but now usually known simply as Central; it is in effect the capital of Hong Kong and contains most of its chief institutions, but it straggles inchoately all along the island's northern edge, following the track worn by the junk crews when, before the British came at all, adverse winds

obliged them to drag their vessels through this strait. Around the two conglomerates the Territory's being revolves: one talks of Kowloon-side or Hong Kong–side, and on an average day more than 115,000 vehicles pass through the underwater tunnels from one to the other.

Once the Territory had a formal urban center. Sit with me now in the Botanical Gardens, those inescapable amenities of the British Empire that have defied progress even here, and still provide shady boulevards, flower beds, and a no more than usually nasty little zoo almost in the heart of Central. From this belvedere, 50 years ago, we could have looked down upon a ceremonial plaza of some dignity, Statue Square. It opened directly upon the harbor, rather like the Piazza d'Italia in Trieste, and to the west ran a waterfront esplanade, called the Praya after its Macau original. The steep green island hills rose directly behind the square, and it was surrounded by structures of consequence— Government House, where the Governor lived; Head Quarter House, where the General lived; a nobly classical City Hall; the Anglican cathedral; the Supreme Court; the Hongkong & Shanghai Bank. The effect was sealed by the spectacle of the ships passing to and fro at the north end of the square, and by the presence of four emblematically imperial prerequisites: a dockyard of the Royal Navy, a cricket field, the Hong Kong Club, and a statue of Queen Victoria.

It has all been thrown away. Today Statue Square is blocked altogether out of our sight by office buildings, and anyway only the specter of a plaza remains down there, loomed over, fragmented by commercialism. Even the waterfront has been pushed back by land reclamation. The surviving promenade is all bits and pieces of piers, and a three-story parking lot obstructs the harbor view. The cricket ground has been prettified into a municipal garden, with turtles in a pond. Government House and the cathedral are hardly visible through the skyscrapers, the Hong Kong Club occupies four floors of a 24-story office block. Queen Victoria has gone.

This is the way of urban Hong Kong. It is cramped by the force of nature, but it is irresistibly restless by instinct. Except for the harbor, it possesses no real center now. The territory as a whole has lately become a stupendous exercise in social design, but no master plan for the harbor cities has ever succeeded—Sir Patrick Abercrombie offered one in the heyday of British town planning after the Second World War, but like so many of his schemes it never came to anything. Proposals to extend that promenade were repeatedly frustrated down the years, notably by the military, who would not get their barracks and dockyards out of the way; all that is left of the idea is the howling expressway that runs on stilts along the foreshore.

Today beyond Statue Square, all along the shoreline, across the harbor, far up the mountain slopes, tall concrete buildings extend without evident pattern or logic. There seems to be no perspective to them either, so that when we shift our viewpoint one building does not move with any grace against another—just a clump here, a splotch there, sometimes a solitary pillar of glass or concrete. Across the water they loom monotonously behind the Kowloon waterfront, square and Stalinesque; they are limited to a height of 12 stories there, because the old Kai Tak airport is nearby. On the sides of distant mountains you may see them protruding from declining ridges like sudden outcrops of white chalk. Many are still meshed in bamboo scaffolding, many more are doomed to imminent demolition. If we look down the hill again, behind the former governor's palace immolated in its gardens, we may see the encampment of blue-and-white awnings, interspersed with bulldozers and scattered with the labor-

ing straw-hatted figures of construction workers, which shows where the foundations of yet another skyscraper, still bigger, more splendid, and more extravagant no doubt than the one before, are even now being laid.

The fundamentals, then, are plain and practical, the design is inchoate, the architecture of a somewhat mixed character; yet Hong Kong is astonishingly beautiful. It is made so partly by its setting, land and sea so exquisitely interacting, but chiefly by its impression of irresistible activity. It is like a cauldron, seething, hissing, hooting, arguing, enmeshed in a labyrinth of tunnels and overpasses, with those skyscrapers erupting everywhere into view, with ferries churning and Hovercraft splashing and great jets flying in, with fleets of ships lying always offshore, with double-decker buses and clanging tramcars, with a car it seems for every square foot of roadway, with a pedestrian for every square inch of sidewalk, and funicular trains crawling up and down the mountainside, and small scrubbed-faced policemen scudding about on motorbikes—all in all, with a pace of life so unremitting, a sense of movement and enterprise so challenging, that one's senses are overwhelmed by the sheer glory of human animation.

— By Jan Morris

Jan Morris is the author of more than 20 books, including such best-sellers as *Journeys, Destinations,* and *Manhattan '45.* This excerpt comes from her book *Hong Kong: Epilogue to an Empire.*

FOOD AND DRINK IN HONG KONG AND MACAU

I F YOU ARE COMING to Hong Kong for the first time, you must leave certain misconceptions at home. Hong Kong does not, for example, have some of the best Chinese food in the world. It has *the* best Chinese food in the world.

Such a statement may not find immediate acceptance in Taiwan or the People's Republic of China, but, as they say in the West, the proof is in the pudding, and those Taiwanese and mainland Chinese who can afford it come to Hong Kong to eat. It is historical fact that chefs were brought from Canton to Peking to serve in the Chinese emperors' kitchens, and that for many centuries the Cantonese were acknowledged as the Middle Kingdom's finest cooks.

An old Chinese maxim tells you where to find the prettiest girls, where to get married, where to die, where to eat, and so forth. The answer to "where to eat" is Canton (now called Guangzhou in the official romanization of Chinese names that also changed Peking to Beijing).

Hong Kong's 6-million-plus population is 98% Chinese, of whom the vast majority are Cantonese. This includes a significant group of Chiu Chow people, whose families originated around the port city of Swatow. Food is a subject of overriding importance to the Cantonese, and it can be said, as it is of the French, that they live to eat rather than eat to live. Find out how true this is on a culinary tour of Hong Kong.

The Cantonese made an art out of a necessity, and in times of hardship they used every part of an animal, fish, or vegetable. Some dishes on a typical Hong Kong menu will sound strange, even unappetizing— goose webs, for example, or cockerels' testicles, cows' innards, snakes (in season), pigs' shanks, and other things that may not be served back home. But why not succumb to new taste experiences? Who scorns the French for eating snails and frogs' legs, or the Japanese for eating raw fish?

There is no such thing, by the way, as a fortune cookie in a Hong Kong restaurant;

the overseas Chinese came up with that novelty. Chop suey was invented abroad, too. Its exact origin is disputed: some say it began in the California goldfields; others give credit (or blame) to Australian gold miners.

Your first destination must be a dim-sum palace. Served from before dawn to around 5 or 6 PM, these Cantonese daytime snacks are miniature works of art. There are about 2,000 kinds of dim sum in the Cantonese repertoire, and most dim-sum restaurants prepare 100 varieties daily. Generally served steaming in bamboo baskets, the buns, crepes, and cakes are among the world's finest hors d'oeuvres. Many are minor engineering achievements—like a soup with prawns served in a translucent rice-pastry shell, or a thousand-layer cake, or the ubiquitous spring roll.

Hong Kong has hundreds of dim-sum restaurants. The monthly *Essential HK,* published by the Hong Kong Tourist Association (HKTA), has color photos of some of the most popular dim sum (as well as other dishes) and "how-to" illustrations on chopsticks. (If you can't handle them, ask for a knife and fork; the object is to get the food to your mouth, not show off your dexterity.) The HKTA's *Official Dining, Entertainment and Shopping Directory* lists dozens of restaurants. Many of the top-rated Chinese restaurants in hotels and some of the better independent restaurants provide (somewhat incongruously) elegant settings for lunchtime dim sum, with bilingual check sheets, waiter service, and private tables. Such class costs about HK$15 or more per basket.

History-minded snackers will prefer, however, to visit the culinary shrine of the **Luk Yu Teahouse,** at 24 Stanley Street in Central, preferably with some Cantonese comrades. Luk Yu is more than a restaurant; it is one of Hong Kong's few historical monuments. It opened in the early 20th century as a wood-beamed, black-fanned, brass-edged place for Chinese gentlemen to partake of tea, dim sum, and gossip. When it was forced to relocate in the 1980s, everything was kept intact—marble-back chairs, floor spittoons, kettle warmers, brass coat hooks, and lockup liquor cabinets for regular patrons. Despite the addition of air-conditioning, fans still decorate a plain ceiling that looks down on elaborately framed scrolls, carved-wood booth partitions, and colored-glass panels. The ancient wooden staircase still creaks as Hong Kong's more traditional gentlemen ascend to the upper floors to discuss business and government.

Modernity has brought Luk Yu the English language, at least in the form of bilingual menus (though not for the individually served dim sum items), but you may have trouble making yourself understood.

As far as the Cantonese are concerned, anything that "keeps its back to heaven" is fit for cooking. Bird tastings in Hong Kong should include a feast of quails; smooth, salted chicken; sweet roasted chicken in lemon sauce; and minced pigeon served in lettuce-leaf "bowls" (rolled up with plum sauce). Pigeons appear on many menus, but the **Lung Wah,** a venerable and famous restaurant in Shatin, specializes in pigeon and serves it in dozens of forms.

Fish is plentiful everywhere. Hong Kong is a major port with numerous fishing communities, a fact easily forgotten by the urbane traveler. Go to the islands—to **Lamma** especially, where the small village of Sok Kwu Wan has a waterfront lined with restaurants offering fine seafood feasts. At **Leiyuemun** you choose your dinner from the massive fish tanks of the fishmongers lining the street, who then deliver it; or you can carry your choice (live, of course) to the restaurant to be cooked and served alfresco. Feel free to haggle over the price.

Hong Kong's most famous dining experience is the **Jumbo Floating Restaurant,** at Aberdeen, which is moored to another floating seafood house covered with gaudy multicolored carvings and murals that form a sight in themselves. The Jumbo, a 2,000-seat three-decker, is a marvel of outrageous ostentatiousness. The excitement here is about not the food, which is average, but about the environment and, if you're lucky enough to have a table on the periphery, about the view. Many Hong Kong Harbour tours end their trips here.

THERE IS NO SUCH thing as "Chinese" cooking in China. Every good "Chinese" chef has his (occasionally her) own repertoire, which will in turn reflect his clan's origin. Most Hong Kong restaurants are Cantonese; others prepare Pekingese or northern dishes, Shanghai specialties, or Szechuan (Sichuan) or Chiu Chow fare.

Crowds fill the new eating places in **Wanchai,** once the fictional home of Suzie Wong and now a struggling nightlife area that has run out of sailors. Restaurants of every description, along with Western-style bars and pub, have appeared to fill the gaps—almost replacing the topless bars, hostess-filled nightclubs, and dance halls that have long been expensive ways to get a drink.

"Old" **Tsim Sha Tsui,** on both sides of Nathan Road from the Peninsula Hotel up to the Jordan Road junction, has another batch of established restaurants. And the skyscrapers in Tsim Sha Tsui East burst with eateries, from grand Cantonese restaurants to cheerful little cafés. Here, as everywhere, you'll find not only Cantonese fare but Korean barbecues, Singaporean satays, Peking duck, Shanghainese breads and eel dishes, fine Western cuisine, and, of course, Western junk food.

The **Harbour City** complex, along Canton Road, has many fine restaurants tucked into shopping arcades or courtyards. **Central,** which once felt like a morgue at night, is now a bustling dining district with a warren of trendy bistros and good Indian restaurants up the hillside lanes, on and off Wyndham Street and Lan Kwai Fong.

Another up-and-coming area is Hong Kong's own **SoHo** (South of Hollywood Road), accessed via the long outdoor escalator to Midlevels. Along the escalator are about 60 or 70 restaurants of just about every conceivable ethnic stripe.

Then there are the hotels, culinary competitors full of stylish salons—so stylish that it's now hard to find a simple, old-fashioned coffee shop. Travel away from the downtown districts and you find more temptations: every housing estate and community center now boasts at least one brass-and-chrome home of good Cantonese cuisine, often as chic as it is wholesome.

N SIMPLE TERMS, northern or Peking cuisine is designed to fill and warm—noodles, dumplings, and breads are more evident than rice. Mongolian or Manchurian hot pots (a sort of fondue-cum-barbecue) are northern specialties, and firm flavors, such as garlic, ginger, and leek, are popular. Desserts, generally of little interest to the Cantonese, are heavy and sweet. Feasts have long been favored in the north, and not just by emperors holding weeklong banquets with elaborate centerpieces such as Peking duck (a three-course marvel of skin slices, sautéed meat, a rich soup of duck bones, and Tien Tsin cabbage). Beggar's chicken, about whose origins you'll hear varying legends, is another culinary ceremony, in which a stuffed, seasoned, lotus-leaf–wrapped, clay-baked bird releases heavenly aromas when its clay is cracked open.

Farther south, the Shanghai region (including Hangzhou) developed tastes similar to Peking's but with an oilier, sweeter style that favored preserved meats, fish, and vegetables. In Hong Kong the Shanghainese cafés are generally just that—unostentatious cafés with massive "buffet" displays of preserved or fresh snacks that are popular with late-nighters.

The phenomenal development of a Hong Kong middle class in recent years has prompted the appearance of grander, glitzier restaurants for Shanghainese and all other major regional cuisines. Those run by the Maxim's group are always reliable, moderately priced, and welcoming. Chiu Chow restaurants also come alive late at night, especially in the Chiu Chow areas of the Western District or in parts of western Kowloon. As with Shanghainese and Cantonese cuisine, the Chiu Chow repertoire emphasizes marine traditions, especially shellfish. The exotic-sounding "bird's nest" is the great Chiu Chow delicacy: it's the refined, congealed saliva of nest-building swallows (mainly gathered from nests built into Gulf of Siam cliffs). It may sound revolting to the uninitiated, but it's often exquisitely flavored—and, like many of China's most expensive foods, is said to be an aphrodisiac. A visit to any Chinese department store should include a (shocked) glance at the "medicine" counter's natural foods: the prices of top-grade bird's nest, shark's fins, deer horns, ginseng roots, and other time-tested fortifications are staggering representations of the laws of supply and demand.

The food of the Szechuan region is known as the hottest and spiciest of all of China's cuisines. At first taste, the fiery chili dishes, somewhat akin to both Thai and Indian cuisines, can sear your tongue. Once your taste buds have blossomed again, the subtleties of Szechuan spices will be apparent—particularly in the classic smoked duck, where camphor wood chips and red tea leaves add magical tinges to a finely seasoned duck that's been marinated for a full day.

Other regional variations, such as those of Hunan or the Hakka people, are not as distinctive as the major cuisines and are rare in Hong Kong. But other Chinese-influenced Asian cuisines are well represented. Even before the exodus of ethnic Chinese from Vietnam, that nation's exciting blend of native, French, and Chinese cooking styles was popular in Hong Kong. Now there are many cafés and a few smart restaurants specializing in prawns on sugarcane, mint-leaved meals, Vietnamese-style (labeled VN) salamis, omelets, and fondues. Look, too, for Burmese restaurants.

The most ubiquitous Asian cuisine is the multi-ethnic "Malaysian," a budget diner's culinary United Nations that includes native Malay, Indian, and Straits Chinese dishes, as well as "European" meals and the Sino-Malay culinary cross-culture of *nonya* cooking.

Indian restaurants are also popular, and not just with Hong Kong's immigrant population from the subcontinent. The Indian kitchens usually concentrate on the northern Moghul styles of cooking, with reliable tandoori dishes; and vegetarians will find them a boon. Spicy Thai fare is readily available, as are the contrasting Indonesian and Vietnamese cuisines.

As for Northeast Asia, Hong Kong has some of the world's finest Japanese restaurants, which thrive on local seafood and still tempt big spenders with imports of the highly prized Kobe or Matsukaya beef (marbled slices with a fine flavor produced by beer-massaged and pampered steers). Smaller spenders welcome the many local Korean cafés, whose inexpensive *bulgogi* (barbecues) provide that country's distinctive garlicky, marinated meats and the minibuffet of preserved kimchi selections.

From Europe, Hong Kong has a wonderland of fine French restaurants (mostly in the top hotels), British pubs, German wining-and-dining havens, delis, and a sprinkling of pleasingly offbeat eating experiences—from Mexican and Californian to Austrian and Spanish-Filipino.

The Cantonese may be the world's finest cooks, but they're among the least polite servers. They're a proud people—some say arrogant—and their language has an abruptness that often translates poorly into English. Don't expect smiles or obsequiousness; Hong Kong is not Bangkok or Manila. It's friendly in its own way, and it's certainly efficient; so if you meet smiles as well, be fully appreciative and tip accordingly. Note that tips are not expected at local corner cafés and (the few remaining) roadside food stalls.

Wherever you eat, at the top or bottom end of the culinary scale, always check prices beforehand, especially for live fish, which is always expensive but becomes a serious luxury item when scarce. "Seasonal" prices apply to many dishes and can be steep, and some of the most prized Chinese delicacies—shark's fin, abalone, bird's nest, bamboo fungus—can cost an emperor's ransom. Although few Hong Kong restaurants set out to rip off tourists (and certainly not those that are sign-bearing members of the HKTA), waiters will of course try to "sell up."

Finally, don't settle for safe, touristy standbys. Sweet-and-sour pork, chop suey, and fried rice can be marvelous here, but the best dishes are not on the menu: they're seasonal specialties written in Chinese on table cards. Ask for translations, ask for interesting recommendations, try new items—show that you're adventurous and you'll get the respect and the food you deserve.

— Barry Girling

A food, travel, and entertainment columnist, Barry Girling has lived in Hong Kong since 1977.

DOING BUSINESS IN HONG KONG

THIS TERRITORY is returning to its roots in more than one way. The most obvious transition came at midnight on June 30, 1997, when the Union Jack was lowered and the red flag of the People's Republic of China was hoisted in front of the Hong Kong Convention and Exhibition Centre. At the stroke of midnight, Hong Kong changed from a British Crown Colony to a Special Administrative Region of the PRC, and China regained sovereignty over Hong Kong for the first time since 1842.

Indirectly related to Hong Kong's becoming once more a part of China is a subtler change: an ongoing economic transformation that has the onetime colony becoming closely integrated with the mainland and especially with Guangdong Province, the part of China that Hong Kong abuts.

China's opening to world commerce under Deng Xiaoping in the late 1970s came at the perfect time for Hong Kong. Though its population was growing, the Territory had reached its peak as a manufacturing center. Soon, however, Hong Kong factories were being shuttered up and moved to Guangdong Province, where labor costs were much cheaper; and Hong Kong became the principal gateway to China, benefiting from the more than 20% annual growth on the southern mainland. Hong Kong's economy shifted to embrace a clean and lucrative set of industries revolving around trade and financial services.

Hong Kong and China began to merge economically even before the political day of destiny arrived: China's influence grew while Britain's weakened. The decision in 1996 by Swire Pacific, an old-line British *hong* (trading company) to sell major parts of its Cathay Pacific Airways and Dragonair to mainland interests typified the transition. The Hong Kong Jockey Club, long the essence of colonial British rule, dropped "Royal" from its name, as did the Hong Kong Golf Club and other such institutions, and various government departments.

Name changes are one thing, but will the essence of Hong Kong—its business culture—also be transformed? It's still too early to say; but if it does change, it's not hard to guess which habits will be the first to go. Business dress in Hong Kong, as formal as ever, is much closer to British tradition than to the more laid-back styles of other Southeast Asian business centers such as Singapore and Kuala Lumpur. True, those cities are intensely hot and humid year-round, but a sultry summer day in Hong Kong is more than muggy enough to make you wonder whether a suit is really warranted. Business fashion in China is generally less formal, but it remains to be seen whether China will begin dressing up or Hong Kong dressing down.

Until Hong Kong fashion changes substantially, you should wear the lightest possible suit materials you can afford, and always carry an extra supply of handkerchiefs—you'll need them to towel off the sweat. Have an umbrella handy in the summer, and keep one eye out for typhoon warning flags in the lobbies of hotels and office buildings. When the No. 8 flag is hoisted, the city closes down, and the safest thing to do is return to your hotel as quickly as possible.

Harder to gauge than the changeover's sartorial ramifications is its effect on language requirements in business. For decades, Beijing has sought to make Mandarin the official language in deed as well as in word on mainland China; but the southern Chinese, especially those in Guangdong Province, have insisted on retaining their Cantonese dialect, which is as different from the official language as French is from Spanish. Mandarin, or *putonghua*—the people's language—has made inroads despite the resistance; television newscasts in Hong Kong now come in both languages, as well as English. Indeed, the most obvious change since the handover has been the increased use of Mandarin, although most of that is by mainlanders who have moved to the territory. While many more Hong Kongers have taken to studying Mandarin for doing business on the mainland, they rarely (if ever) use it as their conversational tongue in Hong Kong.

Surprisingly, the changeover is not apt to affect the use of English in Hong Kong. Even Malaysia—the former British colony that bitterly rejected the English language after the nation was formed from a polyglot of British colonies and outposts in 1957—has returned to using English on purely utilitarian grounds. With ethnic Chinese holding strong economic influence throughout the Pacific Rim, various Chinese dialects are unquestionably useful, but English remains, arguably, the language of business in Asia.

One Hong Kong tradition that's unlikely to change anytime soon is its denizens' devotion to lucre. An American businessman remarked, "I'm from Minnesota. When I wake up in the morning, I'm thinking about fishing. When a Chinese person wakes up, he's thinking about ways to make money." This is important to keep in mind whether you're considering how much *laisee* money to give staff at the Chinese New Year or contemplating gifts for a new business partner. Resist the temptation to skimp.

Hong Kongers also have a keen sense of hierarchy in the office. Egalitarianism can be insulting rather than admired. Let the tea lady get the tea and coffee—that's what she's there for. Your assistant or Chinese colleague has better things to do than make copies or deliver messages. You'll only engender animosity if you assign such tasks without appreciating which job descriptions they fall under; and if you do these things yourself, you may unwittingly imply that the person assigned to do them is incompetent. It's easy to offend in unfamiliar ways.

Hierarchy and status go hand in hand, and business cards are tangible evidence of both. For your part, have plenty of cards available, ideally printed in English on one side and Chinese on the other. Exchange cards by proffering yours with both hands and a slight bow, and receiving the other person's in the same way. Examine the card you get immediately upon receiving it, still holding it with two hands, and comment on some aspect of it: for example, that your colleague's title is impressive or that the card itself is of high quality. Such a response gives the person you're greeting "face": his or her prestige and personal dignity have been publicly acknowledged.

DON'T BE SURPRISED, no matter how late in the day it is, if you're invited to a meal after making an impressive showing on your first meeting with a business associate. Hong Kongers work late, and they often don't get around to eating dinner until well into the evening. A full day of meetings followed by dinner at 10 PM is not unusual, so it's a good idea to make dinner reservations even when you think you're unlikely to find any restaurant still open.

Western silverware is common in Hong Kong, but it might be seen as another respectful, face-enhancing gesture if you try your hand at chopsticks. After all, business conversation is often conducted in English; learning to use chopsticks is a fairly easy way to reciprocate a cultural interest.

Of course, all of these customs—dress, language, business cards, chopsticks—pale next to some of the changeover's meatiest questions. How does Hong Kong's status as China's newest city affect foreigners doing business here? Hong Kong is, as you'll see from the moment you arrive, an international crossroads unlike any other city in China. More to the point, the laws governing Hong Kong the SAR are pretty much the same as the laws that governed Hong Kong the British Crown Colony. The Basic Law, the mini-constitution drafted by China, allows the SAR to function under common law—British common law, on which American law is founded—a system not used on the mainland. Businesses and travelers in Hong Kong thus have the same rights and protections they had prior to July 1, 1997. The law remains a common playing field for local companies, foreign companies, and individuals alike, administered by a neutral judiciary. Suits can be brought against the government, and the judiciary can rule against it—indeed, *has* ruled against the new SAR government. And, unlike China, the SAR is one of the least corrupt countries in the world. Of course, you need only worry about the law if trouble strikes, whether in the form of a business contract or a traffic accident.

Of all the political questions hanging over the new Hong Kong, none is likely to have a greater impact on business than the fate of the rule of law. Mainland China is definitely moving in Hong Kong's direction on this issue, attempting to establish a legal framework in which laws are written and contracts enforced in a way that is quite new to the world's oldest culture. Hong Kong is the greater-China headquarters of choice for a variety of multinational American, European, and Asian firms, and that alone is a powerful incentive for China to want to let Hong Kong be—don't tinker with success. But some wonder whether Beijing will be able to keep its hands entirely off its expensive new toy, and whether the toy might be damaged by simple handling. For example, China has no real tradition of zoning. How will a mainland developer feel when told that he can't build in Hong Kong because a law prohibits it? Such a case may go a long way toward determining whether Hong Kong is ultimately ruled by laws or by people.

Hong Kong's currency has been pegged to the U.S. dollar since 1982, at a rate that fluctuates narrowly around 7.8 Hong Kong dollars to one U.S. dollar. The peg has unquestionably been responsible for a good portion of Hong Kong's inflation, which has fluctuated between 7% and 10% for most of the 1990s (though it fell below 5% in '98); but Hong Kong officials, backed by China, insist that the peg will stay.

As for taxes, China has pledged not to change Hong Kong's reputation as a tax haven for businesses. The territory has been able to keep its flat tax rate at 15%, partly because it hasn't had to pay for its defense (the British garrison provided protection) and hasn't chosen to spend much on social welfare. And Beijing made it clear before the handover that China does not want to inherit an expanding welfare state.

In spite of the uncertainties, it would be shortsighted not to see the Chinese takeover of Hong Kong as precisely what the city needs, at least economically. There is no question that China's growth has fueled Hong Kong's economy since the early 1980s. When China opened itself up to the outside world, nearly half of Hong Kong's workers were employed in manufacturing; today, the fraction is barely one-sixth. In the same period, employment in trade, tourism, and services has gone from 30% to 55%.

Clearly, if Hong Kong is to continue its stunning rebound from the Asian crisis that affected it from 1997 to 1999 it will be on the back of China, which will provide the muscular economy to absorb all of Hong Kong's highly skilled services. The big question now is whether Hong Kong will remain an international city that caters to foreign interests looking for a comfortable conduit to China, or whether it will be swallowed by the mainland.

If you need business assistance or research facilities while in Hong Kong, the Hong Kong Development Council runs a huge trade-inquiry service where overseas buyers can trace manufacturers or products. The local chambers of commerce are also helpful and have good libraries and briefings. And freedom of the press means you can keep up with events around the world, uncensored

— By Tim Healy; updated by Sean Rocha

Tim Healy has reported, written, and edited business news since the 1980s. He currently writes for *Aisaweek*, a weekly newsmagazine published in Hong Kong.

BOOKS AND PERIODICALS

J AMES CLAVELL'S *Tai-Pan* and *Noble House* are blockbuster novels covering the early history of the British colony and the multifaceted culture of Hong Kong in the 1950s. Both books are insightful, if at times sensational. Robert S. Elegant's *Dynasty* is another epic novel, tracing the development of a powerful Eurasian family. It simplifies history a bit, but it does help reveal the Hong Kong world view. Another best-seller set here is John Le Carre's *The Honorable Schoolboy,* a superb spy thriller. On a smaller scale is Han Suyin's *A Many Splendoured Thing.* Richard Mason's classic *The World of Suzie Wong* depicts an American's adventures with a young woman in the Wanchai bar area. Austin Coates's *Myself a Mandarin* is a lively and humorous account of a European magistrate handling Chinese society, and his *City of Broken Promises* is a rags-to-riches biography of an 18th-century woman from Macau.

Maurice Collis's beautifully written classic *Foreign Mud* covers the early opium trade and China wars. Colin N. Crisswell's *The Taipans: Hong Kong's Merchant Princes* describes the historical inspiration for novels exploring that era. G. B. Endicott's *History of Hong Kong* traces Hong Kong from its birth to the riot-wracked 1960s, but Frank Welsh's *A History of Hong Kong* is far more readable. Trea Wiltshire's *Hong Kong: Improbable Journey* is another readable history and has superb photographs.

Jan Morris's *Hong Kong: Social Life and Customs* and *Hong Kong: Xianggang* are primers on the region's daily interpersonal interactions. Younger readers might enjoy Nancy Durrell McKenna's *A Family in Hong Kong,* part of a series describing families all over the world. G. S. Hey-

wood's *Rambles in Hong Kong* is a personal reflection. Books on the post-1997 future proliferate; a reading list might include Jamie Allen's *Seeing Red,* Mark Roberti's *The Fall of Hong Kong,* Robert Cottrell's *The End of Hong Kong,* Jonathan Dimbleby's *The Last Governor,* and Chris Patten's own *East and West.* Stephen Vines's *Hong Kong: China's New Colony* looks at the situation well past the handover.

For businesspeople, the American Chamber of Commerce publishes *Living in Hong Kong, Doing Business in Hong Kong,* and *Establishing an Office in Hong Kong,* all of which are available to nonmembers. The *Far Eastern Economic Review Yearbook* and the *Hong Kong Government Yearbook* are essential reference books; the *Monthly Digest,* from the U.S. Census and Statistics Department, may also be useful. *Hong Kong Tax Planning* is useful in cutting through tax-related legalese. The China Phone Book Co. publishes a slew of useful publications on China in addition to its telephone and telex directories. The Hong Kong Trade Development Council publishes trade directories and has a good library.

Newspapers

Newspapers and magazines from all over the world are readily available in Hong Kong. The *Asian Wall Street Journal,* the *Financial Times,* the *International Herald Tribune,* and *USA Today International* print international editions in Hong Kong to supplement the two English-language dailies, the *South China Morning Post* and the *Hongkong Standard.* The *Far Eastern Economic Review* leads the pack of business publications. *Time* and *Newsweek* both print in Hong Kong, joined by the native *Asiaweek.*

INDEX

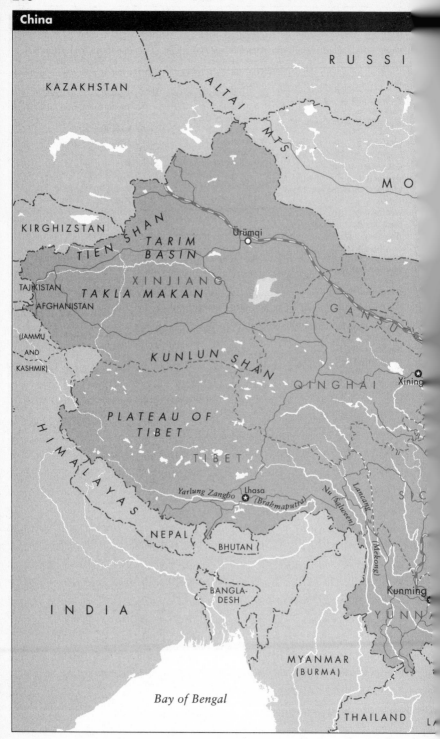

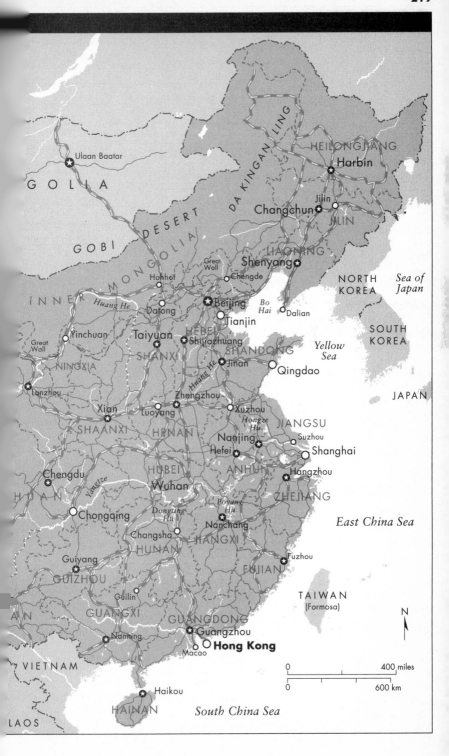

NOTES

NOTES

NOTES